Table of Contents

Literacy Plus

**Teacher
Reference
Book
to Words
in Semantic
Clusters**

Robert J. Marzano
Diane E. Paynter
John S. Kendall
Debra Pickering
Lorraine Marzano

Zaner-Bloser, Inc.

How to Use This Book

This book is a resource text to 12,409 words ranging from grades K-12, organized in 61 major semantic clusters. To understand the cluster approach to vocabulary instruction and how it relates to the teaching of reading and writing, read Chapter 1 of this text. Chapter 2 contains technical information about the 12,409 words, such as where they came from, how they were organized into clusters, and how grade levels were assigned and can be excluded from your reading without greatly affecting comprehension. Chapter 3 contains a detailed discussion of how this reference text relates to four companion student wordbooks and should be read carefully. As part of this program students have their own wordbooks with the words organized in the 61 semantic clusters. However, their wordbooks do not contain all 12,409 words. Each of the four levels of student wordbooks contains only those words appropriate to certain grade levels. For example, the Level I student wordbook contains words in grades K, 1 and 2; the Level II student wordbook contains words in grades 2, 3, and 4 and so on. Consequently, you can use the words in this reference book to add to and supplement the words in the student wordbooks. Appendix A contains all 12,409 words organized in the 61 major clusters, and Appendix B contains those same words listed in alphabetic order so that the category to which any of the 12,409 words belongs can be easily identified.

Developed in cooperation with the
Mid-Continent Regional Educational Laboratory

Acknowledgements

McREL Staff
C.L. Hutchins, *executive director*
Jo Sue Whisler, *product development unit manager*
Shae Isaacs, *production manager*
Carol Meyer, *desktop publishing*
Jeanne Deak, *production assistant*

ISBN 0-88309-948-9

Zaner-Bloser, Inc., P.O. Box 16764, Columbus, Ohio 43216-6764

Printed in the United States of America

1 The Nature of Words In Semantic Clusters

This book is meant as a reference for teachers who wish to help students develop their vocabulary in a systematic, yet flexible, way. It is part of a comprehensive program for teaching reading, writing, vocabulary and reasoning in an integrated fashion. That program is described in the book, *Literacy Plus: An Integrated Approach to Teaching Reading, Writing, Vocabulary and Reasoning* (Marzano, Marzano, Paynter, & Pickering 1989). In that program, vocabulary development is approached using semantic clusters. The semantic cluster approach is a dramatic new way of teaching and reinforcing vocabulary.

Simply stated, a semantic cluster is a group of related words. The relationship among words in a cluster is not necessarily that of synonymy. Rather, words within a semantic cluster generally have important characteristics in common. To illustrate, consider Figure 1.1.

Figure 1.1

A Semantic Cluster

governor
mayor
congressman
congresswoman
senator
candidate
councilman
councilwoman
politician
delegate
tribune
incumbent

All of the words in Figure 1.1 share the characteristic that they refer to individuals in power who are commonly elected or appointed. Teaching and presenting words in semantic clusters can greatly enhance the efficiency and utility of vocabulary learning.

Although the rationale and theory behind a semantic cluster approach to learning vocabulary is explained in depth in *A Cluster Approach to Elementary Vocabulary Instruction* (Marzano & Marzano 1988), we will briefly describe it here. Basically, there are two major reasons why it is useful to teach vocabulary using a semantic cluster approach.

1. Learning new words is easier when the words are presented in semantic clusters.

The task of learning a new word in context is very difficult. Some theorists (e.g., Nagy 1988) point out that the context surrounding a word commonly doesn't provide much information as to the meaning of a word. That is, when you encounter a new word in a passage, you usually have relatively little information to help you figure out what the word means. For example, assume you do not know what the word *delegate* means, but encounter it in the following sentence:

Jana is a *delegate* to the convention.

From the context alone you would have some (but not many) clues as to the meaning of the word *delegate*. Given the information in the sentence, Jana could be a *newcomer* to the convention, a *spy* at the convention, or a *janitor* at the convention. In other words, you must piece together a lot of unknowns to determine the meaning of the word *delegate* in this sentence. Of course, in a story you would have much more information with which to figure out the meaning of the word than that presented in the sentence above. However, research indicates that even with the added information provided by the content of a story, context alone would commonly not provide enough information to determine the meaning of many unknown words.

Now reconsider Figure 1.1 and assume that you first encountered the word *delegate* within that cluster and were told that it was similar or related in meaning to the other words in the cluster. Although you did not know the word *delegate*, you might know the words *mayor*, *governor* and *senator*. You could, therefore, conclude that *delegate* probably has something to do with officials or people in power or people in public offices. In other words, semantic clusters provide students with built-in sets of clues that guide them to an understanding of new words.

It is important to note that we do not mean to imply that students should not learn words from context. On the contrary, learning words from context should be the primary means of increasing vocabulary. Nagy (1988) explains the apparent contradiction that while encountering words in context does not provide good clues as to the meaning of unknown words, it should be the primary vehicle for vocabulary learning. The answer has to do with quantity. Specifically, Nagy and his colleagues (Nagy, Anderson & Herman 1987) estimated that students learn about one new word for every 20 unfamiliar words they encounter during reading. This doesn't sound like much. However, if students read 20 minutes a day for 200 days a year, they will encounter about 20,000 unfamiliar words a year. If one in 20 of those words is learned, this amounts to about 1,000 new words per year. As Nagy and Anderson (1984) note, this is far more words than could be learned from even the most ambitious program of direct vocabulary instruction.

Consequently, it is our recommendation that students be continually engaged in wide reading and language-rich activities that allow them to encounter and determine the

2

meaning of a variety of new words. Additionally, students should systematically be presented with words in semantic clusters to augment their vocabulary development.

2. Semantic clusters provide a useful structure for deepening the understanding of new words encountered during wide reading.

In addition to systematically providing students with new words in such a way as to offer strong clues to their meaning, semantic clusters can also be used as a structure for deepening students' understanding of new words encountered in wide reading. We have just seen that students learn about one in every 20 unknown words they encounter in their wide reading simply by using context. However, Nagy (1988) noted that a word must be learned at a relatively deep level to be a part of one's working vocabulary so that it might be used at a later date to facilitate comprehension. In other words, research and theory indicate that students must interact with a new word at a somewhat deep level to most effectively use it.

A powerful way of increasing one's depth of understanding of words learned from context is to integrate them into semantic clusters. Specifically, suppose you recorded (wrote down) those new words you encountered and learned during your wide reading. Each day you might record only one or two such words. At the end of the week, however, you could then determine into which semantic clusters these new words fit. As you did this, you would be learning the words in greater depth by making connections with words already in the semantic clusters. For example, assume that you encountered the word *incumbent* in your reading and from context determined that it had something to do with being in political office. As you tried to determine which category the word *incumbent* fit into, you would be forced to think about the word in new ways. (What is *incumbent* similar to? What are some of the characteristics of an *incumbent*?)

Once you found a category that the word seemed to fit into (like the one in Figure 1.1), you could then engage in a number of activities to deepen your knowledge of the word even further (e.g., compare and contrast it with other words in the cluster; form generalizations about the words in that cluster). In short, integrating new words into semantic clusters forces one to engage in a level of processing that deepens understanding of the words and provides an opportunity to engage in a variety of activities that can generate a very rich understanding of the words.

Of course, such activities assume that you already have words organized into semantic clusters. That is where this reference book comes in. It organizes over 12,000 words students will commonly encounter into 61 major semantic categories. Virtually any new word students encounter in their wide reading can be integrated into these semantic clusters.

Of course, students aren't given all the words at once. Rather, they are presented with words arranged in clusters that are at a level appropriate to their development. Specifically, students are provided with their own personal wordbooks in which words are arranged in semantic clusters. These are described in depth in a subsequent chapter of this text. Each of the four student wordbooks (Levels I, II, III, and IV) contains words appropriate to students' experiences and development in grades K through 8. As students encounter words in their wide reading, they then integrate these words into their own personal wordbooks. The words already in their books represent important words for them to consider. Thus, there is a certain amount of focus to their vocabulary development efforts. However, since students continually add words encountered during their wide reading, there is a great deal of subjectivity and flexibility in their vocabulary development. As students add more words to their wordbooks, their wordbooks become more personalized, more relevant, and more valuable.

In summary, semantic clusters are a valuable tool for presenting new words to students and helping them deepen their understanding of words they learn from their wide reading.

2   **What This Book Contains**

This reference book contains 12,409 words organized into semantic clusters. It contains all of the words found in the four levels of student wordbooks, plus some additional words not found in the student wordbooks. All words are listed in Appendix A where, in addition, you will find information on: (1) the recommended grade level for each word, (2) the first appearance of each word in content reading material, and (3) the grade level at which each word first appears on one of several standardized tests.

In this section, we provide some background information on the semantic clusters and additional information for each word within a semantic cluster.

Where Did the 12,409 Words Come From?

The words found in the semantic clusters came from a variety of sources. The first source was Harris and Jacobson's (1972) list of 7,661 words drawn from 14 elementary school textbook series. Specifically, six basal series and two series each in the fields of English, social studies, mathematics and science were used in the Harris and Jacobson study. Given that these series were somewhat dated, 60 elementary school teachers reviewed the list to: (1) delete any words they did not believe were currently useful in an instructional sense, and (2) add words they believed were necessary but not included.[*]

This revised list was then organized into semantic clusters by a single individual. This process produced three levels of semantically related words: super-clusters, clusters and mini-clusters. (These are described in detail in the next section.) The super-clusters, clusters and mini-clusters were then reviewed by the 60 elementary school teachers who were asked to reclassify any words that "did not fit from an instructional perspective." In other words, teachers were asked to think of the super-clusters, clusters and mini-clusters from the perspective of their instructional utility — could the groupings be used to help students learn words in the super-clusters, clusters and mini-clusters? Words were reclassified until there was 99.5% agreement among the teachers. That is, words were reclassified until teachers identified as miscategorized only five words in 1,000. The results of these efforts were published by the International Reading Association as a text entitled *A Cluster Approach to Elementary Vocabulary Instruction* (Marzano & Marzano 1988).

---

[*] An attempt was also made to change the sexist stereotypes in the list since it was based on materials written before publishers began to reduce sex stereotyping in books. However, even with these changes there are still sex stereotypes in the list (e.g., there is an entry for "fireman," but not for "firefighter").

This initial list of words in semantic clusters was then supplemented by adding words from a study of the basic words in the English language. Specifically, a study done by Becker, Dixon and Anderson-Inman (1980) was consulted. This study identified 8,109 basic words students encounter in grades K through 12. A basic word, according to Becker, is one that cannot be derived from knowledge of another word. To illustrate, the word *beauty* is basic, but the word *beautiful* is not. If you know the word *beauty*, you can figure out what the word *beautiful* means, even if you've never encountered it before. However, there is no word, the knowledge of which will help you figure out what *beauty* means. You simply have to know it — it is basic.

Given that Becker et al. identified 8,109 of these basic words that are found in K through 12 material, it seemed important that they be added to the semantic clusters. The basic words not already included were systematically added to the super-clusters, clusters and mini-clusters into which they most logically fit. This work was done primarily by two raters who continued to classify the new words until they disagreed on less than five words in 1,000.

When the Becker et al. words were integrated, the final list came to 12,409 words organized into the three levels of semantic clusters.

How the Semantic Clusters Are Organized

The 12,409 words are organized into 61 major semantic clusters referred to as **Super-Clusters**. These are reported in their entirety in Appendix A. The names of the 61 super-clusters are reported in Figure 2.1.

Within each super-cluster, words are further subdivided into semantic groups referred to as **Clusters**. To illustrate, consider Figure 2.2 which contains a listing of the clusters within Super-Cluster 17 entitled "Clothing." Clusters can be thought of as subtopics within super-clusters. That is, the broad category of clothing (the title of Super-Cluster 17) can be further divided into subtopics like "Parts of Clothing," "Accessories to Clothing," and so on. The various clusters within each super-cluster are described in some detail in Chapter 4.

Finally, the clusters within super-clusters are further subdivided into groups referred to as **Mini-Clusters**. For example, Figure 2.3 contains two mini-clusters from Cluster G (entitled "Accessories to Clothing") within Super-Cluster 17.

Occasionally, a mini-cluster itself requires further division. To illustrate, consider Figure 2.4. Here, Mini-Cluster 2E2 is subdivided into two groups of words: 2E2.0 and 2E2.1. Mini-clusters are commonly broken up into groups when words differ in their parts of speech. *Complete* in 2E2.0, for example, denotes a process or activity that is similar to the verbal ideas described by *finish*, *culminate*, and other words in the same mini-cluster. The noun form of the word, *completion*, is placed in the related, but separate, Mini-Cluster 2E2.1 since it denotes a condition rather than the activity that produced the condition. Similarly, the word *deed*, although it has no exact verbal counterpart in Mini-Cluster 2E2.0, does convey the noun form of the ideas expressed there, so it joins the word *completion* as a part of Mini-Cluster 2E2.1.

Figure 2.1

The 61 Super-Clusters

1. Occupations/Pursuits
2. Types of Motion/Activity
3. Size/Quantity/Weight
4. Animals
5. Feelings/Attitudes
6. Food Types/Meal Types
7. Time
8. Machines/Engines/Tools
9. Types of People
10. Communication
11. Transportation
12. Mental Actions/Thinking
13. Human Traits/Behavior
14. Location/Direction
15. Literature/Writing
16. Water/Liquids
17. Clothing
18. Places Where People Might Live/Dwell
19. Noises/Sounds
20. Land/Terrain
21. Dwellings/Shelters
22. Materials and Building
23. The Human Body
24. Vegetation
25. Groups of Things
26. Value/Correctness
27. Similarity/Dissimilarity
28. Money/Finance
29. Soil/Metal/Rock
30. Rooms/Furnishing/Parts of Dwellings/Buildings
31. Attitudinals
32. Shapes/Dimensions
33. Destructive and Helpful Actions
34. Sports/Recreation
35. Language
36. Ownership/Possession
37. Disease/Health
38. Light
39. Causality
40. Weather
41. Cleanliness/Uncleanliness
42. Popularity/Familiarity
43. Physical Traits of People
44. Touching/Grabbing Actions
45. Pronouns
46. Contractions
47. Entertainment/The Arts
48. Walking/Running Actions
49. Mathematics
50. Auxiliary/Helping Verbs
51. Events
52. Temperature/Fire
53. Images/Perceptions
54. Life/Survival
55. Conformity/Complexity
56. Difficulty/Danger
57. Texture/Durability
58. Color
59. Chemicals
60. Facial Expressions/Actions
61. Electricity/Particles of Matter

Figure 2.2

Names of Clusters Within Super-Cluster 17, "Clothing"

17A Clothing (General)	17F Coats
17B Parts of Clothing	17G Accessories to Clothing
17C Shirts/Pants/Skirts	17H Armor
17D Things Worn on the Head	17I Actions Related to Clothing
17E Things Worn on the Hands/Feet	17J Characteristics of Clothes and Wearing of Clothes
	17K Fabrics

Figure 2.3

Mini-Clusters From Cluster 17G, "Accessories to Clothing"

17G Accessories to Clothing	
17G3.0	17G4.0
pin	brush
buckle	comb
hairpin	razor

Figure 2.4

Categories Within Mini-Cluster 2E2

2E2.0	2E2.1
finish	completion
complete	deed
graduate	
accomplish	
fulfill	
consummate	
culminate	

As can be inferred from Figures 2.1 through 2.4, words in the mini-cluster have the strongest semantic ties. To illustrate, consider once again the words in Figure 2.3. Specifically, consider the level of relatedness among the words in Mini-Cluster 17G3.0. These are all types of things commonly used as fasteners. Similarly, the words in Mini-Cluster 17G4.0 are also very closely related semantically. They represent items commonly used as tools for taking care of oneself. But now consider the name for Cluster 17G, "Accessories to Clothing." The mini-clusters, in general, all fit under this heading, but we might say that the mini-clusters are less related to the cluster name than the words in mini-clusters are related to one another. Finally, reconsider Figure 2.2 which contains the names of the clusters in Super-Cluster 17. Although the clusters generally fit under the heading "Clothing" (the name of the super-cluster), the relationships are stretched a bit at this level. For example, Cluster 17H has "Armor" for its heading. Although the words in Cluster 17H can be generally associated with clothing (e.g., *shield*), the relationship is not strong.

In short, the larger the organization category, the looser the relationship among components. This looseness, however, does not create a problem in vocabulary learning. The purpose of presenting words in super-clusters, clusters and mini-clusters is to provide students with initial links for words they don't know. Students later expand on these initial links to create an in-depth knowledge of words. We have found that all of the levels of semantic clusters (super-clusters, clusters and mini-clusters) provide strong enough links for students to learn new words. That is, regardless of whether students are presented with words organized into super-clusters, clusters, or mini-clusters, they can use the semantic relationships among the words to enhance their vocabulary learning.

Information for Words in Semantic Clusters: Appendix A

For each word in Appendix A, three types of information are presented: (1) the recommended grade level for the word, (2) the first appearance of the word in content reading material, and (3) the grade level at which the word first appears on any of four standardized tests.

Recommended Grade Level

The task of assigning a grade level to words has always been problematic. Historically it has been very difficult to determine a valid process for assigning grade levels to words. The most common approach has been to use frequency as the major indicator of grade level. The most frequently encountered words are placed at the early grade levels; the less frequently encountered words are assigned to later grade levels; and so on. The only problem with this approach is that frequency levels change from one type of material to another. That is, you obtain different frequency levels based on the material you analyze to obtain your frequency counts. For example, if you analyze basal readers, a specific word might be found quite frequently at the fourth grade level. However, if you analyze children's literature, that same word might be found frequently at the second grade level.

The best way to assign grade levels is to consider a number of sources and then combine the information from those various sources. To assign the grade levels for words in this reference book, the process described below was used. (For a more detailed description of the process, see Marzano, Kendall & Paynter 1989.)

Step 1: Each word in Appendix A was cross-referenced using *The American Heritage Word Frequency Book* (WFB) to determine its earliest occurrence in reading material. The WFB is a study published in 1971 (Carroll, Davies, & Richman) that examined some 1,000 publications containing over five million words of text found in reading materials commonly used in Grades 3 through 9. The grade level at which a word first appeared within that study was considered the lower limit for the grade level at which the word should be introduced to students.

The WFB was also used to calculate the modal grade level — the grade at which the word most frequently appeared. This modal grade was considered the highest grade level (upper limit) at which the word should be introduced. That is, the modal grade provided a rough guide for the grade at which one could say confidently the word should be mastered by most students and would probably no longer be the subject of instruction, but rather could be used to develop other words or concepts. Based on the lower and upper limits, an initial grade level estimate was established. This level represented an initial guess as to the grade at which students might be able to learn the words on their own (or with a little guidance from the teacher) using a semantic cluster approach.

Step 2: The occurrence of each word on standardized tests was then determined. Specifically, the grade level at which each word first appeared on the following tests was identified:

- **The California Achievement Tests (CAT)** (1986; Form E; Levels 10 through 20, inclusive)
- **The Comprehensive Test of Basic Skills (CTBS)** (1984; Form U; Levels A, B, C, D, E, F, G, H, J, K)
- **Science Research Associates (SRA) Survey of Basic Skills Objectives** (1984; Form P; Levels 20, 21, 22, 23, 34, 35, 36, 37)
- **The Stanford Achievement Tests** (Gardner, Rudman, Karlsen & Merwin 1981; Form E; Levels K1, K2, P1, P2, P3, I1, I2, A, T1, T2)

This was done by listing each word in each test (including the words in the directions to students). The words for each test were then compared, and the first occurrence of each word identified.

These grade levels of first occurrence on standardized tests served either to confirm or disconfirm the initial grade level estimates. If there was a great discrepancy in the grade level assigned as a result of Step 1 described above and the grade level at which a word was introduced on standardized tests, the grade level estimate for the word was adjusted accordingly.

Step 3: Five professional teachers representing grades 2, 4, 5 and 6 were then asked to verify the grade level designations for each word resulting from Steps 1 and 2. If the designation for a given word was challenged by the participating teachers, the grade level was re-examined by the raters and, if appropriate, a new grade level assigned that reflected the recommendations of the teachers.

The final level assigned after Step 3 was considered the grade level at which students can learn a word when it is presented within a semantic cluster. These final grade level estimates appear in the first column (Column A) after each word in Appendix A.

First Appearance in Reading Material

The first appearance of each word in student reading material is listed in the second column (Column B) after each word (immediately following the recommended grade level). As described in Step 1 of the previous section, the first appearance of words in student reading material was determined using *The American Heritage Word Frequency Book*. This book lists the first occurrence of each word within a number of content areas (e.g., science, mathematics, literature). The earliest grade level of these occurrences was considered the first appearance of the word in student reading material.

First Appearance on Standardized Tests

Immediately following the grade level indicating the first appearance of each word in student reading materials is listed the first appearance of each word on one or more of the following standardized tests: the CAT, the CTBS, the SRA, and the Stanford. Recall that these tests were used to aid in the identification of grade level designations (described in Step 2 of the process for assigning the recommended grade level). If a word does not appear on any of these tests, a dash appears after the word in Column C. To illustrate, consider Figure 2.5.

Figure 2.5

Information for Words in Semantic Clusters

SUPER-CLUSTER
1. Occupations/Pursuits

1B Supervisors/Assistants

1B1.0	A	B	C
assistant	4	3	6
attendant	5	5	6
apprentice	6	4	6
journeyman	8	4	-
peon	8	3	-

In Figure 2.5, Column A stands for the recommended grade level designated as a result of the three-step process described previously. Column B lists the grade level at which the word first appears in student reading material. Column C identifies the earliest grade of occurrence on the CAT, the CTBS, the SRA, or the Stanford. As Figure 2.5 illustrates, the words *assistance*, *attendant*, and *apprentice* all appear first at the sixth-grade level on one or more of the four tests. A dash in Column C indicates that the word does not appear on the standardized tests. Since the words *journeyman* and *peon* do not appear on the CAT, CTBS, SRA or the Stanford, they have dashes listed in Column C.

This Standardized test information is meant to be used to help teachers identify those words that might be important to emphasize. That is, if a word appears on a standardized test students will take, then it might be useful to expose them to that word as a part of regular vocabulary instruction.

Words in Alphabetical Order: Appendix B

In addition to the words in Appendix A listed within super-clusters and mini-clusters, each word is also listed in alphabetical order in Appendix B. Following each word in Appendix B is a code that designates the super-cluster, cluster and mini-cluster to which the word belongs. To illustrate, consider the word *deadline*. Consulting Appendix B, you would find that *deadline* has the identification number 2E1. The number 2 indicates that the word belongs to Super-Cluster 2 entitled "Types of Motion/ Activity." The letter E indicates that *deadline* appears in Cluster E within that super-cluster. Turning to Appendix A, you find Cluster 2E which is entitled "Completion." Looking through the mini-clusters, you would discover the word *deadline* under mini-cluster 1.0. Appendix B, then, can be used to locate the super-cluster and cluster in which any of the 12,409 words can be found.

In summary, this textbook contains over 12,000 words organized in such a way that each word can be presented along with related words. Additionally, for each word, valuable supplemental information is presented, such as a recommended grade level, and the grade level at which the word first appears in student reading material as well as on selected standardized tests.

3   How to Use This Reference

This book is meant to be used as a reference text to supplement students' use of their individual wordbooks. There are four levels of individual student wordbooks. Level I wordbooks contain words from grades K, 1 and 2 organized into the 61 super-clusters; Level II wordbooks contain words in grade levels 2, 3 and 4 organized into the 61 super-clusters; Level III wordbooks contain words in grade levels 4, 5 and 6 organized into 61 super-clusters; Level IV wordbooks contain words in grade levels 5 through 10 organized in the same format. Thus, as students progress from one level to the next, there is at least a one-grade level overlap. This is to insure that within a super-cluster, cluster, or mini-cluster, there will always be familiar words to which students can relate the meanings of unfamiliar words.

There are, however, differences in the number of words within each wordbook. Specifically, the Level I book contains 1,381 words, the Level II book includes 4,559 words, the Level III book, 6,231 words and the Level IV book, 6,994 words.

Another difference in the student wordbooks exists between the Level I versus the Level II, III and IV wordbooks. The Level II, III and IV wordbooks are subdivided into super-clusters, clusters and mini-clusters. Within these levels, each super-cluster and cluster is named, however mini-clusters are not. To illustrate, consider Figure 3.1 which contains a page from the Level III wordbook.

In Figure 3.1, "Water/Liquids" is the name of the super-cluster and appears at the top of the page. "Different Forms of Water/Liquids" is the name of the first cluster (16A) within that super-cluster. There are five mini-clusters within the cluster. These

Figure 3.1

16. Water/Liquids

16A. Different Forms of Water/Liquids	glacier	cascade
fluid	hail	surge
moisture	hailstone	
aqua	iceberg	
	berg	
	icecap	oooze
	slush	ebb
	floe	seep
drizzle		
vapor		
	16B. Actions Related to Water/Liquids	dissolve
	dribble	evaporate
		thaw
sleet		
	secrete	
	squirt	ford
	gush	wade
snowcap	slosh	snorkel
	spatter	
	spurt	
	swash	

are signified by the five boxes, each with one or more words. (Note that when a mini-cluster contains only one word, part of the job of the student is to add words to that mini-cluster that are related to the word already there.) "Actions Related to Water/Liquids" is the second cluster (16B) within the super-cluster. It contains five mini-clusters on that page. (Note that when a box continues from one column to the next, as is the case with the second mini-cluster within 16B, it indicates that all words are within the same mini-cluster. Thus, *cascade* and *surge* belong to the same mini-cluster as *swash*, *spurt*, and so on.)

Level I wordbooks contain super-cluster names but not cluster or mini-cluster names. Additionally, the super-cluster names in the Level I wordbooks are worded somewhat differently from those used in the Level II, III and IV books. Figure 3.2 contains the super-cluster names used in the Level I student wordbooks.

Figure 3.2

Level I Super-Cluster Names

1. What People Do	21. Places for People, Animals and Things	41. Clean or Dirty
2. Going, Moving and Stopping	22. Things We Make	42. Things that Happen
3. Sizes and Amounts	23. Your Body	43. How People Look
4. Animals	24. Trees and Plants	44. Moving Hands and Arms
5. Feelings	25. Groups of Things and People	45. Pronouns
6. Food	26. Good and Bad	46. Contractions
7. Time	27. Same and Different	47. Things to Do
8. Things We Use	28. Money	48. Moving Feet and Legs
9. People	29. Things in the Ground	49. Arithmetic
10. Talking	30. Rooms and Furniture	50. Helping Verbs
11. Travel	31. How You Think	51. People Together
12. Thinking	32. Shapes	52. Heat and Cold
13. How People Act	33. Helping and Hurting	53. How Things Look
14. Places	34. Sports and Games	54. Living
15. Writing	35. Language	55. Average and Special
16. Water	36. Finding and Keeping	56. Trouble and Safety
17. Clothes	37. How You Feel	57. How Things Feel
18. Places People Live	38. Light	58. Color
19. Noises and Sounds	39. Why Things Happen	59. Gases
20. Land and Country	40. Weather	60. Our Faces
		61. Electricity

If you compare these names with those in Figure 2.1 from Chapter 2, you will note that the Level I super-cluster names are simply more easily understood versions of those used in Levels II, III and IV. Additionally, Level I wordbooks do not contain names for clusters or mini-clusters simply because, in many cases, there are not enough words within clusters at that level to warrant a title. Consequently, at Level I, students are presented with super-cluster titles only, although the words themselves are organized so as to suggest cluster groups. To illustrate, consider Figure 3.3 which contains a page from the Level I wordbook.

Although students have only the title for the super-cluster, "What People Do," the words on the page suggest five different types of words that fall under the general heading "What People Do." The first group would be words that somehow go with *job* and

Figure 3.3

1. What People Do	
job **housework**	**cowboy** **cowgirl** **farmer**
king	
	artist
runner	**painter**

housework. The second group would be words that somehow go with *king*; the third would be words that somehow go with *runner* and so on.

Within all levels of student wordbooks, words are ordered by grade level. That is, the first words presented within each mini-cluster are at the lowest grade levels, and the last words within each mini-cluster are at the highest grade levels.

As students progress through their individual wordbooks, this reference book can be used to add words to mini-clusters, clusters and super-clusters that are not in the student wordbooks. For example, assume that a student is working on Cluster 1J1.0 within Super-Cluster 1 in the Level II wordbook. The cluster contains the following words:

detective
sheriff
marshal
inspector
officer
patrolman

However, if you refer to Cluster 1J1.0 within Appendix A of this text, you will find a number of other words, each with its grade level information (see Figure 3.4). Recall that Column A is the recommended grade level at which students can learn the words in clusters; Column B is the grade level at which the word first appears in student reading material; and Columns C is the grade level at which the word first appears on the CAT, CTBS, SRA or Stanford.

Figure 3.4

Words in Cluster 1J1.0

1J Public Servants

1J1.0	A	B	C
fireman	1	3	-
policeman	1	3	-
policewoman	1	-	-
detective	3	3	2
marshal	3	5	-
officer	3	3	3
sheriff	3	3	6
inspector	4	3	4
patrolman	4	7	-
trooper	5	5	-
constable	6	4	-
sergeant	6	3	8
coroner	8	-	-
lawmaker	8	3	-
notary	8	8	-
sleuth	8	-	-

After consulting the words in Appendix A, you might decide that you want to expose students to some more advanced words than those prescribed in the Level II wordbook (e.g., *trooper, constable, sergeant*) or some relatively simple words (e.g., *fireman policeman, policewoman*) that students would encounter at an earlier grade level than those covered in the Level II wordbook.

In summary, this text is a comprehensive listing of 12,409 words organized into super-clusters, clusters and mini-clusters. In addition, each word listed includes a grade-level designation that indicates the level at which the word might be introduced. Also listed after each word is the grade level at which each word first appears in student reading material and the grade level at which it first appears on one or more of four major standardized tests. Finally, the text contains an alphabetical list of the words and a coding scheme that allows you to locate the super-cluster, cluster and mini-cluster to which each word belongs. Consequently, this reference book can be used to greatly enhance student learning of vocabulary presented in semantic clusters and encountered in their wide reading.

4   A Preview of the Super-Clusters

Although the semantic clusters are presented in their entirety in Appendix A, this chapter provides an overview of what you will find in each super-cluster. Specifically, this chapter provides a brief summary of each of the 61 super-clusters and the composition of the various clusters within each super-cluster.

1. Occupations/Pursuits

Super-Cluster 1, "Occupations/Pursuits," is the largest super-cluster. Most words in this super-cluster are job titles (e.g., *carpenter, ballplayer*) or job class titles (e.g., *craftsman, professional*). The clusters are formed by grouping together occupations that share one or more features. The cluster "Outdoor Professions," for example, contains the words *fisherman* and *farmer*. Both *fisherman* and *farmer* share the characteristic of describing people who have outdoor professions.

Although the majority of words within this super-cluster are nouns, some of the mini-clusters include verbs or verbal ideas related to occupations. For example, words like *hire* and *retire* are found in a mini-cluster within the cluster entitled "Work-related Actions." There are 31 clusters within this super-cluster. They are:

A. Occupations (General)
B. Supervisors/Assistants
C. Royalty/Statesmen
D. Names of People in Sports
E. Reporters/Writers
F. Outdoor Professions
G. Artists
H. Entertainers/Performers
I. Teachers/Students
J. Public Servants
K. Areas of Work
L. Scientists/Discoverers
M. People Who Buy and Sell
N. Small Business
O. People Who Work in Offices
P. Builders
Q. Publishing
R. People Who Clean Up
S. Occupations Related to Money
T. Occupations Related to Imprisonment/Slavery
U. Occupations Related to Medicine
V. Occupations Related to Transportation
W. Clergy/Religious
X. Repairmen/Construction Workers
Y. Legal Participants and Occupations
Z. Servants
a. Occupations Related to Restaurants
b. Messengers
c. Occupations Usually Held by Youth
d. Work-related Actions
e. Hobbies

Because there are so many clusters within this super-cluster, some clusters necessarily utilize a small letter rather than a capital to signify the cluster (e.g., a, b, c, d and e).

2. Types of Motion/Activity

This super-cluster contains words grouped according to the motion or activity they describe. Most words are fairly closely related to the title of the cluster to which they are assigned; however, in some cases, words that express a more remote sense of an activity signified by the cluster title are also included. The word *boycott*, for example, can be found under the cluster "Halting" along with the words *stop* and *obstruct*. The words *stop* and *obstruct* are obviously actions closely related to the general heading "Halting," whereas the word *boycott* is more indirectly related. There are 24 clusters within this super-cluster. They are:

A. General Motion	M. Shifting Motion
B. Lack of Motion	N. Jerking Motion
C. Beginning Motion	O. Ascending Motion
D. The Act of Occurring	P. Descending Motion (General)
E. Completion	Q. Descending Motion Done by
F. Halting	Human Beings
G. General Actions Involving	R. Reduction
Coming/Going	S. Expansion
H. Pursuit	T. Force
I. Taking/Giving	U. Closing/Opening Actions
J. Tossing/Catching Actions	V. Joining Actions
K. Pushing/Pulling Actions	W. Separating Actions
L. Vibration	X. Circular/Angular Motions

3. Size/Quantity/Weight

Super-Cluster 3 is comprised of words that are terms of measure, as well as words for tools or instruments that are used to obtain measurement. The last three clusters, "Specifiers," "Diminishers" and "Intensifiers," are made up of words or short expressions that change the scope of the words they modify. The cluster "Specifiers," for example, lists determiners like *a* and *the*. Similarly, words like *roughly* and *mainly* are found under "Diminishers," and *most* and *especially* under the cluster entitled "Intensifiers." *Roughly* and *mainly*, when used before adjectives and verbs, diminish the impact of those elements, for example: He was *mainly* interested in sports. The words *most* and *especially*, when used before adjectives and verbs, intensify the impact of those elements, for example: He was *most* interested in sports. There, are 11 clusters within this super-cluster. They are:

A. Size/Weight	G. General Amounts
B. Measurement Actions	H. Cardinal/Ordinal Numbers
C. Measurement Devices	I. Specifiers
D. Things Commonly Measured	J. Diminishers
E. Specific Units of Measurement	K. Intensifiers
F. Partitives	

4. Animals

Super-Cluster 4, "Animals," lists words that name living things other than human beings. There are 15 clusters within this super-cluster. The last four clusters consist of words that describe actions or objects that are primarily associated with animals. The clusters in this super-cluster are:

A. Animals (General)
B. Cats/Dogs
C. Reptiles/Mythical Animals
D. Baby Animals
E. Land Animals (General)
F. Rodents
G. Primates
H. Sea Animals
I. Shellfish and Others
J. Birds
K. Insects
L. Parts of Animals
M. Animal Dwellings
N. Animal Equipment
O. Actions Related to Animals

5. Feelings/Attitudes

This super-cluster, "Feelings/Attitudes," focuses on human emotions. The first cluster addresses general names for feelings (e.g., *mood*, *sense*, *impulse*). The clusters that follow are organized around a specific emotion or related emotions. The last cluster, "Human Traits (General)," includes words such as *skill*, *attitude* and *personality* which are general labels for human traits. The 18 clusters within this super-cluster are:

A. Names for Feelings (General)
B. Fear
C. Actions Associated with Fear
D. Worry/Guilt
E. Anger
F. Meanness/Cruelty
G. Irritability
H. Sadness
I. General Upset
J. Excitement
K. Fun/Joy
L. Comfort/Contentment
M. Jealousy/Envy
N. Hope/Doubt
O. Caring/Trusting
P. Neglecting Actions
Q. Desire
R. Human Traits (General)

6. Food Types/Meal Types

Super-Cluster 6, "Food Types/Meal Types," groups food in several ways: food and drink, the four food groups, foods that are prepared, and ingredients that are used to prepare foods. Like many others, Super-Cluster 6 ends with clusters that describe actions or activities related to the general topic of the super-cluster. There are 14 clusters within this super-cluster. They are:

A. Types of Meals
B. Food Types
C. Sweets
D. Prepared Foods
E. Meats
F. Dairy Products
G. Ingredients Used to Prepare Foods
H. Things to Drink
I. Fruits
J. Vegetables
K. Actions Done to/with Food

L. Food Tastes
M. Eating/Drinking Actions

N. Hunger/Thirst

7. Time

This super-cluster contains words that describe time as well as words for the devices that measure time. Three clusters, G, H and I, contain relationship markers—words that serve to indicate the relationship between two or more events. For example, words like *while* and *then*, and expressions like *at first* are found in these three clusters. The word *while* usually indicates that events occurred simultaneously, for example: Bill played *while* Mary worked. The word *then* commonly indicates that one event occurred subsequent to another event, for example: Bill played, *then* Mary played. The phrase *at first* indicates that one event occurred prior to other events, for example: *At first* Jana was startled. The last two clusters of this super-cluster contain words that describe speed, duration and frequency. There are 11 clusters within this super-cluster. They are:

A. Time (General)
B. Devices Used to Measure Time
C. Parts of a Day
D. Other Periods of Time
E. Months and Days
F. Relative Time
G. Prior Action (Relationship Markers)
H. Subsequent Action (Relationship Markers)
I. Concurrent Action (Relationship Markers)
J. Speed
K. Duration/Frequency

8. Machines/Engines/Tools

Like most super-clusters, this one begins with a group of the most general words that fall within the topic treated by the super-cluster. In the first cluster, "Machines," are such words as *machine, equipment* and *mechanism*. Other clusters (e.g., "Fuels/Lubricants," "Cutting/Abrasive Actions," "Fasteners" and "Handles") include elements necessary to run machines and the types of actions for which machines or tools are employed. This super-cluster also includes a cluster for eating utensils and one for weaponry. There are 14 clusters within this super-cluster. They are:

A. Machines
B. Engines and Parts of Engines
C. Fuels/Lubricants
D. Appliances
E. Tools (General)
F. Tools Used for Cutting
G. Cutting/Abrasive Actions
H. Fasteners
I. Handles
J. Miscellaneous Devices
K. Equipment Related to Vision
L. Electronic Equipment
M. Utensils Used for Cooking/Eating
N. Weapons

9. Types of People

Super-Cluster 9 includes words that are used to describe people. However, unlike Super-Cluster 1, words that refer to occupations are not included. Rather, characteristics ranging from age to family relationship to financial status are used to form specific clusters. There is also a cluster of names for spiritual or mythological characters. The 15 clusters included in this super-cluster are:

A. People (General Names)
B. Names for Women
C. Names for Men
D. Names Indicating Age
E. Names Indicating Friendship/Camaraderie
F. Names for Spiritual or Mythological Characters
G. Names Indicating Negative Characteristics about People
H. Names Indicating Lack of Permanence for People
I. Names Indicating Permanence for People
J. Names Indicating Size of People
K. Names Indicating Fame
L. Names Indicating Knowledge of a Topic
M. Names Indicating Financial Status
N. Family Relationships
O. Names Indicating Political Disposition

10. Communication

Words in the "Communication" super-cluster are grouped according to the general content of information or how that information is presented. For example, one cluster is entitled "Communication Involving Confrontation or Negative Information." It includes words that signify negative or confrontational activities such as *argue*, *warn* and *blame*. Often the form of communication provides the focus for a cluster. This is the case in clusters such as "Persuasion," "Questions" and "Promises." One cluster entitled "Recording or Translating Information" treats the conversion of information from speech to writing. The 11 clusters within this super-cluster are:

A. Communication (General)
B. Communication Involving Confrontation or Negative Information
C. Communication Involving General Presentation of Information
D. Communication Involving Positive Information
E. Persuasion
F. Questions
G. Communication Involving Supervision/Commands
H. Giving Out Information Previously Withheld
I. Promises
J. Recording or Translating Information
K. Exclamations (General)

11. Transportation

This super-cluster lists various types of vehicles related to transportation (e.g., "Work-related Vehicles" and "Vehicles Used for Air Transportation"). In addition, it contains a cluster on the actions and characteristics of vehicles (Cluster G) that includes both verbs that are commonly associated with vehicles (e.g., *ride*, *sail*, *drive*) and adjectives that indicate a type of vehicle (e.g., *seagoing*). Cluster G also contains a section on the names for people in vehicles (e.g., *driver*, *stowaway*) and words to describe vehicles in groups (e.g., *transport*, *convoy*). The eight clusters within this super-cluster are:

A. Types of Transportation
B. Work-related Vehicles
C. Vehicles Used in Snow
D. Vehicles Used for Air Transportation
E. Vehicles Used for Sea Transportation
F. Parts of Vehicles
G. Actions and Characteristics of Vehicles
H. Things Traveled On

12. Mental Actions/Thinking

Super-Cluster 12 begins with a cluster that describes mental processes in a general way. The second cluster, "Subject/Topics," contains words that are common labels for subjects or topics of thought such as *scheme* and *objective*. The remaining clusters describe particular types of mental activity ("Mental Explorations," "Choice"), states of mind ("Consciousness," "Interest"), descriptions of ability ("Intelligence"), and viewpoint ("Beliefs"). The 12 clusters within this super-cluster are:

A. Thought/Memory (General)
B. Subjects/Topics
C. Mental Exploration
D. Mental Actions Involving Conclusions
E. Consciousness
F. Interest
G. Teaching/Learning
H. Processes and Procedures
I. Definition
J. Choice
K. Intelligence
L. Beliefs

13. Human Traits/Behavior

Since words for human emotions are listed in an earlier super-cluster (Super-Cluster 5, "Feelings/Attitudes"), Super-Cluster 13 deals with human traits that, for the most part, describe nonemotional traits or capabilities. The 16 clusters within this super-cluster are:

A. Kindness/Goodness
B. Eagerness/Dependability
C. Lack of Initiative
D. Freedom/Independence
E. Confidence/Pride
F. Patience
G. Luck/Probability
H. Strictness/Stubbornness
I. Humor
J. Spirituality
K. Prudence
L. Shyness
M. Dishonesty
N. Loyalty/Courage
O. Instability
P. Caution

14. Location/Direction

This super-cluster contains words that are used to describe position and direction. Most clusters within this super-cluster contain fairly specific indications of position and direction. For example, there is one cluster devoted to words that relate to the dimensions of back, front and middle. The cluster "Boundaries" includes words such as *corner*, *side* and *horizon*. Although there are a number of nouns in this super-cluster, the majority of the words are adverbs and/or prepositions, like *here*, *there*, *under* and *close*. There are 12 clusters within this super-cluster. They are:

A. Location (General)
B. Boundaries
C. Planes
D. Non-specific Locations
E. Directions
F. Back-Front-Middle
G. Direction To/From
H. In/Out and Inward/Outward
I. Up/On
J. Down/Under
K. Distances
L. Presence/Absence

15. Literature/Writing

The words in this super-cluster include those that are commonly associated with written language. For example, this super-cluster contains a cluster, "Types of Literature," with words that describe general types of written materials, such as *fiction* and *essay*. It also contains a cluster, "Reading/Writing/Drawing Actions," with words that describe physical acts of writing and drawing such as *scribble* and *sketch*. Additionally, the cluster "Rules/Laws" emphasizes principles of culture and society, especially as they relate to written precepts. There are nine clusters within this super-cluster. They are:

A. Names/Titles
B. Types of Literature
C. Types of Publications
D. Poems/Songs
E. Drawings/Illustrations
F. Messages
G. Things to Write On/With
H. Rules/Laws
I. Reading/Writing/Drawing Actions

16. Water/Liquids

This super-cluster contains a cluster whose words describe water and liquids in the different forms they take (e.g., *ice*, *snow*, *vapor*). It also contains a cluster whose words describe actions associated with liquids (e.g., *drip* and *pour*). Additionally, the cluster "Directions Related to Water" contains words like *ashore* and *underwater* that indicate directionality as it relates specifically to water. There are nine clusters within this super-cluster. They are:

A. Different Forms of Water/Liquids
B. Actions Related to Water/Liquids
C. Equipment Used with Liquids
D. Moisture
E. Slime
F. Bodies of Water
G. Places Near Water
H. Directions Related to Water
I. Man-made Places For/Near Water

17. Clothing

Super-Cluster 17 groups together words for articles of clothing, parts of clothing (e.g., *button*, *pocket*), and actions related to clothing. Also within this super-cluster are clusters that cover accessories to clothing (e.g., *tie*, *ribbon*), and fabric (e.g., *cotton*, *wool*). Additionally, one cluster is entitled "Armor." There are 11 clusters within this super-cluster. They are:

A. Clothing (General)
B. Parts of Clothing
C. Shirts/Pants/Skirts
D. Things Worn on the Head
E. Things Worn on the Hands/Feet
F. Coats
G. Accessories to Clothing
H. Armor
I. Actions Related to Clothing
J. Characteristics of Clothes and Wearing of Clothes
K. Fabrics

18. Places Where People Might Live/Dwell

This super-cluster lists words that identify political and social units (e.g., *neighborhood*, *county*). It also contains words that signify unique places where people might live (e.g., *heaven*, *hell*, *utopia*). The last two clusters list the 50 states and major U.S. cities. The four clusters within this super-cluster are:

A. Places Where People Might Live
B. Continents/Countries
C. States
D. Cities

19. Noises/Sounds

Super-Cluster 19 begins with general concepts about sounds and noise (e.g., *echo*, *loud*, *silence*), then lists together electrical and mechanical devices that produce or reproduce sounds (e.g., *horn*, *gong*, *phone*). Next follows a cluster on words for human sounds (e.g., *roar*, *cheer*, *gasp*), then one on animal noises (e.g., *quack*, *peep*, *bark*), and finally one on mechanical sounds (e.g., *ring*, *tick*, *clop*, *zoom*, *clang*). The five clusters within this super-cluster are:

A. Noises (General)
B. Devices That Produce/ Reproduce Sound
C. Noises Made by People
D. Animal Noises
E. Noises Made by Objects

20. Land/Terrain

This super-cluster focuses on geography. It starts with a cluster that describes areas of land in a general way (e.g., *lot*, *expanse*). The next cluster, "Characteristics of Places," lists words that range from *geographic* and *rural* to *municipal* and *developed*. Most of the remaining clusters deal with specific types of land or terrain. Finally, the cluster entitled "Bodies in Space" includes planets and satellites. There are eight clusters within this super-cluster. They are:

A. Areas of Land
B. Characteristics of Places
C. Valleys/Craters
D. Mountains/Hills
E. Forests/Woodlands
F. Fields/Pastures
G. Yards/Parks
H. Bodies in Space

21. Dwellings/Shelters

Most of the dwellings and shelters listed within Super-Cluster 21 are man-made. The first cluster, "Man-made Structures," contains the most general terms for structures, such as *tower* and *skyscraper*. The clusters that follow deal with specific types of dwellings or shelters. The last cluster, "Monuments," is a little different from the other clusters in that some items might not be man-made (e.g., *landmark*) or designed for shelter (e.g., *totem*). There are 13 clusters within this super-cluster. They are:

A. Man-made Structures
B. Places to Live
C. Places of Protection/Incarceration
D. Places Where Goods Are Bought and Sold
E. Mills/Factories/Offices
F. Places for Learning/Experimentation
G. Places for Sports/Entertainment
H. Medical Facilities
I. Places for Worship/Meetings
J. Places Related to Transportation
K. Places Used for Storage
L. Farms/Ranches
M. Monuments

22. Materials and Building

This super-cluster organizes words that are associated with everyday objects, materials and the process of building. Clusters deal with containers, materials used to cover things and objects in general (e.g., *thing, object, substance*). Clusters on building materials are divided into wooden and other types of materials. Clusters on the activity of building (e.g., *make, build*) and the activity of wrapping or covering (e.g., *wrap, pack*) end this super-cluster. There are seven clusters within this super-cluster. They are:

A. Containers
B. Materials/Objects Used to Cover Things
C. Wooden Building Materials
D. Other Building Materials
E. General Names for Objects
F. Building/Repairing Actions
G. Wrapping/Packing Actions

23. The Human Body

The majority of clusters within this super-cluster on the human body list body parts and organs. The cluster entitled "Body Coverings" includes such words as *skin, scalp, hair* and *freckle*. However, it does not include clothing (which is covered in Super-Cluster 17). There are 11 clusters within this super-cluster. They are:

A. The Body (General)
B. Body Coverings
C. The Head
D. Mouth/Throat
E. Eyes/Ears/Nose
F. Limbs
G. Legs/Feet
H. Organs of the Body
I. Body Fluids
J. Bones/Muscles/Nerves
K. Body Systems

24. Vegetation

This super-cluster begins with words that describe vegetation in general (e.g., *tree, bush, growth, vegetation*). The clusters that follow list types of trees and bushes, and names for the features that are associated with them (e.g., *bark, branch*). Flowers and plants have a separate cluster. The last cluster, "Other Vegetation," contains words like *fungus*, and more general terms like *root* and *stalk*. There are five clusters within this super-cluster. They are:

A. Vegetation (General)
B. Types of Trees/Bushes
C. Parts of Trees/Bushes
D. Flowers/Plants
E. Other Vegetation

25. Groups of Things

Words that describe groups make up this super-cluster. The types of objects or people that are grouped provide the subject for the clusters. General names for groups of objects or ideas are listed in the first cluster. Words that describe groups of people or animals form the next cluster. The last three clusters group words according to whether they describe political or social groups, groups in uniform, or social or business groups. There are five clusters within this super-cluster. They are:

A. General Names for Groups of Things
B. Groups of People/Animals
C. Political/Social Groups
D. Groups in Uniform
E. Social/Business Groups

26. Value/Correctness

Words in this super-cluster include concepts of right and wrong, success and failure, value and lack of value. There are four clusters within this super-cluster. They are:

A. Right/Wrong
B. Success/Failure
C. Importance/Value
D. Lack of Value

27. Similarity/Dissimilarity

In addition to grouping terms that express similarity or dissimilarity, this super-cluster lists a number of relationship markers. While Super-Cluster 7, "Time," introduces relationship markers that signify relative time, this super-cluster contains relationship markers for addition (e.g., *with, as well as*) and contrast (e.g., *yet, else, instead*). Addition relationship markers indicate that ideas or concepts are somehow similar, for example: He was intelligent *as well as* good looking. Contrast relationship markers indicate that concepts or ideas are in some way different or antithetical, for example: She was determined *yet* flexible. There are four clusters within this super-cluster. They are:

A. Likeness
B. Addition (Relationship Markers)
C. Difference
D. Contrast (Relationship Markers)

28. Money/Finance

Words that are common in the world of business and finance form this super-cluster. The cluster divisions are based on the concepts of obtaining and spending money, types of money and valuables, trading money and goods, how things are described in terms of money (e.g., *wasteful*, *costly*, *cheap*), and where money and valuables are stored. There are six clusters within this super-cluster. They are:

A. Money/Goods You Receive
B. Money/Goods Paid Out
C. Types of Money/Goods

D. Money/Goods Related to Actions
E. Money Related to Characteristics
F. Places Where Money/Goods Are Kept

29. Soil/Metal/Rock

The subject of this super-cluster is geology. The first four clusters deal with various types of geological entities (e.g., *metals*, *jewels*, *rocks*) and characteristics and actions associated with these objects. The last two word clusters, "Soil" and "Actions Done to Soil/Crops," deal with cultivation. There are six clusters within this super-cluster. They are:

A. Metals
B. Jewels/Rocks
C. Characteristics of Rocks/Soil

D. Actions of Metals
E. Soil
F. Actions Done to Soil/Crops

30. Rooms/Furnishings/Parts of Dwellings/Buildings

Super-Cluster 30 covers all types of rooms, as well as features of rooms (e.g., *hall*, *doorway*, *aisle*). The cluster "Fences/Ledges" lists items that may be found outside a house but form part of a dwelling. The six clusters within this super-cluster are:

A. Rooms
B. Parts of a Home
C. Fences/Ledges

D. Furniture
E. Decorations
F. Linens

31. Attitudinals

This super-cluster is comprised of adverbs that express a speaker's attitude toward his subject. For example, attitudinals indicating truth signal that the speaker or writer strongly asserts that his subject is true and/or accurate, for example: *Truly*, he was a gentleman. There are eight clusters within this super-cluster. They are:

A. Attitudinals (Truth)
B. Attitudinals (Lack of Truth/Doubt)
C. Attitudinals (Expected/Unexpected)
D. Attitudinals (Fortunate/Unfortunate)

E. Attitudinals (Satisfaction/Dissatisfaction)
F. Attitudinals (Correctness/Incorrectness)
G. Attitudinals (Wisdom/Lack of Wisdom)
H. Other Attitudinals

32. Shapes/Dimensions

This super-cluster groups names for shapes and forms of all kinds—regular geometrical shapes (e.g., *cone*, *sphere*, *square*, *rectangle*), curved shapes (e.g., *bend*, *curl*), and the attributes of sharpness, bluntness, straightness and crookedness. Included in this super-cluster is a cluster on fullness or emptiness (e.g., *swollen*, *hollow*). The eight clusters within this super-cluster are:

A. Shapes (General Names)
B. Circular or Curved Shapes
C. Rectangular or Square Shapes
D. Straightness/Crookedness
E. Sharpness/Bluntness
F. Dimension
G. Fullness/Emptiness
H. Inclination

33. Destructive and Helpful Actions

Super-Cluster 33 organizes words that describe helpful or destructive acts. The first cluster, "Actions Destructive to Nonhumans," lists words that are primarily used to describe actions destructive to objects (although the words might sometimes be used to describe actions destructive to humans or animals). The second cluster lists only those words that are used to describe actions that are harmful to living things. The four clusters within this super-cluster are:

A. Actions Destructive to Nonhumans
B. Actions Destructive to Humans
C. Fighting
D. Actions Helpful to Humans

34. Sports/Recreation

Super-Cluster 34 first groups words that describe sports and/or general recreational activities (e.g., hobby, game, race). Following this are two clusters that list specific sports and equipment used in sports. The last two clusters are "Magic" (e.g., trick, stunt) and "Board and Other Games." There are six clusters within this super-cluster. They are:

A. Sports/Recreation
B. Specific Sports
C. Equipment Used in Sports/Recreation
D. Exercising
E. Magic
F. Board and Other Games

35. Language

This super-cluster contains words that describe various aspects of language in general. Words that emphasize oral or written language are found in the Communication (10) and the Literature/Writing (15) Super-Clusters, respectively. There are three clusters within this super-cluster. They are:

A. Language and Language Conventions
B. Words/Sentences
C. Letters/Alphabet

36. Ownership/Possession

Super-Cluster 36 groups words that describe the action or state of owning or having—how we obtain things, how we lose things. Not all actions or states relate to items or material, however. To illustrate, note the cluster entitled "Freedom/Lack of Freedom." There are six clusters within this super-cluster. They are:

A. Losing/Giving Up
B. Freedom/Lack of Freedom
C. Possession/Ownership
D. Winning/Losing
E. Taking/Receiving Actions
F. Finding/Keeping

37. Disease/Health

The first cluster in this super-cluster deals with disease or health in a general sense. The next four clusters group words according to specific diseases, symptoms, or germs. The cluster entitled "Actions Related to Injury/Disease" contains words like *burn* and *sprain*. The cluster on medicine lists both activities (e.g., *operate*, *diagnose*) and medicines (e.g., *iodine*, *aspirin*) that are concerned with disease and health. The six clusters within this super-cluster are:

A. Disease
B. Specific Diseases/Ailments
C. Symptoms of Diseases
D. Specific Types of Germs/Genes
E. Actions Related to Injury/Disease
F. Medicine

38. Light

This super-cluster begins with words that indicate the source or type of light (e.g., *lamplight*, *sunshine*) and descriptions of the effect of light (e.g., *bright*, *radiant*). The cluster entitled "Producers of Light" lists both man-made and natural sources of light. The last cluster, "Clarity," groups together words that describe qualities or characteristics effected by light or its absence (e.g., *transparent*, *dim*). There are five clusters within this super-cluster. They are:

A. Light/Lightness
B. Actions of Light
C. Darkness
D. Producers of Light
E. Clarity

39. Causality

The first cluster within this super-cluster lists words one uses when talking about causes (e.g., *result*, *effect*, *conclusion*). The second cluster lists relationship markers that describe how one action may or may not be related causally to another, for example: He left *because* Mary left. The two clusters within this super-cluster are:

A. Causality
B. Causality (Relationship Markers)

40. Weather

The super-cluster on weather first lists words that describe weather and nature in a very general sense (e.g., *climate, environment*). Clusters on storms, clouds and natural catastrophes follow. Clusters on characteristics of weather (e.g., *dry, foggy, sunny*) are also included. The five clusters in Super-Cluster 40 are:

- A. Weather/Nature (General)
- B. Storms/Wind
- C. Clouds
- D. Natural Catastrophes
- E. Characteristics of Weather

41. Cleanliness/Uncleanliness

The first cluster in this super-cluster lists objects (e.g., *wastebasket, trash*) and actions (e.g., *pollute, infect*) that relate to cleanliness. Cleaning actions (e.g., *rinse, launder*) and the results of cleaning (e.g., *sterile, sanitary*) are found in the second cluster. The last cluster lists tools commonly used for cleaning (e.g., *cleaner, broom, brush*). The three clusters in this super-cluster are:

- A. Filth/Uncleanliness
- B. Cleanliness
- C. Tools for Cleaning

42. Popularity/Familiarity

The first cluster within this super-cluster contains words that describe the degree to which people or things are known or popular, whereas the second cluster lists words dealing with lack of familiarity or popularity. The last cluster groups words that describe the likelihood or probability that an event may happen. The three clusters within this super-cluster are:

- A. Popularity/Familiarity
- B. Lack of Popularity/Familiarity
- C. Likelihood

43. Physical Traits of People

Where earlier super-clusters deal with human emotions (Super-Cluster 5), mental characteristics or abilities (Super-Cluster 12), and personality traits of people (Super-Cluster 13), this super-cluster groups together words that are used to describe people in physical terms. The four clusters within this super-cluster are:

- A. Physical Traits
- B. Neatness
- C. Attractiveness
- D. Size as a Physical Trait

44. Touching/Grabbing Actions

The first two clusters within this super-cluster list general words for touching or grabbing (e.g., *feel, grab*). The last cluster lists specific actions (e.g., *point, wave*). The three clusters within this super-cluster are:

A. Feeling/Striking Actions
B. Grabbing/Holding Actions
C. Specific Actions Done with the Hands

45. Pronouns

In this super-cluster, pronouns are broken down into five clusters. Interrogative and indefinite adverbs make up the last section. The six clusters within this super-cluster are:

A. Pronouns and Reflexive Pronouns
B. Possessive Pronouns
C. Relative Pronouns
D. Interrogative Pronouns
E. Indefinite Pronouns
F. Interrogative/Indefinite Adverbs

46. Contractions

The first cluster in this super-cluster lists words contracted with the word *not*, while the last five clusters list the contracted forms of modals and the verb *to be*. The six clusters within this super-cluster are:

A. Contractions (Not)
B. Contractions (Have)
C. Contractions (Will)
D. Contractions (Is)
E. Contractions (Would)
F. Contractions (Are)

47. Entertainment/The Arts

This super-cluster begins with a wide-ranging cluster, "Plays/Movies," that includes words such as *act, tryout, cartoon, stage* and *plot*. The last cluster, "Art," focuses on the visual arts and includes words like *painting, woodcut* and *statue*. The four clusters in this super-cluster are:

A. Plays/Movies
B. Music/Dance
C. Instruments
D. Art

48. Walking/Running Actions

This super-cluster organizes words that describe physical activity generally performed by the legs and feet. The five clusters in this super-cluster are:

A. Running/Walking Actions
B. Lurking/Creeping
C. Kicking
D. Jumping
E. Standing/Stationary Actions

49. Mathematics

The first cluster, "Branches of Mathematics," within this super-cluster includes such general words as *arithmetic, mathematics* and *math*. Within the cluster "Mathematical Quantities" are words like *maximum, total* and *fraction*. The cluster "Mathematical Terms" includes such words as *denominator* and *numerator*. Finally, the cluster entitled

"Mathematical Operation" has words like *addition* and *divide*. The four clusters within this super-cluster are:

A. Branches of Mathematics
B. Mathematical Quantities
C. Mathematical Terms
D. Mathematical Operations

50. Auxiliary/Helping Verbs

The first cluster within the "Auxiliary/Helping Verbs" super-cluster lists forms of the verb *to be*. The cluster entitled "Primary Auxiliaries" lists conjugated forms of the verbs *to do* and *to have*. The "Modals" cluster includes *will, can* and *may*. The "Semi-Auxiliaries" cluster contains verbal constructs that behave like auxiliaries. Within this cluster are phrases like *is going to* and *had better*. The final cluster lists linking verbs. The five clusters within this super-cluster are:

A. Auxiliary Verbs
B. Primary Auxiliaries
C. Modals
D. Semi-Auxiliaries
E. Linking Verbs

51. Events

This super-cluster deals with general terms for events as well as terms for specific types of events. The three clusters within this super-cluster are:

A. Dates/Events (General)
B. Festive/Recreational Events
C. Political Events

52. Temperature/Fire

The super-cluster on temperature/fire includes general words related to temperature and heat as well as specific words related to fire. The cluster "Products of Fire" contains words like *ash* and *cinder*, while "Fire Products" groups words like *firewood, matchbox* and *cigar*. The five clusters in this super-cluster are:

A. Temperature
B. Insulation
C. Fire
D. Products of Fire
E. Fire Products

53. Images/Perceptions

Super-Cluster 53 divides the idea of perception into two clusters: (1) the act of showing or the object being shown (e.g., *image, sight, represent*), and (2) the perspective of the subject or perceiver (e.g., *look, notice, appear, loom*). The two clusters in this super-cluster are:

A. Visual Images/Perception
B. Looking/Perceiving Actions

54. Life/Survival

Words that describe the beginnings of life and its end are the focus of the first cluster within this super-cluster, while the maintenance of life is the theme for the second. The two clusters are:

A. Life, Birth, Death

B. Survival/Growth

55. Conformity/Complexity

The first cluster within this super-cluster groups together words that do not describe a norm but imply one (e.g., *special, original, strange*). The second cluster lists words that describe ranges of complexity (e.g., *ornate, maze, plain*). The two clusters are:

A. Conformity to a Norm

B. Complexity/Order

56. Difficulty/Danger

Cluster A within this super-cluster lists words along the dimension of difficulty-ease, while Cluster B lists words along the dimension of danger-safety. The two clusters are:

A. Difficulty/Ease

B. Danger/Safety

57. Texture/Durability

The first cluster in Super-Cluster 57 contains words that describe various kinds of texture. The cluster on durability includes both tactile and abstract terms (e.g., *brittle, subtle*). Words describing degree of density or viscosity are found under the cluster "Consistency." The three clusters in this super-cluster are:

A. Texture

B. Durability

C. Consistency

58. Color

The first cluster within this super-cluster deals with different types of color. The cluster on paint contains words like *tint, whitewash* and *dye*. The two clusters are:

A. Color

B. Paint

59. Chemicals

General terms related to chemicals (e.g., *compound, chemical*) are found in this super-cluster, as well as gases and chemical actions (e.g., *chlorinate, ferment*). The two clusters are:

A. Chemicals

B. Acids

60. Facial Expressions/Actions

This super-cluster deals with general and specific actions associated with the face. The four clusters are:

A. Facial Expressions
B. Actions Associated with the Nose
C. Actions Associated with the Mouth
D. Breathing

61. Electricity/Particles of Matter

This super-cluster lists words associated with energy of different kinds. The two clusters are:

A. Electricity
B. Molecules/Atoms

REFERENCES

Becker, W. C., Dixon, R., & Anderson-Inman, L. (1980). *Morphographic and root word analysis of 26,000 high frequency words*. Eugene, OR: University of Oregon, College of Education.

California Achievement Tests (CAT) (1986). (Form E). Monterey, CA: CTB/McGraw-Hill.

Carroll, J., Davies, P., & Richman, B. (1971). *The American Heritage word frequency book*. Boston: Houghton Mifflin.

Comprehensive Tests of Basic Skills (CTBS) (1984). (Form U). Monterey, CA: CTB/McGraw-Hill.

Gardner, E. F., Rudman, H. C., Karlsen, B., & Merwin, J. C. (1981). *Stanford Achievement Test*. (Form E). U.S.A.: Harcourt Brace Jovanovich.

Harris, A., & Jacobson, M. (1972). *Basic elementary reading vocabulary*. New York: Macmillan.

Marzano, R. J., Kendall, J. S., & Paynter, D. E. (1989). *A study of basic words and their related grade levels*. Aurora, CO: Mid-continent Regional Educational Laboratory.

Marzano, R. J., & Marzano, J. S. (1988). *A cluster approach to elementary vocabulary instruction*. Newark, DE: International Reading Association.

Marzano, R. J., Marzano, L., Paynter, D. E., & Pickering, D. J. (1989). *Literacy plus: An integrated approach to teaching reading, writing, vocabulary and reasoning*. Aurora, CO: Mid-continent Regional Educational Laboratory.

Nagy, W. E. (1988). *Teaching vocabulary to improve reading comprehension*. Urbana, IL: National Council of Teachers of English.

Nagy, W. E., & Anderson, R. (1984). How many words are there in printed school English? *Reading Research Quarterly, 19*, 303-330.

Nagy, W. E., Anderson, R., & Herman, P. (1987). Learning words from context during normal reading. *American Educational Research Journal, 24*, 237-270.

Science Research Associates (SRA) Survey of Basic Skills Objectives (1984). (Form P). Chicago, IL: Science Research Associates, Inc.

Appendix A: Words in Semantic Clusters

1. Occupations/Pursuits

1A Occupations (General)

1A1.0	A	B	C
homemaker	3	4	-
worker	3	3	3
workman	3	3	-
workingman	4	-	-
employee	5	3	7
laborer	5	5	6
professional	5	3	5
breadwinner	6	-	-
craftsman	6	5	-
factotum	13	-	-

1A2.0	A	B	C
craft	3	3	4
career	4	3	5
occupation	4	3	5
employment	5	3	7
livelihood	5	3	5
profession	5	4	5
role	5	3	5
sideline	5	6	-
vocation	8	5	10
lifework	10	6	-

1A3.0	A	B	C
job	1	3	1
housework	2	3	-
errand	3	3	-
housekeeping	3	3	6
task	3	3	5
chore	4	4	5
production	5	3	6

1B Supervisors/Assistants

1B1.0	A	B	C
assistant	4	3	6
attendant	5	5	6
apprentice	6	4	6
journeyman	8	4	-
peon	8	3	-

1B2.0	A	B	C
boss	3	3	3
owner	3	3	3
landowner	4	3	-
manager	4	3	3
employer	5	3	6
foreman	5	3	-
landlady	5	3	-
landlord	5	3	4
landholder	6	8	-
floorwalker	10	-	-
padrone	13	-	-

1B3.0	A	B	C
leader	3	3	3
director	4	3	4
chairman	5	3	-
chairperson	5	-	5
chairwoman	5	-	-
headmaster	5	4	-
headmistress	5	-	-
administrator	6	4	-
overseer	6	3	-
superintendent	6	3	-
supervisor	6	7	6

1B4.0	A	B	C
producer	4	3	5
sponsor	4	4	9
founder	5	4	5
impresario	13	-	-

1C Royalty/Statesmen

1C1.0	A	B	C
governor	3	3	4
mayor	3	3	3
congressman	4	4	-
congresswoman	4	-	5
senator	4	3	4
candidate	5	3	5
councilman	5	-	-
councilwoman	5	-	-
politician	5	5	7
delegate	6	6	7
tribune	6	5	-

A: Grade level; B: Earliest Grade of Occurrence in Textbooks; C: Earliest Grade of Occurrence on Standardized Tests.

	A	B	C
incumbent	8	5	-
lawgiver	8	7	-
demagogue	10	7	-

1C2.0	A	B	C
ambassador	5	4	5
officeholder	5	-	-
official	5	3	5
dignitary	6	4	-
diplomat	6	4	7
statesman	6	5	7
consul	8	7	-
councilor	8	3	-
envoy	8	7	-
magistrate	8	5	-
legate	10	-	-
prefect	10	-	-
praetor	13	-	-
reeve	13	3	-

1C3.0	A	B	C
king	1	3	K
prince	3	3	3
princess	3	3	3
queen	3	3	6
duke	4	4	K
lord	4	3	5
duchess	5	6	-
earl	5	4	7
knight	5	3	6
monarch	5	3	12
sire	5	3	-
sultan	5	4	-
baron	6	5	-
czar	6	6	-
emperor	6	3	7
empress	6	3	7
nobleman	6	3	7
squire	6	6	-
marquis	8	7	-
sheik	8	-	8
liege	10	5	-
patrician	10	3	-
hidalgo	13	7	-

1C4.0	A	B	C
chief	3	3	3
president	3	3	3
vice president	4	3	-
figurehead	5	3	-
dictator	8	3	9
liberator	8	-	-
chancellor	10	5	-
despot	10	-	-
provost	10	-	-

	A	B	C
regent	10	5	-
triumvir	10	-	-

1D Names of People in Sports

1D1.0	A	B	C
loser	3	3	-
winner	3	3	3
underdog	5	5	-

1D2.0	A	B	C
runner	2	3	2
boxer	3	3	6
player	3	3	3
acrobat	4	4	6
athlete	4	3	4
diver	4	4	4
horseman	4	3	-
horsewoman	4	-	-
skater	4	3	12
swimmer	4	3	5
wrestler	4	3	-
daredevil	5	4	-
fighter	5	3	-
gymnast	5	-	7
skier	5	5	7
contestant	6	3	7
racer	6	4	7
equestrian	8	4	-
heavyweight	8	4	-

1D3.0	A	B	C
catcher	3	3	3
ballplayer	4	3	-
baseman	4	3	4
batter	4	3	4
fielder	4	3	-
goalkeeper	4	-	-
shortstop	4	3	4
quarterback	5	5	5
halfback	6	6	-
lineman	8	4	-
southpaw	8	3	-

1D4.0	A	B	C
coach	3	3	3
lifeguard	3	3	9
trainer	3	3	3
umpire	4	3	5
lifesaver	6	6	9
referee	6	6	7
timekeeper	6	7	-

1D5.0	A	B	C
sharpshooter	4	-	-
archer	6	4	9

A: Grade level; B: Earliest Grade of Occurrence in Textbooks; C: Earliest Grade of Occurrence on Standardized Tests.

marksman	6	4	-
markswoman	6	-	6

1E Reporters/Writers

1E1.0	A	B	C
announcer	4	3	5
weatherman	4	3	-
sportscaster	5	7	-
newscaster	6	-	7

1E2.0	A	B	C
author	3	3	3
reporter	3	3	3
writer	3	3	3
newspaperman	4	5	-
poet	4	3	5
scribe	6	3	-
critic	8	5	10
historian	8	4	10
playwright	8	3	7
gazetteer	10	-	-

1E3.0	A	B	C
narrator	4	4	8
speaker	5	3	4
spokesman	5	5	-
spokesperson	5	-	-
spokeswoman	5	-	-

1F Outdoor Professions

1F1.0	A	B	C
camper	4	4	-
fisher	4	4	4
fisherman	4	3	7
hunter	4	3	3
sportsman	5	6	-
sportswoman	5	-	-
trapper	5	3	5

1F2.0	A	B	C
digger	4	3	-
gravedigger	4	-	-
miner	4	3	4
stonecutter	5	3	-

1F3.0	A	B	C
cowboy	2	3	5
cowgirl	2	-	-
cowhand	3	3	-
shepherd	3	3	3
rancher	4	3	4
cattleman	5	-	-
herdsman	5	5	-
ranger	5	3	7

roughrider	6	-	-
stockman	6	-	-
swineherd	8	7	-

1F4.0	A	B	C
farmer	2	3	2
gardener	3	3	3
milkmaid	3	6	-
grower	5	3	-
picker	5	4	-
sharecropper	6	3	-
serf	8	6	7

1F5.0	A	B	C
woodcutter	4	3	-
woodsman	4	3	-
forester	5	4	-
logger	5	4	-
lumberjack	5	4	5
lumberman	5	8	-

1G Artists

1G1.0	A	B	C
artist	2	3	2
painter	2	3	K
designer	5	5	10
potter	5	3	-
architect	6	3	5
photographer	6	4	6
sculptor	6	3	8
lapidary	10	-	-

1G2.0	A	B	C
singer	3	3	3
conductor	4	3	3
drummer	4	3	12
musician	5	3	6
composer	6	3	7
soloist	6	6	-
soprano	6	4	-
violinist	6	6	-
minstrel	8	4	9
tenor	8	4	-
troubadour	8	4	-
virtuoso	10	7	-

1H Entertainers/Performers

1H1.0	A	B	C
dancer	2	3	K
actor	3	3	3
actress	3	4	3
model	4	3	4
performer	4	3	4

1H2.0	A	B	C
clown	1	3	K
ringmaster	3	3	-
comic	4	3	3
juggler	4	4	-
magician	4	3	5
fortuneteller	5	3	-
ventriloquist	5	4	-
mime	6	-	-
barker	10	3	-
harlequin	10	6	-

1H3.0	A	B	C
entertainer	5	3	-
showman	5	4	-

1I Teachers/Students

1I1.0	A	B	C
teacher	1	3	1
librarian	2	3	8
schoolteacher	2	3	9
professor	3	3	3
principal	4	3	4
instructor	5	3	-
schoolmaster	5	4	-
schoolmistress	5	-	-
counselor	5	7	6
dean	6	5	4
tutor	6	4	6
adviser	6	7	5
mentor	8	-	11
pedagogue	13	-	-
proctor	13	-	-

1I2.0	A	B	C
pupil	3	3	4
student	3	3	3
freshman	4	3	7
graduate	5	3	9
sophomore	6	3	-
alumnus	8	-	-
disciple	8	4	-

1J Public Servants

1J1.0	A	B	C
fireman	1	3	-
policeman	1	3	-
policewoman	1	-	-
detective	3	3	2
marshal	3	5	11
officer	3	3	3
sheriff	3	3	3
inspector	4	3	4
patrolman	4	7	-
trooper	5	5	-
constable	6	4	-
sergeant	6	3	7
coroner	8	-	-
lawmaker	8	3	-
notary	8	8	-
sleuth	8	-	-

1J2.0	A	B	C
captain	3	3	3
soldier	3	3	4
redcoat	4	3	-
airman	5	4	-
cavalryman	5	6	-
rifleman	5	5	-
colonel	6	3	6
corporal	6	5	-
guerilla	8	5	11
mercenary	10	5	-
sentinel	10	6	-
sentry	10	5	-
doughboy	13	-	-

1J2.1	A	B	C
martial	8	7	-

1K Areas of Work

1K1.0	A	B	C
science	2	3	3
medicine	2	3	4
business	3	3	3
education	3	3	4
law	3	3	3
religion	3	3	4
agriculture	4	3	6
industry	4	3	5
military	5	3	5
politics	5	3	5
technology	5	3	5

1L Scientists/Discoverers

1L1.0	A	B	C
scientist	3	3	4
engineer	4	3	4
vet	4	3	3
veterinarian	4	7	-
astronaut	5	3	5
mathematician	5	4	9
meteorologist	5	4	9
archeologist	6	4	-
astronomer	6	3	7
biologist	6	5	5

A: Grade level; B: Earliest Grade of Occurrence in Textbooks; C: Earliest Grade of Occurrence on Standardized Tests.

	A	B	C
chemist	6	3	-
frogman	6	4	7
geographer	6	4	6
geologist	6	3	11
naturalist	8	3	12
botanist	10	5	-
curator	10	5	-

1L2.0	A	B	C
spaceman	3	3	-
explorer	4	3	4
inventor	4	3	5
frontiersman	5	5	-
frontierswoman	5	-	-
discoverer	6	5	-
researcher	8	5	9

1L3.0	A	B	C
geography	4	3	4
astronomy	5	4	9
biology	5	5	7
chemistry	5	3	5
ecology	5	7	11
economics	5	4	5
geology	5	5	12
taxidermy	6	-	-
anatomy	8	4	-
anthropology	8	5	7
archeology	8	7	-
architecture	8	3	7
botany	8	6	11
obstetrics	8	-	-
physics	8	3	9
psychology	8	5	7
zoology	8	7	-
paleontology	10	7	-
pediatrics	10	8	-
physiology	10	5	-
demography	13	-	-
entomology	13	-	-
etymology	13	5	-
morphology	13	-	-
ontology	13	-	-
ornithology	13	3	-
pathology	13	7	-
topology	13	4	-

1M People Who Buy and Sell

1M1.0	A	B	C
customer	3	3	3
shopper	3	3	3
buyer	4	3	6
client	6	4	10
patron	10	4	-

1M2.0	A	B	C
peddler	4	3	-
salesclerk	4	-	-
salesman	4	3	6
salesperson	4	-	2
saleswoman	4	-	-
shopkeeper	4	3	7
storekeeper	4	3	3
trader	4	4	4
agent	5	3	5
merchant	5	3	7
middleman	5	-	-
seller	5	3	6
tradesman	5	8	-
broker	6	3	6
vendor	6	4	9

1N Small Business

1N1.0	A	B	C
shoemaker	3	3	4
blacksmith	4	3	4
clockmaker	4	-	-
goldsmith	4	3	10
locksmith	4	5	-
smith	4	4	3
watchmaker	4	-	-
brazier	5	-	-
cobbler	5	3	-
gunsmith	5	8	-
silversmith	5	4	5
cabinetmaker	6	7	-
coppersmith	6	6	-
bootblack	10	6	-
wheelwright	10	4	-

1N2.0	A	B	C
baker	2	3	3
butcher	2	3	3
milkman	2	3	-
grocer	3	3	-
bodyguard	4	6	-
barber	5	3	7
pastry cook	5	-	-
saloonkeeper	5	-	-
florist	6	-	9
fishmonger	10	5	-

1N3.0	A	B	C
dressmaker	4	3	-
weaver	4	4	7
miller	6	3	11
tailor	6	3	7
tanner	8	5	9

---

haberdasher	10	-	-
milliner	10	4	-
mercer	13	-	-

1O People Who Work in Offices

1O1.0	A	B	C
businessman	4	3	6
businesswoman	4	-	-

1O2.0	A	B	C
secretary	4	3	4
typist	4	5	9
clerk	6	3	6
receptionist	6	-	7

1O2.1	A	B	C
stenography	8	-	-

1P Builders

1P1.0	A	B	C
builder	3	3	4
shipbuilder	3	5	-
manufacturer	5	3	5
contractor	6	7	7

1P1.1	A	B	C
shipbuilding	5	3	-

1Q Publishing

1Q1.0	A	B	C
editor	4	3	4
printer	4	3	4
publisher	4	3	4

1R People Who Clean Up

1R1.0	A	B	C
garbageman	2	-	-
janitor	4	3	5
caretaker	6	4	8
custodian	6	-	7

1S Occupations Related to Money

1S1.0	A	B	C
banker	2	4	2
bookkeeper	5	-	-
accountant	6	-	9
cashier	6	3	-
teller	6	3	7

pawnbroker	10	7	-
croupier	13	-	-

1T Occupations Related to Imprisonment/Slavery

1T1.0	A	B	C
prisoner	3	3	3
slave	3	3	3
bondman	5	-	-
bondservant	6	-	-
gladiator	6	4	-
inmate	8	6	-
chattel	10	5	-
thrall	10	7	-

1T2.0	A	B	C
guard	3	3	4
bondsman	5	-	-
slaveholder	5	-	-
hangman	6	7	-
warden	6	4	9
watchman	6	3	6
turnkey	8	-	7

1U Occupations Related to Medicine

1U1.0	A	B	C
doctor	2	3	K
nurse	3	3	2
dentist	4	3	3
physician	5	4	5
intern	6	7	-
psychiatrist	6	7	-
surgeon	6	3	7
apothecary	8	-	-
therapist	13	-	-

1V Occupations Related to Transportation

1V1.0	A	B	C
driver	2	3	2
pilot	3	3	4
flier	4	3	-
skipper	5	4	4
copilot	6	5	7
aeronaut	10	-	-

1V2.0	A	B	C
shipowner	4	-	-
brakeman	5	3	-
seaman	5	3	11
shipmate	5	-	-

A: Grade level; B: Earliest Grade of Occurrence in Textbooks; C: Earliest Grade of Occurrence on Standardized Tests.

switchman	5	-	-
porter	6	3	-
stevedore	6	7	-
stewardess	6	3	-
steward	8	4	-
boatswain	10	-	-
longshoreman	10	-	-
coxswain	13	7	-

1W Clergy/Religious

1W1.0	A	B	C
missionary	4	3	-
nun	4	7	-
bishop	5	3	-
minister	5	3	5
pastor	5	4	-
pope	5	3	-
priest	5	3	5
prophet	5	3	-
abbot	6	5	-
apostle	6	6	-
clerical	6	7	8
deacon	6	-	-
hermit	6	3	7
monk	6	4	-
parson	6	5	-
rabbi	6	3	-
cardinal	8	3	-
churchwarden	8	-	-
clergyman	8	3	7
friar	8	6	-
layperson	8	-	-
rector	8	-	5
dervish	10	-	-
pontiff	10	-	-
eremite	13	-	-
hierarch	13	-	-
prelate	13	3	-

1X Repairmen/Construction Workers

1X1.0	A	B	C
mechanic	4	3	4
plumber	4	3	5
repairman	4	4	-
cameraman	5	4	-
surveyor	5	4	4
draftsman	6	7	-
draftsperson	6	-	-
technician	6	9	7

1X2.0	A	B	C
carpenter	3	3	4
bricklayer	4	5	-
mason	5	3	5
stagehand	5	4	-
stonemason	5	7	-
shipwright	10	-	-
wright	10	3	4

1Y Legal Participants and Occupations

1Y1.0	A	B	C
judge	2	3	2
lawyer	2	4	2
attorney	5	7	6
counselor	8	7	6
defendant	8	5	9
juror	8	7	11
prosecutor	8	7	12

1Y1.1	A	B	C
forensic	10	-	-

1Z Servants

1Z1.0	A	B	C
maid	3	3	3
butler	4	3	-
doorkeeper	4	4	5
doorman	4	3	-
housekeeper	4	3	4
servant	4	3	10
bellhop	5	-	-
gatekeeper	5	3	-
usher	5	4	7
chambermaid	6	-	-
chauffeur	6	5	-
coachman	6	3	-
handmaid	6	-	-
redcap	6	-	-
caddie	8	5	-
valet	8	4	-
vassal	8	7	7
cupbearer	10	-	-
gamekeeper	10	6	-
lackey	10	-	-
scullion	10	6	-

1Z1.1	A	B	C
menial	8	5	-

1a Occupations Related to Restaurants

1a1.0	A	B	C
dishwasher	3	3	3
waiter	3	3	8
waitress	3	7	-
bartender	5	-	-
chef	5	7	6
busboy	6	-	-

1b Messengers

1b1.0	A	B	C
mailman	1	3	-
messenger	4	3	4
operator	4	3	6
postmaster	4	3	-
news carrier	6	-	-
telegrapher	6	-	-
courier	10	4	-

1c Occupations Usually Held by Youth

1c1.0	A	B	C
babysitter	1	-	-
paperboy	1	-	-
nursemaid	5	4	-

1d Work-related Actions

1d1.0	A	B	C
work	K	3	K
effort	4	3	4
labor	4	3	7
strive	4	5	-
toil	5	6	4
drudge	6	4	-
overwork	6	6	-
travail	6	-	-
endeavor	8	6	-

1d2.0	A	B	C
hire	3	3	3
employ	5	3	6
engage	6	3	6

1d3.0	A	B	C
quit	2	3	2
layoff	6	-	-
retire	6	4	6
depose	8	5	-
lockout	8	-	-

	A	B	C
resign	8	3	10
abdicate	10	7	10

1d4.0	A	B	C
featherbedding	8	-	-
nepotism	10	-	-
simony	10	-	-
sinecure	13	-	-

1e Hobbies

1e1.0	A	B	C
collector	4	3	6
bibliophile	8	-	-

SUPER CLUSTER
2. Types of Motion/Activity

2A General Motion

2A1.0	A	B	C
play	K	3	K
action	3	3	3
traffic	3	3	3
activity	4	3	5
motion	4	3	4
movement	4	3	5
osmosis	6	7	-

2A1.1	A	B	C
movable	3	3	-
kinetic	5	6	5
mobile	6	3	-
portable	8	3	8

2B Lack of Motion

2B1.0	A	B	C
motionless	5	3	-
standstill	5	3	-
static	5	3	5
inert	6	5	-
stagnant	6	3	9
stationary	6	4	10
deadlock	10	-	-

2B2.0	A	B	C
hang	1	3	1
dangle	5	5	9
hover	6	3	-
suspend	6	6	9
adjourn	8	3	-

A: Grade level; B: Earliest Grade of Occurrence in Textbooks; C: Earliest Grade of Occurrence on Standardized Tests.

2B2.1	A	B	C
probation	6	7	6
suspension	6	3	6
abeyance	10	5	-

2B3.0	A	B	C
wait	1	3	1
stay	2	3	K
remain	3	3	1
await	4	3	7
hesitate	4	3	6
pause	4	3	4
postpone	4	4	-
procrastinate	4	-	-
putter	4	5	-
falter	5	7	-
lag	5	5	2
linger	5	3	7
bide	8	3	-
dally	8	-	-
dawdle	8	3	-
loiter	8	6	-
tarry	10	4	-

2B4.0	A	B	C
interrupt	4	3	4
delay	5	3	5
waylay	5	-	-
defer	6	6	12
detain	6	7	-
hinder	6	3	7
impede	8	8	-
intervene	8	7	-

2B4.1	A	B	C
interruption	6	K	-
filibuster	10	7	-
hiatus	13	-	-

2B5.0	A	B	C
rest	2	3	2
relax	3	3	3
settle	3	3	2
lounge	5	5	-
bask	10	6	10

2C Beginning Motion

2C1.0	A	B	C
begin	1	3	1
start	1	3	1
try	2	3	2
introduce	4	3	7
embark	8	4	9
inaugurate	8	-	-

	A	B	C
originate	8	6	12
induct	10	-	-

2C1.1	A	B	C
inchoate	13	-	-
incipient	13	-	-

2C1.2	A	B	C
prelude	8	4	-
preamble	10	8	8
prologue	10	-	-
exordium	13	-	-

2C2.0	A	B	C
beginning	2	3	3
origin	5	3	5
source	5	3	5
genesis	6	7	6
onset	8	-	-

2C3.0	A	B	C
baptism	3	3	-
introduction	4	3	5
initiation	6	6	11
preface	6	5	7

2D The Act of Occurring

2D1.0	A	B	C
do	K	3	K
use	1	3	1
apply	5	3	K
function	5	3	6
commit	6	3	6
exert	8	6	11

2D2.0	A	B	C
happen	1	3	K
occur	4	3	6
undergo	6	4	10
ensue	10	5	-
recur	10	9	-
transpire	10	-	-
supervene	13	-	-

2D3.0	A	B	C
react	6	3	7

2D3.1	A	B	C
reaction	6	3	7
backlash	10	-	-

2E Completion

2E1.0	A	B	C
last	1	3	1
end	2	3	K
final	3	3	5
deadline	4	9	-

2E2.0	A	B	C
finish	2	3	2
complete	3	3	2
graduate	4	3	9
accomplish	5	3	5
fulfill	6	3	-
consummate	10	-	-
culminate	10	8	-

2E2.1	A	B	C
completion	6	3	7
deed	6	3	11

2F Halting

2F1.0	A	B	C
stop	K	3	K
cancel	4	4	7
quit	4	3	2
cease	5	5	6
halt	5	3	2
extinguish	5	-	10
lapse	6	5	-
terminate	6	8	-
abolish	8	3	9
abort	8	-	-
desist	10	6	-
stanch	10	6	-

2F2.0	A	B	C
prevent	4	3	3
obstruct	5	4	-
boycott	6	5	6
prohibit	6	-	7
deter	8	3	11
preempt	8	-	-
preclude	10	-	-
thwart	10	4	-
obviate	13	-	-

2F2.1	A	B	C
obstacle	5	3	6

2F3.0	A	B	C
dodge	3	3	4
avoid	4	3	4
abstain	6	8	-
refrain	6	3	-
shirk	8	-	-
elude	10	-	12
eschew	10	-	-

2F4.0	A	B	C
resist	5	3	6
restrain	6	3	11
intercept	8	3	-
parry	10	4	-

2F5.0	A	B	C
smother	4	3	4
clog	5	4	7
congest	6	4	-
muffle	6	-	7
stifle	6	3	-
repress	8	-	-

2G General Actions Involving Coming/Going

2G1.0	A	B	C
arrival	5	3	6
oncoming	5	3	-
advent	10	3	12
ingress	10	-	-

2G2.0	A	B	C
trip	1	3	2
travel	2	3	3
flight	3	3	2
journey	3	3	3
voyage	3	3	3
sightseeing	4	4	-
expedition	5	3	5
hitchhike	5	7	-
tour	5	3	3
exploration	6	3	6
migration	6	3	10
commute	8	5	11
excursion	8	3	-
junket	8	-	-
safari	8	6	10
traverse	8	5	9
trek	8	5	7
jaunt	10	-	-
transit	10	7	11

2G3.0	A	B	C
adventure	3	3	3
jag	8	-	-
quest	8	3	-
spree	8	7	-

2G3.1	A	B	C
nomadic	5	6	-
wayfaring	10	-	-
errant	13	-	-

2G4.0	A	B	C
leave	1	3	1
exit	3	4	3
depart	5	8	9
takeoff	5	4	6
withdraw	5	3	5
vacate	8	5	-
abscond	10	-	-
recede	10	5	8
retract	10	3	-

2G4.1	A	B	C
departure	5	3	6
exodus	10	5	11
egress	13	-	-

2G5.0	A	B	C
disappear	3	3	3
dissolve	5	3	5
vanish	5	3	5

2G6.0	A	B	C
wander	2	3	2
roam	3	3	2
migrate	5	3	4
stray	5	3	7
meander	8	8	-
rove	8	-	6
straggle	8	-	-

2G7.0	A	B	C
come	K	3	K
visit	2	3	2
appear	3	3	3
arrive	3	3	3

2G8.0	A	B	C
go	K	3	K
step	1	3	1
approach	4	3	2
access	5	3	8
advance	5	3	7
proceed	5	3	-
headway	6	3	-
progress	6	3	7
encroach	10	7	-
impinge	10	-	-

2H Pursuit

2H1.0	A	B	C
pursuit	6	4	7

2H2.0	A	B	C
follow	1	3	2
chase	2	3	2
track	2	3	2
pursue	5	4	5

2I Taking/Giving

2I1.0	A	B	C
get	K	3	K
take	K	3	1
bring	1	3	2
carry	2	3	2
move	2	3	K
fetch	4	3	-
trundle	4	3	-
bear	5	3	1
import	5	3	5
shuttle	6	6	5
tote	8	6	-
waft	8	7	-

2I2.0	A	B	C
return	2	3	1
homecoming	4	4	10
retrieve	6	8	8
remand	8	-	-

2I3.0	A	B	C
mail	1	3	1
send	1	3	1
airmail	3	3	-
ship	3	3	2
dispatch	5	3	9
export	5	3	5

2I4.0	A	B	C
relay	5	3	4
transfer	6	3	2
transplant	8	7	11
devolve	13	-	-

2I5.0	A	B	C
remove	3	3	3
rid	3	3	6
eliminate	6	3	7
oust	8	6	-
uproot	8	-	-
deport	10	8	-
evict	10	-	-
exorcise	13	-	-

A: Grade level; B: Earliest Grade of Occurrence in Textbooks; C: Earliest Grade of Occurrence on Standardized Tests.

2I6.0	A	B	C
put	K	3	K
give	1	3	K
place	2	3	K
set	2	3	1
provide	3	3	3
furnish	4	3	6
supply	4	3	5
purvey	13	-	-

2I7.0	A	B	C
deliver	2	3	3
present	2	3	1
deposit	4	3	5
bestow	6	4	-
consign	8	7	-
dispense	8	4	7
distribute	8	3	11
ration	8	4	9

2J Tossing/Catching Actions

2J1.0	A	B	C
pass	1	3	3
toss	1	3	3
throw	2	3	K
pitch	3	3	3
cast	4	3	K
chuck	4	3	3
fling	4	3	6
flip	4	3	-
heave	4	3	-
flick	5	3	-
hurl	6	5	6
thrust	6	3	6
catapult	8	6	-
jettison	13	-	-

2J2.0	A	B	C
catch	1	3	K
snag	6	7	-
enmesh	10	-	-
trammel	10	-	-

2K Pushing/Pulling Actions

2K1.0	A	B	C
push	1	3	1
shove	3	3	4
insert	5	3	8
propel	5	4	5
inject	6	5	-
excrete	8	7	-
extrude	10	-	-

2K2.0	A	B	C
pull	1	3	K
drag	3	3	5
haul	4	3	5
tow	4	3	6
yank	5	5	-
lug	6	3	-

2K2.1	A	B	C
gravity	4	3	3
traction	8	7	-

2L Vibration

2L1.0	A	B	C
shake	2	3	1
shiver	3	3	11
tremble	3	3	3
quiver	4	3	4
vibrate	4	3	5
shudder	5	4	7
throb	5	3	7
wobble	5	5	-
jitter	5	-	-
quake	6	3	9
totter	6	-	-
undulate	6	-	-
quaver	8	-	-
twitter	8	3	-
dodder	10	6	-
oscillate	10	-	-
palpitate	10	-	-

2L2.0	A	B	C
flutter	3	3	10
wiggle	3	3	-
wriggle	3	3	-
sputter	4	3	-
squirm	4	3	-
teeter	4	-	-
waver	5	6	5
flit	8	3	-
fluctuate	10	-	-
vacillate	10	-	-
writhe	10	-	-

2L2.1	A	B	C
vibration	5	3	5

2L3.0	A	B	C
juggle	4	4	4
scramble	4	3	-
jumble	6	3	-

2M Shifting Motion

2M1.0	A	B	C
slide	2	3	2
rock	3	3	K
fishtail	4	-	-
shift	4	3	-
skid	4	3	7
slip	4	3	4
sway	4	3	5
jostle	8	4	-
scud	8	-	-
careen	10	-	-
skew	10	4	-
yaw	10	3	-

2N Jerking Motion

2N1.0	A	B	C
jerk	3	3	3
snap	3	3	3
budge	4	3	2
bob	5	3	1
fidget	5	3	-
lurch	5	4	-
twitch	5	3	4
flounce	6	-	-
jolt	6	4	-
spasm	8	6	-
fillip	13	-	-

2N2.0	A	B	C
bounce	3	3	4
deflect	6	4	-
jounce	6	5	-
ricochet	8	-	-

2O Ascending Motion

2O1.0	A	B	C
order	3	3	3
rank	5	3	5
rate	5	3	4

2O2.0	A	B	C
lift	2	3	2
raise	2	3	2
load	3	3	3
hoist	5	5	5
pry	5	3	-
elevate	6	-	6
boost	8	3	-

2O3.0	A	B	C
climb	2	3	2
blast-off	3	5	-
mount	4	3	-
rise	4	3	3
skyrocket	4	3	-
arise	6	4	11
ascend	6	3	6
clamber	8	-	7
emerge	8	3	7
escalate	8	-	-

2O3.1	A	B	C
ascent	6	4	11

2P Descending Motion (General)

2P1.0	A	B	C
fall	K	3	1
tumble	4	3	3
collapse	5	3	5
descend	5	3	5
landslide	5	4	-
plunge	5	3	9
topple	6	3	-
plummet	8	-	-
swoon	10	-	-

2P1.1	A	B	C
descent	6	3	-

2P2.0	A	B	C
lay	1	3	K
drop	2	3	2
dump	3	3	4
lower	3	3	3
tilt	5	3	-
dunk	6	7	-
cumber	10	-	-
lade	10	-	-

2P3.0	A	B	C
dip	4	3	4
sag	4	4	-
droop	5	3	-
slump	5	3	8
slouch	6	5	-

2Q Descending Motion Done by Human Beings

2Q1.0	A	B	C
sit	K	3	1
crouch	4	3	-

	A	B	C
squat	4	3	5
stoop	5	3	9

2Q2.0	A	B	C
flop	3	4	5
lie	3	3	3
sprawl	5	6	5

2R Reduction

2R1.0	A	B	C
shrink	3	4	3
diminish	5	7	11
dwindle	5	6	3
wither	5	5	5
shrivel	5	-	-
letup	6	3	-
wilt	6	3	7
subside	8	7	-
abate	10	-	7
wizen	10	-	-

2R1.1	A	B	C
contraction	4	3	-
compression	6	5	-
closure	8	5	-
stricture	10	-	-

2R2.0	A	B	C
shorten	3	3	2
reduce	4	3	4
extenuate	10	-	-
retrench	10	-	-
mitigate	13	7	-

2R3.0	A	B	C
tighten	3	3	4
condense	5	3	9
compress	6	6	-
cramp	6	3	-
cram	8	3	-
tamp	8	4	-
constrict	10	-	-

2R4.0	A	B	C
corrugate	5	-	-
crumble	5	3	4
crumple	5	K	-
crinkle	6	7	-
crimp	8	-	-

2S Expansion

2S1.0	A	B	C
explosion	5	3	9
expansion	6	3	6

	A	B	C
diffusion	8	5	-
extension	8	3	9

2S2.0	A	B	C
enlarge	4	5	4
magnify	4	5	7
swell	4	3	4
expand	6	3	7
bloat	8	7	-
dilate	8	-	-
extend	8	3	7
inflate	8	-	8
splay	10	-	-

2S3.0	A	B	C
protrude	4	-	11
bulge	5	4	10
jut	6	-	5
billow	8	-	-
protuberant	13	-	-

2S4.0	A	B	C
burst	3	3	4
blast	4	3	5
erupt	4	4	11
explode	5	3	-
discharge	6	3	6
emit	8	5	-
expel	8	7	7
detonate	10	-	-
emanate	13	-	-
fulminate	13	-	-

2S5.0	A	B	C
scatter	3	3	4
spread	3	3	K
diffuse	8	3	10
dispel	8	8	-
disperse	8	5	10
disseminate	10	-	-
dissipate	10	7	-
intersperse	10	-	-
strew	10	6	10

2T Force

2T1.0	A	B	C
force	3	3	3
pressure	4	3	4
inertia	6	3	-
propulsion	6	5	-
onrush	10	5	-

A: Grade level; B: Earliest Grade of Occurrence in Textbooks; C: Earliest Grade of Occurrence on Standardized Tests.

2U Closing/Opening Actions

2U1.0	A	B	C
open	1	3	K
ajar	5	-	8
gape	8	4	-

2U2.0	A	B	C
shut	2	3	2
abridge	8	-	-
curtail	8	-	9
restrict	8	5	7
occlude	10	-	-
shutdown	10	8	-

2V Joining Actions

2V1.0	A	B	C
connection	4	4	5
seam	4	3	K
bond	6	3	6
hookup	6	3	-
liaison	8	-	-

2V2.0	A	B	C
join	2	3	1
marry	3	3	6
wed	3	3	-
attach	4	3	3
federate	4	-	-
splice	4	-	-
accompany	5	3	5
combine	5	3	9
connect	5	3	7
link	5	3	7
unite	5	3	9
associate	6	4	6
engage	6	3	6
fuse	6	3	-
graft	6	7	6
merge	6	3	6
adjoin	8	3	-
annex	8	3	7
conjugate	8	9	-
consolidate	8	5	-
integrate	8	-	-
affiliate	10	5	-
consort	10	-	-
coalesce	13	-	-
concatenate	13	-	-

2V2.1	A	B	C
synthesis	4	3	8
union	4	3	4
fusion	8	4	11

2V3.0	A	B	C
wedding	4	3	4
marriage	6	3	7
betroth	8	-	-
matrimony	8	-	-
bigamy	10	-	-
nuptial	10	7	-
polygamy	10	-	-
connubial	13	-	-

2V4.0	A	B	C
consist	4	4	6
constitute	4	3	-
contain	4	3	4
include	5	3	7
involve	5	3	5
comprise	6	4	-

2V5.0	A	B	C
intersect	5	4	6
dovetail	10	-	-
jibe	10	-	-

2V6.0	A	B	C
meet	2	3	K
collide	6	5	6
converge	8	4	7
encounter	8	3	9
mingle	8	3	7
rendezvous	8	3	-
convene	10	6	-

2V7.0	A	B	C
stick	2	3	2
fasten	4	3	4
hitch	4	3	3
tether	4	3	-
affix	6	7	4
shackle	6	3	-
cleave	8	4	-
fetter	8	5	-
cohere	10	-	-

2W Separating Actions

2W1.0	A	B	C
split	2	3	2
separate	3	3	5
disconnect	5	7	6
divorce	5	5	-
detach	6	7	7
bisect	6	6	8
diverge	8	4	7
divert	8	7	12
segregate	8	-	7

A: Grade level; B: Earliest Grade of Occurrence in Textbooks; C: Earliest Grade of Occurrence on Standardized Tests.

sunder	10	-	-
winnow	10	-	-
sequester	13	-	-

2W1.1	A	B	C
fission	8	5	-
dichotomy	10	-	-
schism	10	-	-

2W2.0	A	B	C
loosen	3	3	3
unfasten	3	7	-
unscrew	3	4	-
unwind	5	4	-

2W3.0	A	B	C
ravel	8	8	7

2X Circular/Angular Motions

2X1.0	A	B	C
circulation	5	3	7
rotation	5	3	5
torque	8	7	11

2X2.0	A	B	C
spin	1	3	K
roll	2	3	2
orbit	3	3	2
pinwheel	4	3	-
twirl	4	4	-
whirl	4	3	4
rotate	5	3	6
revolve	6	4	6
gyrate	8	-	-
pirouette	10	-	-

2X2.1	A	B	C
clockwise	6	4	11
counterclockwise	6	3	11
orbital	6	3	-

2X3.0	A	B	C
invert	5	3	-
reverse	5	3	7
reciprocal	6	4	6
recoil	8	7	-
regress	10	-	-
retrograde	10	8	-

2X4.0	A	B	C
turn	1	3	1
swirl	3	3	3
twist	3	3	4
windup	3	3	-
swerve	6	3	12

swivel	6	4	-
pivot	8	5	-
refract	8	-	-
veer	8	6	-

2X5.0	A	B	C
surround	4	3	4
enclose	5	4	5
encircle	6	6	6
encompass	8	3	-
gird	8	7	-
ambient	13	7	-
environ	13	-	-

2X6.0	A	B	C
about	1	3	1
around	2	3	K

SUPER CLUSTER

3. Size/Quantity/Weight

3A Size/Weight

3A1.0	A	B	C
size	2	3	2
greatness	4	3	-
measurement	4	3	6
bulk	5	3	-
dimension	8	5	12
extent	8	3	-

3A2.0	A	B	C
little	K	3	K
small	1	3	1
tiny	1	3	K
wee	4	3	9
lightweight	5	3	5
miniature	5	4	10
compact	6	4	7
stubby	6	4	-
petite	6	5	-
microscopic	8	4	-

3A3.0	A	B	C
big	K	3	K
huge	1	3	K
giant	2	3	3
great	2	3	K
large	2	3	2
grand	3	3	3
enormous	4	3	2
jumbo	5	3	-
mammoth	5	3	5
vast	5	3	5
immense	6	3	6

	A	B	C
massive	6	3	6
monstrous	6	4	-
colossus	8	4	-
titanic	8	7	7
ponderous	10	3	9

3B Measurement Actions

3B1.0	A	B	C
measure	2	3	2
weigh	3	3	3
fathom	5	4	4

3C Measurement Devices

3C1.0	A	B	C
ruler	3	3	3
scale	3	3	K
thermometer	3	3	3
yardstick	3	3	-
compass	4	3	3
gauge	5	3	5
protractor	5	5	-
speedometer	5	3	-
seismograph	8	5	-
galvanometer	10	5	-

3D Things Commonly Measured

3D1.0	A	B	C
latitude	5	3	6
longitude	5	3	6

3D2.0	A	B	C
angle	5	3	5
circumference	5	4	7
diameter	5	3	6
radius	5	3	5
meridian	6	3	7
caliber	8	5	-
vertex	8	4	-

3D3.0	A	B	C
census	5	3	5
birthrate	8	7	-

3E Specific Units of Measurement

3E1.0	A	B	C
foot	2	3	K
mile	2	3	3
yard	2	3	K
inch	3	3	3
meter	3	3	2
centimeter	4	3	4
kilometer	4	5	3
mil	6	-	10
decimeter	8	7	-
furlong	8	4	-

3E2.0	A	B	C
volt	6	5	7
watt	6	3	7
ohm	10	8	-

3E3.0	A	B	C
pound	3	3	4
ton	3	3	3
gram	4	6	2
kilogram	4	6	2
ounce	4	3	4
dram	8	7	-
kilo	10	7	-

3E3.1	A	B	C
metric	4	5	4
troy	13	-	4

3E4.0	A	B	C
grade	3	3	3
degree	4	3	4

3E5.0	A	B	C
gallon	2	3	3
quart	2	3	2
liter	3	4	2
pint	3	3	3
tablespoon	3	3	6
teaspoonful	3	3	-
bushel	4	3	9

3E6.0	A	B	C
spoonful	2	3	5
cupful	3	3	-
handful	4	3	5
mouthful	4	3	-
pinch	4	3	9

3F Partitives

3F1.0	A	B	C
dot	1	3	3
bit	2	3	2
fluff	4	3	-
speck	4	3	4
powder	5	3	5
speckle	5	-	-
gob	5	4	-
particle	6	4	9
fleck	8	6	-

A: Grade level; B: Earliest Grade of Occurrence in Textbooks; C: Earliest Grade of Occurrence on Standardized Tests.

	A	B	C
jot	8	3	-
mote	8	7	-
whit	8	5	-
wisp	8	3	-
pip	10	6	-
iota	13	-	-
scintilla	13	-	-

3F2.0

	A	B	C
type	3	3	3
version	6	4	7

3F3.0

	A	B	C
part	1	3	1
piece	2	3	2
item	3	3	3
member	3	3	4
section	3	3	3
factor	4	3	5
fragment	5	3	4
module	5	3	-
portion	5	3	8
segment	5	3	5
species	5	3	7
subset	5	3	7
component	8	7	11
quota	8	3	-

3F4.0

	A	B	C
sample	3	3	K
specimen	8	3	8

3F5.0

	A	B	C
flake	2	4	-
chunk	3	3	-
slice	3	3	5
crumb	4	3	-
slab	4	3	-
splinter	4	4	-
sawdust	4	3	3
scrap	5	3	6
sliver	5	7	-
morsel	6	6	-
fallout	8	7	-
cantle	13	7	-
shard	13	-	-

3F6.0

	A	B	C
department	3	3	3
category	6	5	7

3G General Amounts

3G1.0

	A	B	C
amount	3	3	3
unit	3	3	3

	A	B	C
volume	4	3	4
capacity	4	3	4
quantity	5	3	8

3G2.0

	A	B	C
all	K	3	1
whole	3	3	3
entire	4	3	4

3G3.0

	A	B	C
countless	5	3	7
abundant	6	3	6
extensive	6	3	7
unlimited	6	3	7
numerous	6	3	9
infinite	8	4	7
myriad	8	3	9
copious	10	3	-

3G4.0

	A	B	C
plenty	3	3	3
abundance	5	3	11
plethora	10	-	-

3G4.1

	A	B	C
ample	6	3	6
lush	6	3	9
lavish	8	4	9
profuse	10	7	12

3G5.0

	A	B	C
extra	3	3	3
remainder	3	3	9
spare	3	3	3
leftover	4	3	-
excess	5	4	5
stub	5	3	7
surplus	6	3	7
residue	8	4	-
redundant	10	-	-
superfluous	10	-	11
surfeit	13	-	-

3G5.1

	A	B	C
exceed	5	3	9
outnumber	6	6	-

3G6.0

	A	B	C
other	1	3	K
another	2	3	2
several	3	3	3
additional	6	3	6

3G7.0

	A	B	C
increase	4	3	4
enhance	8	7	-

	A	B	C
accretion	10	-	-
augment	10	-	-

3G8.0

	A	B	C
decrease	4	4	4
deduct	6	8	-
attrition	8	3	-
wane	10	4	-
attenuate	13	-	-

3G9.0

	A	B	C
many	1	3	1
more	1	3	K
lot	2	3	1
most	2	3	2
majority	6	3	7
brunt	8	7	-

3G10.0

	A	B	C
both	1	3	K
two	1	3	K
half	2	3	2
pair	2	3	3
twice	2	3	3
double	3	3	3
couple	4	3	6
binary	6	4	-
mate	6	3	6
duplex	8	-	-
deuce	10	-	-
moiety	13	-	-

3G11.0

	A	B	C
only	1	3	1
lone	3	3	2
single	3	3	4
particular	4	3	5
sole	5	3	2

3G12.0

	A	B	C
little	K	3	K
few	2	3	3
less	2	3	3
least	3	3	3

3G13.0

	A	B	C
partial	4	3	5
fractional	5	3	-
finite	8	4	-
meager	8	3	9
scant	8	4	-
sparse	8	3	11

3G14.0

	A	B	C
lack	4	3	4
shortage	5	3	5

	A	B	C
scarcity	8	3	-
dearth	10	7	-

3G15.0

	A	B	C
plural	4	3	6
singular	4	3	7

3H Cardinal/Ordinal Numbers

3H1.0

	A	B	C
one	1	3	K
two	1	3	K
three	1	3	K
four	1	3	1
five	1	3	K
six	1	3	1
seven	1	3	1
eight	1	3	1
nine	1	3	1
ten	1	3	1
eleven	2	3	4
twelve	2	3	2
thirteen	2	3	3
fourteen	2	3	3
fifteen	2	3	3
sixteen	2	3	2
seventeen	2	3	6
eighteen	2	3	7
nineteen	2	3	5
twenty	2	3	2
thirty	2	3	3
forty	2	3	3
fifty	2	3	3
sixty	2	3	3
seventy	2	3	3
eighty	2	3	5
ninety	2	3	3
hundred	2	3	2
thousand	3	3	3
million	3	3	3
billion	4	3	6
trillion	5	5	-

3H2.0

	A	B	C
first	1	3	K
second	1	3	1
third	1	3	1
fourth	1	3	1
fifth	1	3	2
sixth	1	3	2
seventh	1	3	2
eighth	1	3	5
ninth	1	3	3
tenth	1	3	4
eleventh	2	3	-

	A	B	C
twelfth	2	3	-
thirteenth	2	3	-
fourteenth	2	3	5
fifteenth	2	3	5
sixteenth	2	3	5
seventeenth	2	3	5
eighteenth	2	3	9
nineteenth	2	3	7
twentieth	2	3	5
fiftieth	2	3	11
sixtieth	2	7	-
eightieth	2	-	-
thousandth	3	5	7
millionth	3	7	-

3H2.1	A	B	C
dozen	3	3	3
fourscore	5	4	-
trice	5	3	-
triple	5	4	9
threescore	6	6	-
secondary	8	3	8
subordinate	8	7	12
triad	8	4	-
trinity	8	4	-
tertiary	10	-	-
quint	10	-	-

3H3.0	A	B	C
number	2	3	3
digit	3	3	3
numeral	3	3	3
decimal	4	3	5
data	5	3	5
integer	5	5	-
numeration	6	5	-

3I Specifiers

3I1.0	A	B	C
a	K	3	K
an	K	3	K
no	K	3	K
the	K	3	K
each	2	3	K
every	2	3	2
either	3	3	4

3I2.0	A	B	C
that	K	3	K
this	K	3	1
these	1	3	K
those	1	3	1

3J Diminishers

3J1.0	A	B	C
broadly	5	4	-
general(ly)	5	3	-
roughly	5	3	-
approximate(ly)	6	4	-
overall	6	5	6
circa	13	-	-

3J2.0	A	B	C
alone	1	3	K
just	1	3	K
only	1	3	1
exactly	3	3	3
particularly	4	3	5
simply	4	3	6
in particular	6	-	-
purely	6	3	9
exclusively	8	5	8
precisely	8	3	11
specifically	8	5	9

3J3.0	A	B	C
mostly	2	3	1
mainly	3	3	3
insofar	5	3	-
largely	5	3	7

3J4.0	A	B	C
enough	2	3	1
kind of	3	-	-
quite	3	3	4
rather	3	3	3
sort of	3	-	-
more or less	4	-	-
adequate	5	3	5
sufficiently	8	3	11

3J5.0	A	B	C
mild(ly)	4	3	-
partly	4	3	4
somewhat	4	3	5
slightly	5	3	5
at least	5	-	-
mere(ly)	6	3	-
piecemeal	6	4	-
in part	8	-	-
in some respect	8	-	-
inasmuch	8	7	-
moderate(ly)	8	3	-
to some extent	8	-	-

3J6.0	A	B	C
a bit	2	-	-
a little	2	-	-

A: Grade level; B: Earliest Grade of Occurrence in Textbooks; C: Earliest Grade of Occurrence on Standardized Tests.

hardly	2	3	1
in the least bit	4	-	-
barely	5	3	6
in the slightest	6	-	-
scarcely	6	3	6

3J7.0	A	B	C
almost	2	3	2
nearly	2	3	2
practically	4	3	6
as good as	5	-	-
probable	5	4	5
virtually	8	3	9
quasi	13	-	-

3K Intensifiers

3K1.0	A	B	C
most	2	3	2
altogether	3	3	5
especially	3	3	4
quite	3	3	4
complete(ly)	4	3	-
fully	4	3	4
perfectly	4	3	5
downright	5	4	-
entire(ly)	5	3	-
thorough(ly)	5	3	-
totally	5	5	7
widely	5	3	6
absolute(ly)	6	3	-
extreme(ly)	6	3	-
utmost	6	5	6
utter(ly)	6	3	-
eminent	8	5	-
exceedingly	8	3	9
exceptionally	8	4	8
in all respects	8	-	-
outright	8	3	-
ultimate	8	5	11
ultra	8	8	-

3K2.0	A	B	C
so	K	3	1
too	K	3	K
more	1	3	K
much	1	3	1
sure	1	3	1
very	1	3	K
well	1	3	K
highly	2	3	2
such	2	3	2
badly	3	3	4
deeply	3	3	3
greatly	4	3	5

terribly	4	3	-
a great deal	5	-	-
by far	5	-	-
intense(ly)	6	4	-
notably	6	5	-
galore	8	3	-

SUPER CLUSTER

4. Animals

4A Animals (General)

4A1.0	A	B	C
pet	K	3	K
animal	1	3	2
beast	3	3	3
creature	3	3	3
wildlife	3	3	4
mascot	4	-	5
livestock	4	3	4
fauna	8	7	-
vermin	8	7	-

4A2.0	A	B	C
mammal	3	3	3
amphibian	5	3	5
invertebrate	5	5	5
aquatic	6	4	9
carnivorous	8	6	-
primate	8	7	-
biped	10	-	-
quadruped	10	-	-
ungulate	13	7	-

4A2.1	A	B	C
fossil	3	3	3

4B Cats/Dogs

4B1.0	A	B	C
cat	K	3	K
lion	1	3	1
tiger	1	3	2
leopard	3	3	3
cougar	4	5	-
tomcat	4	4	-
wildcat	4	3	-
lioness	5	4	-
panther	5	3	6
puma	5	5	-
bobcat	6	3	8
puss	6	-	-
feline	8	3	-
tabby	8	7	-

4B2.0	A	B	C
wolf	1	3	1
fox	2	3	1
coyote	4	3	4
dingo	5	4	-
hyena	6	4	-
jackal	6	6	-

4B3.0	A	B	C
dog	K	3	K
hound	3	3	3
watchdog	3	3	9
beagle	4	3	5
bulldog	4	3	5
collie	4	3	5
foxhound	4	4	-
greyhound	4	3	-
mutt	4	3	-
poodle	4	3	6
spaniel	4	3	-
terrier	4	3	-
bloodhound	5	5	-
pug	5	3	-
wolfhound	5	4	-
bitch	8	7	-
canine	8	7	11

4C Reptiles/Mythical Animals

4C1.0	A	B	C
snake	1	3	K
reptile	3	3	3
rattlesnake	4	3	4
serpent	6	3	9
anaconda	8	6	-
blacksnake	8	-	-
copperhead	8	3	-

4C2.0	A	B	C
dragon	2	3	2
monster	3	3	3
mermaid	4	3	4
unicorn	4	4	6
nymph	6	3	5
chimera	10	-	-
satyr	10	-	-

4C3.0	A	B	C
frog	1	3	1
turtle	1	3	1
bullfrog	2	3	-
toad	2	3	2
alligator	2	3	4
crocodile	3	3	4
dinosaur	3	3	4

lizard	3	3	3
tortoise	3	3	-

4D Baby Animals

4D1.0	A	B	C
kitten	K	3	K
puppy	K	3	K
bunny	1	3	1
calf	1	3	K
cub	2	3	2
kitty	2	4	3
pup	2	3	4
tadpole	2	3	5
chick	3	3	4
colt	3	3	3
duckling	3	3	-
fawn	4	3	-
yearling	5	5	-
dogie	5	3	-

4E Land Animals (General)

4E1.0	A	B	C
deer	2	3	3
reindeer	2	3	3
caribou	3	3	3
antelope	4	4	-
elk	4	3	-
doe	5	4	-
gazelle	5	4	-
stag	5	4	-

4E2.0	A	B	C
horse	1	3	K
pony	1	3	1
donkey	2	3	2
ass	3	3	-
burro	3	3	3
mule	3	3	4
zebra	3	3	9
stallion	4	3	-
bronco	5	3	-
horseflesh	5	3	-
jackass	5	3	-
mare	5	3	7
mustang	5	3	-
pinto	5	3	5
racehorse	5	-	-
stud	5	4	-
steed	6	3	-
hackney	8	-	-
sorrel	8	3	-
thoroughbred	8	4	10

A: Grade level; B: Earliest Grade of Occurrence in Textbooks; C: Earliest Grade of Occurrence on Standardized Tests.

4E3.0	A	B	C
cow	K	3	K
buffalo	3	3	3
cattle	3	3	4
ox	3	3	9
steer	3	3	3
bull	4	3	7
bison	6	3	9
longhorn	8	6	-
shorthorn	8	-	-
bovine	10	-	-

4E4.0	A	B	C
goat	1	3	K
lamb	1	3	1
sheep	1	3	1
llama	4	3	4
bighorn	6	-	-
ram	6	3	9

4E5.0	A	B	C
pig	1	3	1
hog	5	3	-
sow	6	3	7
swine	8	7	-
razorback	10	-	-

4E6.0	A	B	C
kangaroo	3	3	4
anteater	5	3	7
opossum	5	K	-
platypus	5	4	7
sloth	8	3	10

4E7.0	A	B	C
bear	1	3	1
elephant	1	3	1
giraffe	3	3	4
yak	4	3	-
camel	5	3	4

4E8.0	A	B	C
rabbit	1	3	K
skunk	3	3	3
raccoon	4	3	-
weasel	4	3	-
badger	5	4	-
cottontail	5	5	-
hare	5	3	8
hedgehog	5	4	-
mink	5	4	8
mole	5	3	6
polecat	6	-	-

4F Rodents

4F1.0	A	B	C
beaver	3	3	3
porcupine	4	3	7
woodchuck	5	3	-

4F2.0	A	B	C
mouse	1	3	K
squirrel	1	3	1
chipmunk	3	3	-
hamster	3	3	3
rat	3	3	4
muskrat	5	3	7
rodent	6	6	-
shrew	6	3	-

4G Primates

4G1.0	A	B	C
monkey	1	3	2
ape	3	3	6
baboon	3	3	-
chimpanzee	3	3	4
gorilla	3	4	5
anthropoid	10	7	-

4H Sea Animals

4H1.0	A	B	C
seal	1	3	K
whale	1	3	K
porpoise	4	3	5
walrus	4	3	5
dolphin	5	3	5
humpback	5	3	K
swordfish	5	3	-
shark	5	3	5
hammerhead	6	4	6

4H2.0	A	B	C
fish	K	3	K
goldfish	3	3	K
cod	4	3	7
guppy	4	4	-
salmon	4	3	4
seahorse	4	4	3
minnow	4	3	-
bass	5	3	7
carp	5	3	-
codfish	5	4	-
flounder	5	3	-
herring	5	3	5
smelt	5	3	-
snapper	5	3	5

A: Grade level; B: Earliest Grade of Occurrence in Textbooks; C: Earliest Grade of Occurrence on Standardized Tests.

	A	B	C
sunfish	5	3	-
trout	5	3	5
tuna	5	3	5
catfish	8	3	9
flying fish	8	-	-
halibut	8	5	10
lungfish	8	7	-
pike	8	3	-
sardine	8	3	-
whitefish	8	-	-
bluefish	8	-	9

4I Shellfish and Others

4I1.0	A	B	C
jellyfish	4	3	5
sponge	4	3	4
eel	5	3	5
stingray	5	-	-

4I2.0	A	B	C
crab	3	3	1
shellfish	3	3	4
shrimp	3	3	3
lobster	4	3	5
crayfish	5	3	5

4I3.0	A	B	C
shell	2	3	2
clam	3	3	3
coral	3	3	4
starfish	3	3	5
mollusk	4	6	4
cockle	5	-	-
oyster	5	3	8
scallop	6	3	-
barnacle	8	7	-
cockleshell	8	-	-

4I4.0	A	B	C
snail	4	3	3
octopus	5	3	5
squid	6	3	-

4J Birds

4J1.0	A	B	C
bird	K	3	K
crow	2	3	1
eagle	2	3	2
jay	2	3	2
owl	2	3	2
parrot	2	3	2
robin	2	3	4
falcon	3	6	7

	A	B	C
hawk	3	3	3
pigeon	3	3	3
woodpecker	3	3	4
blackbird	4	3	-
blue jay	4	K	-
bluebird	4	3	4
canary	4	3	5
cuckoo	4	3	-
dove	4	3	4
finch	4	3	4
lark	4	3	4
oriole	4	3	-
ostrich	4	3	7
sparrow	4	3	9
turtledove	4	-	-
vulture	4	3	7
hummingbird	5	3	-
meadowlark	5	3	-
mockingbird	5	3	-
parakeet	5	3	9
raven	5	3	-
songbird	5	3	-
wren	5	3	7
skylark	6	-	-
starling	6	3	-
bullfinch	8	3	-
cowbird	8	3	-
fantail	8	-	-
kingfisher	8	3	-
nightingale	8	4	9
peregrine	8	-	7
redbreast	8	-	-
redwing	8	-	-
sapsucker	8	-	-
snipe	8	7	-
sparrow hawk	8	-	-
tern	10	4	-

4J2.0	A	B	C
chicken	1	3	K
hen	1	3	1
fowl	2	3	K
rooster	2	3	3
turkey	2	3	2
partridge	3	3	-
gander	4	4	-
pheasant	4	5	8
cock	6	3	-
wildfowl	8	8	11

4J3.0	A	B	C
duck	1	3	K
goose	2	3	3
gull	3	3	2
seagull	3	3	-

	A	B	C
quail	4	3	10
swan	4	3	8
crane	5	3	K
drake	5	4	7
mallard	5	4	-
waterfowl	5	4	11
albatross	6	3	10
sandpiper	8	3	-
shorebird	8	-	-
gannet	10	3	-
plover	10	3	-

4K Insects

4K1.0	A	B	C
fly	K	3	K
bee	1	3	1
butterfly	1	3	2
bumblebee	2	4	-
ladybug	2	3	2
cricket	3	3	K
honeybee	3	3	7
insect	3	3	5
mosquito	3	3	5
moth	3	3	4
flea	4	3	8
grasshopper	4	3	5
housefly	4	3	5
wasp	4	3	4
yellow jacket	4	-	-
dragonfly	5	5	-
hornet	5	4	9
drone	6	3	6
firefly	6	4	9
gnat	6	3	-
blue bottle	8	-	-
cicada	8	3	8
damselfly	8	-	-
gadfly	8	5	-
mayfly	8	7	-
swallowtail	8	7	-

4K2.0	A	B	C
ant	1	3	1
bug	2	3	1
caterpillar	2	3	3
spider	2	3	3
worm	2	3	5
beetle	3	3	-
earthworm	3	3	3
larva	3	3	3
centipede	4	4	-
glowworm	4	3	-
slug	4	3	-
termite	4	6	4

	A	B	C
cockroach	5	6	-
mite	5	3	-
silkworm	5	3	-
millipede	5	-	-
mantis	6	3	-
mealworm	8	-	-
silverfish	8	3	-

4K2.1	A	B	C
parasite	5	7	7
flatworm	6	7	11
hookworm	8	7	9
roundworm	8	7	-
tapeworm	8	7	11
louse	10	7	11

4L Parts of Animals

4L1.0	A	B	C
bearskin	3	3	-
deerskin	3	3	-
goatskin	3	3	-
horsehide	3	5	-
sealskin	3	3	-
cowhide	4	3	6
hide	4	3	K
pelt	5	3	10
doeskin	6	4	-
rawhide	6	3	-

4L2.0	A	B	C
fur	1	3	1
whisker	2	3	4
horsehair	3	3	-
mane	4	3	4
bristle	5	5	-
fleece	5	3	7
hackle	8	7	-
withers	8	3	9

4L3.0	A	B	C
feather	2	3	2
plume	5	3	-
quill	5	3	5
eider	8	4	-
eiderdown	8	-	-
pinna	13	-	-

4L4.0	A	B	C
beak	3	3	5
bill	3	3	K
snout	5	3	5
duckbill	8	3	7

4L5.0	A	B	C
tail	1	3	1
paw	2	3	1
claw	3	3	3
fin	4	3	5
flipper	4	4	-
hoof	4	3	-
talon	6	3	-
bobtail	8	5	-
scut	10	-	-

4L6.0	A	B	C
antenna	5	3	5
antler	5	3	7
ivory	6	K	-
tusk	6	6	6
whalebone	6	4	-

4L7.0	A	B	C
pouch	5	3	5
cud	6	4	-
gill	6	3	-
sac	6	4	-

4M Animal Dwellings

4M1.0	A	B	C
zoo	K	3	K
birdhouse	2	3	-
doghouse	2	3	-
farmyard	2	3	-
pigpen	2	3	-
corral	3	3	4
kennel	3	3	-
stable	3	3	5
aquarium	4	3	3
coop	4	3	-
henhouse	4	3	-
pigsty	4	4	-
stall	4	3	5
stockyard	5	5	-
hencoop	8	-	-
livery	8	4	-
paddock	8	6	-
sty	8	3	-
warren	8	3	8
dovecote	10	-	-
pinfold	10	-	-
cote	13	-	-

4M2.0	A	B	C
nest	1	3	1
beehive	2	4	3
cocoon	3	3	-
hive	3	3	3

lair	5	5	-
roost	5	3	6
honeycomb	6	3	6
aviary	8	3	-
aerie	13	-	-

4M2.1	A	B	C
eggshell	3	4	5
beeswax	4	3	-

4N Animal Equipment

4N1.0	A	B	C
collar	3	3	4
horseshoe	3	3	6
saddle	3	3	5
rein	4	3	-
bridle	5	3	6
chaps	5	4	-
halter	5	3	-
harness	5	3	-
leash	5	3	5
muzzle	5	3	-
stirrup	5	3	6
saddlebag	6	4	-
yoke	8	3	-

4O Actions related to Animals

4O1.0	A	B	C
fly	1	3	K
soar	3	3	2
sting	4	3	4
swarm	5	3	8
swoop	5	3	5

4O2.0	A	B	C
graze	4	3	4
forage	10	6	-

4O3.0	A	B	C
gallop	4	3	-
buck	5	3	8
stampede	5	4	6
canter	8	5	-

4O4.0	A	B	C
fish	1	3	K
hunt	2	3	3

4O4.1	A	B	C
trap	1	3	1
mousetrap	3	3	-
snare	5	3	5
birdlime	10	-	-

A: Grade level; B: Earliest Grade of Occurrence in Textbooks; C: Earliest Grade of Occurrence on Standardized Tests.

4O5.0	A	B	C
horseback	4	3	4
bareback	5	3	8
horseless	5	3	-
roughshod	10	-	-

SUPER CLUSTER

5. Feelings/Attitudes

5A Names for Feelings (General)

5A1.0	A	B	C
feeling	2	3	3
sense	3	3	2
mood	4	3	5
impulse	5	4	9
sensation	5	3	5
emotion	6	5	7
impression	6	3	6
sentiment	8	5	-
whim	8	7	-
heartstrings	8	-	-
caprice	10	-	-

5B Fear

5B1.0	A	B	C
alarm	2	3	3
fear	2	3	2
dread	3	4	6
shock	3	3	7
terror	3	3	3
horror	4	4	5
panic	5	3	8
fright	6	3	7
hysteria	8	5	8
trepidation	10	-	-

5B1.1	A	B	C
frightful	4	3	-
bloodcurdling	5	-	-
eerie	5	3	-

5B2.0	A	B	C
afraid	1	3	1
fearful	3	3	5
cautious	4	4	5
frantic	5	4	5
craven	10	-	-
timorous	10	-	-
pusillanimous	13	-	-

5C Actions Associated with Fear

5C1.0	A	B	C
frighten	2	3	2
scare	2	3	2
startle	4	4	4
terrify	4	5	4
cringe	5	5	-
haunt	5	6	7
horrify	5	5	-
flinch	6	5	-
petrify	6	-	-
cower	8	-	-
daunt	8	-	-
wince	8	4	-
obsess	10	-	-

5D Worry/Guilt

5D1.0	A	B	C
shame	4	3	8
embarrassment	5	4	7
guilt	5	5	7
humiliation	8	6	7
chagrin	10	7	-

5D1.1	A	B	C
guilty	5	3	5

5D2.0	A	B	C
worry	2	3	2
fret	4	3	6
strain	4	3	5
concern	5	3	5
anxiety	6	4	8
suspense	6	5	6
tension	6	3	9
qualm	8	-	9
scruple	8	9	-
compunction	10	-	-
punctilio	13	-	-

5D3.0	A	B	C
anxious	3	3	3
uncomfortable	4	3	5
uneasy	4	3	8
tense	5	3	5
distraught	8	7	-

5E Anger

5E1.0	A	B	C
anger	3	3	5
rage	4	3	5
temper	4	3	-

	A	B	C
fury	5	3	-
huff	6	3	-
revenge	6	5	6
wrath	6	6	-
ire	8	3	-
seethe	8	-	-
tantrum	8	8	-
vengeance	8	4	-
dander	10	3	-
umbrage	10	7	-
choler	13	-	-

5E2.0	A	B	C
bitterness	4	3	4
hatred	5	3	-
scorn	5	4	11
contempt	6	5	-
indignation	8	4	-
revulsion	8	9	-
acrimony	10	-	-
antipathy	10	-	-
rancor	10	-	-
asperity	13	-	-
misanthropy	13	-	-

5E3.0	A	B	C
hate	2	3	3
dislike	3	3	4
resent	5	4	11
despise	6	5	7
abhor	8	-	9
detest	8	-	8
disdain	8	3	-
execrate	10	-	-

5E4.0	A	B	C
displease	4	-	4
irritate	5	4	9
offend	5	3	-
disgust	6	4	7
incense	6	3	6
outrage	6	5	-
aggravate	8	-	9
agitate	8	6	9
enrage	8	-	7
peeve	8	-	-
pique	8	7	-
provoke	8	6	9
gall	10	7	-
rile	10	-	-

5E5.0	A	B	C
angry	1	3	K
furious	4	3	4
hostile	5	3	7
warlike	5	3	6

	A	B	C
adverse	8	4	7
belligerent	8	7	-
bellicose	10	-	-
indignant	10	3	-
vehement	10	5	-
inimical	13	-	-

5F Meanness/Cruelty

5F1.0	A	B	C
meanness	4	4	-
cruelty	5	3	-
malice	8	3	-
aggression	10	5	10

5F1.1	A	B	C
mean	1	3	1
cruel	3	3	4
unkind	3	3	4
merciless	6	3	7
vicious	6	3	5
abusive	8	7	-
vile	8	6	-
mordant	10	-	-
odious	10	7	-
sardonic	10	-	-
truculent	13	-	-
vituperative	13	-	-

5F2.0	A	B	C
fierce	3	3	3
destructive	5	3	10
savage	5	3	6
violent	5	3	6
drastic	6	5	7
ferocious	6	3	7
bloodthirsty	8	6	-

5G Irritability

5G1.0	A	B	C
grumpy	2	3	3
unfriendly	3	3	4
unpleasant	3	3	4
disagreeable	4	7	6
bad tempered	5	3	-
gruff	5	3	7
irritable	6	4	9
scornful	6	3	11
cantankerous	8	6	-
petulant	10	5	-

5G2.0	A	B	C
rude	3	3	3
saucy	5	4	-

impertinent	6	-	-
brusque	8	7	-
captious	8	7	-
curt	8	6	7
impudent	8	3	-
pert	8	6	-
surly	8	3	-
insolent	10	6	-

5H Sadness

5H1.0	A	B	C
sadness	3	3	3
gloom	4	3	5
letdown	4	-	-
discomfort	5	6	6
heartache	5	3	-
heartbreak	5	5	-
sorrow	5	3	5
dismay	6	3	5
doldrums	6	5	-
loneliness	6	4	-
misery	6	3	12
remorse	6	4	-
woe	6	3	-
anguish	8	5	12
tribulation	8	4	-
despond	10	-	-
dolor	13	-	-

5H2.0	A	B	C
sad	K	3	K
sorry	1	3	1
unhappy	1	3	2
miserable	3	3	2
contrite	5	-	-
downhearted	5	-	-
forlorn	5	4	-
sorrowful	5	3	5
wretched	5	3	-
grief-stricken	6	5	-
heartsick	6	7	-
pitiful	6	3	8
desolate	8	3	10
downcast	8	3	-
hangdog	8	-	-
heartrending	8	-	-
melancholy	8	4	9
penitent	8	-	-
pensive	8	4	-
wistful	8	7	-
morose	10	-	-
poignant	10	-	12
lachrymal	13	-	-

| lugubrious | 13 | - | - |
| mawkish | 13 | - | - |

5H3.0	A	B	C
regret	4	3	7
suffer	4	3	-
grieve	5	4	-
mourn	5	5	5
sulk	5	3	-
repent	6	3	11
deplore	8	-	-
lament	8	3	-
mope	8	-	-
rue	8	3	-

5I General Upset

5I1.0	A	B	C
upset	2	3	2
bother	3	3	4
disturb	3	4	3
disappoint	4	3	9
discourage	4	3	9
frustrate	4	8	-
depress	5	-	9
balk	6	3	-
deject	6	-	-
disrupt	6	7	6
impose	6	5	12
infringe	6	4	-
interfere	6	3	7
molest	6	6	-
exasperate	8	-	-
harass	8	3	12
harry	8	6	K
henpeck	8	-	-
intrude	8	6	8
meddle	8	6	7
perturb	8	-	-
vex	8	-	-
beleaguer	10	-	-
disconcert	10	-	-
interlope	10	-	-
irk	10	-	-
abash	13	-	-
incommode	13	-	-
obtrude	13	-	-

5I2.0	A	B	C
serious	3	3	3
earnest	5	3	9
solemn	5	3	7
somber	5	3	7
dour	6	5	-

sullen	6	5	-
aloof	8	4	-

5I3.0	A	B	C
distress	5	3	10
discontent	6	3	-

5I4.0	A	B	C
alone	1	3	K
lonely	2	3	2
homesick	3	3	5
dissatisfied	5	3	7
lovesick	8	-	-

5J Excitement

5J1.0	A	B	C
excitement	3	3	3
astonishment	4	3	4
hubbub	4	3	-
awe	4	3	7
amazement	5	3	6
disbelief	5	3	10
ecstasy	6	5	-
passion	6	4	-
jubilation	8	5	-

5J2.0	A	B	C
surprise	1	3	K
amaze	4	3	4
astonish	5	4	7
appall	6	7	-
marvel	6	4	6
boggle	8	-	-
fascinate	8	6	12
astound	10	-	-

5J2.1	A	B	C
thunderstruck	6	6	-
aghast	8	3	-
agog	10	-	-

5J3.0	A	B	C
excite	3	3	9
thrill	4	3	4
tingle	4	3	-
rejoice	5	4	9
arouse	6	4	5
enchant	8	-	-
enliven	8	5	-
enthuse	8	-	-
exult	8	-	-
kindle	8	7	11
tantalize	8	-	-
whet	8	7	-
elate	10	-	-

enthrall	10	-	-
exhilarate	10	-	11
ravish	10	-	-
rejuvenate	10	-	-

5K Fun/Joy

5K1.0	A	B	C
fun	K	3	K
joy	1	3	3
happiness	2	3	4
pleasure	2	3	5
delight	3	3	6
enjoyment	3	3	6
glee	5	3	-
mirth	6	3	-
bliss	8	3	-
felicity	10	-	-
levity	10	-	-

5K2.0	A	B	C
gay	1	3	K
glad	1	3	K
happy	1	3	K
silly	1	3	2
cheerful	2	3	4
jolly	2	3	3
merry	2	3	3
joyful	3	3	4
joyous	3	3	3
playful	3	3	3
enjoyable	4	3	5
carefree	5	3	5
jubilant	6	7	5
rollicking	6	4	-
blithe	8	5	-
genial	8	3	7
gleeful	8	-	-
jaunty	8	5	-
jovial	8	7	10

5K3.0	A	B	C
humor	2	3	5
please	2	3	K
amuse	3	3	3
entertain	3	3	4
pamper	6	6	-
coddle	8	-	-
indulge	8	8	-
pander	10	-	-
regale	10	-	-

5K4.0	A	B	C
play	K	3	K
celebrate	3	3	2

A: Grade level; B: Earliest Grade of Occurrence in Textbooks; C: Earliest Grade of Occurrence on Standardized Tests.

frolic	5	5	-
revel	8	7	-

5K5.0	A	B	C
joke	2	3	2
riddle	4	3	3
gag	5	8	5
jest	5	3	5
antic	6	3	-
wisecrack	6	7	-
farce	8	6	6
irony	8	4	9
lampoon	8	-	-
sarcasm	8	7	-
tomfoolery	8	7	-
quip	10	-	-
repartee	13	-	-

5L Comfort/Contentment

5L1.0	A	B	C
comfort	3	3	4
relief	3	3	2
contentment	6	4	6
welfare	8	3	7
equanimity	13	-	-

5L2.0	A	B	C
pity	4	3	4
sympathy	5	3	7
empathy	8	-	-

5L3.0	A	B	C
calm	3	3	3
satisfy	3	3	5
tame	4	3	3
civilize	5	5	11
pacify	8	-	5
suffice	8	6	-
becalm	10	-	-
sate	13	-	-

5L4.0	A	B	C
soothe	4	4	5
console	6	3	-
sympathize	6	6	-
empathize	8	-	-
assuage	10	-	-
conciliate	10	-	-
mollify	10	-	-
quell	10	-	6
placate	10	8	-
condole	13	-	-

5L5.0	A	B	C
comfortable	3	3	3
content	3	3	3
cozy	3	3	3
peaceful	4	3	4
snug	4	3	-
undisturbed	4	4	5
mellow	5	3	5
placid	8	4	6

5M Jealousy/Envy

5M1.0	A	B	C
jealousy	4	4	7
envy	5	3	5
grudge	6	6	9
gloat	8	4	-
spite	8	3	8

5M2.0	A	B	C
jealous	5	4	5
possessive	5	4	-

5N Hope/Doubt

5N1.0	A	B	C
hope	2	3	2
trust	3	3	3
belief	4	3	4
faith	4	3	11
optimism	8	6	-

5N2.0	A	B	C
desperate	4	3	5
hopeless	4	3	6
crestfallen	8	-	-

5N3.0	A	B	C
disappointment	4	3	4
doubt	4	3	4
despair	6	3	7
desperation	6	3	-
pessimism	8	-	-

5O Caring/Trusting

5O1.0	A	B	C
care	1	3	1
like	1	3	K
love	1	3	2
enjoy	2	3	3
respect	3	3	4
value	3	3	4
admire	4	3	3
appreciate	4	3	5

favor	4	3	4
prefer	4	3	4
regard	4	3	7
fond	5	3	7
adore	6	4	8
romance	6	3	12
cherish	8	7	12
dote	8	9	-
esteem	8	4	10
revere	8	3	2
amour	10	-	-
venerate	10	-	-
adulate	13	-	-

5O2.0	A	B	C
appreciation	4	3	8
affection	5	3	7
gratitude	5	3	6
admiration	6	3	7
mania	6	4	-
fetish	8	-	-
homage	8	6	-

5O3.0	A	B	C
believe	2	3	K
approve	3	4	3
depend	4	3	4
rely	4	4	6
support	4	3	4
entrust	6	5	-
advocate	8	5	7
bolster	8	3	-
condone	8	5	-
devote	8	3	-
sustain	8	4	7
vouch	8	6	-
endorse	10	-	-

5O4.0	A	B	C
forgive	3	3	6
pardon	4	4	4
remit	8	-	-
absolve	10	-	-

5P Neglecting Actions

5P1.0	A	B	C
omit	4	3	4
overlook	5	3	5
neglect	6	5	7
derelict	8	3	-
remiss	8	-	-

5P2.0	A	B	C
exclude	6	7	-
isolate	6	7	6

maroon	8	7	7
seclude	8	-	-
blackball	10	-	-

5Q Desire

5Q1.0	A	B	C
miss	1	3	K
need	1	3	K
want	1	3	K
wish	1	3	K
desire	3	3	3
expect	4	3	5
seek	4	3	4
anticipate	5	7	5
crave	5	7	8
hanker	6	-	-
yearn	6	7	-
aspire	8	7	-
covet	8	5	-
lust	8	7	-
woo	8	7	-
flirt	8	8	-
ogle	10	-	-
philander	10	-	-

5Q1.1	A	B	C
greed	6	5	7
avarice	10	8	-

5Q2.0	A	B	C
selfish	2	3	5
greedy	3	3	3
lascivious	10	-	-
venal	10	-	-
prurient	13	-	-

5R Human Traits (General)

5R1.0	A	B	C
skill	3	3	5
ability	4	3	4
talent	4	4	6
capacity	5	3	4
flair	5	3	-
knack	5	4	-
capability	8	7	-
faculty	8	6	7

5R2.0	A	B	C
attitude	3	3	5
behavior	3	3	4
manner	3	3	6
discipline	4	4	5
personality	5	3	5

	A	B	C
bearing	6	3	11
etiquette	8	4	7
guise	8	4	-

5R3.0	A	B	C
characteristic	5	3	7
quality	5	3	4
attribute	6	4	-
trait	6	3	9
aspect	8	3	11
idiosyncrasy	10	-	-

SUPER CLUSTER

6. Food Types/Meal Types

6A Types of Meals

6A1.0	A	B	C
breakfast	1	3	1
lunch	1	3	K
dinner	2	3	3
meal	2	3	3
supper	2	3	3
buffet	4	7	4
chow	4	3	-
refreshment	5	4	-
brunch	8	-	-
repast	10	6	-

6A2.0	A	B	C
picnic	2	3	1
feast	3	3	3
banquet	4	4	3

6A3.0	A	B	C
treat	2	3	3
dessert	3	3	4
canape	8	5	-
caviar	8	4	-
souffle	8	-	-
tidbit	8	7	9

6B Food Types

6B1.0	A	B	C
food	K	3	K
nutrition	5	4	9
hash	6	3	-
nourishment	6	3	6
aliment	8	-	7
delicacy	8	5	-
comestible	10	-	-
culinary	10	-	11
viand	10	-	-

6B2.0	A	B	C
crop	3	3	3
diet	4	3	4
supplies	5	3	4
cuisine	8	8	9
foodstuff	8	5	-
provisions	8	6	11
victuals	8	7	-

6B3.0	A	B	C
fruit	2	3	K
meat	2	3	3
vegetables	2	3	2
sweets	3	3	-
seafood	4	3	6
relish	5	3	5
garnish	6	7	-
legume	6	5	-
pulp	6	4	-

6B4.0	A	B	C
calorie	4	4	5
carbohydrate	4	3	7
cellulose	5	5	7
protein	5	3	4
glucose	6	4	7

6C Sweets

6C1.0	A	B	C
honey	1	3	1
jam	1	3	1
syrup	2	3	3
marmalade	4	3	10
molasses	5	3	7

6C2.0	A	B	C
cake	1	3	1
cookie	1	3	K
cupcake	2	7	11
doughnut	2	3	-
gingerbread	2	3	-
pie	2	3	K
brownie	3	4	3
popover	4	-	-
pastry	5	3	7
tart	5	5	7
shortcake	6	7	-
wafer	6	4	-
gingersnap	8	-	-
mousse	8	-	-
cruller	10	-	-
ladyfinger	10	6	-
macaroon	10	-	-

6C3.0	A	B	C
candy	2	3	2
gum	2	3	4
pudding	2	3	-
fudge	3	3	3
lollipop	3	3	-
marshmallow	3	5	6
sundae	3	4	-
caramel	4	3	-
gumdrop	4	3	-
sherbet	4	3	6
lozenge	5	-	-
patty	5	4	-
taffy	5	4	-
toffee	5	-	-
bonbon	6	3	-
confection	8	6	-
custard	8	3	-
parfait	8	-	-
sweetmeats	8	6	-
tapioca	8	-	-

6C4.0	A	B	C
chocolate	3	3	3
cocoa	4	3	5
licorice	4	4	-
peppermint	4	3	5
butterscotch	5	-	-
spearmint	5	3	-
vanilla	5	3	6

6D Prepared Foods

6D1.0	A	B	C
macaroni	4	3	-
noodles	4	5	7
spaghetti	4	3	3
vermicelli	8	-	-

6D2.0	A	B	C
cereal	2	3	2
mush	3	3	2
oatmeal	3	3	-
porridge	4	3	-
gruel	6	4	-
pap	8	7	-
farina	10	-	-
pabulum	10	-	-

6D3.0	A	B	C
bread	1	3	1
bun	2	4	2
crust	2	3	4
pancake	2	3	4
pizza	2	3	3
toast	2	3	3
loaf	3	3	2
waffle	3	4	-
loaves	4	3	7
muffin	4	3	-
biscuit	5	3	-
cornbread	5	4	-
flapjack	5	5	-
johnnycake	5	3	-
tortilla	5	4	-
crepe	8	3	-
crouton	8	7	-
fritter	8	-	-
hardtack	8	4	-
rusk	8	9	8
scone	8	9	-
pone	10	6	-
timbale	10	9	-

6D4.0	A	B	C
chips	2	3	2
cracker	2	3	-
snack	2	3	6
pretzel	8	8	-

6D5.0	A	B	C
hamburger	2	3	K
sandwich	2	3	2
frankfurter	8	4	10
croquette	10	-	-

6D6.0	A	B	C
salad	2	3	2
watercress	6	7	-
sauerkraut	8	4	-
slaw	8	-	6

6E Meats

6E1.0	A	B	C
ham	1	3	1
beef	2	3	7
sausage	2	3	7
bacon	3	3	3
poultry	4	3	4
steak	4	3	4
beefsteak	5	3	-
bologna	5	7	7
lard	6	4	-
mutton	6	3	8
pemmican	6	3	-
pork	6	3	6
brisket	8	-	-
giblet	8	-	-
gizzard	8	7	-
porterhouse	8	-	-

A: Grade level; B: Earliest Grade of Occurrence in Textbooks; C: Earliest Grade of Occurrence on Standardized Tests.

6F (cont.)	A	B	C
suet	8	3	-
sweetbread	8	-	-
tripe	8	3	-
veal	8	3	-
venison	8	3	-
cutlet	10	-	-
flitch	10	-	-

6F Dairy Products

6F1.0	A	B	C
egg	1	3	K
butter	2	3	3
cheese	2	3	K
yolk	2	3	-
cream	3	3	3
margarine	3	3	6
curd	5	3	-
lactic	8	4	-
glair	10	-	-

6G Ingredients Used to Prepare Foods

6G1.0	A	B	C
dough	2	3	4
flour	2	3	2
mix	2	3	2
batter	3	3	4
graham	3	3	7
yeast	3	3	6
cornmeal	4	3	-
gelatin	5	4	-
starch	5	3	4
sugarcane	5	4	-
cornstarch	6	3	7
brine	8	4	7
leaven	8	-	-
sourdough	8	7	-

6G2.0	A	B	C
pepper	2	3	5
salt	2	3	2
sugar	2	3	3
mustard	4	3	3
spice	4	3	11
cinnamon	5	3	5
garlic	5	3	7
cloves	6	3	-
ginger	6	3	12
herb	6	6	5
nutmeg	6	4	6
parsley	6	3	6
allspice	8	5	-
cress	8	-	-
curry	8	4	-

	A	B	C
peppercorn	8	6	-
saccharine	8	-	-
tartar	8	5	-
mace	10	7	-

6G3.0	A	B	C
gravy	2	3	-
sauce	2	3	2
catsup	4	4	-
vinegar	4	3	4
mayonnaise	5	4	-
aspic	8	-	-
horseradish	8	9	-
condiment	10	-	-

6H Things to Drink

6H1.0	A	B	C
milk	1	3	K
pop	1	3	2
juice	2	3	3
lemonade	3	3	3
soda	3	3	4
tea	3	3	2
buttermilk	4	4	4
coffee	4	3	4
cider	5	3	-
nectar	5	3	5
beverage	6	6	3
whey	8	4	-
libation	10	-	-

6H2.0	A	B	C
beer	4	3	-
alcohol	5	3	5
wine	5	3	4
champagne	6	6	-
gin	6	3	-
liquor	6	7	-
whiskey	6	5	-
ale	8	3	-
brandy	8	3	-
cocktail	8	5	-
grog	8	3	-
maraschino	8	-	-
mead	8	5	8
moonshine	8	7	-
rum	8	5	7
scotch	8	4	-
sherry	8	8	4
vodka	8	7	-
highball	10	-	-
malmsey	10	-	-
toddy	10	-	-

	A	B	C
vermouth	10	-	-
potation	13	-	-

6H3.0	A	B	C
soup	2	3	2
chili	3	3	-
stew	3	3	4
broth	5	5	-
chowder	5	5	7
bouillon	8	5	7
consommé	10	-	-

6I Fruits

6I1.0	A	B	C
apple	1	3	1
peach	2	3	2
pear	2	3	3
apricot	4	4	7

6I1.1	A	B	C
applesauce	5	3	-

6I2.0	A	B	C
grape	3	3	8
raisin	3	3	-
plum	4	3	3
fig	5	3	3
prune	5	3	-

6I3.0	A	B	C
cherry	2	3	2
strawberry	2	3	6
berry	3	3	4
blackberry	3	3	-
blueberry	3	3	3
cranberry	3	3	-
raspberry	3	3	-
elderberry	8	5	-
gooseberry	8	3	-
dewberry	10	-	-

6I4.0	A	B	C
orange	2	3	3
grapefruit	3	3	11
lemon	3	3	3
lime	4	3	3
tangerine	5	7	-

6I5.0	A	B	C
banana	2	3	3
pineapple	4	3	-
coconut	5	3	3

6I6.0	A	B	C
watermelon	3	3	4
melon	4	4	3
honeydew	5	3	-

6J Vegetables

6J1.0	A	B	C
bean	1	3	1
carrot	2	3	3
celery	3	3	6
cucumber	3	3	-
olive	3	3	3
onion	3	3	3
peas	3	3	3
potato	3	3	3
radish	3	3	4
tomato	3	3	3
beet	4	3	3
cabbage	4	3	6
pickle	4	4	5
spinach	4	3	3
turnip	4	3	6
eggplant	6	4	-
yam	6	-	4
succotash	8	3	-

6J2.0	A	B	C
lettuce	3	3	3
pumpkin	3	3	4
squash	4	3	8

6J3.0	A	B	C
corn	2	3	2
popcorn	2	3	2
grain	3	3	5
rice	3	3	3
wheat	3	3	3
corncob	4	3	-
oats	4	3	7
soybean	4	3	-
maize	5	6	-
malt	5	3	3
barley	6	3	7
bran	6	3	9
rye	6	4	9
buckwheat	8	3	-
hominy	8	5	-
grist	10	-	-

6J4.0	A	B	C
peanut	1	3	1
nut	2	3	K
seed	2	3	1
acorn	4	3	-

chestnut	4	3	-
kernel	4	3	-
almond	5	3	-
cashew	5	-	-
nutshell	5	7	-
pecan	5	3	-
walnut	5	3	-
beechnut	8	4	-
butternut	8	-	-
filbert	8	-	-
hazelnut	8	7	-

6K Actions Done to/with Food

6K1.0	A	B	C
cook	1	3	1
bake	2	3	1
boil	2	3	3
barbecue	3	3	7
fry	3	3	3
roast	3	3	3
brew	4	4	6
grill	4	3	5
broil	5	4	-
poach	5	-	-
scald	6	5	-
simmer	6	7	-
skewer	6	4	-
blanch	8	-	-
braise	8	-	-
concoct	8	-	-
distill	8	5	12
sauté	8	-	-
decoct	10	-	-
fricassee	10	-	-
shirr	10	-	-

6K2.0	A	B	C
churn	3	3	3
serve	3	3	3
sift	4	6	5
knead	5	7	-
cater	8	-	-
shuck	8	4	-

6K3.0	A	B	C
spoil	3	3	3
ripen	3	3	5
rot	4	4	4
decay	5	3	5
deteriorate	6	3	-
taint	8	7	-

6K3.1	A	B	C
ptomaine	8	-	-

6L Food Tastes

6L1.0	A	B	C
taste	2	3	2
flavor	4	3	4
tang	5	4	12
savor	6	7	-
bland	8	7	7
gustatory	10	-	-

6L2.0	A	B	C
sweet	2	3	2
delicious	3	3	3
tasty	3	3	7
delectable	8	4	-
luscious	8	5	-

6L2.1	A	B	C
sweetness	4	3	-
bitterness	5	3	4
ambrosia	8	6	-

6L3.0	A	B	C
bitter	3	3	5
sour	3	3	3
bittersweet	8	8	-
rancid	8	7	7
sec	8	9	-
brackish	10	5	-

6L4.0	A	B	C
juicy	3	3	8
ripe	3	3	2
succulent	6	3	-

6L5.0	A	B	C
greasy	3	3	7
rotten	4	3	9
stale	4	3	-

6M Eating/Drinking Actions

6M1.0	A	B	C
bite	2	3	2
chew	3	3	3
swallow	3	3	4
gnaw	4	3	4
munch	4	3	-
nibble	4	3	5
masticate	10	-	-

6M2.0	A	B	C
eat	1	3	K
feed	1	3	K
dine	4	3	K
devour	5	4	-

A: Grade level; B: Earliest Grade of Occurrence in Textbooks; C: Earliest Grade of Occurrence on Standardized Tests.

gorge	5	3	6
sup	5	5	-
consume	6	3	11
ingest	8	-	-
cloy	10	-	-
glut	10	-	-
sate	10	-	-

6M3.0	A	B	C
drink	1	3	2
sip	3	3	12
gargle	5	-	-
guzzle	5	-	-
tipple	8	-	-
imbibe	10	-	-
swill	10	-	-
quaff	13	-	-

6M3.1	A	B	C
quench	8	3	-
inebriate	10	-	-
slake	10	-	-

6N Hunger/Thirst

6N1.0	A	B	C
hunger	3	3	4
thirst	3	3	3
appetite	4	3	4

6N1.1	A	B	C
hungry	2	3	K
thirsty	2	3	4
ravenous	8	3	12
voracious	10	7	-

6N2.0	A	B	C
starve	3	3	7
famish	8	-	-
emaciate	13	-	-

SUPER CLUSTER
7. Time

7A Time (General)

7A1.0	A	B	C
time	1	3	K
bedtime	2	3	3
daytime	2	3	4
dinnertime	2	3	-
lunchtime	2	3	1
springtime	2	3	-
summertime	2	3	6
suppertime	2	3	4

wintertime	2	3	-
lifetime	4	3	5
mealtime	4	4	5
peacetime	4	3	-
wartime	5	5	-

7B Devices Used to Measure Time

7B1.0	A	B	C
clock	1	3	1
watch	1	3	K
calendar	4	3	3
stopwatch	4	7	-
wristwatch	4	6	-
hourglass	5	5	-
sundial	5	4	-
timepiece	5	-	-
water clock	10	-	-

7B1.1	A	B	C
o'clock	3	3	1
date	4	3	3

7C Parts of a Day

7C1.0	A	B	C
day	K	3	K
morning	1	3	K
afternoon	2	3	1
noon	2	3	1
noontime	2	3	3
sunrise	3	3	3
dawn	4	3	3
noonday	4	3	-
daybreak	5	4	5
sunup	5	3	-
workday	5	3	7
midday	6	3	-

7C2.0	A	B	C
night	1	3	K
evening	2	3	2
tonight	2	3	2
midnight	4	3	3
overnight	4	3	4
sunset	4	3	3
dusk	5	3	-
nightfall	5	3	7
sundown	5	3	-
twilight	6	3	-
vesper	8	-	-
eve	8	3	11

A: Grade level; B: Earliest Grade of Occurrence in Textbooks; C: Earliest Grade of Occurrence on Standardized Tests.

7C3.0	A	B	C
hour	1	3	2
second	1	3	1
minute	2	3	3
moment	3	3	2
instant	4	3	5

7D Other Periods of Time

7D1.0	A	B	C
age	2	3	2
season	2	3	5
period	3	3	3
cycle	4	3	3
lifelong	5	4	-
meantime	5	3	7
term	5	3	4
countdown	6	3	-
duration	6	3	12
generation	6	3	7
interval	6	4	7
epoch	8	7	-
interim	8	5	-
interlude	8	7	-
phase	8	5	7
posterity	8	4	8
ides	10	-	9
longevity	10	-	-

7D2.0	A	B	C
fall	1	3	1
spring	1	3	K
summer	1	3	1
winter	1	3	1
autumn	2	3	3
yule	6	3	-
equinox	8	6	-
vernal	8	5	-

7D3.0	A	B	C
week	1	3	2
year	1	3	1
month	2	3	2
weekday	2	3	-
weekend	2	3	2
century	4	3	4
decade	6	3	9
centennial	8	5	7
era	8	3	7
millennium	8	5	-

7E Months and Days

7E1.0	A	B	C
January	2	3	2
February	2	3	3
March	2	3	2
April	2	3	2
May	2	3	1
June	2	3	1
July	2	3	2
August	2	5	3
September	2	3	1
October	2	3	3
November	2	3	4
December	2	3	2

7E2.0	A	B	C
Monday	1	3	1
Tuesday	1	3	1
Wednesday	1	3	1
Thursday	1	3	1
Friday	1	3	1
Saturday	1	3	1
Sunday	1	3	1

7F Relative Time

7F1.0	A	B	C
today	1	3	K
everyday	2	3	8
tomorrow	2	3	2
present	3	3	1
someday	3	3	7
future	4	3	4
eternity	5	3	9
morrow	6	5	10

7F2.0	A	B	C
past	2	3	3
yesterday	2	3	2
bygone	6	4	-

7F2.1	A	B	C
relic	6	4	-
anachronism	13	-	-

7F3.0	A	B	C
boyhood	4	4	6
childhood	4	3	5
youth	4	3	5
adolescence	8	7	11
puberty	8	-	-

7F4.0	A	B	C
old	1	3	K
ancient	4	3	3

A: Grade level; B: Earliest Grade of Occurrence in Textbooks; C: Earliest Grade of Occurrence on Standardized Tests.

	A	B	C
antique	5	5	5
secondhand	5	3	-
obsolete	8	7	11
timeworn	8	-	-
superannuated	10	-	-
vintage	10	-	-
hoar	13	-	-

7F5.0	A	B	C
colonial	4	3	4
prehistoric	4	3	5
historic	5	3	6
historical	5	3	4
primitive	5	3	7
medieval	6	3	-
primal	8	5	-
paleolithic	10	7	-
pristine	10	-	-
primordial	13	4	-

7F5.1	A	B	C
history	4	3	4
ancestry	6	5	8

7G Prior Action (Relationship Markers)

7G1.0	A	B	C
ago	1	3	K
early	1	3	1
already	3	3	K
lately	4	3	4
prior to	6	-	-

7G1.1	A	B	C
earlier	2	3	2
former	5	3	6
previous	5	3	6
anterior	8	-	-
precede	8	6	9
antecedent	10	7	-
precursor	10	-	-

7G2.0	A	B	C
as yet	4	-	-
at first	4	-	-
before now	4	-	-
before that	4	-	-
in the beginning	4	-	-
so far	4	-	-
until then	4	-	-
up to now	4	-	-
beforehand	6	4	9
heretofore	6	7	-
hitherto	6	4	-

	A	B	C
initially	8	7	9
aforementioned	10	-	-
aforesaid	10	-	-

7G3.0	A	B	C
original	4	3	4
source	4	3	5
initial	5	3	4
introductory	6	7	-
preliminary	8	4	8

7G4.0	A	B	C
fresh	1	3	1
new	1	3	K
young	2	3	2
modern	3	3	4
brandnew	4	3	-
current	4	3	4
recent	5	3	5

7G4.1	A	B	C
ready	1	3	K
due	5	3	6

7G5.0	A	B	C
after	1	3	K
since	2	3	3
now that	4	-	-
subsequent to	8	-	-

7H Subsequent Action (Relationship Markers)

7H1.0	A	B	C
soon	1	3	K
shortly	3	3	4
eventually	6	3	6
momentarily	6	3	9
forthwith	8	-	-
straightway	8	4	-
imminent	10	-	-

7H2.0	A	B	C
then	K	3	K
next	1	3	K
later	2	3	2
after that	3	-	-
in the end	3	-	-
afterwards	5	3	6
henceforth	5	6	-
henceforward	5	-	-
latter	5	3	-
thereafter	5	3	7
hereafter	6	6	-
hereinafter	6	-	-
subsequently	6	5	-

7H2.1	A	B	C
late	1	3	1
tardy	4	5	2
eventual	5	6	-

7H3.0	A	B	C
before	1	3	K
until	1	3	1

7I Concurrent Action (Relationship Markers)

7I1.0	A	B	C
now	1	3	K
at this point	4	-	-
immediately	4	3	3
nowadays	5	3	-
presently	5	3	11

7I2.0	A	B	C
at	K	3	K
on	K	3	K
of	K	3	K
thereof	5	3	-

7I3.0	A	B	C
as	K	3	2
when	1	3	K
during	2	3	2
while	2	3	K
whilst	6	5	-

7I4.0	A	B	C
together	2	3	1
at the same time	4	-	-
in the meantime	4	-	-
meanwhile	4	3	6
simultaneously	6	3	7
concurrently	8	-	-
in the interim	8	-	-
contemporaneously	10	-	-
coeval	13	-	-
concomitant	13	-	-

7J Speed

7J1.0	A	B	C
speed	2	3	2
pace	5	3	6
tempo	5	3	-
velocity	6	5	8

7J2.0	A	B	C
bustle	5	3	-
fuss	5	3	-
haste	5	3	5
flurry	6	3	-
frenzy	6	5	-
spate	8	-	-

7J3.0	A	B	C
hurry	1	3	1
race	1	3	3
rush	2	3	1
charge	3	3	2
dash	3	3	2
scoot	4	3	-
accelerate	6	5	-
hasten	6	4	9
hustle	6	4	-
scurry	6	3	10
whisk	6	3	-
hotfoot	8	-	-
hurtle	8	-	-
hie	10	-	5

7J3.1	A	B	C
slow	2	3	1
slowdown	3	7	-
decelerate	10	-	12

7J4.0	A	B	C
fast	1	3	K
quick	2	3	3
speedy	3	3	-
brisk	4	3	4
rapid	4	3	5
swift	4	3	4
jiffy	5	3	-
fleet	6	3	10
presto	6	3	-
posthaste	8	-	-

7J5.0	A	B	C
sudden	2	3	4
brief	4	3	3
immediate	4	3	9
instant	4	3	5
automatic	5	3	11
abrupt	6	4	7
prompt	6	4	12
spontaneous	6	7	9

7J5.1	A	B	C
hastily	4	3	5
automatically	5	3	-
offhand	6	-	-
cursory	10	-	-
extempore	10	-	-

7J5.2	A	B	C
headfirst	4	3	-
helter-skelter	5	3	-
hasty	6	3	7
headlong	6	3	-

7K Duration/Frequency

7K1.0	A	B	C
always	1	3	K
long	1	3	K
forever	3	3	2
constant	5	3	5
endless	5	3	2
everlasting	5	3	7
permanent	5	3	5
continuous	6	3	-
eternal	6	4	7
chronic	8	7	11
perpetual	8	4	-
incessant	10	3	8

7K2.0	A	B	C
rare	2	3	5
sometimes	2	3	1
awhile	3	3	4
occasional	4	3	4
temporary	5	3	6
infrequent	6	4	10
irregular	6	3	11
momentary	6	7	-
periodic	8	4	7
piecemeal	8	4	-
sporadic	8	5	-
tentative	8	7	-

7K3.0	A	B	C
longtime	5	5	-
longstanding	6	3	-

7K4.0	A	B	C
again	1	3	K
once	1	3	1
twice	1	3	3
encore	8	8	-

7K5.0	A	B	C
nightly	2	3	-
weekly	2	3	7
daily	3	3	4
hourly	3	4	6
quarterly	8	-	-
circadian	13	-	-
diurnal	13	7	-

7K5.1	A	B	C
often	2	3	2
ever	3	3	3
forevermore	6	-	-

7K6.0	A	B	C
anymore	2	3	2
never	2	3	1
seldom	4	3	5
nevermore	6	7	-

7K7.0	A	B	C
continue	3	3	3
persist	6	5	12
persevere	8	-	-
resume	8	5	9
perpetuate	10	6	-
protract	10	7	-

7K7.1	A	B	C
practice	2	3	2
repeat	4	3	7
rehearse	5	4	2
iterate	10	-	-

7K8.0	A	B	C
common	3	3	4
regular	3	3	4
annual	4	3	4
general	4	3	4
usual	4	3	3
customary	5	4	9
frequent	5	3	5
continual	6	5	-
habitual	8	7	10
inveterate	8	7	-

SUPER CLUSTER

8. Machines/Engines/Tools

8A Machines

8A1.0	A	B	C
equipment	3	3	3
machine	3	3	3
hardware	4	3	6
machinery	4	3	5
appliance	5	5	9
apparatus	6	4	12

8A1.1	A	B	C
equip	5	3	-
automate	8	-	-

A: Grade level; B: Earliest Grade of Occurrence in Textbooks; C: Earliest Grade of Occurrence on Standardized Tests.

8A1.2	A	B	C
mechanical	5	3	5

8A2.0	A	B	C
clockwork	5	4	-
mechanism	5	4	-
contraption	6	3	-
gadget	6	4	7
rig	6	3	-

8B Engines and Parts of Engines

8B1.0	A	B	C
battery	3	3	4
engine	3	3	3
motor	3	3	4

8B2.0	A	B	C
brake	4	3	-
gear	4	3	5
starter	4	3	-
generator	5	3	5
compressor	6	4	-
crankshaft	6	3	-
piston	6	3	-
throttle	6	3	-
cog	8	6	-
dynamo	8	-	-
flywheel	8	7	-
gasket	8	6	-
gearbox	8	4	-
sprocket	8	7	-
transmission	8	6	10

8B3.0	A	B	C
jet	1	3	1
turbine	6	4	9

8C Fuels/Lubricants

8C1.0	A	B	C
oil	2	3	2
fuel	3	3	3
gas	3	3	3
gasoline	3	3	4
petroleum	5	3	6
diesel	6	3	7
turpentine	6	3	9
kerosene	8	3	9

8C1.1	A	B	C
refuel	5	5	-

8C2.0	A	B	C
grease	4	3	5
lubricate	6	4	-

	A	B	C
tallow	6	3	10
lubrication	8	4	-

8D Appliances

8D1.0	A	B	C
oven	2	3	3
stove	2	3	K
toaster	2	3	5
cook stove	4	4	-
griddle	4	4	-
flatiron	10	5	-

8D2.0	A	B	C
heater	3	3	3
burner	4	3	7
furnace	4	3	4
boiler	5	3	-
kiln	5	3	-
radiator	6	3	10
crucible	10	4	-

8D3.0	A	B	C
refrigerator	3	3	4
freezer	4	3	4
icebox	4	3	-

8D4.0	A	B	C
TV	1	3	-
radio	2	3	3
television	2	3	2
phonograph	4	3	5
stereo	5	5	8
jukebox	8	-	-
shortwave	8	7	-
turntable	8	8	-
wireless	8	3	7

8E Tools (General)

8E1.0	A	B	C
tool	2	3	2
instrument	3	3	3
aid	4	3	3
device	5	3	5
implement	5	5	7
utensil	6	7	11

8E2.0	A	B	C
drill	4	3	3
screwdriver	4	3	6
pliers	5	3	6
wrench	6	3	7
auger	8	7	7
gimlet	10	-	-

A: Grade level; B: Earliest Grade of Occurrence in Textbooks; C: Earliest Grade of Occurrence on Standardized Tests.

8E3.0

8E3.0	A	B	C
crowbar	4	3	-
jack	4	3	1
lever	4	3	6
wedge	4	3	6
chock	8	-	-
handspike	8	-	-
jimmy	10	-	3
shim	10	-	-

8E4.0	A	B	C
hammer	2	3	2
sledge	6	4	-
gavel	8	3	-
pestle	8	3	-
triphammer	10	-	-

8E5.0	A	B	C
saw	1	3	K
jigsaw	3	3	-
hacksaw	8	4	-

8E6.0	A	B	C
shovel	2	3	2
rake	3	3	5
hoe	4	3	5
pitchfork	5	4	-
spade	6	3	-
trowel	8	7	-
dibble	10	-	-

8E7.0	A	B	C
chisel	5	3	2
sandpaper	5	3	7
scraper	5	4	8
awl	8	3	-
gouge	8	6	-
rasp	8	7	-

8F Tools Used for Cutting

8F1.0	A	B	C
ax	4	3	8
axe	4	4	-
hatchet	4	3	2
scythe	6	4	6
sickle	6	4	9

8F2.0	A	B	C
knife	2	3	3
scissors	2	3	4
jackknife	4	4	-
pocketknife	4	6	-
razor	4	3	9
lawnmower	5	5	-
trimmer	5	4	-

	A	B	C
clipper	8	3	-
lathe	8	6	-
mower	8	3	-
scalpel	8	7	-
straightedge	8	3	8

8F3.0	A	B	C
blade	4	3	6
barb	6	3	-

8G Cutting/Abrasive Actions

8G1.0	A	B	C
peck	4	3	7
pierce	5	3	5
prick	5	3	-
stab	5	3	-
transfix	8	7	-
impale	10	-	-
incise	10	-	-

8G2.0	A	B	C
rub	2	3	1
scratch	2	3	2
scrape	3	3	4
shave	3	3	-
grate	4	4	7
chafe	5	-	-
whittle	5	4	5
scuff	8	3	-
abrade	10	-	-

8G3.0	A	B	C
chop	2	3	2
mow	3	4	-
grind	4	3	4
shred	4	5	5
slash	4	3	4
gnash	5	-	10
hack	6	4	-
mince	6	3	-
hew	8	6	-
lacerate	8	-	-

8G4.0	A	B	C
cut	1	3	K
peel	2	3	3
carve	3	3	3
clip	3	3	3
slice	4	3	5
snip	4	3	-
cutoff	5	4	-
shear	5	3	11
slit	5	3	-
crosscut	6	4	-
pare	6	4	-

	A	B	C
amputate	8	-	-
sever	8	4	9
tonsure	10	-	-

8G5.0	A	B	C
dig	2	3	2
burrow	4	3	5
scoop	4	3	7
bulldoze	5	-	-
dredge	6	5	-
excavate	6	5	11
exhume	10	-	-

8H Fasteners

8H1.0	A	B	C
nail	2	3	2
hook	3	3	4
fishhook	4	4	-
hinge	4	5	4
latch	4	3	6
screw	4	3	9
spike	4	3	-
brad	5	5	5
peg	5	3	1
slot	5	3	2
rivet	6	7	-
dowel	8	7	-
hasp	8	-	-
hobnail	8	-	-
thumbscrew	8	-	-

8H2.0	A	B	C
clamp	5	3	-
clothespin	5	4	-
forceps	8	-	-
ferrule	10	-	-

8H3.0	A	B	C
pin	K	3	1
glue	2	3	3
needle	2	3	3
staple	4	3	7
tack	4	3	4
thumbtack	4	3	-
mucilage	8	4	-

8H4.0	A	B	C
chain	1	3	K
rope	1	3	1
string	1	3	K
shoestring	2	3	-
lasso	3	3	-
shoelace	3	5	5
strap	3	3	4
tether	3	3	-

	A	B	C
cable	4	3	4
clothesline	4	3	5
cord	4	3	3
fishline	4	4	-
lariat	4	3	-
thong	4	4	-
twine	4	3	-
drawstring	5	3	-

8H4.1	A	B	C
knot	3	3	2

8H5.0	A	B	C
key	2	3	2
lock	2	3	K
handcuff	4	4	-
keyhole	5	3	-
bolt	6	3	9
manacle	8	-	-

8I Handles

8I1.0	A	B	C
handle	2	3	2
doorknob	3	3	-
grip	4	3	-
knob	5	3	5
hilt	6	4	-
haft	10	-	-
helve	10	-	-

8J Miscellaneous Devices

8J1.0	A	B	C
pedal	3	3	6
switch	3	3	3
dial	4	3	5
trigger	5	3	-
toggle	6	6	-

8J2.0	A	B	C
crank	3	3	9
windlass	6	4	-
winch	8	7	-

8J3.0	A	B	C
fulcrum	3	3	11
roller	3	3	5
pulley	4	3	-
spool	5	3	11
spindle	6	3	-

8J4.0	A	B	C
ladder	2	3	2
platform	4	3	3
stepladder	4	3	-

A: Grade level; B: Earliest Grade of Occurrence in Textbooks; C: Earliest Grade of Occurrence on Standardized Tests.

	A	B	C
easel	5	3	-
springboard	5	4	-
sawhorse	6	3	-
anvil	8	6	-
gantry	8	6	-
pallet	8	3	-
scaffold	8	-	11
tripod	8	5	-

8J5.0	A	B	C
baton	4	4	-
pointer	5	3	11
wand	5	3	-

8K Equipment Related to Vision

8K1.0	A	B	C
microscope	3	3	3
telescope	4	3	7
binoculars	5	3	12
eyepiece	5	5	-
spyglass	5	4	-
periscope	8	4	7

8K2.0	A	B	C
camera	3	3	3
lens	4	3	5

8L Electronic Equipment

8L1.0	A	B	C
transistor	5	4	-
transmitter	8	3	10

8L2.0	A	B	C
computer	3	3	6
robot	3	3	7
terminal	6	3	6
thermostat	6	4	-
electroscope	8	5	-
teletype	8	5	-

8M Utensils Used for Cooking/Eating

8M1.0	A	B	C
fork	2	3	3
knife	2	3	3
spoon	2	3	3
teaspoon	3	3	4
silverware	4	3	-
tablespoon	4	3	6
tableware	4	3	-
chopsticks	5	3	4

8M2.0	A	B	C
pan	1	3	1
pot	2	3	1
teakettle	3	3	7
teapot	3	3	4
kettle	4	3	5
saucepan	4	3	-
skillet	4	4	-
crock	5	4	-
stewpan	5	-	-
cauldron	8	7	-

8M3.0	A	B	C
scoop	3	3	7
dipper	4	3	4
ladle	4	3	-
spatula	4	4	-
tong	4	3	-
sieve	5	3	9
colander	8	-	-

8M4.0	A	B	C
nutcracker	4	3	5
opener	5	3	5
corkscrew	8	3	-

8M5.0	A	B	C
bowl	1	3	K
cup	1	3	1
glass	1	3	K
teacup	2	3	-
mug	4	4	-
glassware	5	5	-
water glass	5	-	-
goblet	6	6	-
stein	6	4	5
compote	8	-	-
tankard	8	5	-
wineglass	8	-	-
tureen	10	4	-

8M6.0	A	B	C
dish	1	3	K
plate	1	3	K
dishpan	3	3	-
saucer	3	3	-
tray	3	3	3
casserole	4	7	6
china	4	3	4
platter	4	3	5
chinaware	5	3	-
kitchenware	5	4	-
saltcellar	10	-	-
salver	10	-	-

A: Grade level; B: Earliest Grade of Occurrence in Textbooks; C: Earliest Grade of Occurrence on Standardized Tests.

8M7.0	A	B	C
beater	3	3	-
turnspit	10	-	-

8N Weapons

8N1.0	A	B	C
firearms	5	3	-
weapon	5	3	5
arms	5	3	3
artillery	8	3	-
ballistics	10	3	-

8N2.0	A	B	C
sword	3	3	3
harpoon	4	3	-
spear	4	3	5
tomahawk	4	3	-
cutlass	5	3	-
dagger	5	4	-
javelin	6	5	9
lance	6	4	4
broadsword	8	-	-
rapier	8	5	-
saber	8	4	-
poniard	10	-	-
stiletto	10	6	-
trident	10	3	-
poleax	13	-	-

8N3.0	A	B	C
gun	1	3	3
holster	3	5	-
pistol	4	3	6
rifle	4	3	6
cannon	5	3	-
revolver	5	4	-
shotgun	5	5	6
musket	6	4	-
firelock	8	6	-
flintlock	8	4	-
gunstock	8	-	-
matchlock	8	4	-

8N3.1	A	B	C
bomb	4	3	-
bombshell	4	4	-
bullet	4	3	6
gunshot	4	-	-
ammunition	5	4	5
cannonball	5	5	-
missile	5	3	5
pellet	5	3	9
torpedo	5	6	6
buckshot	8	-	-

	A	B	C
shrapnel	8	-	-
warhead	8	6	-
brickbat	10	-	-

8N4.0	A	B	C
firecracker	3	3	-
fireworks	3	3	6
dynamite	5	3	9
grenade	5	5	-
gunpowder	5	3	5
explosive	6	4	10
fireball	8	7	-
incendiary	10	5	-
squib	10	-	-

8N5.0	A	B	C
arrow	3	3	3
bow	3	3	3
arrowhead	4	3	-
dart	4	3	5
boomerang	5	3	-
sling	5	3	-
slingshot	5	4	-
bowstring	6	4	-
crossbow	6	5	-
mangonel	13	-	-

8N6.0	A	B	C
whip	3	3	-
blackjack	8	-	-
cudgel	10	4	-
truncheon	10	-	-

8N7.0	A	B	C
guillotine	6	5	-
noose	6	5	-

SUPER CLUSTER

9. Types of People

9A People (General Names)

9A1.0	A	B	C
person	1	3	1
self	2	4	3
being	3	3	3
human	3	3	4
chap	4	4	5
character	4	3	4
individual	4	3	5

9A1.1	A	B	C
people	1	3	K
folk	4	3	5

A: Grade level; B: Earliest Grade of Occurrence in Textbooks; C: Earliest Grade of Occurrence on Standardized Tests.

	A	B	C
mankind	5	3	-
gentlefolk	8	7	-

9A2.0	A	B	C
highness	5	4	-
majesty	5	3	6

9B Names for Women

9B1.0	A	B	C
lady	1	3	7
woman	1	3	1
female	3	3	4
housewife	3	3	-
squaw	4	4	-
widow	4	3	4
belle	5	4	-
dame	5	3	-
feminine	5	5	9
gentlewoman	5	-	-
ma'am	5	3	-
mistress	5	3	-
spinster	5	-	-
hostess	6	4	9
madam	6	3	7
madame	6	3	-
vamp	8	-	-
womenfolk	8	-	-
bluestocking	10	-	-
coquette	10	-	-
soubrette	13	-	-

9B2.0	A	B	C
girl	1	3	K
lass	4	3	-
schoolgirl	4	5	-
tomboy	4	4	-
maiden	5	4	-

9C Names for Men

9C1.0	A	B	C
man	1	3	K
fellow	3	3	6
male	3	3	5
sir	3	3	4
gentleman	4	3	-
gentlemen	4	3	7
guy	4	4	7
master	4	3	4
mister	4	3	-
señor	4	3	4
masculine	5	5	9
dude	5	4	-
bachelor	6	3	6

	A	B	C
host	6	3	7
schoolfellow	6	6	-
menfolk	8	-	-
eunuch	10	-	-

9C2.0	A	B	C
boy	K	3	K
lad	3	3	2
schoolboy	3	3	-
junior	4	3	5
urchin	6	6	12
gamin	10	-	-

9D Names Indicating Age

9D1.0	A	B	C
baby	1	3	K
babe	3	5	5
newborn	4	3	5
papoose	4	4	-
toddler	4	3	-
infant	5	3	6
tot	5	7	6
embryo	6	4	-
fetus	8	9	-

9D2.0	A	B	C
child	1	3	K
kid	4	3	4
minor	4	3	3
juvenile	5	6	4
orphan	5	3	-
youngster	5	3	9
teen	6	4	12
adolescent	8	5	9
waif	8	7	-
whippersnapper	8	-	-

9D3.0	A	B	C
adult	3	3	3
grown-up	3	3	-
senior	5	6	5
elder	6	3	6
octogenarian	10	-	-

9E Names Indicating Friendship/Camaraderie

9E1.0	A	B	C
friend	1	3	K
neighbor	2	3	3
pal	3	3	9
buddy	4	3	-
classmate	4	3	8
partner	4	3	4

playmate	4	3	4
roommate	4	3	11
schoolmate	4	3	4
teammate	4	3	3
chum	5	4	-
peer	5	3	5
playfellow	5	-	-
acquaintance	6	4	10
ally	6	3	9
bedfellow	8	-	-
cohort	8	4	-
comrade	8	6	-
merrymaker	8	9	-
crony	10	-	-
kith	10	-	-
messmate	10	7	-
confrere	13	-	-

9E2.0	A	B	C
boyfriend	4	5	-
girlfriend	4	8	-
darling	5	3	-
lover	5	3	-
suitor	5	4	-
fiance	6	5	-
mate	6	3	6
sweetheart	6	5	-
ladylove	8	-	-
playboy	8	-	-
amour	10	-	-

9F Names for Spiritual or Mythological Characters

9F1.0	A	B	C
fairy	2	3	3
elf	3	3	3
elves	3	3	3
pixy	4	3	-
sandman	6	-	-

9F2.0	A	B	C
ghost	3	3	2
genie	4	4	-
spook	4	3	-
specter	8	8	-
wraith	10	-	-

9F3.0	A	B	C
god	1	3	7
angel	2	3	-
cupid	2	4	-
devil	3	3	11
saint	5	4	6
soul	6	3	10

cherub	8	-	-
deity	8	6	-
godhead	8	-	-
joss	8	6	-

9F4.0	A	B	C
goblin	4	3	-
demon	5	3	7
imp	5	3	3
phantom	5	5	-
crossbones	6	-	7
ghoul	6	3	-
bugaboo	8	6	-
gnome	8	-	-
hobgoblin	8	-	-

9F5.0	A	B	C
witch	3	3	4
monster	3	3	3
wizard	4	3	9
hag	6	7	-
clairvoyant	10	-	-

9G Names Indicating Negative Characteristics about People

9G1.0	A	B	C
gossip	4	4	4
liar	4	4	-
storyteller	4	6	7
telltale	4	3	-
busybody	6	-	-
chatterbox	8	8	-
gadabout	8	-	-
talebearer	8	-	-
fishwife	10	-	-
monger	10	-	-
scandalmonger	10	-	-
termagant	13	-	-

9G2.0	A	B	C
fool	3	3	3
pest	3	3	3
slowpoke	3	3	-
coward	4	3	4
dunce	4	-	7
blockhead	5	5	-
dolt	5	4	-
dope	5	3	-
delinquent	6	-	11
moron	6	8	-
nuisance	6	3	6
scatterbrain	6	-	7
buffoon	8	7	-
bumpkin	8	3	-

A: Grade level; B: Earliest Grade of Occurrence in Textbooks; C: Earliest Grade of Occurrence on Standardized Tests.

fop	8	-	-
frump	8	-	-
imbecile	8	-	-
lout	8	-	-
ninny	8	-	-
popinjay	8	7	-
sot	8	-	-
boor	10	-	-
churl	10	-	-
coxcomb	10	-	-
degenerate	10	7	-
recreant	10	-	-
poltroon	13	-	-

9G3.0	A	B	C
enemy	3	3	3
bully	4	3	7
attacker	5	-	-
brute	5	3	-
cad	5	7	3
foe	5	4	6
opponent	5	3	5
rascal	5	3	-
rival	5	3	5
scamp	5	3	-
hothead	6	7	-
ruffian	6	5	-
scoundrel	6	3	7
dastard	8	-	-
henchman	8	-	-
knave	8	7	-
ringleader	8	-	-
rogue	8	4	-
anathema	10	-	-
blackguard	10	-	-
huckster	10	-	-
pariah	10	-	-
roughneck	10	-	-

9G4.0	A	B	C
suspect	4	3	5
hunchback	5	3	-
prey	5	3	5
victim	5	3	5
captive	6	3	-
castaway	6	4	-
hostage	6	6	9
invalid	6	5	-
addict	8	7	-
castoff	8	-	-
leper	8	-	-
martyr	8	6	-
lazar	10	-	-

9G4.1	A	B	C
wallflower	5	5	-

9G5.0	A	B	C
snob	3	8	-
bigot	8	-	-
cynic	8	-	-
prude	8	-	-
recluse	8	-	-
gourmand	10	-	-
introvert	10	-	-
parvenu	10	-	-
prig	10	-	-
sycophant	10	-	-
teetotaler	10	-	-

9G6.0	A	B	C
bandit	2	3	K
robber	2	3	2
burglar	3	3	-
killer	3	3	6
pirate	3	3	5
thief	3	3	3
crook	4	3	5
gunfighter	4	-	-
rustler	4	3	-
cannibal	5	3	7
convict	5	5	-
jailbird	5	-	-
outlaw	5	4	6
vandal	5	4	-
criminal	6	5	9
lawbreaker	6	4	-
pickpocket	6	-	-
tyrant	6	3	5
villain	6	4	-
wrongdoer	6	7	-
assassin	8	8	11
culprit	8	3	8
cutthroat	8	7	-
evildoer	8	-	-
felon	8	-	-
fiend	8	5	-
thug	8	-	-
malefactor	10	-	-
prostitute	10	-	-
miscreant	13	-	-

9H Names Indicating Lack of Permanence for People

9H1.0	A	B	C
guest	3	3	4
stranger	3	3	3
visitor	3	3	5
tourist	5	3	5
vacationer	5	3	-

A: Grade level; B: Earliest Grade of Occurrence in Textbooks; C: Earliest Grade of Occurrence on Standardized Tests.

9H2.0	A	B	C
gypsy	4	3	-
hobo	4	3	4
runaway	4	3	-
wanderer	5	3	-
fugitive	6	6	9
rover	6	5	-
vagabond	6	5	-
nomad	8	4	9
vagrant	8	8	-
wayfarer	8	-	-

9H3.0	A	B	C
passenger	4	3	4
spectator	6	6	7

9I Names Indicating Permanence for People

9I1.0	A	B	C
pilgrim	3	5	9
pioneer	3	3	4
settler	4	3	-
colonist	5	5	-
newcomer	5	3	-
puritan	5	4	8
townsman	6	6	-
backwoodsman	8	-	-

9I2.0	A	B	C
caveman	3	3	-
townsfolk	4	3	-
villager	4	4	-
dweller	5	3	6
townspeople	5	3	-
inhabitant	6	3	-
tenant	6	3	-
tribesman	6	4	-
bushman	8	6	-
denizen	10	-	-

9I3.0	A	B	C
citizen	4	3	4
native	4	3	4
aborigine	5	3	-
ethnic	8	3	9
indigenous	10	5	-
endemic	10	7	-

9I3.1	A	B	C
foreigner	5	3	-
alien	6	4	9
immigrant	8	3	8

9I4.0	A	B	C
countryman	5	4	-
countrywoman	5	-	-
taxpayer	6	8	5
traitor	6	6	7
veteran	6	3	9
freeman	8	6	-
patriot	8	3	6
renegade	8	7	11
turncoat	10	3	-

9J Names Indicating Size of People

9J1.0	A	B	C
giant	2	3	3
dwarf	3	3	7
midget	3	3	-
troll	3	3	-
runt	4	4	-
pygmy	5	3	-

9K Names Indicating Fame

9K1.0	A	B	C
star	1	3	1
savior	4	3	-
celebrity	5	5	7
heroine	5	3	-
idol	6	4	-
torchbearer	8	9	-
upstart	8	8	-
cynosure	13	-	-

9L Names Indicating Knowledge of a Topic

9L1.0	A	B	C
ace	4	3	3
expert	4	3	4
genius	5	3	6
pro	5	4	7
scholar	5	4	-
gamesman	6	-	-
veteran	6	3	9
academic	8	3	7
highbrow	8	6	-
sage	8	3	7
specialist	8	5	9
connoisseur	10	7	-
epicure	10	-	-
savant	10	5	-
sophist	10	-	-

| sophisticate | 10 | - | - |
| polyglot | 13 | 7 | - |

9L2.0	A	B	C
beginner	2	5	4
virgin	5	4	-
rookie	5	5	-
amateur	6	3	6
novice	6	7	11
greenhorn	8	5	-
tenderfoot	8	7	-
dilettante	13	-	-
neophyte	13	-	-
tyro	13	-	-

9M Names Indicating Financial Status

9M1.0	A	B	C
beggar	3	3	-
bum	3	3	-
peasant	6	3	6
miser	8	7	7
niggard	8	-	-
pauper	8	-	-
spendthrift	8	7	7
mendicant	10	-	-
proletarian	10	-	-

9M2.0	A	B	C
millionaire	5	4	7
bondholder	8	5	-
moneymaker	8	-	-
tycoon	8	-	-

9N Family Relationships

9N1.0	A	B	C
family	2	3	2
household	4	3	7

9N2.0	A	B	C
relative	4	3	4
ancestor	5	3	5
heir	5	4	-
descendant	6	3	6
offspring	6	3	12
pedigree	6	3	-
kin	8	4	-
kinfolk	8	-	-
primogenitor	10	-	-
progeny	10	7	-
scion	10	-	-

9N3.0	A	B	C
dad	1	3	1
daddy	1	3	1
father	1	3	K
papa	1	3	4
pa	2	3	6
godfather	5	-	-
patriarch	6	5	-
paternal	8	-	-

9N4.0	A	B	C
parent	2	3	3
guardian	6	3	6
ward	8	3	10

9N5.0	A	B	C
mama	1	3	4
mamma	1	6	-
mom	1	3	1
mother	1	3	K
ma	2	4	9
godmother	5	3	-
maternal	8	6	-

9N6.0	A	B	C
brother	2	3	K
sister	2	3	2
daughter	3	3	4
son	3	3	3
sissy	4	3	-
godchild	6	-	-
goddaughter	6	-	-
godson	6	7	-
fraternal	8	5	-
sibling	8	-	-
filial	10	-	-

9N7.0	A	B	C
husband	3	3	3
wife	3	3	9
harem	8	7	-
helpmate	8	-	-
matron	8	5	-
spouse	8	-	-

9N7.1	A	B	C
bride	4	3	5
groom	4	3	3
bridegroom	6	5	-
bridesmaid	6	9	-

9N8.0	A	B	C
grandfather	2	3	2
grandma	2	4	1
grandmother	2	3	1
grandpa	2	3	5

A: Grade level; B: Earliest Grade of Occurrence in Textbooks; C: Earliest Grade of Occurrence on Standardized Tests.

granny	2	7	-
grandchildren	3	3	-
granddaughter	3	4	4
grandparent	3	5	-
grandson	3	3	5
grandnephew	6	-	-

9N9.0	A	B	C
aunt	2	3	K
uncle	2	3	1
nephew	3	3	3
niece	3	3	8
cousin	4	3	3

9O Names Indicating Political Disposition

9O1.0	A	B	C
confederate	6	4	6
communist	8	5	9
feudal	8	3	11
nationalist	8	5	-
socialist	8	5	-

9O1.1	A	B	C
fascism	8	4	-
feudalism	8	3	7

9O2.0	A	B	C
democratic	6	3	6
republican	6	3	6

SUPER CLUSTER

10. Communication

10A Communication (General)

10A1.0	A	B	C
statement	3	3	3
comment	4	3	5
remark	4	3	4
declaration	5	5	4
exclamation	5	3	-
expression	5	3	K
proclamation	5	3	5
testimony	5	6	-
proposal	6	4	6
deposition	8	7	-

10A1.1	A	B	C
maxim	8	4	-
aphorism	10	-	-
platitude	10	-	-
tautology	13	-	-

10A2.0	A	B	C
talk	1	3	K
speak	2	3	2
communicate	4	3	4
discuss	4	3	7
chat	5	4	5
converse	6	5	7
negotiate	6	5	-
brainstorm	6	-	-
commune	8	5	9
parley	8	4	-
hobnob	10	-	-

10A3.0	A	B	C
conversation	4	3	4
discussion	5	3	8
powwow	5	5	-
dialogue	6	3	7
discourse	8	6	-
telepathy	8	-	-
colloquy	10	-	-
symposium	10	-	-

10A4.0	A	B	C
speech	3	3	3
sermon	4	4	-
lecture	5	3	8
homily	8	5	-
monologue	8	7	6
valedictory	8	-	-
disquisition	10	-	-
eulogy	10	7	-
harangue	10	-	-

10A5.0	A	B	C
talkative	5	3	7
eloquent	6	3	7
vocal	6	3	6
fluent	8	-	-
verbose	8	-	7
voluble	10	6	-
excursive	13	-	-
garrulous	13	-	-
loquacious	13	5	-
prolix	13	-	-

10A6.0	A	B	C
jabber	4	-	-
drawl	5	4	-
blab	6	-	-
digress	8	-	7
maunder	10	-	-
prattle	10	-	-
expatiate	13	-	-

10A7.0	A	B	C
concise	8	7	9
explicit	8	5	-
succinct	10	-	-
terse	10	-	-
laconic	13	5	-

10B Communication Involving Confrontation or Negative Information

10B1.0	A	B	C
argue	3	3	3
complain	3	3	3
object	3	3	3
protest	3	3	5
challenge	4	3	8
disagree	4	3	4
debate	6	6	5
gripe	6	-	-
squabble	6	5	12
bicker	8	7	-
contradict	8	7	7
dissent	8	8	-
haggle	8	-	-
rebut	8	-	-
litigate	10	-	-
plaint	10	-	-
remonstrate	10	-	-
inveigh	13	-	-

10B2.0	A	B	C
disobey	3	5	6
decline	5	4	4
rebel	5	4	5
revolt	5	3	5
defy	6	4	-
reject	6	6	12
oppose	6	8	9
jilt	8	-	-
contravene	10	-	-
spurn	10	-	11

10B2.1	A	B	C
insurrection	10	6	-
sedition	10	5	-

10B3.0	A	B	C
cheat	3	3	7
betray	5	3	-
exaggerate	5	4	9
con	6	3	10
deceive	6	6	7
distort	6	6	-
delude	8	6	-
dissemble	8	-	-
swindle	8	7	-
collude	10	-	-
connive	10	-	-
conspire	10	5	11
prevaricate	10	-	-
cozen	13	-	-
mulct	13	-	-
tergiversate	13	-	-

10B4.0	A	B	C
swear	4	4	-
curse	5	4	9
damn	5	7	-
profane	6	4	-
blaspheme	10	-	-
imprecate	13	-	-

10B5.0	A	B	C
argument	4	3	5
complaint	4	4	4
quarrel	4	3	4
spat	4	3	-
criticism	5	4	4
dispute	5	4	4
objection	6	3	9
trial	6	3	6
controversy	8	6	8
discord	8	3	-
lawsuit	8	6	9
contumely	10	-	-
tirade	10	-	-
contretemps	13	-	-
polemic	13	-	-

10B6.0	A	B	C
annoy	3	3	5
dare	3	3	3
tease	3	3	9
threaten	5	3	-
menace	6	5	7
browbeat	8	-	-
confront	8	7	-
accost	10	-	-

10B7.0	A	B	C
caution	3	3	3
warn	3	3	3
warning	3	3	3
threat	5	3	5
fortunetelling	8	7	-
omen	8	3	-
oracle	8	6	5
premonition	8	-	-
prophecy	8	5	8
bode	10	7	-

A: Grade level; B: Earliest Grade of Occurrence in Textbooks; C: Earliest Grade of Occurrence on Standardized Tests.

monition	10	-	-
portend	10	-	-
presage	10	-	-
harbinger	13	-	-

10B8.0	A	B	C
blame	2	3	2
scold	3	3	3
accuse	4	3	4
criticize	5	5	9
nag	5	4	-
condemn	6	6	7
denounce	6	5	-
sue	6	3	2
chastise	8	-	-
indict	8	-	6
ostracize	8	-	-
reproach	8	4	9
reprove	8	-	-
castigate	10	-	-
impugn	10	-	-
reprehend	10	-	-

10B9.0	A	B	C
embarrass	4	6	11
mock	4	4	3
insult	5	5	7
ridicule	5	6	-
scoff	5	6	4
jeer	6	6	6
slur	6	3	-
affront	8	-	11
banter	8	-	-
chide	8	9	-
degrade	8	-	-
deprecate	8	-	-
downgrade	8	5	-
gibe	8	-	-
heckle	8	-	-
mortify	8	-	-
taunt	8	7	-
twit	8	-	-
upbraid	8	-	-
deride	10	-	-
derogate	10	-	-
disparage	10	-	-
asperse	13	-	-

10B10.0	A	B	C
disgrace	5	3	9
detract	8	7	9
slander	8	5	-
libel	10	-	-
calumny	13	-	-
traduce	13	-	-

10B11.0	A	B	C
fib	3	4	-
lie	3	3	3
nonsense	3	3	2
foolishness	4	3	6
deceit	5	7	-
exaggeration	5	3	-
falsehood	5	3	-
rumor	5	5	-
hearsay	6	3	-
hyperbole	6	-	-
alibi	8	3	-
bogus	8	6	-
charade	8	-	-
drivel	8	-	-
fraud	8	6	11
guise	8	4	-
hypocrisy	8	-	-
pretext	8	7	-
propaganda	8	5	9
sham	8	6	11
twaddle	8	7	-
gibberish	10	-	-
palter	10	-	-
bombast	13	-	-
cant	13	3	-
claptrap	13	-	-
mendacity	13	-	-
plagiary	13	-	-

10C Communication Involving General Presentation of Information

10C1.0	A	B	C
tell	1	3	1
describe	3	3	4
explain	3	3	5
exhibit	4	3	4
present	4	3	1
demonstrate	5	3	9
inform	5	3	7
notify	5	5	7
acquaint	6	6	7
apprise	8	-	-
articulate	8	5	11
recount	8	6	7
relate	8	3	11
explicate	10	-	-
expound	10	-	-

10C2.0	A	B	C
say	K	3	K
state	2	3	K
mention	3	3	5

refer	5	3	4
convey	6	5	6
indicate	6	3	6
specify	6	7	6
advert	8	-	-
cite	8	4	-
imply	8	5	11
signify	8	7	7
allude	10	6	11

10C3.0	A	B	C
telegraph	4	3	4
broadcast	6	3	5
transmit	6	5	8
telecast	8	5	9

10C4.0	A	B	C
announce	3	3	3
boast	3	4	3
exclaim	3	3	4
pronounce	3	3	4
recite	3	3	2
brag	4	4	6
express	4	3	4
preach	4	4	6
advertise	5	3	5
claim	5	3	5
declare	5	3	6
utter	6	4	-
affirm	8	-	-
allege	8	-	-
assert	8	5	11
attest	8	-	7
bluster	8	7	-
contend	8	7	-
herald	8	6	11
postulate	8	6	-
proclaim	8	3	10
profess	8	7	-
purport	8	4	-
testify	8	7	-
vouch	8	6	-
orate	10	-	-
promulgate	10	-	-
tout	10	-	-
aver	10	-	-

10C5.0	A	B	C
accent	4	3	5
emphasize	5	3	4
stress	5	3	5
enunciate	8	7	-
inflect	8	-	-

10D Communication Involving Positive Information

10D1.0	A	B	C
agree	3	3	4
cooperate	4	4	4
participate	4	4	5
concur	8	-	-

10D1.1	A	B	C
teamwork	5	3	-
concord	8	-	5
rapport	8	6	11
rapprochement	13	9	-

10D2.0	A	B	C
awe	4	3	7
charm	4	3	3
soothe	4	4	5
assure	5	5	-
encourage	5	4	5
flatter	5	5	-
inspire	5	6	8

10D3.0	A	B	C
greet	2	3	3
praise	3	3	2
compliment	5	4	5
congratulate	5	6	-
acknowledge	6	3	9
commend	8	4	9
extol	8	4	-
laud	10	6	-

10D4.0	A	B	C
welcome	2	3	5
greeting	3	3	4
congratulations	4	3	8
accolade	10	-	-

10D5.0	A	B	C
thank	1	3	K
bless	2	3	2
pray	3	3	-
worship	4	3	5

10D5.1	A	B	C
apology	3	3	7
blessing	3	3	12
prayer	3	3	12
tribute	5	3	-
benediction	8	4	-
panegyric	13	-	-

A: Grade level; B: Earliest Grade of Occurrence in Textbooks; C: Earliest Grade of Occurrence on Standardized Tests.

10E Persuasion

10E1.0

	A	B	C
convince	4	4	4
influence	4	3	4
sway	4	3	5
bait	5	3	4
tempt	5	6	5
bias	6	5	-
bribe	6	7	-
lure	6	3	5
persuade	6	3	6
blackmail	8	-	-
convert	8	3	9
corrupt	8	5	11
debauch	8	-	-
deprave	8	-	-
enlist	8	7	9
entice	8	-	9
induce	8	7	11
seduce	8	-	-
dissuade	10	-	12
incite	10	-	-
instigate	10	-	-
proselyte	10	-	-
inveigle	13	-	-

10E2.0

	A	B	C
beg	3	3	-
plead	4	5	4
coax	5	3	-
urge	5	4	4
appeal	6	3	7
petition	6	5	7
beseech	8	5	-
conjure	8	5	-
entreat	8	9	-
exhort	8	6	-
impel	8	7	-
implore	8	-	-
solicit	8	-	-
supplicate	8	-	-
cajole	10	-	-
canvass	10	3	11
importune	10	-	-
wheedle	10	-	-

10E3.0

	A	B	C
suggest	4	3	5
advise	5	3	6
cue	5	3	7
recommend	5	3	6
insinuate	10	-	-

10E3.1

	A	B	C
hint	4	3	11
innuendo	10	-	-

10F Questions

10F1.0

	A	B	C
answer	2	3	2
reply	3	3	2
respond	4	3	5
comeback	6	7	-
retort	6	4	-

10F2.0

	A	B	C
ask	1	3	K
call	1	3	K
question	2	3	2
invite	3	3	3
offer	3	3	4
bid	4	3	4
poll	4	4	4
beckon	6	-	6
propose	6	4	6
request	6	3	7

10F3.0

	A	B	C
test	2	3	K
quiz	3	3	8
examination	4	3	4

10F4.0

	A	B	C
consult	5	4	5
inquire	5	3	-
interview	5	4	5
confer	6	4	-
interrogate	8	-	-

10G Communication Involving Supervision/Commands

10G1.0

	A	B	C
advice	3	3	3
direction	3	3	3
instruction	4	3	6
suggestion	4	3	4
counsel	5	3	-
guideline	5	5	-
auspices	10	6	-

10G2.0

	A	B	C
command	3	3	3
insist	4	3	4
demand	5	3	5
require	5	3	5
decree	6	5	-

A: Grade level; B: Earliest Grade of Occurrence in Textbooks; C: Earliest Grade of Occurrence on Standardized Tests.

summon	6	3	-
commission	8	3	9
dictate	8	6	9
instill	8	6	-
invoke	8	6	-
mandate	8	4	-
prescribe	8	8	-
arraign	10	-	-
countermand	10	-	-
subpoena	10	-	-

10G3.0	A	B	C
let	1	3	K
allow	3	3	5
excuse	3	3	4
permit	4	3	4
license	5	3	7
certify	8	3	-
exempt	8	5	12
franchise	8	-	6
ratify	8	3	-
sanction	8	4	-
deign	10	-	-
reinstate	10	-	-
vouchsafe	10	-	-

10G4.0	A	B	C
obey	3	3	4
yield	5	3	1
conform	6	4	11
consent	6	3	10
submit	6	5	7
assent	8	5	-
cede	8	5	11
comply	8	6	11
compromise	8	5	7
relent	8	-	-
heed	8	3	11
accede	10	-	-
comport	10	-	-
truckle	10	-	-

10G5.0	A	B	C
correct	2	3	2
direct	3	3	5
remind	3	3	3
control	4	3	4
manage	4	3	4
administer	5	6	5
govern	5	3	6
reign	5	3	7
preside	6	4	-
regulate	6	3	7
supervise	6	3	-
admonish	8	-	-
superintend	8	8	-

suppress	8	-	-
relegate	10	-	-

10G5.1	A	B	C
force	3	3	3
compel	5	5	-
enforce	6	5	9
constrain	8	-	-
exploit	8	3	11
manipulate	8	5	11
coerce	10	-	-
conscript	10	-	-
oppress	10	-	-
ramrod	10	4	-

10G6.0	A	B	C
authority	5	3	5
leadership	5	3	5
hegemony	13	-	-

10G7.0	A	B	C
refuse	3	3	3
deny	4	4	7
forbid	4	5	6
revoke	4	3	-
ban	5	5	2
repeal	6	5	7
demote	8	-	-
impeach	8	-	-
negate	8	-	-
rebuff	8	7	-
rebuke	8	-	-
repress	8	-	-
reprimand	8	-	-
veto	8	3	7
annul	10	-	-
censor	10	5	-
interdict	10	-	-
renounce	10	7	-
repudiate	10	-	-
subjugate	10	-	-
abjure	13	-	-
abrogate	13	-	-

10G7.1	A	B	C
proscribed	8	-	-
taboo	8	7	-

10H Giving Out Information Previously Withheld

10H1.0	A	B	C
tattle	2	-	-
expose	5	3	6

	A	B	C
reveal	5	3	5
divulge	8	-	12

10H2.0	A	B	C
admit	4	3	6
apologize	4	3	4
confess	5	4	8
confide	6	5	-
unbosom	8	-	-

10I Promises

10I1.0	A	B	C
promise	1	3	1
vow	5	3	-
guaranty	6	-	-
plea	6	6	7
pledge	6	3	6
pact	8	5	-
gage	10	7	-

10I1.1	A	B	C
breach	8	7	-

10J Recording or Translating Information

10J1.0	A	B	C
recording	4	3	3
quotation	6	3	9
translation	6	3	-
interpretation	8	3	12

10J1.1	A	B	C
score	2	3	2
bookkeeping	8	7	-
registers	8	6	-

10J1.2	A	B	C
enroll	8	7	8
matriculate	10	-	-

10J2.0	A	B	C
record	2	3	K
interpret	5	4	6
translate	5	4	4
quote	6	4	12
interpolate	8	-	-

10K Exclamations (General)

10K1.0	A	B	C
oh	1	3	1
ah	3	3	9
aha	3	3	-
beware	3	3	3
ha	3	3	10
hey	3	3	5
ho	3	3	7
hurrah	3	3	-
la	3	3	3
ow	3	3	7
pooh	3	3	-
wow	3	3	4
aw	4	3	-
olé	4	3	-
ooh	4	3	-
ugh	4	3	-
ay	5	3	7
bravo	5	3	7
gee	5	3	7
alas	6	3	-
dickens	8	6	8
haw	8	3	-
gad	10	9	-

10K2.0	A	B	C
no	K	3	K
yes	K	3	K
maybe	1	3	K
ok	3	4	-
okay	3	3	5
aye	4	3	-

10K3.0	A	B	C
hello	1	3	3
hi	1	3	3
bye	2	5	5
good-bye	2	3	-
goodby	2	3	-
farewell	5	3	7
howdy	5	3	-
begone	10	3	-

SUPER CLUSTER

11. Transportation

11A Types of Transportation

11A1.0	A	B	C
car	K	3	K
automobile	3	3	3
auto	4	3	5
rattletrap	4	3	-
vehicle	4	3	9
motorcar	5	-	-
jalopy	6	3	-

11A2.0	A	B	C
truck	1	3	1
van	2	3	4
jeep	3	3	7
trailer	3	3	3
pickup	4	3	4
sedan	6	7	9
lorry	8	9	-

11A3.0	A	B	C
bus	1	3	K
ambulance	3	3	6
cab	3	3	3
taxi	3	3	-
taxicab	3	3	3
subway	4	3	2
streetcar	5	3	-
trolley	6	3	-
hearse	8	6	-
limousine	8	7	7
motorbus	8	-	-
omnibus	8	5	-
tram	8	-	-

11A4.0	A	B	C
bike	1	3	1
bicycle	2	3	2
motorcycle	3	3	6
scooter	4	4	-
tricycle	4	3	5
unicycle	5	-	7
tandem	8	-	-

11A5.0	A	B	C
train	1	3	1
caboose	4	3	-
locomotive	5	3	3

11A6.0	A	B	C
cart	1	3	K
wagon	1	3	K
buggy	3	3	-
carriage	4	3	8
chariot	4	3	6
stagecoach	4	3	4
hayrack	5	-	-
horsecar	5	-	-
surrey	8	4	-
tumbrel	10	7	-

11B Work-related Vehicles

11B1.0	A	B	C
tractor	2	3	3
bulldozer	3	3	-

	A	B	C
wheelbarrow	3	3	-
barrow	4	3	-
steamshovel	4	-	-
forklift	5	3	-
reaper	5	4	-
derrick	6	7	5
harrow	8	3	-
wain	10	-	-

11B2.0	A	B	C
elevator	2	3	2
escalator	3	6	-
conveyor	5	5	-
travois	8	3	-

11C Vehicles Used in Snow

11C1.0	A	B	C
sled	1	3	1
sleigh	2	3	7
dogsled	3	-	-
snowplow	3	3	-
toboggan	3	3	-
bobsled	4	5	-

11D Vehicles Used for Air Transportation

11D1.0	A	B	C
airplane	1	3	K
plane	1	3	K
helicopter	2	3	4
airline	4	3	4
airliner	4	3	-
aircraft	5	3	5
seaplane	5	-	5

11D2.0	A	B	C
balloon	1	3	1
kite	1	3	K
airship	4	3	-
glider	5	3	8
blimp	6	-	-
dirigible	8	7	-

11D3.0	A	B	C
rocket	1	3	K
spaceship	2	3	4
spacecraft	3	3	4

A: Grade level; B: Earliest Grade of Occurrence in Textbooks; C: Earliest Grade of Occurrence on Standardized Tests.

11E Vehicles Used for Sea Transportation

11E1.0

	A	B	C
boat	1	3	K
ship	1	3	2
houseboat	3	4	-
ark	4	3	3
vessel	5	4	5
whaleboat	5	-	-
icebreaker	6	3	-
longboat	8	-	-
scow	8	5	-
flotilla	10	-	-

11E2.0

	A	B	C
ferry	4	4	6
flatboat	5	3	-
liner	5	3	-
barge	6	3	6
ferryboat	6	4	-
freighter	6	3	6
tanker	6	3	-
keelboat	8	8	-

11E3.0

	A	B	C
battleship	4	5	7
carrier	4	3	3
sub	4	3	-
submarine	4	3	3
warship	5	4	-
flagship	6	6	-
destroyer	8	5	8
gunboat	8	7	-
privateer	8	-	-

11E4.0

	A	B	C
showboat	6	-	-
steamboat	6	3	9
steamer	6	4	10
steamship	6	3	-

11E5.0

	A	B	C
lifeboat	3	4	-
tug	3	3	2
tugboat	5	4	-
dinghy	6	6	-
lightship	8	5	-

11E6.0

	A	B	C
sailboat	4	3	9
yacht	5	6	-
cutter	6	3	7
schooner	6	5	6
galleon	8	4	-

sloop	8	4	-
yawl	8	4	-

11E7.0

	A	B	C
canoe	2	3	2
motorboat	3	3	-
raft	4	3	5
kayak	5	4	11
rowboat	5	3	10
gig	8	-	-
gondola	8	5	12
pontoon	8	3	-
skiff	8	6	-
dory	10	3	-

11E8.0

	A	B	C
shipwreck	6	4	10
hulk	8	4	-

11F Parts of Vehicles

11F1.0

	A	B	C
deck	3	3	3
anchor	4	3	4
buoy	4	4	-
gangplank	4	3	-
mast	4	3	5
mainstay	5	3	-
porthole	5	3	-
rudder	5	3	5
gunwale	6	3	-
helm	6	5	-
outboard	6	7	9
prow	6	6	-
afterdeck	8	-	-
bulkhead	8	6	-
galley	8	3	-
halyard	8	4	-
hatchway	8	6	-
hull	8	3	-
keel	8	3	-
lifeline	8	5	-
mooring	8	6	-
poop	8	5	-
quarterdeck	8	-	-
skysail	8	-	-
topsail	8	7	-
crosstrees	10	-	-

11F1.1

	A	B	C
paddle	3	3	-
oar	4	3	9
masthead	8	6	-
oarlock	8	8	-
rowlock	10	-	-

11F2.0	A	B	C
tire	2	3	1
wheel	3	3	4
axle	4	3	4
hub	6	3	-

11F3.0	A	B	C
mirror	2	3	5
seatbelt	2	-	-
trunk	2	3	2
headlight	4	4	-
windshield	4	3	-
dashboard	8	3	11

11F4.0	A	B	C
tail	1	3	1
wing	1	3	K
parachute	4	3	9
propeller	4	3	5
cockpit	5	3	-
rotor	6	3	-
fuselage	8	5	-

11F4.1	A	B	C
wingspread	6	3	9
wingspan	8	-	-

11G Actions and Characteristics of Vehicles

11G1.0	A	B	C
fly	1	3	K
ride	1	3	1
row	1	3	3
drive	2	3	2
sail	2	3	2
glide	3	3	4
launch	4	4	4
cruise	5	5	5
navigate	5	3	6

11G1.1	A	B	C
marine	5	3	6
naval	5	3	5
aerial	6	5	-
airborne	6	3	-
nautical	8	4	-
seafaring	8	3	9
seagoing	8	3	8
seaworthy	8	6	-

11G2.0	A	B	C
rider	3	3	4
passenger	4	3	4

	A	B	C
cabdriver	5	-	-
stowaway	6	-	-

11G3.0	A	B	C
transport	5	3	5
convoy	8	6	-

11G3.1	A	B	C
transportation	3	3	3
aviation	6	5	9

11H Things Traveled On

11H1.0	A	B	C
road	1	3	1
street	1	3	K
avenue	3	3	4
highway	3	3	3
lane	3	3	2
freeway	4	7	9
parkway	4	3	9
roadway	4	6	5
boulevard	6	5	7
byway	6	7	-
causeway	6	5	-
highroad	6	3	-
bypass	8	7	-
expressway	8	3	9
roadbed	8	5	8
thoroughfare	8	7	-
turnpike	8	5	-

11H1.1	A	B	C
racetrack	4	8	-
speedway	4	3	-
racecourse	5	5	-

11H2.0	A	B	C
intersection	5	3	6
crossroad	6	3	-
crossway	8	4	-

11H3.0	A	B	C
way	1	3	2
pass	2	3	3
course	3	3	4
passage	3	3	3
detour	4	3	-
passageway	4	3	5
route	4	3	4
shortcut	5	6	-
fairway	8	-	-

11H4.0	A	B	C
driveway	2	3	6
alley	3	3	6

A: Grade level; B: Earliest Grade of Occurrence in Textbooks; C: Earliest Grade of Occurrence on Standardized Tests.

	A	B	C
wayside	5	3	-
roadside	6	3	6
towpath	8	3	-

11H5.0	A	B	C
bridge	2	3	2
drawbridge	4	3	-
span	6	3	7
tollgate	8	-	-
viaduct	8	3	10
trestle	10	3	-

11H6.0	A	B	C
track	2	3	2
railroad	3	3	3
rail	4	3	-
railway	4	3	7
sidetrack	5	4	-
tramway	8	-	-

11H7.0	A	B	C
tunnel	3	3	3
ramp	4	3	7
chute	5	3	5

11H8.0	A	B	C
path	2	3	2
mall	3	3	6
pathway	3	4	6
sidewalk	3	3	2
trail	3	3	2
archway	5	-	-
catwalk	8	7	-
gangway	8	4	-

11H9.0	A	B	C
waterway	5	3	-
airway	6	4	-
seaway	6	9	-

11H10.0	A	B	C
airfield	5	5	-
airstrip	5	4	-
runway	5	3	5

SUPER CLUSTER
12. Mental Actions/Thinking

12A Thought/Memory (General)

12A1.0	A	B	C
idea	2	3	2
thought	2	3	K
imagination	4	3	6
memory	4	3	4

	A	B	C
reflection	5	3	5
conscience	6	3	7
cognition	8	-	-
contemplation	8	8	-

12A2.0	A	B	C
concentrate	4	3	4
memorize	6	3	11
visualize	8	6	10

12A3.0	A	B	C
think	1	3	K
wonder	2	3	2
consider	4	3	4
meditate	5	4	-
ponder	6	4	-
reckon	6	3	-
contemplate	8	7	10
deliberate	8	3	10
mull	8	-	-
muse	8	7	-
cogitate	10	-	-
introspect	10	-	-
ruminate	10	-	-

12A4.0	A	B	C
forget	1	3	2
remember	3	3	3
recall	5	4	4
recollect	6	3	-
reminisce	8	-	-
retrospect	10	8	-

12A5.0	A	B	C
amnesia	6	-	9
nostalgia	8	6	-

12B Subjects/Topics

12B1.0	A	B	C
core	4	3	4
subject	4	3	4
topic	4	3	4
theme	5	3	5
essence	6	3	-
keynote	6	6	-
thesis	8	5	-

12B2.0	A	B	C
plan	2	3	2
objective	4	4	7
scheme	5	4	5
strategy	5	4	6
viewpoint	5	5	5
layout	6	7	-
scope	6	6	-

12C Mental Exploration

12C1.0	A	B	C
exam	3	4	7
examination	4	3	4
inspection	5	3	5
investigation	5	4	7
experimentation	6	4	9
reconnaissance	8	6	-
scrutiny	8	7	9

12C2.0	A	B	C
examine	3	3	2
experiment	3	3	4
explore	3	3	3
search	3	3	3
inspect	4	4	-
research	4	3	6
analyze	5	5	5
investigate	5	3	6
probe	5	3	11
review	5	3	4
survey	5	3	5
rummage	6	5	-
assay	10	-	-
delve	10	-	-

12C3.0	A	B	C
homework	2	3	2
lesson	2	3	2
assignment	3	3	7
schoolwork	4	3	6

12D Mental Actions Involving Conclusions

12D1.0	A	B	C
design	3	3	2
compose	4	3	-
create	4	3	5
invent	4	3	5
intend	4	3	5
devise	6	4	-
improvise	6	3	7
conceive	8	7	-
contrive	8	4	-

12D2.0	A	B	C
solve	4	3	3
calculate	5	5	7
compute	5	3	11
conclude	5	3	11
determine	5	4	6
abstract	6	4	7
derive	6	4	9

	A	B	C
infer	6	4	-
deduce	8	8	-
deem	8	6	-
educe	10	-	-
extrapolate	10	-	-

12D3.0	A	B	C
prove	3	3	4
confirm	5	7	6
resolve	6	4	6
corroborate	8	-	9
evince	8	-	-
refute	8	-	-
adduce	10	-	-

12D3.1	A	B	C
hunch	4	4	9
theory	5	3	7
prediction	6	4	7
suspicion	6	3	7
inkling	8	3	-

12D4.0	A	B	C
guess	1	3	1
estimate	4	3	3
suppose	4	3	4
assume	5	3	7
forecast	5	4	6
revise	5	4	-
suspect	5	3	5
conjecture	6	5	9
foresee	6	4	6
predict	6	4	6
speculate	6	4	-
appraise	8	-	11
assess	8	5	-
postulate	8	6	-
presume	8	6	7
surmise	8	7	-

12D5.0	A	B	C
clue	3	3	2
discovery	3	3	3
fact	3	3	3
information	3	3	4
evidence	4	3	3
invention	4	3	5
proof	4	3	4
principle	5	3	7
solution	5	3	6
calculation	6	3	9
indication	6	4	7
indicator	6	5	7
axiom	8	9	-
criterion	8	-	-
statistics	8	3	11

A: Grade level; B: Earliest Grade of Occurrence in Textbooks; C: Earliest Grade of Occurrence on Standardized Tests.

12D5.1	A	B	C
mystery	3	3	3
enigma	6	5	-
paradox	8	6	-

12E Consciousness

12E1.0	A	B	C
awake	3	3	K
conscious	5	4	5
insomnia	8	-	-

12E2.0	A	B	C
asleep	2	3	3
drowsy	3	3	9
weary	3	3	2
unconscious	6	5	6
careworn	8	7	-
somnolent	13	-	-
soporific	13	-	-

12E3.0	A	B	C
dream	1	3	1
dreamland	3	3	-
fairyland	3	3	-
nightmare	4	4	-
vision	5	3	5
fantasy	6	3	7
trance	6	3	-
figment	8	-	-
hallucination	8	9	-
illusion	8	5	7
mirage	8	5	9
oblivion	8	5	-
reverie	10	-	-

12E4.0	A	B	C
nap	1	3	2
sleep	1	3	K
hibernate	3	3	6
slumber	3	4	7
daze	4	3	6
doze	4	3	11
snooze	4	3	-
hypnosis	6	-	-
stupor	6	7	-
lethargy	8	5	-
loll	8	-	-
repose	8	4	7
ennui	10	-	-

12E5.0	A	B	C
wake	2	3	2
waken	4	3	4
rouse	6	4	-

12E6.0	A	B	C
pretend	3	3	3
daydream	4	3	7
fantasize	6	-	-
hallucinate	8	-	-

12F Interest

12F1.0	A	B	C
interest	3	3	3
intrigue	6	7	-
engross	8	-	-

12F1.1	A	B	C
rapt	10	-	-

12F2.0	A	B	C
attention	3	3	3
concentration	4	3	4
curiosity	4	3	4

12G Teaching/Learning

12G1.0	A	B	C
direction	2	3	3
advice	3	3	3
instruction	4	3	6
suggestion	4	3	4

12G2.0	A	B	C
coach	2	3	3
teach	2	3	3
educate	4	3	12
instruct	4	3	6
enlighten	8	-	10
edify	10	-	-
inculcate	13	-	-

12G2.1	A	B	C
didactic	10	-	-

12G3.0	A	B	C
learn	1	3	1
discover	3	3	4
study	3	3	3
realize	4	3	5
glean	6	-	-
apprehend	8	9	-
discern	8	6	11
lucubrate	13	-	-

12G4.0	A	B	C
trick	1	3	K
fake	3	7	6
decoy	5	3	6
outsmart	5	-	-

outwit	6	3	-
feign	8	-	-
hoodwink	8	-	-
loophole	8	7	-
ploy	8	-	-
artifice	10	6	-
chicanery	10	-	-
ruse	10	7	-
subterfuge	10	7	-

12G5.0	A	B	C
complicate	5	-	10
confuse	5	4	7
confound	6	7	-
mystify	6	6	-
baffle	8	6	11
bewilder	8	-	12
consternate	8	-	-
derange	8	-	-
fluster	8	-	-
fuddle	8	-	-
garble	8	-	-
nonplus	8	-	-
perplex	8	6	9
addle	10	-	-
confute	10	-	-
mesmerize	10	-	-
stultify	13	-	-

12G6.0	A	B	C
know	1	3	K
understand	2	3	3
comprehend	5	6	9

12G6.1	A	B	C
knowledge	3	3	3
breakthrough	6	5	7
lore	6	4	-
intuition	8	4	9
ken	10	7	-
afflatus	13	-	-

12H Processes and Procedures

12H1.0	A	B	C
method	3	3	4
system	3	3	4
process	4	3	4
recipe	4	3	4
routine	4	3	6
tactics	5	3	-
logic	6	5	7
procedure	6	4	9
technique	6	4	6
maneuver	8	4	7
protocol	8	-	-

rote	8	-	-
syllogism	8	-	-
rigmarole	10	-	-

12I Definition

12I1.0	A	B	C
meaning	3	3	3
definition	4	3	4
semantics	8	5	-

12I2.0	A	B	C
define	4	5	4
represent	4	3	4
interpret	5	4	6
symbolize	6	5	7
construe	8	-	-

12J Choice

12J1.0	A	B	C
pick	1	3	1
choose	2	3	2
decide	2	3	2
select	3	3	2
sort	3	3	5
weed	4	3	2
discriminate	6	5	-
cull	8	-	-
destine	8	-	-

12J1.1	A	B	C
choice	2	3	K
decision	3	3	4
selection	3	4	6
judgement	5	5	7
verdict	6	3	7
predilection	13	-	-

12J2.0	A	B	C
judge	2	3	2
misjudge	5	-	-
arbitrate	8	-	-

12J3.0	A	B	C
assign	4	4	6
appoint	5	6	6
dedicate	5	5	6
allot	8	3	-
anoint	8	5	-
ordain	8	8	8
allocate	10	-	12
depute	10	-	-

12K Intelligence

12K1.0	A	B	C
wisdom	3	3	3
ignorance	4	5	9
intelligence	4	3	4
stupidity	4	4	7
intellect	5	4	9
wit	5	4	7
prescience	10	-	-

12K1.1	A	B	C
smart	2	3	2
wise	2	3	2
brilliant	4	3	4
intelligent	4	3	5
shrewd	6	5	-
farseeing	8	5	-
literate	8	6	-
erudite	10	9	-
gnostic	10	-	-
omniscient	10	-	-
sapient	10	-	-

12K1.2	A	B	C
dumb	2	3	5
stupid	2	3	-
ignorant	5	3	6
uneducated	5	5	-
unskilled	5	3	6
crude	6	3	6
naive	6	7	9
vulgar	6	7	-
crass	8	-	-
gauche	8	-	-
callow	10	-	-

12K2.0	A	B	C
alert	3	3	4
aware	3	3	5
curious	3	3	3
astute	8	6	-

12K3.0	A	B	C
scientific	4	3	4
practical	4	3	6
intelligible	5	7	-
logical	6	3	7
rational	6	4	11
perspicuous	10	-	-
cogent	13	-	-

12K4.0	A	B	C
able	2	3	2
clever	3	3	3
capable	4	4	4
skillful	4	3	7
competent	5	6	4
adept	6	7	-
deft	6	4	-
adroit	8	8	-
canny	8	8	-
proficient	8	7	9
versatile	8	5	10
trenchant	10	-	-

12K5.0	A	B	C
creative	4	3	3
imaginative	5	4	7

12L1.0	A	B	C
belief	3	3	4
opinion	3	3	3
ideal	4	3	7
superstition	5	4	6
creed	6	5	-
doctrine	6	4	-
mythology	6	3	7
philosophy	6	5	7
dogma	8	5	-
ethics	8	9	-
ism	8	-	-
tenet	8	-	-
theism	10	-	-

12L2.0	A	B	C
practice	2	3	2
habit	3	3	3
custom	4	3	4
instinct	5	3	6
tradition	5	3	5
vice	6	5	9
mores	8	7	-
usage	10	3	11

SUPER CLUSTER

13. Human Traits/Behavior

13A Kindness/Goodness

13A1.0	A	B	C
forgiveness	3	3	6
goodness	3	3	6
kindness	3	3	4
charity	5	3	6
mercy	5	3	4
altruism	10	-	-
philanthropy	10	-	9

13A2.0	A	B	C
courtesy	4	3	4
grace	4	3	3
consideration	5	4	9
hospitality	6	3	-
tact	8	6	7
amenity	10	-	-
comity	10	-	-

13A3.0	A	B	C
gentle	1	3	1
thoughtful	2	3	4
tender	3	3	3
sensitive	4	3	6
sympathetic	5	3	6
liberal	6	3	9
clement	6	3	-
lenient	8	4	-
exorable	13	-	-

13A4.0	A	B	C
thankful	2	3	3
grateful	4	3	4

13A5.0	A	B	C
kind	1	3	1
nice	1	3	K
pleasant	3	3	3
kindhearted	4	4	-
social	4	3	2
affable	8	-	11
amiable	8	6	-
benevolent	8	5	7
benign	8	7	-
convivial	10	8	-
gregarious	10	-	9

13A6.0	A	B	C
affectionate	5	3	5
attentive	6	5	8

13A7.0	A	B	C
generous	4	3	4
unselfish	4	3	5
willing	4	3	4
magnanimous	8	6	-
munificent	10	-	-

13A8.0	A	B	C
polite	3	3	3
courteous	4	4	7
gracious	4	3	-
respectful	4	3	7
civil	5	3	5
noble	5	4	9
tactful	6	8	-

	A	B	C
chivalrous	8	7	-
cordial	8	6	9
debonair	8	-	-
genial	8	3	7
suave	8	-	-
couth	10	-	-

13B Eagerness/Dependability

13B1.0	A	B	C
sincerity	5	6	7
dependability	5	-	-
reliability	6	4	9
trustworthiness	6	-	-

13B2.0	A	B	C
eagerness	4	3	7
enthusiasm	4	3	4
ambition	5	3	6
determination	5	3	5
spirit	5	3	5
zeal	8	3	-
alacrity	13	-	-

13B3.0	A	B	C
service	4	3	4
duty	5	3	5
responsibility	5	4	6
devoir	10	-	-

13B4.0	A	B	C
efficient	5	4	4
productive	5	3	7
diligent	6	4	7
effective	6	3	6
industrious	6	6	9
thorough	6	3	9
sedulous	10	-	-
assiduous	13	-	-

13B5.0	A	B	C
dependable	4	3	3
responsible	4	3	4
earnest	5	3	9
reliable	5	3	5
sincere	5	5	5
trustworthy	5	6	9
credible	8	-	-
heartfelt	8	6	-
obsequious	10	7	-

13B5.1	A	B	C
depend	4	3	4
rely	4	4	6
oblige	8	4	-

13B6.0	A	B	C
busy	3	3	3
eager	3	3	4
active	4	3	4
lively	4	3	3
enthusiastic	5	4	7
ambitious	6	4	6
animated	6	5	-
energetic	6	5	8
vigorous	6	3	9
avid	8	7	-
compulsive	8	-	-
fervent	8	5	-
wholehearted	8	-	-
exuberant	10	-	12

13B7.0	A	B	C
pep	5	5	-
vigor	5	4	-
zest	6	3	7
verve	8	7	-
vim	8	-	-
vivacity	8	7	-

13C Lack of Initiative

13C1.0	A	B	C
lazy	2	3	2
idle	4	3	4
easygoing	5	3	-
dormant	6	5	-
inactive	6	5	7
lax	6	5	7
listless	6	5	7
indolent	8	-	-
passive	8	7	11
lackadaisical	10	-	-
torpid	10	-	-
dilatory	13	-	-

13C2.0	A	B	C
casual	5	4	-
aimless	6	4	-
blasé	8	-	-
complacent	8	5	-
nonchalant	8	3	-
callous	10	-	-

13C3.0	A	B	C
apathy	8	5	10
insouciance	13	-	-

13D Freedom/Independence

13D1.0	A	B	C
freedom	4	3	5
liberty	4	3	4
independence	5	3	4
autonomy	8	8	-
impunity	8	8	-
volition	8	-	-
amnesty	10	-	-

13D1.1	A	B	C
free	2	3	2
independent	5	5	5
voluntary	5	5	12
freeborn	8	-	-

13D2.0	A	B	C
imprison	6	5	-
confine	8	6	8
impound	8	-	-
incarcerate	10	-	-
immure	13	-	-

13D3.0	A	B	C
dependent	4	3	7
obedient	4	3	-

13E Confidence/Pride

13E1.0	A	B	C
proud	1	3	1
sure	1	3	1
certain	3	3	3
hopeful	4	3	3
confident	5	3	5
frank	6	4	7
sanguine	10	9	-

13E1.1	A	B	C
confidence	4	3	4
pride	4	3	7
conceit	6	5	7
poise	8	4	8
vainglory	8	-	-
effrontery	10	-	-
ostentation	10	-	-

13E2.0	A	B	C
smug	5	3	-
vain	5	3	5
haughty	6	4	9
arrogant	8	7	9
cavalier	8	4	-
cocksure	8	9	-
supercilious	10	-	-

13F Patience

13F1.0	A	B	C
expectant	4	4	11
impatient	4	3	3
patient	4	3	4
restless	4	3	4

13F1.1	A	B	C
patience	4	3	4

13G Luck/Probability

13G1.0	A	B	C
lucky	2	3	2
fortunate	4	3	4
successful	4	3	4
prosperous	5	3	5

13G1.1	A	B	C
unfortunate	5	3	5

13H Strictness/Stubbornness

13H1.0	A	B	C
headstrong	4	4	-
ornery	4	3	-
steadfast	4	3	-
stubborn	4	3	5
obstinate	6	3	-
resolute	6	4	-
adamant	8	5	-
perverse	8	5	-
recalcitrant	8	7	8
staunch	8	-	-
hidebound	10	-	-
obdurate	10	-	-
recusant	13	-	-

13H1.1	A	B	C
rigor	6	8	7
tenacity	8	7	-

13H2.0	A	B	C
sober	4	3	7
stuffy	4	3	-
grave	5	3	-
sedate	10	4	-
stolid	10	4	-

13H3.0	A	B	C
strict	4	3	11
severe	5	3	5
stern	5	3	-
austere	8	5	-
fastidious	8	7	-

	A	B	C
finicky	8	-	-
stringent	8	5	-
ascetic	10	-	-

13I Humor

13I1.0	A	B	C
funny	1	3	K
humorous	4	4	4
hilarious	5	7	9
witty	5	4	-
wry	6	5	7
droll	8	-	-
facetious	10	-	11

13J Spirituality

13J1.0	A	B	C
holy	4	3	11
religious	4	3	5
sacred	5	3	5
spiritual	5	3	-
divine	6	4	-
pious	8	5	-
hieratic	10	-	-
orthodox	10	6	-
supernal	10	-	-

13J2.0	A	B	C
heathen	5	4	-
agnostic	8	7	-
freethinker	8	-	-
pagan	8	3	-
skeptic	8	5	-

13J3.0	A	B	C
artistic	5	3	4
aesthetic	10	9	12

13K Prudence

13K1.0	A	B	C
modest	3	3	2
sensible	4	3	4
chaste	6	5	-
discreet	6	5	-
demure	8	-	10
celibate	10	-	-
circumspect	10	-	-

13K1.1	A	B	C
modesty	5	7	-
prudence	8	5	12
thrift	8	7	-

A: Grade level; B: Earliest Grade of Occurrence in Textbooks; C: Earliest Grade of Occurrence on Standardized Tests.

13K2.0	A	B	C
bawdy	8	-	-
carnal	8	-	-
obscene	8	-	-
profligate	10	-	9
promiscuous	10	-	-
ribald	10	-	-
licentious	13	-	-

13L Shyness

13L1.0	A	B	C
helpless	3	3	5
mild	3	3	4
shy	3	3	4
skittish	4	4	-
timid	4	3	7
bashful	5	-	5
coy	5	5	-
meek	5	3	5
docile	8	3	11
fainthearted	8	3	-
squeamish	8	-	11
tractable	8	-	8
diffident	10	-	-
reticent	10	-	-

13M Dishonesty

13M1.0	A	B	C
unfair	3	3	9
dishonest	4	4	4
naughty	4	3	-
sly	4	3	4
tricky	4	3	6
mischievous	5	4	5
underhanded	6	6	-
unfaithful	6	-	6
phony	8	-	-
unscrupulous	8	5	-
insidious	10	7	12

13M2.0	A	B	C
mischief	5	3	-
cunning	6	3	6
disloyalty	6	7	8
treason	6	5	-
guile	8	6	-
treachery	8	6	-
apostasy	8	-	-

13N Loyalty/Courage

13N1.0	A	B	C
friendship	3	3	5
obedience	4	4	9
allegiance	5	3	-
loyalty	5	3	9
devotion	6	4	7
fidelity	8	8	-

13N2.0	A	B	C
courage	3	3	4
bravery	4	3	6
grit	5	3	-
chivalry	6	3	-
valor	6	7	-
audacity	10	-	-
temerity	10	-	-

13N3.0	A	B	C
brave	2	3	2
bold	4	3	5
fearless	4	3	6
adventurous	5	3	6
intrepid	8	4	-

13N4.0	A	B	C
courageous	5	3	6
gallant	5	4	-
heroic	5	3	5
doughty	8	7	-
lionhearted	8	-	-

13N5.0	A	B	C
faithful	5	3	7
loyal	5	3	4
patriotic	5	4	7
highborn	8	-	-
truehearted	8	-	-

13N6.0	A	B	C
honest	3	3	4
straightforward	6	4	-
fair-minded	8	-	-
forthright	8	5	11
impartial	8	8	9

13O Instability

13O1.0	A	B	C
wild	1	3	K
crazy	2	3	3
frantic	5	4	5
hectic	5	7	9
uncontrolled	5	6	-
unsettled	5	3	5

A: Grade level; B: Earliest Grade of Occurrence in Textbooks; C: Earliest Grade of Occurrence on Standardized Tests.

	A	B	C
unsteady	5	4	8
amuck	6	4	-
fanatic	6	8	9
fickle	6	4	6
giddy	6	4	-
unstable	6	5	8
barbaric	8	-	9
cock-eyed	8	6	-
daft	8	6	-
demented	8	-	-
fanatical	8	6	-
haywire	8	-	4
moonstruck	8	-	-
tipsy	8	-	-
volatile	8	7	-
zany	8	-	-
quixotic	13	7	-

13P Caution

13P1.0	A	B	C
careful	2	3	2
watchful	3	3	4
cautious	4	4	5
stingy	4	4	9
suspicious	4	3	3
wary	6	3	11
frugal	8	6	-
loath	8	6	-
painstaking	8	4	12
prudent	8	7	-
reluctant	8	4	7
averse	10	-	-
chary	10	-	-

13P1.1	A	B	C
foolhardy	5	3	-
slack	5	5	-
frivolous	8	5	8
impetuous	8	5	9
lax	8	5	7

13P2.0	A	B	C
careless	3	3	3
reckless	5	3	5

SUPER CLUSTER

14. Location/Direction

14A Location (General)

14A1.0	A	B	C
direction	3	3	3
distance	3	3	4
location	3	3	2

	A	B	C
altitude	4	3	4
position	4	3	5
standpoint	6	7	-

14A2.0	A	B	C
place	1	3	K
spot	1	3	2
address	2	3	3
point	2	3	K
axis	5	3	6
destination	5	3	5
whereabouts	5	5	-
antipodes	10	-	-
perihelion	13	-	-

14A2.1	A	B	C
niche	8	6	9
interstice	13	-	-
lacuna	13	-	-

14B Boundaries

14B1.0	A	B	C
corner	1	3	K
edge	1	3	3
side	1	3	K
limit	2	4	2
margin	3	4	9
perimeter	3	4	3
border	4	3	4
boundary	4	3	5
brim	4	3	4
ridge	4	3	11
horizon	5	3	5
rim	5	3	7
verge	5	3	-
brink	6	3	7
flank	6	6	9
battlefront	6	-	-
borderland	8	8	-
periphery	8	-	-

14C Planes

14C1.0	A	B	C
horizontal	4	3	7
diagonal	5	3	-
perpendicular	5	3	5
vertical	5	3	5
transverse	8	9	-

14C2.0	A	B	C
sideways	4	3	7
broadside	6	4	-
lateral	6	6	-

	A	B	C
sidelong	8	6	-
leeway	8	5	-

14D Non-specific Locations

14D1.0	A	B	C
here	K	3	K
there	K	3	K
where	1	3	K
anywhere	2	3	3
everywhere	2	3	1
somewhere	2	3	4
all over	3	4	-
nowhere	3	3	3
someplace	3	4	7
elsewhere	4	3	7

14E Directions

14E1.0	A	B	C
east	2	3	2
north	2	3	2
south	2	3	2
west	2	3	2
northeast	3	3	3
northwest	3	3	5
southeast	3	3	4
southwest	3	3	5
midwest	5	5	5

14E1.1	A	B	C
eastern	3	3	5
northern	3	3	5
southern	3	3	5
western	3	3	5
southland	4	5	-
eastward	5	3	-
northeastern	5	3	10
northerly	5	5	5
northernmost	5	3	-
northland	5	5	7
northward	5	3	6
northwestern	5	3	5
southeastern	5	3	7
southward	5	3	-
southwestern	5	3	-
westernmost	5	3	-
westward	5	3	5
boreal	8	-	-

14E2.0	A	B	C
left	1	3	1
right	1	3	1
starboard	5	4	-
dexter	8	3	-

14F Back-Front-Middle

14F1.0	A	B	C
back	K	3	K
end	K	3	K
rear	3	3	8
background	4	3	4
hind	4	3	4
endpoint	5	3	-
breech	8	7	-
posterior	8	7	-

14F1.1	A	B	C
backward	3	3	6
backwards	3	3	7
astern	8	6	-

14F1.2	A	B	C
behind	1	3	1
last	1	3	1

14F2.0	A	B	C
front	1	3	K
fore	5	3	-
obverse	6	8	-

14F2.1	A	B	C
ahead	2	3	2
forward	2	3	3
forth	3	3	3

14F2.2	A	B	C
ahead of	4	-	-

14F3.0	A	B	C
center	2	3	2
middle	2	3	2
among	3	3	3
halfway	4	3	4
medium	4	3	7
mid	4	3	9
midst	5	3	11
midway	5	3	8
inter	8	5	7
midmost	8	-	-

14F3.1	A	B	C
central	4	3	5

14G Direction To/From

14G1.0	A	B	C
at	K	3	K
from	K	3	K
to	K	3	K
bound	4	3	6

thereto	5	4	-
hither	6	4	-
via	8	5	9

14H In/Out and Inward/Outward

14H1.0	A	B	C
in	K	3	K
into	K	3	K
inside	1	3	1
indoor	3	3	11
indoors	3	3	4
within	3	3	5
inward	4	3	6
inland	5	3	5
interior	5	3	5
internal	6	4	7

14H1.1	A	B	C
incoming	4	3	-
intake	5	5	9

14H2.0	A	B	C
out	K	3	K
outside	2	3	K
outdoors	3	3	3
exterior	5	3	5
outward	5	3	6
overboard	5	3	-
external	6	4	9

14H3.0	A	B	C
across	2	3	2
through	2	3	1
throughout	3	3	5

14H4.0	A	B	C
enter	2	3	2
embark	6	4	9

14I Up/On

14I1.0	A	B	C
on	K	3	K
thereon	4	3	-
hereon	5	-	-

14I1.1	A	B	C
on top of	2	-	-
upon	2	3	3
atop	4	3	6

14I1.2	A	B	C
aboard	3	3	3

14I2.0	A	B	C
over	1	3	K
above	2	3	2
overhead	3	3	5

14I2.1	A	B	C
off	1	3	2

14I3.0	A	B	C
tip	2	3	5
top	2	3	K
peak	4	3	3
summit	5	3	6
topside	5	4	-
pinnacle	6	6	-
acme	8	-	9
apex	8	7	-
cusp	8	-	-
zenith	8	5	9

14I4.0	A	B	C
high	1	3	K
upper	3	3	4

14I5.0	A	B	C
upside-down	3	3	-
upright	4	3	5

14I6.0	A	B	C
up	K	3	K
uphill	3	3	9
upstairs	3	3	3
upward	3	3	2
upland	4	4	-
skyward	5	3	-

14I7.0	A	B	C
overland	5	3	-

14J Down/Under

14J1.0	A	B	C
under	1	3	1
below	2	3	3
low	2	3	2
beneath	3	3	4
underground	3	3	3
underneath	3	3	4
underside	5	3	8
subordinate	8	7	12
nether	10	-	-
subtend	10	-	-

14J1.1	A	B	C
bottom	2	3	2

14J1.2	A	B	C
underfoot	4	4	-

14J2.0	A	B	C
down	K	3	K
downstairs	2	3	3
downhill	3	3	3
downward	4	3	4
downwind	4	3	-

14K Distances

14K1.0	A	B	C
distant	3	3	3
outer	3	3	3
outlying	6	4	11
remote	8	3	12

14K1.1	A	B	C
away	K	3	K
far	1	3	1
faraway	2	3	4
yonder	5	3	-

14K1.2	A	B	C
abroad	5	3	7
overseas	6	3	-

14K1.3	A	B	C
past	3	3	3
beyond	4	3	6

14K2.0	A	B	C
close	1	3	1
near	1	3	K
toward	2	3	3
alongside	3	3	3
nearby	3	3	2
opposite	3	3	3
aside	4	3	3
roundabout	4	3	-
local	5	3	5
nigh	5	3	11
abreast	6	5	-
adjacent	6	3	6
thereabout	6	-	-
thereabouts	6	3	-
proximate	10	-	-

14K2.1	A	B	C
closeness	5	3	9
contact	5	3	5
vicinity	6	3	7
propinquity	13	-	-

14K3.0	A	B	C
homeward	6	3	12

14K4.0	A	B	C
by	K	3	K
between	2	3	3

14L Presence/Absence

14L1.0	A	B	C
absence	4	4	6
attendance	4	4	7
presence	5	3	6

14L1.1	A	B	C
present	2	3	1
absent	4	3	4
truant	6	4	-

14L2.0	A	B	C
available	5	3	5
unavailable	5	-	-

SUPER CLUSTER

15. Literature/Writing

15A Names/Titles

15A1.0	A	B	C
name	K	3	K
title	2	3	2
nickname	3	3	6
brand	4	3	4
denomination	4	5	-
trademark	4	4	-
monogram	6	-	-
alias	8	-	-
euphemism	8	8	11
namesake	8	8	9
pseudonym	8	-	7
appellation	10	-	-
epithet	10	3	-

15A1.1	A	B	C
identify	3	3	4
rename	3	3	5
dub	6	6	-
entitle	8	7	7

15A2.0	A	B	C
mark	2	3	2
label	3	3	2
tag	3	3	4
heading	4	3	4
postmark	4	-	-

	A	B	C
subheading	5	4	-
caption	6	7	-
stigma	6	4	-
inscription	6	3	-
cachet	8	-	-
earmark	8	3	-
colophon	10	-	-
rubric	10	-	-

15A2.1	A	B	C
autograph	3	3	-
signature	3	3	7

15B Types of Literature

15B1.0	A	B	C
fiction	3	3	3
writing	3	3	3
nonfiction	4	5	4
poetry	4	3	6
composition	5	3	5
literature	5	3	5
verse	5	3	6
prose	6	3	12

15B2.0	A	B	C
story	K	3	K
tale	3	3	3
legend	4	3	4
myth	4	3	5
parable	4	3	-
comedy	5	5	7
fable	5	3	11
allegory	8	5	-
epic	8	7	9
parody	8	7	-
saga	8	8	-

15B3.0	A	B	C
adage	8	-	-
apothegm	10	-	-
byword	10	-	-

15C Types of Publications

15C1.0	A	B	C
book	K	3	K
album	3	3	5
storybook	3	3	8
cookbook	4	3	5
schoolbook	4	6	-
textbook	4	4	7
yearbook	4	-	-
catalogue	5	5	-
guidebook	5	-	-

	A	B	C
handbook	5	4	12
manual	5	5	7
primer	5	4	-
script	5	4	5
hymnal	6	-	-
hornbook	8	-	-

15C2.0	A	B	C
report	3	3	3
biography	4	4	7
diary	4	3	5
essay	4	3	6
novel	4	4	5
autobiography	5	6	8
thesis	8	5	-
dissertation	10	-	-

15C3.0	A	B	C
booklet	3	4	4
chapter	4	3	3
paragraph	4	3	3
text	4	4	7
volume	4	3	4
document	5	3	7
edition	5	3	11
episode	5	4	6
issue	5	3	5
pamphlet	5	7	5
paperback	5	8	5
publication	5	4	11
excerpt	6	4	7
manuscript	6	3	-
ledger	8	7	-
monograph	8	-	7
quarto	8	-	-
folio	10	-	-
tome	10	-	-

15C4.0	A	B	C
dictionary	3	3	3
encyclopedia	3	3	4
almanac	4	3	5
atlas	4	3	4
bibliography	4	9	6
thesaurus	6	-	6
lexicon	10	6	-
ephemeris	13	-	-

15C5.0	A	B	C
bible	3	3	-
scripture	4	6	-
testament	5	5	-
apocalypse	8	-	-
koran	10	5	-

A: Grade level; B: Earliest Grade of Occurrence in Textbooks; C: Earliest Grade of Occurrence on Standardized Tests.

15C6.0	A	B	C
newspaper	2	3	2
article	3	3	5
column	3	3	4
front-page	3	3	-
headline	3	3	-
magazine	3	3	3
journal	4	4	5
annals	8	4	-
chronicle	8	5	9
gazette	8	6	6
obituary	8	8	-

15C7.0	A	B	C
index	3	3	5
summary	5	4	9
anthology	8	7	-
syllabus	8	-	-
synopsis	8	8	-
compendium	10	8	-

15D Poems/Songs

15D1.0	A	B	C
poem	3	3	5
rhyme	3	3	7
lyric	5	5	-
stanza	5	3	-
limerick	6	7	7
refrain	6	3	-
epigram	8	-	-
idyll	8	-	-
ode	8	8	-
sonnet	8	6	-
doggerel	10	-	-
strophe	10	-	-

15D1.1	A	B	C
poetic	6	4	7

15D2.0	A	B	C
song	1	3	1
carol	3	3	1
lullaby	3	3	-
anthem	4	4	-
ballad	4	3	7
hymn	4	3	6
ditty	6	7	-
psalm	6	4	-
serenade	6	5	7
aria	8	6	-
dirge	8	7	9
elegy	8	7	-
madrigal	8	5	-
reveille	8	5	-

rhapsody	8	6	-
libretto	10	5	-

15D3.0	A	B	C
music	2	3	2
score	4	3	2

15E Drawings/Illustrations

15E1.0	A	B	C
drawing	1	3	K
map	1	3	2
chart	3	3	3
graph	3	3	3
diagram	4	3	3
illustration	5	3	5
blueprint	8	3	8

15F Messages

15F1.0	A	B	C
letter	1	3	K
note	2	3	2
postcard	2	4	3
valentine	2	3	-
message	3	3	2
telegram	4	4	9
tidings	5	3	-
correspondence	6	4	10
memo	6	7	6
billet	8	-	-
epistle	8	3	-
missive	10	-	-

15F2.0	A	B	C
ad	3	3	3
poster	3	3	5
announcement	4	3	4
bulletin	4	3	4
commercial	4	3	4
advertisement	5	3	5
handbill	5	5	-
motto	5	3	7
signpost	5	8	-
slogan	5	3	6
billboard	6	8	-
signboard	6	6	-
epitaph	8	3	-
playbill	8	-	-

15G Things to Write On/With

15G1.0	A	B	C
notebook	3	3	5
scrapbook	3	3	-

	A	B	C
stationery	5	4	-
flyleaf	8	-	-

15G2.0	A	B	C
crayon	1	3	1
pen	1	3	1
pencil	1	3	1
brush	2	3	2
ink	2	3	4
paintbrush	2	3	3
press	2	3	1
chalk	3	3	5
typewriter	4	3	9
pastel	5	6	9
stylus	8	5	-

15G2.1	A	B	C
eraser	3	3	4
inkstand	5	5	-
inkwell	6	4	-

15G3.0	A	B	C
page	1	3	1
paper	1	3	K
blackboard	3	3	-
chalkboard	3	3	7
tablet	4	4	-
parchment	5	4	-
pasteboard	5	3	-
ream	6	4	-
scroll	6	3	-
copperplate	8	-	-
letterhead	8	-	-
vellum	8	7	-
quire	10	6	-

15H Rules/Laws

15H1.0	A	B	C
law	3	3	3
rule	3	3	3
commandment	5	5	-
deed	5	3	11
diploma	5	5	-
curfew	6	6	-
regulation	6	4	7
copyright	8	8	-
edict	8	3	-
fiat	8	8	-
precept	8	-	11
assizes	10	-	-
lex	10	-	-

15H2.0	A	B	C
policy	4	3	5
amendment	5	3	9

	A	B	C
charter	5	3	7
constitution	5	3	5
contract	5	3	5
treaty	5	3	6
passport	6	6	9
resolution	6	4	7
warrant	6	6	-
indenture	8	5	-
visa	8	7	-

15I Reading/Writing/Drawing Actions

15I1.0	A	B	C
scribble	3	-	-
trace	3	3	2
doodle	4	3	7
shorthand	4	3	-
jot	5	3	-
scrawl	5	6	-

15I2.0	A	B	C
print	1	3	K
sign	1	3	1
write	1	3	1
copy	2	3	3
rewrite	3	3	4
typewrite	4	7	-
publish	4	3	5
correspond	8	6	9

15I3.0	A	B	C
color	1	3	2
draw	1	3	K
paint	1	3	K
draft	5	3	5
illustrate	5	3	9
sketch	5	3	10
watercolor	5	5	-
etch	6	3	-
stencil	6	-	-
engrave	8	-	8
inscribe	8	-	-
mottle	10	-	-

15I4.0	A	B	C
capitalize	3	3	9
underline	3	3	-
indent	4	3	-
punctuate	4	4	5
italicize	6	-	-
boldface	8	7	-

15I4.1	A	B	C
spell	1	3	2
misspell	4	3	-

15I5.0	A	B	C
read	1	3	1
proofread	4	3	-
skim	4	3	11
scan	5	5	8
browse	5	-	6
edit	8	7	9
emend	10	-	-
peruse	10	-	-

15I6.0	A	B	C
handwriting	3	3	11
penmanship	5	3	8
calligraphy	6	4	-

15I6.1	A	B	C
handwritten	4	7	11
legible	6	6	10

SUPER CLUSTER

16. Water/Liquids

16A Different Forms of Water/Liquids

16A1.0	A	B	C
water	1	3	K
liquid	3	3	4
fluid	4	3	4
moisture	4	3	4
aqua	6	-	-

16A2.0	A	B	C
mist	3	3	7
steam	3	3	3
drizzle	4	4	10
vapor	4	3	4

16A3.0	A	B	C
rain	K	3	K
raindrop	3	3	-
rainfall	3	3	3
rainwater	3	4	3
sleet	4	3	6

16A3.1	A	B	C
rainbow	2	3	3

16A4.0	A	B	C
snow	1	3	1
snowflake	2	4	8
snowfall	3	3	3

16A4.1	A	B	C
snowball	2	3	-
snowman	2	3	-
snowdrift	3	4	-
snowcap	5	-	-

16A5.0	A	B	C
ice	1	3	1
frost	3	3	4
icicle	3	3	3
glacier	4	3	5
hail	4	3	5
hailstone	4	3	-
iceberg	4	4	7
berg	5	-	-
icecap	5	5	-
slush	5	4	6
floe	6	4	-
glacé	10	-	-
hoarfrost	10	-	-

16B Actions Related to Water/Liquids

16B1.0	A	B	C
drip	2	3	-
sprinkle	2	3	2
ripple	3	3	4
trickle	3	4	-
dribble	4	3	-

16B2.0	A	B	C
spill	2	3	3
splash	2	3	K
flush	3	3	7
overflow	3	3	3
splatter	3	8	3
spray	3	3	6
secrete	4	7	4
squirt	4	3	5
gush	5	4	-
slosh	5	4	-
spatter	5	4	-
spurt	5	3	12
swash	5	3	-
cascade	6	6	11
surge	6	3	8
inundate	10	-	-
whelm	10	-	-

16B3.0	A	B	C
drain	2	3	2
flow	3	3	3
leak	3	3	6
ooze	4	4	-
ebb	5	3	-
seep	5	4	-
flux	8	3	-

16B4.0	A	B	C
pour	2	3	2
stir	2	3	4
decant	8	-	-
siphon	8	5	-

16B5.0	A	B	C
boil	2	3	3
melt	2	3	3
bubble	3	3	3
freeze	3	3	4
dissolve	4	3	5
evaporate	4	3	6
thaw	4	3	4
effervesce	10	-	-

16B6.0	A	B	C
swim	1	3	1
dive	2	3	2
float	2	3	2
sink	2	3	2
drift	3	3	4
drown	3	3	-
ford	4	3	7
wade	4	3	5
snorkel	5	3	-
capsize	8	7	-

16B7.0	A	B	C
soak	2	3	2
absorb	4	3	4
penetrate	4	3	4
drench	5	4	5
moisten	5	3	5
submerge	5	3	5
dilute	6	5	-
douse	6	-	3
leach	6	-	-
souse	6	-	-
waterlog	6	-	-
emulsify	8	-	-
engulf	8	3	-
immerse	8	-	-
marinate	8	-	-
percolate	8	-	-
permeate	8	-	-
saturate	8	-	-
sop	8	7	-
suffuse	10	-	-
imbue	13	-	-

16B8.0	A	B	C
wet	K	3	K
damp	3	3	4
slippery	3	3	4
humid	4	4	5
moist	4	3	4
slick	4	3	7
soggy	4	3	7
dank	8	7	-
sodden	8	6	-

16B9.0	A	B	C
waterproof	4	5	5
watertight	5	5	-

16C Equipment Used with Liquids

16C1.0	A	B	C
fountain	3	3	3
hydrant	3	3	-
sprinkler	3	4	6
waterwheel	6	-	-
waterworks	8	6	-

16C1.1	A	B	C
hydraulic	6	3	-
hydrostatic	8	-	-

16C2.0	A	B	C
faucet	3	3	5
hose	3	3	2
pump	3	3	3
nozzle	4	4	-
funnel	5	3	6
spout	5	4	-
valve	6	3	6
spigot	8	-	-

16D Moisture

16D1.0	A	B	C
dew	4	3	6
dewdrop	4	4	-
droplet	4	4	-

16D2.0	A	B	C
evaporation	4	3	5
condensation	5	3	5

16D3.0	A	B	C
cloud	1	3	K
fog	3	3	3
smog	4	3	7

16E Slime

16E1.0	A	B	C
quicksand	3	3	-
slime	3	5	3
sediment	5	3	5
silt	5	4	6
goo	6	-	4
muck	6	3	-
sludge	8	5	-II

16E2.0	A	B	C
foam	4	3	11
scum	4	3	-
froth	6	4	-

16F Bodies of Water

16F1.0	A	B	C
lake	1	3	1
sea	1	3	1
brook	2	3	K
ocean	2	3	2
puddle	2	3	3
river	2	3	2
stream	2	3	K
creek	3	3	2
pond	3	3	3
waterfall	3	3	3
tidewater	4	3	-
geyser	5	5	-
outlet	5	3	6
tributary	5	4	8
backwater	6	5	-
eddy	6	3	-
estuary	6	3	-
gusher	6	8	-
headwaters	6	4	-
millpond	6	3	-
runoff	6	6	-
fountainhead	8	-	-
millrace	8	-	-
runnel	8	-	-
watercourse	8	7	-
tailrace	10	-	-
tarn	10	-	-
rill	10	5	-

16F2.0	A	B	C
swamp	4	3	7
bog	5	3	-
delta	5	3	5
marsh	5	3	9
marshland	5	4	-
lagoon	6	3	9
reef	6	3	8
mire	8	3	-
moorland	8	-	-
shoal	8	6	-

16F3.0	A	B	C
bay	4	3	K
gulf	4	3	4
cove	5	3	-
inlet	5	4	-
fjord	6	4	-
bight	8	-	-

16F4.0	A	B	C
current	4	3	4
tide	4	3	4
surf	5	3	7
waterline	5	3	-
white cap	6	-	-

16F4.1	A	B	C
tidal	5	4	6
navigable	8	3	-

16G Places Near Water

16G1.0	A	B	C
island	2	3	2
peninsula	5	3	11
isthmus	6	4	8
archipelago	8	3	-
atoll	8	6	-
isle	8	4	11

16G2.0	A	B	C
beach	2	3	2
coast	3	3	4
riverbank	3	3	-
seashore	3	3	4
shore	3	3	3
riverside	4	6	4
seacoast	4	3	5
shoreline	4	3	-
waterfront	4	3	11
lakeside	5	6	-
mainland	5	3	10
waterside	5	4	-
coastland	6	-	-

A: Grade level; B: Earliest Grade of Occurrence in Textbooks; C: Earliest Grade of Occurrence on Standardized Tests.

headland	6	6	-
sandbank	6	7	-
seaboard	6	3	-
strand	6	4	9
longshore	8	-	-
promontory	8	6	-

sluice	6	5	-
flume	8	-	-
spillway	8	7	-

SUPER CLUSTER

17. Clothing

16H Directions Related to Water

17A Clothing (General)

16H1.0	A	B	C
ashore	5	3	5
inland	5	3	5

17A1.0	A	B	C
clothes	2	3	K
clothing	3	3	3
costume	3	3	3
suit	3	3	4
outfit	4	3	5
uniform	4	3	5
attire	5	4	11
wardrobe	5	6	-
apparel	6	6	10
array	6	3	-
garb	6	4	7
garment	6	3	9
lingerie	6	5	-
tuxedo	6	6	-
frippery	8	-	-
layette	8	-	-
togs	8	-	-
trousseau	10	-	-
habiliments	13	-	-

16H2.0	A	B	C
underwater	3	3	3
afloat	4	3	-
undersea	4	3	-
downstream	5	3	11
offshore	5	3	-
upstream	5	3	-
midstream	6	6	-
upriver	6	6	-

16I Man-made Places For/Near Water

16I1.0	A	B	C
harbor	3	3	3
port	4	3	3
shipyard	4	3	8
seaport	5	3	5
breakwater	6	6	-
dockyard	8	-	-

17A2.0	A	B	C
design	2	3	2
fashion	4	3	4
fad	5	7	8
style	5	3	5
craze	6	7	-
glamour	6	7	7
vogue	10	8	-

16I2.0	A	B	C
lighthouse	3	3	3

17B Parts of Clothing

16I3.0	A	B	C
dock	3	3	K
wharf	4	3	4
berth	5	3	-
levee	8	5	-
pierhead	8	-	-
quay	8	7	-

17B1.0	A	B	C
button	1	3	1
zipper	2	3	4
buttonhole	3	7	-
buttonhook	8	-	-

16I4.0	A	B	C
pool	1	3	K
aquarium	4	3	3
channel	4	3	5
dam	4	3	5
reservoir	4	3	7
aqueduct	5	4	-
canal	5	3	5
dike	5	3	-
moat	6	3	-

17B2.0	A	B	C
hem	3	3	-
lining	5	3	7
seam	6	3	K

17B3.0	A	B	C
pocket	1	3	K
bib	3	4	-

	A	B	C
collar	3	3	4
sleeve	3	3	5
ruff	4	3	-
ruffle	4	3	-
tassel	4	3	-
cuff	5	3	-
frill	5	3	-
fringe	5	3	6
pom-pom	5	-	-
gusset	8	7	9
placket	8	7	-
epaulet	10	-	-

17C Shirts/Pants/Skirts

17C1.0

	A	B	C
shirt	2	3	2
sweater	3	3	3
vest	3	3	3
blouse	4	3	-
jersey	4	3	4
pullover	4	-	-
cardigan	5	-	-
waistband	5	6	-
brassiere	8	-	-
dickey	8	-	-
shirtband	8	-	-
shirtwaist	8	-	-
tunic	8	7	-

17C2.0

	A	B	C
belt	2	3	3
jeans	2	4	2
pants	2	3	2
diaper	3	3	6
shorts	3	3	7
tights	3	3	-
overalls	4	3	4
slacks	4	7	7
trousers	4	3	-
dungarees	5	3	-
puttee	10	-	-

17C3.0

	A	B	C
dress	1	3	1
skirt	2	3	3
apron	3	3	-
bathrobe	3	3	-
gown	3	3	5
nightdress	3	-	-
nightgown	3	3	-
pajamas	3	3	3
robe	3	3	5
bedclothes	4	3	-
kimono	4	3	-

	A	B	C
nightshirt	4	5	-
petticoat	4	4	-
pinafore	5	4	-
bedgown	8	-	-
chemise	8	-	-
corset	8	-	-
frock	8	7	-
negligee	8	-	-
smock	8	6	-
toga	10	6	-

17D Things Worn on the Head

17D1.0

	A	B	C
hat	K	3	1
cap	1	3	1
hood	2	3	K
mask	2	3	2
bonnet	3	3	3
crown	3	3	3
headband	3	3	-
helmet	3	3	-
headdress	4	4	-
veil	4	3	-
beret	5	3	10
headpiece	5	-	-
turban	5	3	-
visor	5	3	-
headgear	6	5	7
nightcap	6	6	-
tiara	6	-	-
broadbrim	8	-	-
coif	8	5	-
fez	8	3	-
mantilla	8	-	-
havelock	10	-	-
skullcap	10	-	-
wimple	10	-	-
casque	13	-	-
diadem	13	5	4

17D2.0

	A	B	C
glasses	2	3	2
eyeglasses	3	3	11
sunglasses	3	3	5
goggles	4	3	7
spectacles	4	3	-
eyeshade	6	6	-
monocle	10	-	-
lorgnette	13	-	-

17E Things Worn on the Hands/Feet

17E1.0	A	B	C
boot	K	3	K
shoe	1	3	1
skate	2	3	2
slipper	3	3	-
moccasin	4	3	12
sandal	4	3	-
footwear	5	5	-
snowshoe	5	6	-
clodhopper	8	-	-
galosh	8	-	-
insole	10	-	-
brogue	13	-	-
jackboot	13	-	-
patten	13	-	-
sabot	13	-	-

17E1.1	A	B	C
sock	1	3	K
stocking	3	3	-
garter	4	3	-

17E2.0	A	B	C
gloves	3	3	3
mitt	4	3	3
mittens	4	3	-
gauntlet	6	7	-

17F Coats

17F1.0	A	B	C
coat	1	3	K
jacket	2	3	3
overcoat	3	3	-
parka	3	3	4
raincoat	3	3	4
poncho	4	6	-
stole	4	3	3
slicker	6	6	-
topcoat	6	7	-
waistcoat	6	4	-
cutaway	8	4	-
mackinaw	8	-	-
mackintosh	8	5	-
chesterfield	10	-	-
greatcoat	10	4	-
pelisse	13	-	-
spencer	13	4	4

17F2.0	A	B	C
cape	3	3	6
mantle	4	4	4
shawl	4	3	5
cloak	5	3	5
shroud	8	7	-
cowl	10	-	-

17G Accessories to Clothing

17G1.0	A	B	C
ribbon	1	3	1
tie	1	3	1
handkerchief	3	3	4
necktie	3	3	5
scarf	3	3	3
muffler	4	3	-
sash	4	3	-
kerchief	5	-	-
bandanna	6	7	-
ascot	8	-	9
cravat	8	7	-
neckband	8	-	-
neckcloth	8	-	-

17G2.0	A	B	C
fan	K	3	K
umbrella	3	3	5
cane	4	3	5
parasol	5	3	-
sunshade	5	-	-

17G3.0	A	B	C
pin	K	3	1
buckle	3	3	4
hairpin	4	3	8

17G4.0	A	B	C
brush	2	3	2
comb	3	3	3
razor	4	3	9

17G5.0	A	B	C
ring	1	3	1
bead	3	3	3
bracelet	3	3	2
earring	3	3	-
necklace	3	3	2
jewelry	4	3	4
locket	4	3	4
trinket	4	3	-
bangle	5	-	-
corsage	5	-	-
garland	5	5	-
pendant	6	7	9
scepter	6	4	-
sequin	6	4	-
amulet	8	5	-
cameo	8	7	-

A: Grade level; B: Earliest Grade of Occurrence in Textbooks; C: Earliest Grade of Occurrence on Standardized Tests.

bauble	10	-	-
chaplet	10	-	-
gewgaw	10	6	-

17G6.0	A	B	C
perfume	4	3	9
cologne	5	4	-
rosewater	10	-	-

17G7.0	A	B	C
lipstick	4	3	-
cosmetics	5	3	8
rouge	5	3	7

17H Armor

17H1.0	A	B	C
armor	5	3	5
breastplate	5	5	-
sheath	5	4	7
shield	5	3	6
scabbard	10	6	-
cuirass	13	-	-
escutcheon	13	-	-
panoply	13	-	-

17H1.1	A	B	C
bulletproof	6	-	-
ironclad	8	6	-

17I Actions Related to Clothing

17I1.0	A	B	C
fit	1	3	1
wear	2	3	2
zip	3	3	11
clothe	4	3	5
clad	5	3	-
don	6	4	6
accouter	13	-	-

17I1.1	A	B	C
doff	8	9	-
divest	10	-	-

17I2.0	A	B	C
patch	3	3	K
sew	3	3	3
mend	4	3	6
stitch	4	3	3
alter	6	4	6
baste	6	3	11
darn	8	5	-
hemstitch	8	-	-
mercerize	8	-	-
pleat	8	8	-

17I3.0	A	B	C
braid	3	3	11
knit	4	3	-
crochet	5	-	7
embroider	5	-	-
weave	5	3	9
emboss	8	-	-
purl	8	-	-
broadloom	10	-	-
picot	10	-	-

17I3.1	A	B	C
dressmaking	5	-	-
embroidery	5	4	6
crewel	8	-	-
handwork	8	-	-
lacework	8	-	-
needlepoint	8	-	-

17I4.0	A	B	C
fold	2	3	2
tear	2	3	4
rip	3	3	3
unfold	3	3	5
wrinkle	4	3	4
crease	5	4	4
furl	5	5	-
pucker	5	4	-
tatter	5	3	11
ravel	6	8	7
rumple	6	-	-

17J Characteristics of Clothes and Wearing of Clothes

17J1.0	A	B	C
worn	3	3	3
sheer	6	3	11
threadbare	8	-	-

17J2.0	A	B	C
informal	5	5	5
handmade	5	3	7
fashionable	6	5	9
dowdy	8	-	-
garish	8	5	-
sartorial	13	-	-

17J3.0	A	B	C
bare	3	3	3
barefoot	4	3	5
naked	4	3	6
bareheaded	5	6	-
nude	5	9	-

A: Grade level; B: Earliest Grade of Occurrence in Textbooks; C: Earliest Grade of Occurrence on Standardized Tests.

17K Fabrics

17K1.0

	A	B	C
cloth	1	3	K
rag	2	3	2
material	4	3	4
cheesecloth	5	4	11
dry goods	5	4	-
fabric	5	3	8
textile	5	3	7
broadcloth	8	8	-
bunting	8	5	-
haircloth	8	-	-
lisle	13	-	-

17K2.0

	A	B	C
thread	3	3	3
yarn	3	3	3
skein	4	3	-
fiber	5	4	-
tint	5	5	7
texture	6	3	-
woof	8	3	-
clew	13	-	-
packthread	13	-	-

17K3.0

	A	B	C
felt	2	3	1
wool	2	3	2
cotton	3	3	3
lace	3	3	3
leather	3	3	3
satin	3	3	-
silk	3	3	4
velvet	3	3	9
calfskin	4	7	-
flannel	4	3	-
gauze	4	4	-
nylon	4	4	8
pigskin	4	5	4
sheepskin	4	4	-
buckskin	5	3	-
calico	5	3	5
khaki	5	3	7
linen	5	3	5
plaid	5	3	-
suede	5	5	-
terry	5	-	6
plush	6	6	9
chiffon	8	9	-
gunny	8	6	-
oilskin	8	-	-
rayon	8	3	-
sailcloth	8	-	-
tweed	8	7	-
twill	8	8	-
herringbone	10	-	-
sackcloth	10	-	-

17K3.1

	A	B	C
woolen	3	3	6
homespun	4	4	11
tartan	10	-	-

SUPER CLUSTER

18. Places Where People Might Live/Dwell

18A Places Where People Might Live

18A1.0

	A	B	C
hometown	3	4	3
neighborhood	3	3	-
settlement	3	3	3
colony	4	3	4
birthplace	5	3	11
homeland	6	3	9
fatherland	8	8	-
purlieu	13	-	-

18A1.1

	A	B	C
nationwide	4	3	9

18A2.0

	A	B	C
hell	3	3	-
heaven	4	3	-
paradise	6	3	8
wonderland	6	7	-
limbo	8	-	-
perdition	8	-	-
utopia	8	8	9

18A3.0

	A	B	C
city	1	3	1
town	1	3	1
capital	3	3	2
downtown	3	3	3
village	3	3	4
metropolis	6	6	-
burg	8	-	-
hamlet	8	4	9

18A4.0

	A	B	C
outskirts	4	3	-
suburb	5	3	5
barrio	10	-	-
faubourg	13	-	-

18A5.0	A	B	C
camp	1	3	K
campsite	3	4	8
spa	4	-	-
resort	5	3	6

18A6.0	A	B	C
ghetto	5	5	-
slum	5	4	11

18A7.0	A	B	C
county	3	3	3
province	5	3	-
district	6	3	6
borough	8	3	-
burgh	8	-	-
precincts	8	5	-
bailiwick	10	-	-

18A8.0	A	B	C
state	2	3	K
kingdom	3	3	3
empire	4	3	7
reign	5	3	7
realm	8	3	8

18B Continents/Countries

18B1.0	A	B	C
country	2	3	1
nation	3	3	4

18B2.0	A	B	C
continent	4	3	4

18B2.1	A	B	C
continental	4	3	5

18B3.0	A	B	C
Africa	3	3	3
Antarctica	3	3	5
Asia	3	3	4
Australia	3	3	4
Europe	3	3	3
North America	3	4	-
South America	3	4	-

18B4.0	A	B	C
United States	3	3	-
Canada	4	3	2
China	4	3	4
France	4	3	3
Germany	4	3	3
Greenland	4	3	4
Holland	4	3	4
Italy	4	3	3
Japan	4	3	4
Mexico	4	3	4
Spain	4	3	4
Iran	5	3	7
Israel	5	3	9

18B4.1	A	B	C
America	3	3	3
Orient	4	3	-

18C States

18C1.0	A	B	C
Alabama	3	3	5
Alaska	3	3	3
Arizona	3	3	4
Arkansas	3	3	4
California	3	3	4
Colorado	3	3	4
Connecticut	3	3	5
Delaware	3	3	3
Florida	3	3	3
Georgia	3	3	2
Hawaii	3	3	7
Idaho	3	4	6
Illinois	3	3	5
Indiana	3	3	5
Iowa	3	3	5
Kansas	3	3	9
Kentucky	3	3	4
Louisiana	3	3	4
Maine	3	3	5
Maryland	3	3	5
Massachusetts	3	3	5
Michigan	3	3	5
Minnesota	3	3	5
Mississippi	3	3	4
Missouri	3	3	5
Montana	3	3	4
Nebraska	3	4	5
Nevada	3	3	8
New Hampshire	3	3	-
New Jersey	3	3	-
New Mexico	3	3	-
New York	3	3	-
North Carolina	3	3	-
North Dakota	3	3	-
Ohio	3	3	5
Oklahoma	3	3	8
Oregon	3	3	2
Pennsylvania	3	3	3
Rhode Island	3	4	-
South Carolina	3	3	-
South Dakota	3	3	-
Tennessee	3	3	5
Texas	3	3	1

A: Grade level; B: Earliest Grade of Occurrence in Textbooks; C: Earliest Grade of Occurrence on Standardized Tests.

	A	B	C
Utah	3	3	7
Vermont	3	3	5
Virginia	3	3	5
Washington	3	3	2
West Virginia	3	3	-
Wisconsin	3	3	5
Wyoming	3	3	5

18D Cities

18D1.0	A	B	C
Chicago	3	3	3
Dallas	3	4	4
Denver	3	3	3
Houston	3	3	6
Jackson	3	3	4
Los Angeles	3	3	-
Miami	3	3	1
New York City	3	3	-
San Francisco	3	3	-
Washington DC	3	-	-
Columbus	4	3	2
Detroit	4	3	4
Flagstaff	4	4	11
Harrisburg	4	4	-
Hartford	4	4	-
Jacksonville	4	3	5
Memphis	4	3	5
Milwaukee	4	3	9
New Orleans	4	3	-
Omaha	4	4	5
Philadelphia	4	3	5
Phoenix	4	4	4
Pittsburgh	4	3	-
Providence	4	4	-
Richmond	4	3	-
San Antonio	4	4	-
Santa Fee	4	3	-
Seattle	4	3	8
St. Louis	4	3	-
Tampa	4	3	-
Toledo	4	4	-
Topeka	4	4	-
Wichita	4	4	-
Cheyenne	5	4	-
Cincinnati	5	3	5
Cleveland	5	3	5
Des Moines	5	4	-
Duluth	5	5	12
Indianapolis	5	4	9
Kansas City	5	4	-
Lansing	5	4	-
Louisville	5	3	5
Montgomery	5	4	5
Nashville	5	4	-

	A	B	C
Oklahoma City	5	4	-
Peoria	5	4	-
Portland	5	4	5
Salt Lake City	5	3	-
Spokane	5	-	12
Springfield	5	4	6
Helena	6	5	11
Reno	6	8	-
Trenton	6	3	-

SUPER CLUSTER
19. Noises/Sounds

19A Noises (General)

19A1.0	A	B	C
noise	2	3	1
sound	2	3	2
echo	4	3	4
peal	5	4	-
trill	5	4	-
audio	6	7	-
blare	6	3	-
reverberate	10	-	-

19A2.0	A	B	C
silence	2	3	2
stillness	3	3	10
hush	4	3	5
lull	6	4	-

19A3.0	A	B	C
clatter	4	3	-
clamor	5	3	7
commotion	5	3	5
bluster	8	7	-
din	8	3	10
tumult	8	5	9

19A4.0	A	B	C
hear	1	3	1
listen	2	3	2
audible	5	6	10
earshot	5	4	-
hark	5	3	-
eavesdrop	6	-	-
acoustic	8	7	-

19A5.0	A	B	C
loud	2	3	2
noisy	3	3	K
harsh	4	3	5
shrill	4	3	9
deafening	5	4	12
hoarse	5	3	5

boisterous	8	8	-
rowdy	8	4	-
strident	8	7	-
turbulent	8	5	-
raucous	10	6	-
stentorian	13	-	-

19A6.0	A	B	C
quiet	2	3	K
silent	3	3	3
breathless	4	3	5
serene	5	4	7
voiceless	5	5	-
soundproof	6	6	-
tranquil	6	4	-
mum	8	-	-
tacit	8	8	11

19A7.0	A	B	C
pitch	4	3	3
tone	4	3	2
crescendo	5	6	-
intensity	5	5	-

19B Devices That Produce/Reproduce Sound

19B1.0	A	B	C
phone	2	3	K
telephone	3	3	3
sonar	4	3	-
earphone	5	8	-
loudspeaker	5	4	-
radiophone	5	5	-
receiver	5	3	7
switchboard	6	6	-
wiretap	8	-	-

19B2.0	A	B	C
bell	K	3	K
horn	1	3	1
alarm	3	3	3
doorbell	3	3	2
foghorn	4	3	-
gong	4	3	-
siren	4	3	10
chime	5	3	K
firebox	6	3	4
carillon	13	4	-
tocsin	13	-	-

19C Noises Made by People

19C1.0	A	B	C
cheer	2	3	2
roar	2	3	3
laughter	3	3	4
applause	4	3	5
fracas	5	3	-
ruckus	5	4	-
rumpus	5	4	-
uproar	5	4	6
ovation	6	6	-
hullabaloo	8	-	-

19C2.0	A	B	C
gasp	3	3	-
gulp	3	3	-
yawn	3	3	3
belch	4	-	-
burp	4	5	-
cough	4	3	5
hiccup	4	4	-
snore	4	3	-
burr	5	3	-
wheeze	5	5	-

19C3.0	A	B	C
sing	K	3	K
shout	1	3	1
yell	1	3	K
hum	3	3	4
squeal	3	3	-
whistle	3	3	4
whoop	3	3	-
applaud	4	3	5
chant	4	3	7
holler	4	4	-
bellow	5	3	-
screech	5	3	-
shriek	5	3	6
yodel	5	8	5
birdcall	8	-	-
catcall	8	-	-

19C4.0	A	B	C
laugh	1	3	1
chuckle	2	3	2
giggle	3	3	-
snicker	4	3	-
titter	6	-	-
chortle	8	8	-
guffaw	8	-	-
carouse	10	-	-
roister	10	-	-

19C5.0	A	B	C
cry	1	3	K
moan	3	3	2
sigh	3	3	K
sob	3	3	-
weep	3	3	2
whimper	3	3	-
bawl	4	3	-
groan	4	4	3
whine	4	3	9
wail	5	3	5
pule	13	-	4

19C6.0	A	B	C
whisper	2	3	2
chatter	3	3	3
mutter	3	5	4
babble	4	3	-
blurt	4	-	-
mumble	4	3	4
murmur	5	4	-
stammer	5	-	-
stutter	5	-	-
rant	6	6	1
rave	6	6	-
coo	8	-	-
singsong	8	5	-

19D Animal Noises

19D1.0	A	B	C
bark	2	3	1
gobble	2	3	3
peep	2	3	4
quack	2	3	2
baa	3	3	-
buzz	3	3	-
caw	3	3	2
cheep	3	3	-
cluck	3	3	-
growl	3	3	-
honk	3	3	-
howl	3	3	3
meow	3	3	3
moo	3	3	-
purr	3	3	5
squawk	3	3	-
snort	3	3	-
bleat	4	3	-
chirp	4	3	4
croak	4	4	4
grunt	4	3	5
hiss	4	4	-
hoofbeat	4	3	-
hoot	4	3	K

	A	B	C
whinny	4	3	4
yap	4	4	8
cackle	5	-	-
neigh	5	5	-
snarl	5	3	-
yelp	5	3	-
yip	5	-	-
yowl	5	4	-
bray	6	-	-
warble	6	4	-
cockcrow	8	-	-

19E Noises Made by Objects

19E1.0	A	B	C
ring	1	3	1
tick	2	3	2
clop	3	3	-
jingle	3	3	5
squeak	3	3	K
swish	3	3	-
ting	3	3	-
wail	3	3	5
whir	3	3	-
whoosh	3	3	-
clank	4	3	-
click	4	3	10
creak	4	3	5
crunch	4	3	-
gurgle	4	3	-
rattle	4	3	5
rustle	4	3	5
slam	4	3	3
thud	4	3	5
thump	4	3	5
toot	4	3	-
boom	5	3	5
ping	5	4	5
twang	5	3	-
knell	8	3	-

19E2.0	A	B	C
zoom	3	3	-
chug	4	3	-
clang	4	3	-
clink	4	3	-
plop	4	3	-
crackle	5	6	-
fizz	5	6	-
plunk	5	-	-
tinkle	5	3	-
jangle	6	-	-
clack	8	-	12

A: Grade level; B: Earliest Grade of Occurrence in Textbooks; C: Earliest Grade of Occurrence on Standardized Tests.

SUPER CLUSTER

20. Land/Terrain

20A Areas of Land

20A1.0

	A	B	C
lot	3	3	1
acre	5	3	7
acreage	6	3	7
plot	6	3	6
tract	8	6	7

20A2.0

	A	B	C
place	2	3	K
area	3	3	3
surface	3	3	3
clearing	4	3	4
location	4	3	2
expanse	5	3	-
site	5	3	6
premises	6	6	7
topography	10	4	7

20A3.0

	A	B	C
land	1	3	K
region	4	3	4
territory	4	3	4
zone	4	3	3
frontier	5	3	5
terrain	5	3	4
tropics	5	4	6
domain	6	3	9
outback	6	5	-
panhandle	8	3	-
fief	10	-	7
leasehold	10	-	-

20B Characteristics of Places

20B1.0

	A	B	C
geographic	5	4	7
geographical	5	3	-
geological	5	5	-

20B2.0

	A	B	C
polar	4	3	4
tropical	4	3	3

20B3.0

	A	B	C
coastal	4	3	7
mountainous	5	3	7
seagirt	8	-	-
landlocked	10	6	-
littoral	10	-	-

20B4.0

	A	B	C
rural	4	4	4
rustic	5	4	-
underdeveloped	5	4	5
pastoral	8	5	-
sylvan	8	5	-
agrarian	10	4	11
bucolic	10	-	-

20B5.0

	A	B	C
developed	3	3	4
metropolitan	5	3	11
municipal	5	3	7
urban	5	4	5

20B6.0

	A	B	C
desert	3	3	1
wasteland	4	3	-
wilderness	4	3	6
tundra	5	4	7
moor	6	4	-
steppe	6	6	-
heath	8	7	-

20C Valleys/Craters

20C1.0

	A	B	C
valley	3	3	4
cavern	4	3	-
gulley	4	3	-
cove	5	3	-
ravine	5	3	6
dale	6	5	-
glen	6	5	K
gulch	6	-	8
dell	8	7	-
grotto	8	6	-
swale	10	-	-

20C2.0

	A	B	C
hole	2	3	K
manhole	3	3	-
ditch	4	3	4
pit	4	3	3
cavity	5	4	-
shaft	5	3	-
trench	5	4	5
furrow	6	3	-
silo	6	5	-
quarry	8	3	10
fosse	10	-	-

20C3.0

	A	B	C
crack	3	3	3
gap	4	3	7

A: Grade level; B: Earliest Grade of Occurrence in Textbooks; C: Earliest Grade of Occurrence on Standardized Tests.

	A	B	C
notch	4	3	5
cranny	5	3	-
groove	5	3	-
cleft	6	3	-
crevice	6	6	-
rift	6	5	11
rut	6	7	-
fissure	8	6	-
dingle	10	-	-

20C4.0	A	B	C
canyon	3	3	3
crater	5	3	5
chasm	6	4	-
abyss	8	4	-
crevasse	8	-	-

20D Mountains/Hills

20D1.0	A	B	C
hill	K	3	K
mountain	2	3	2
range	3	3	5
alp	4	4	-
butte	4	4	-
dune	4	3	-
mesa	4	3	7
sierra	4	3	8
volcano	4	3	4
foothill	5	8	10
tableland	5	3	-
highland	6	3	6
knoll	6	3	11
watershed	6	4	-

20D2.0	A	B	C
cliff	3	3	2
hillside	3	3	3
mountaintop	3	3	6
hilltop	4	3	-
mountainside	4	3	6
ridge	4	3	11
bluff	5	3	10
crag	5	3	-
crest	5	3	-
embankment	5	4	-
slope	5	3	5
precipice	8	7	9
scarp	8	4	-
escarp	10	-	-

20E Forests/Woodlands

20E1.0	A	B	C
forest	2	3	K
jungle	3	3	3
grove	5	3	6
thicket	5	3	-
woodland	5	3	7
backwoods	6	3	-
timberland	6	4	-
greenwood	8	3	10
copse	10	-	-

20E2.0	A	B	C
glade	5	4	-
savanna	8	4	-
veld	8	6	-

20F Fields/Pastures

20F1.0	A	B	C
field	2	3	2
cornfield	3	3	-
meadow	3	3	2
orchard	3	3	4
pasture	3	3	6
farmland	4	4	6
hayfield	4	4	-
prairie	4	3	4
countryside	5	3	6
paddy	5	3	-
vineyard	5	3	-
grassland	6	3	8
lowland	6	3	-
cropland	8	-	-
lea	8	3	-

20F1.1	A	B	C
battlefield	5	4	9
battleground	5	5	-

20G Yards/Parks

20G1.0	A	B	C
garden	2	3	1
park	2	3	K
yard	2	3	K
barnyard	3	3	5
playground	3	3	3
schoolyard	3	3	-
churchyard	4	4	-
courtyard	4	3	-
tiltyard	8	-	-
parterre	10	-	-

20G1.1	A	B	C
cemetery	3	3	7
brickyard	4	4	-
graveyard	4	3	-
catacomb	8	-	-
necropolis	13	-	-

20G2.0	A	B	C
patio	4	4	9
plaza	4	3	4
dooryard	5	4	-
terrace	8	6	-

20H Bodies in Space

20H1.0	A	B	C
world	2	3	2
globe	3	3	4
planet	3	3	3

20H1.1	A	B	C
global	5	5	-

20H2.0	A	B	C
sky	1	3	K
space	3	3	3
universe	4	3	3
galaxy	5	3	6
cosmos	6	4	-

20H3.0	A	B	C
sun	K	3	K
star	1	3	1
constellation	4	3	5
lodestar	8	-	-
nova	8	8	8
polestar	8	-	-
sol	8	3	3

20H4.0	A	B	C
lunar	4	3	7
solar	4	3	4
celestial	5	6	5
stellar	6	7	-
astral	10	-	-
empyreal	10	-	-
sidereal	10	-	-

20H5.0	A	B	C
Earth	3	3	3
Mercury	4	3	4
Venus	4	3	4
Mars	4	3	4
Jupiter	4	3	4
Saturn	4	3	4
Uranus	4	3	6
Neptune	4	3	6
Pluto	4	3	5

20H6.0	A	B	C
moon	1	3	K
comet	4	4	4
meteor	4	3	4
satellite	4	3	4

20H7.0	A	B	C
eclipse	5	3	6

SUPER CLUSTER

21. Dwellings/Shelters

21A Man-made Structures

21A1.0	A	B	C
tower	2	3	5
building	3	3	K
skyscraper	3	3	5
icehouse	4	3	-
structure	4	3	6
silo	6	5	-
watchtower	8	-	-

21A2.0	A	B	C
construction	4	3	7
establishment	6	3	7
installation	6	6	7

21B Places to Live

21B1.0	A	B	C
home	1	3	K
house	1	3	K
farmhouse	2	3	-
apartment	3	3	K
cabin	3	3	3
hotel	3	3	3
cottage	4	3	4
countryhouse	4	-	-
chalet	5	3	-
dwelling	5	4	11
habitat	5	3	-
homestead	5	3	8
suite	5	3	10
summerhouse	5	-	-
barracks	6	3	7
bungalow	6	4	-
dormitory	6	4	10
hovel	6	5	-
shanty	6	4	-
villa	6	5	11
abode	8	6	-

	A	B	C
boardinghouse	8	8	-
domicile	8	4	-
penthouse	8	-	-

21B2.0	A	B	C
castle	3	3	2
palace	3	3	3
manor	5	4	7
mansion	5	3	7
estate	6	4	11

21B3.0	A	B	C
tent	3	3	3
igloo	4	3	-
teepee	4	3	9
wigwam	4	4	-
hogan	5	3	-

21B4.0	A	B	C
inn	3	3	3
motel	3	3	-
lodge	4	3	8
bunkhouse	5	3	-

21C Places of Protection/Incarceration

21C1.0	A	B	C
fort	4	3	6
blockhouse	5	3	-
dugout	5	3	-
fortress	5	4	11
garrison	5	4	-
outpost	5	3	-
pueblo	5	3	4
acropolis	6	4	-
bunker	6	5	-
fortification	6	7	-
stronghold	6	5	7
breastwork	8	-	-
bridgehead	8	-	-
redoubt	8	7	-
turret	8	3	-

21C1.1	A	B	C
shelter	3	3	4
haven	5	3	12
refuge	5	3	11
windbreak	5	5	-
retreat	6	3	-
lee	8	3	2

21C2.0	A	B	C
cage	1	3	1
cell	3	3	5
jail	3	3	5

	A	B	C
dungeon	4	3	7
prison	4	3	5
quarantine	4	3	5
stockade	4	3	-
poorhouse	6	-	-
lockup	8	-	-
reformatory	8	7	-

21C3.0	A	B	C
guardhouse	5	7	-
guardroom	6	-	-

21D Places Where Goods Are Bought and Sold

21D1.0	A	B	C
store	1	3	K
market	3	3	3
booth	4	3	4
salon	5	5	9
franchise	8	-	6
mart	8	9	6
emporium	10	-	-
kiosk	13	-	-

21D2.0	A	B	C
grocery	2	3	3
bakery	3	3	3
drugstore	3	3	5
supermarket	3	3	7
barbershop	4	5	-
bookstore	5	-	5
pharmacy	5	5	6
bookshop	8	-	-
commissary	8	-	-
pawnshop	8	-	-

21D3.0	A	B	C
lunchroom	3	3	3
restaurant	3	3	5
cafe	5	6	5
cafeteria	5	3	5
saloon	5	6	8
smokehouse	5	3	-
coffeehouse	6	-	-
barroom	8	-	-
casino	8	-	-
poolroom	8	-	-
taproom	8	6	-
tavern	8	3	-
teahouse	8	-	-
tearoom	8	-	-
alehouse	10	-	-

21E Mills/Factories/Offices

21E1.0	A	B	C
shop	1	3	1
office	3	3	2
headquarters	4	3	7
countinghouse	8	-	-

21E1.1	A	B	C
workroom	3	3	-
studio	5	3	5
workhouse	5	6	-
workshop	5	3	6
sweatshop	8	-	-

21E2.0	A	B	C
factory	3	3	3
mill	3	3	3
windmill	3	3	9
sawmill	4	3	-
lumberyard	5	5	-
tannery	5	5	-
refinery	6	3	6
gristmill	8	3	-
treadmill	8	4	-

21F Places for Learning/Experimentation

21F1.0	A	B	C
school	1	3	K
classroom	3	3	3
kindergarten	3	3	-
schoolhouse	3	3	-
schoolroom	3	3	-
college	4	3	4
campus	5	5	5
university	5	3	6
academy	6	4	9
seminary	6	4	-
lycée	10	-	-

21F2.0	A	B	C
library	2	3	2
museum	3	3	3
gallery	6	3	6
archive	8	6	-

21F3.0	A	B	C
lab	4	4	9
laboratory	4	3	7
planetarium	4	3	4
observatory	5	4	-
reactor	6	6	9

21G Places for Sports/Entertainment

21G1.0	A	B	C
auditorium	4	3	4
arena	5	3	6
coliseum	5	3	-
grandstand	5	3	6
opera	5	3	8
stadium	5	3	5
theater	5	5	5
ringside	6	7	-
pavilion	8	5	11
cabaret	10	-	-
hippodrome	10	-	-

21G2.0	A	B	C
clubhouse	3	3	-
court	3	3	4
playhouse	3	3	-
rink	3	3	2
gym	4	3	5

21H Medical Facilities

21H1.0	A	B	C
hospital	3	3	3
clinic	5	6	9
ward	6	3	10
infirmary	8	-	-
madhouse	8	7	-

21H2.0	A	B	C
morgue	6	-	-
mortuary	6	-	-

21I Places for Worship/Meetings

21I1.0	A	B	C
church	3	3	3
chapel	4	3	-
mission	4	3	4
temple	4	3	3
monastery	5	5	-
cathedral	6	3	7
convent	6	9	-
shrine	6	3	7
synagogue	6	3	6
cloister	8	9	-
tabernacle	8	-	-
sanctum	10	-	-

21I2.0	A	B	C
capitol	4	3	7
courthouse	4	3	4

courtroom	5	7	9
forum	8	7	-
guildhall	10	-	-

21J Places Related to Transportation

21J1.0	A	B	C
station	2	3	4
airport	3	3	3
hangar	3	3	-
depot	4	3	9
terminal	5	3	6

21K Places Used for Storage

21K1.0	A	B	C
barn	1	3	2
hut	2	3	2
shed	3	3	5
storeroom	3	3	3
boathouse	4	4	-
hayloft	4	3	-
shack	4	3	-
storehouse	4	3	-
woodshed	4	3	-
warehouse	5	4	5
arsenal	6	5	-
roundhouse	8	-	-

21K1.1	A	B	C
greenhouse	4	4	1
hothouse	6	7	-

21L Farms/Ranches

21L1.0	A	B	C
farm	1	3	K
ranch	2	3	1
dairy	3	3	4
plantation	6	3	7
grange	8	9	8

21L1.1	A	B	C
fishery	6	7	-

21M Monuments

21M1.0	A	B	C
memorial	4	4	8
landmark	5	3	8
monument	5	3	7
sphinx	5	4	-
totem	5	5	5
monolith	8	-	-

obelisk	10	-	-
stele	10	-	-
cairn	13	4	-

21M2.0	A	B	C
gravestone	5	5	-
headstone	5	3	-
tomb	5	4	5
tombstone	6	5	-
crypt	8	-	-
mausoleum	8	6	-
cenotaph	10	-	-

SUPER CLUSTER

22. Materials and Building

22A Containers

22A1.0	A	B	C
container	3	3	3
folder	3	3	3
holder	3	3	11
carton	4	3	3
packet	4	3	6

22A2.0	A	B	C
capsule	4	3	4
cartridge	5	3	7
compartment	5	4	7
cubbyhole	5	-	-
socket	6	3	9

22A3.0	A	B	C
box	K	3	K
case	3	3	2
coffin	4	4	-
crate	4	3	-
pillbox	5	5	-
tinderbox	5	3	-
bandbox	8	-	-
coffer	8	3	-
snuffbox	8	3	-

22A4.0	A	B	C
dropper	4	3	5
test tube	5	-	-
syringe	8	-	-
vial	8	-	11

22A5.0	A	B	C
package	3	3	3
envelope	4	3	4
parcel	4	3	6
cargo	5	3	4
freight	5	3	6

A: Grade level; B: Earliest Grade of Occurrence in Textbooks; C: Earliest Grade of Occurrence on Standardized Tests.

22A5.1	A	B	C
shipload	4	3	-
shipment	4	4	2
wagonload	4	3	-
carload	6	7	-
cartload	6	-	8

22A6.0	A	B	C
barrel	4	3	4
cask	5	3	-
hogshead	5	-	-
hopper	5	3	-
keg	5	3	-
bin	6	3	-
tun	13	-	-

22A7.0	A	B	C
bag	1	3	1
basket	2	3	K
sack	3	3	5
sandbag	4	-	-
breadbasket	5	-	-
hamper	5	5	-
gunnysack	8	-	-
creel	10	-	-
pannier	13	-	-

22A8.0	A	B	C
bottle	2	3	2
jar	2	3	K
pitcher	3	3	3
flask	4	3	3
jug	4	3	7
waterbottle	4	-	-
canteen	5	3	-
coffeepot	5	7	-
wide-mouthed	5	-	-
flagon	8	3	-
carafe	10	-	-
cruet	10	-	-
cruse	10	-	-
ewer	10	-	-
magnum	10	7	-

22A8.1	A	B	C
bucket	2	3	2
pail	3	3	3
scuttle	6	3	-

22A9.0	A	B	C
bath	3	3	3
bathtub	3	3	4
tub	3	3	K
basin	4	3	4
tank	4	3	3
washbasin	4	4	-
washbowl	4	3	-
cistern	5	4	-
trough	5	3	5
vat	5	5	5
washtub	5	3	-
winepress	8	-	-
hod	10	8	-

22A10.0	A	B	C
luggage	4	4	7
suitcase	4	3	5
baggage	5	3	9
knapsack	6	4	6
packsack	6	6	-
valise	6	7	-
carpetbag	8	7	-
satchel	8	5	-

22B Materials/Objects Used to Cover Things

22B1.0	A	B	C
cover	2	3	2
lid	2	3	2
mask	3	3	2
plug	3	3	4
cork	4	3	K
stopper	4	3	-
thimble	4	4	-
wrapper	4	3	5
bung	6	3	-

22B2.0	A	B	C
canvas	5	3	4
tarpaulin	6	3	-

22B3.0	A	B	C
foil	3	3	7
tinfoil	3	3	-
cellophane	4	3	-

22C Wooden Building Materials

22C1.0	A	B	C
wood	3	3	3
lumber	4	3	3
basswood	5	4	-
hardwood	5	3	-
plywood	5	4	-
sandalwood	5	4	-
timber	5	3	6
veneer	6	5	-
ebony	8	4	8
heartwood	8	-	-
rosewood	8	-	8

	A	B	C
satinwood	8	-	8
teakwood	8	7	-

22C2.0	A	B	C
stick	2	3	2
board	3	3	2
log	3	3	2
driftwood	4	3	-
pillar	4	3	-
palette	5	5	-
panel	5	3	6
plank	5	3	-
shingle	5	4	5
slat	5	3	-
wallboard	5	3	-
batten	8	4	-
wattle	8	6	-
excelsior	10	-	-
lath	10	-	-

22D Other Building Materials

22D1.0	A	B	C
paste	2	3	4
brick	3	3	3
cardboard	3	3	3
plastic	3	3	3
tin	3	3	4
wire	3	3	1
cement	4	3	3
pavement	4	3	5
plaster	4	3	11
adobe	5	3	12
asbestos	5	3	-
brickwork	5	6	-
ceramic	5	5	11
concrete	5	3	6
grout	5	-	-
porcelain	5	3	6
putty	5	4	-
tar	5	3	7
tile	5	4	5
brownstone	6	-	-
clapboard	6	6	-
mortar	6	3	10
stucco	6	6	-
quicklime	8	-	-
stonework	8	4	-

22D1.1	A	B	C
cornerstone	6	4	-
buttress	8	6	-
keystone	8	6	-

22D2.0	A	B	C
pipe	2	3	2
tube	3	3	3
drainpipe	4	4	-
sewer	4	4	11
culvert	5	4	-
duct	5	5	7
pipeline	5	3	7
waterspout	5	-	-
conduit	8	8	8

22D3.0	A	B	C
bar	2	3	6
flagpole	3	3	6
pole	3	3	2
rod	3	3	6
crossbar	4	4	-
rung	4	4	4
stilt	5	3	-
joist	8	-	-

22D4.0	A	B	C
support	4	3	4
prop	5	3	5
pedestal	6	5	-
cantilever	8	3	-
mainstay	8	3	-
lintel	10	-	-
stanchion	10	5	-

22D4.1	A	B	C
hoop	3	3	-
brace	5	3	2
bracket	6	3	-
crosspiece	6	6	-
flange	8	7	-
mortise	10	-	-
tenon	10	7	-

22E General Names for Objects

22E1.0	A	B	C
thing	1	3	K
matter	3	3	4
object	3	3	3
substance	3	3	3
material	4	3	4
entity	8	4	-

22F Building/Repairing Actions

22F1.0	A	B	C
construction	4	3	7
earthwork	5	-	-

	A	B	C
formation	5	4	5
groundwork	6	5	-

22F2.0	A	B	C
make	1	3	1
found	2	3	1
build	3	3	2
prepare	3	3	2
produce	3	3	3
construct	4	3	7
create	4	3	5
establish	4	3	5
manufacture	4	3	6
generate	5	3	9
constitute	8	3	-
fabricate	8	3	12

22F3.0	A	B	C
form	3	3	2
mold	3	3	3
shape	3	3	3
develop	4	3	4
pave	4	-	-
forge	5	4	10
install	5	5	6
process	5	3	4
sculpt	8	-	-

22F4.0	A	B	C
glaze	4	4	-
calk	8	-	-
laminate	8	-	-

22F5.0	A	B	C
fix	2	3	1
repair	3	3	1
replace	3	3	3
adjust	4	3	6
modernize	5	3	5
modify	5	4	8
preserve	5	3	5
qualify	5	3	6
rearrange	5	4	-
rebuild	5	3	7
restore	5	4	4
strengthen	5	3	7
rehabilitate	6	5	-
streamline	6	3	-
rectify	8	-	-
revamp	8	-	-
tinker	8	3	-
furbish	10	-	-

22F5.1	A	B	C
maintenance	6	5	7

22G Wrapping/Packing Actions

22G1.0	A	B	C
tape	2	3	2
pack	3	3	K
wrap	3	3	3
bind	5	3	6
furl	6	5	-
swathe	8	-	-
truss	8	3	-
swaddle	10	-	-

22G2.0	A	B	C
uncover	3	7	4
unload	3	3	3
unlock	3	3	-
unpack	3	3	-
unroll	3	3	-
untie	3	3	2
unravel	5	3	-

SUPER CLUSTER

23. The Human Body

23A The Body (General)

23A1.0	A	B	C
body	2	3	K
trunk	2	3	2
torso	8	-	-

23A1.1	A	B	C
mental	4	3	7
physical	5	3	5

23A2.0	A	B	C
belly	3	3	3
chest	3	3	3
neck	3	3	2
breast	4	3	7
thorax	4	3	-
bosom	5	3	-
limbs	5	3	6
rump	5	3	-
teat	5	-	3
udder	5	7	-
nape	6	-	-
scruff	6	-	-
loin	8	9	-

23A2.1	A	B	C
spinal	6	4	6
pectoral	8	-	-
ventral	8	-	12

A: Grade level; B: Earliest Grade of Occurrence in Textbooks; C: Earliest Grade of Occurrence on Standardized Tests.

23A2.2	A	B	C
lap	3	3	4
waist	3	3	3
waistline	4	3	-

23B Body Coverings

23B1.0	A	B	C
skin	3	3	4
flesh	4	3	5
scalp	4	3	-
blubber	5	3	-
dandruff	5	-	7
pore	5	4	9
tissue	5	3	5
membrane	6	4	9
cutaneous	10	-	-
derma	10	-	-
adipose	13	-	-
integument	13	-	-
subcutaneous	13	-	-

23B2.0	A	B	C
suntan	4	3	8
complexion	5	4	-

23B2.1	A	B	C
ruddy	5	3	-
albino	8	-	-
swarthy	8	4	-

23B3.0	A	B	C
hair	2	3	2
beard	3	3	7
wig	3	3	1
mustache	4	3	7
pigtail	4	5	-
redhead	4	4	-
sideburns	4	3	-
tuft	5	3	-
cowlick	6	7	-
hairline	6	8	-
tress	6	3	6
plait	8	-	-
toupee	8	-	-

23B3.1	A	B	C
bald	3	3	7
bearded	4	4	-
redhaired	4	3	-
hirsute	13	-	-

23B4.0	A	B	C
bump	2	3	2
lump	3	3	3
scar	3	3	2

	A	B	C
bruise	4	3	4
freckle	4	4	-
birthmark	5	3	-
hump	5	3	11
pimple	5	7	-
rash	5	5	7
tumor	5	5	11
wart	5	4	-
blackhead	6	5	-
blemish	6	5	-
pock	6	-	-
contusion	8	-	-
node	8	-	-
excrescence	13	-	-

23C The Head

23C1.0	A	B	C
head	1	3	K
brain	3	3	5
skull	5	3	5

23C2.0	A	B	C
mind	3	3	4
ego	6	7	-
psyche	8	6	-

23C3.0	A	B	C
cheek	2	3	K
chin	2	3	2
face	2	3	K
forehead	4	3	-
countenance	6	4	-
visage	10	6	-
physiognomy	13	-	-

23C4.0	A	B	C
cerebellum	8	6	-
cerebrum	8	5	11
cranium	8	5	-
medulla	8	-	-

23D Mouth/Throat

23D1.0	A	B	C
mouth	2	3	2
teeth	2	3	2
tooth	2	3	2
gum	3	3	4
lip	3	3	4
tongue	3	3	4
jaw	4	3	5
fang	5	3	-
cuspid	6	5	11
molar	6	7	-

jowl	8	7	-
palate	8	9	-
orifice	8	7	-
maw	10	-	-

23D1.1	A	B	C
dental	4	4	5
oral	6	3	K
guttural	8	4	-
labial	13	-	-

23D2.0	A	B	C
throat	2	3	2
voice	2	3	2
windpipe	4	4	10
gullet	8	5	-

23E Eyes/Ears/Nose

23E1.0	A	B	C
ear	2	3	K
eardrum	3	4	-
earlobe	4	-	-
lobe	5	9	9
auricle	8	4	-

23E2.0	A	B	C
eye	1	3	1
brow	4	3	4
eyeball	4	6	-
eyebrow	4	4	-
eyelash	4	3	-
eyelid	4	6	5
retina	5	3	-

23E2.1	A	B	C
eyesight	4	3	7
optic	8	6	-
ocular	10	7	-

23E3.0	A	B	C
nose	2	3	K
nostril	5	5	-

23F Limbs

23F1.0	A	B	C
arm	3	3	2
elbow	3	3	-
wrist	3	3	3
shoulders	4	3	5
armpit	5	-	-
biceps	6	9	-

23F2.0	A	B	C
hand	1	3	K
finger	2	3	2
thumb	2	3	2
fingernail	3	3	-
fingerprint	3	3	-
fingertip	3	4	-
fist	3	3	3
nails	3	3	3
palm	3	3	3
knuckle	4	3	7
thumbnail	4	7	-
cuticle	5	3	-

23G Legs/Feet

23G1.0	A	B	C
feet	1	3	1
foot	2	3	K
toe	2	3	2
heel	3	3	2
ankle	4	3	5
arch	4	3	4
flatfoot	6	-	-

23G2.0	A	B	C
leg	1	3	1
hips	3	3	-
knee	3	3	2
calves	4	3	6
crotch	5	6	-
shank	5	5	-
shin	5	4	2
thigh	5	3	8
haunch	8	4	-
shinbone	8	-	-

23H Organs of the Body

23H1.0	A	B	C
heart	3	3	3
stomach	3	3	4
gut	4	6	-
intestine	4	3	7
kidney	4	4	-
liver	4	3	7
diaphragm	5	3	-
gland	5	4	-
lung	5	3	-
ovary	5	3	7
bowel	6	6	-
spleen	6	-	-
innards	8	7	-
womb	8	7	-
entrails	10	6	-

A: Grade level; B: Earliest Grade of Occurrence in Textbooks; C: Earliest Grade of Occurrence on Standardized Tests.

23I Body Fluids

23I1.0	A	B	C
pus	3	3	-
blood	4	3	5
perspiration	4	3	-
sweat	4	3	-
bloodstream	5	5	-
mucus	5	4	5
saliva	5	3	5
hemoglobin	6	5	-
bile	8	7	-
lifeblood	8	9	-
phlegm	8	8	-
urine	8	4	-
gore	10	7	-
sputum	10	-	-

23I2.0	A	B	C
capillary	4	4	-
vein	4	3	9
vessel	4	4	5
artery	5	3	9
ventricle	6	5	12

23I3.0	A	B	C
bleed	3	3	3
circulate	5	7	-
hemorrhage	10	-	-

23I4.0	A	B	C
clot	5	5	-
coagulate	8	-	-

23J Bones/Muscles/Nerves

23J1.0	A	B	C
bone	3	3	3
rib	3	3	2
backbone	5	3	5
breastbone	5	3	-
cheekbone	5	3	-
collarbone	5	-	-
spine	5	3	6
jawbone	6	3	-
vertebrae	6	7	6
marrow	8	5	-

23J2.0	A	B	C
muscle	4	3	7
cartilage	5	5	-
ligament	6	9	-
sinew	6	4	-
tendon	6	3	-
gristle	8	7	-
thews	10	-	-

23J3.0	A	B	C
nerve	6	4	7
neuron	8	6	-

23K Body Systems

23K1.0	A	B	C
circulatory	6	4	6
digestive	6	5	6
reproductive	6	6	6
respiratory	6	7	6
sensory	6	5	9
skeletal	6	6	-
genital	8	7	-
salivary	8	5	-

23K1.1	A	B	C
circulation	5	3	7
digestion	6	3	-

23K1.2	A	B	C
digest	5	3	6
perspire	5	3	-

SUPER CLUSTER

24. Vegetation

24A Vegetation (General)

24A1.0	A	B	C
bush	1	3	1
tree	1	3	K
flower	2	3	1
plant	2	3	K
weed	2	3	2
oasis	4	4	4
shrub	4	3	4
arbor	5	4	-
hedgerow	8	4	-

24A2.0	A	B	C
growth	3	3	3
vegetation	4	3	7
flora	5	4	12
greenery	5	3	7
underbrush	5	3	-
undergrowth	5	3	-
bower	8	5	-

24B Types of Trees/Bushes

24B1.0	A	B	C
elm	3	3	5
fir	3	3	4

A: Grade level; B: Earliest Grade of Occurrence in Textbooks; C: Earliest Grade of Occurrence on Standardized Tests.

	A	B	C
mulberry	3	3	-
oak	3	3	3
pine	3	3	3
poplar	3	3	3
rosebush	3	3	-
willow	3	3	3
aspen	4	4	5
birch	4	3	5
cedar	4	3	7
cottonwood	4	3	-
maple	4	3	3
redwood	4	3	11
balsa	5	4	8
beech	5	3	5
boxwood	5	5	-
citrus	5	3	8
dogwood	5	4	-
hickory	5	3	5
laurel	5	4	4
locust	5	3	6
spruce	5	3	-
eucalyptus	6	4	8
evergreen	6	3	6
hemlock	6	3	6
teak	6	4	-
blackthorn	8	-	-
breadfruit	8	6	5
brushwood	8	6	-
mahogany	8	3	8
sequoia	8	3	-
snowberry	8	-	-
wormwood	8	-	-
cordwood	10	-	-

24C Parts of Trees/Bushes

24C1.0	A	B	C
bark	1	3	1
branch	2	3	2
leaf	2	3	2
twig	2	3	2
limb	3	3	3
stem	3	3	4
treetop	3	4	6
bough	4	3	-
knothole	4	3	-
stump	4	3	5
thorn	4	3	9
wicker	4	5	-
broadleaf	5	4	8
offshoot	5	-	-
sprig	5	6	-
foliage	6	5	9
gnarl	8	-	5
withe	8	-	-

24C2.0	A	B	C
rubber	3	3	3
sap	3	3	3
latex	5	4	6
pith	5	5	-
resin	5	4	-

24D Flowers/Plants

24D1.0	A	B	C
blossom	2	3	2
bud	3	4	4
petal	3	3	5
bouquet	4	4	-
pod	4	3	5

24D2.0	A	B	C
seed	1	3	1
bulb	3	3	5
pistil	3	3	5
pollen	3	3	4
stamen	3	4	5
cottonseed	4	3	-
spore	4	3	12
sprout	4	3	5
tuber	5	4	-
linseed	6	6	-

24D3.0	A	B	C
rose	2	3	1
daffodil	3	3	4
daisy	3	4	3
dandelion	3	3	-
lilac	3	3	-
poppy	3	3	-
tulip	3	3	4
buttercup	4	5	-
carnation	4	3	-
geranium	4	3	9
goldenrod	4	3	4
lily	4	3	6
marigold	4	-	7
petunia	4	6	-
rosebud	4	5	-
snapdragon	4	-	-
sunflower	4	3	5
wildflower	4	3	-
bluebell	5	9	-
chrysanthemum	5	3	-
cowslip	5	-	-
flytrap	5	-	5
foxglove	5	-	-
gardenia	5	4	-
honeysuckle	5	5	-
larkspur	5	3	-

	A	B	C
anemone	6	7	9
aster	8	5	7
nightshade	8	4	-
sweetbrier	8	-	-
windflower	8	-	-
wintergreen	8	-	-

24D4.0	A	B	C
berry	3	3	4
holly	4	3	-
huckleberry	4	4	-
thistle	4	3	-
brier	5	5	-

24D5.0	A	B	C
flax	5	3	-
hemp	6	3	-
jute	6	4	-
sisal	10	6	-

24E Other Vegetation

24E1.0	A	B	C
fern	3	3	3
moss	3	3	4
mushroom	3	3	3
algae	4	3	5
fungus	4	3	5
toadstool	4	5	10
kelp	5	3	-
mildew	5	-	-
thatch	5	3	6
lichen	6	7	9
duff	8	9	-

24E2.0	A	B	C
cob	3	3	2
root	3	3	3
beanstalk	4	3	-
grapevine	4	4	-
stalk	4	3	-
vine	4	3	4

24E3.0	A	B	C
cornhusk	4	4	-
husk	5	3	-
rind	5	4	-
chaff	8	3	-

24E4.0	A	B	C
grass	1	3	1
clover	3	3	5
hay	3	3	3
straw	3	3	12
alfalfa	4	3	7
bamboo	4	3	5

	A	B	C
cornstalk	4	4	-
reed	4	3	6
horsetail	8	7	-
sedge	8	7	-
thistledown	8	-	-
tussock	10	-	-

24E4.1	A	B	C
lawn	3	3	3
haystack	4	3	-

24E5.0	A	B	C
cattail	3	3	-
sagebrush	4	3	5
seaweed	4	3	5
milkweed	5	3	6
ragweed	5	6	-
chickweed	8	-	-
duckweed	8	6	-

SUPER CLUSTER

25. Groups of Things

25A General Names for Groups of Things

25A1.0	A	B	C
group	2	3	2
kit	3	3	5
assortment	4	3	8
collection	4	3	5
array	5	3	-
collective	5	4	-
matrix	8	9	-
miscellany	8	-	-
quorum	8	-	-
gamut	8	7	-
corpus	10	9	11
menagerie	10	4	7
congeries	13	-	-

25A2.0	A	B	C
list	3	3	3
schedule	3	3	6
arrangement	4	3	5
directory	4	4	4
file	4	3	4
menu	4	3	5
series	4	3	4
setup	4	4	4
curriculum	5	3	-
inventory	5	4	-
invoice	5	-	-
roster	5	5	-
timetable	5	3	6

A: Grade level; B: Earliest Grade of Occurrence in Textbooks; C: Earliest Grade of Occurrence on Standardized Tests.

	A	B	C
chronology	6	4	-
classification	6	4	9
sequence	6	3	6
itinerary	8	-	-
docket	10	-	-

25A3.0	A	B	C
blend	3	3	5
combination	4	3	4
compound	4	3	7
mixture	4	3	3
alloy	5	3	7
composite	5	3	6
medley	5	3	11
hybrid	6	6	-
aggregate	8	7	-
amalgam	8	3	-
crossbred	8	-	-
potpourri	8	-	-
salmagundi	13	9	-

25A4.0	A	B	C
web	4	3	5
network	5	3	9

25A5.0	A	B	C
pile	2	3	2
bunch	3	3	4
heap	3	3	4
stack	3	3	2
bale	4	4	-
batch	4	3	-
clump	4	3	-
cluster	4	3	-
stock	4	3	2
sheaf	5	4	-
wad	5	5	-
swath	6	3	-

25A6.0	A	B	C
gather	2	3	1
arrange	3	3	3
bundle	3	3	3
collect	4	3	3
organize	4	3	5
summarize	4	5	7
assemble	5	4	7
classify	5	3	6
muster	5	3	-
cumulate	6	-	-
compile	8	7	11
congregate	8	-	-
federate	8	-	-
glomerate	8	-	-
scavenge	8	5	-

	A	B	C
accrue	10	-	-
convoke	10	-	-
pigeonhole	10	-	-
queue	10	5	-

25B Groups of People/Animals

25B1.0	A	B	C
crowd	3	3	1
gang	4	3	5
huddle	4	3	4
faction	5	5	-
horde	5	3	-
mass	5	3	4
mob	5	4	9
throng	5	4	-
rabble	8	-	-
riffraff	10	-	-
canaille	13	-	-

25B2.0	A	B	C
band	2	3	2
chorus	4	3	4
quartet	4	3	-
trio	4	4	-
ensemble	6	5	-
quintet	6	4	-

25B3.0	A	B	C
herd	3	3	3
cowherd	4	3	-
flock	4	3	5
brood	5	3	K
covey	5	5	-
pod	5	3	5
bevy	6	-	-
gaggle	6	-	-

25B4.0	A	B	C
class	1	3	K
club	3	3	4
brotherhood	5	3	-
fraternity	5	7	-
denomination	6	5	-
clique	8	-	-
elite	8	5	9
entourage	8	7	-
pantheon	8	-	-
sorority	8	-	-
coterie	10	-	-

25B4.1	A	B	C
species	4	3	7
phylum	6	7	10
genus	8	4	10

A: Grade level; B: Earliest Grade of Occurrence in Textbooks; C: Earliest Grade of Occurrence on Standardized Tests.

25B5.0	A	B	C
team	3	3	3
crew	4	3	7
posse	5	4	-
varsity	8	6	-

25C Political/Social Groups

25C1.0	A	B	C
confederacy	5	4	-
democracy	5	3	7
federation	5	5	-
republic	5	3	5
protectorate	6	5	-
aristocracy	8	5	12
autocracy	8	-	-
commonwealth	8	3	11
junta	8	3	-
oligarchy	8	5	-
plutocracy	10	-	-

25C2.0	A	B	C
country	2	3	1
nation	3	3	4

25C2.1	A	B	C
national	4	3	4
international	5	3	6

25C3.0	A	B	C
government	3	3	3
congress	5	3	5
legislature	5	3	6
parliament	5	3	5
senate	5	3	5
regime	6	5	-
embassy	8	3	7

25C4.0	A	B	C
lawmaking	4	3	-
federal	5	3	5
legislative	5	3	5
political	5	3	5

25C5.0	A	B	C
community	3	3	3
civilization	4	3	5
culture	4	3	5
society	5	3	6
dynasty	8	5	12

25C6.0	A	B	C
family	2	3	2
tribe	3	3	2
clan	5	3	5
caste	6	4	-

	A	B	C
cult	6	5	-
sect	6	5	-

25C6.1	A	B	C
tribal	5	3	7
civic	6	5	3

25D Groups in Uniform

25D1.0	A	B	C
police	2	3	2
army	3	3	3
air force	4	-	-
navy	4	3	4
infantry	5	5	-
marines	5	3	-

25D2.0	A	B	C
patrol	4	3	4
troop	4	3	3
squad	5	3	9
squadron	5	3	-
brigade	6	5	-
corp	6	6	9
detail	6	3	7
legion	6	7	8
regiment	6	3	6
platoon	8	7	-

25E Social/Business Groups

25E1.0	A	B	C
company	3	3	3
committee	4	3	5
council	4	3	4
organization	4	3	5
staff	4	3	4
union	4	3	4
association	5	3	7
auxiliary	5	3	-
foundation	5	3	5
league	5	3	6
troupe	5	4	11
commission	6	3	9
institute	6	5	8
cartel	8	-	-
guild	8	6	8
syndicate	8	7	-
synod	10	-	-

25E1.1	A	B	C
corporate	8	7	-

A: Grade level; B: Earliest Grade of Occurrence in Textbooks; C: Earliest Grade of Occurrence on Standardized Tests.

25E2.0	A	B	C
conference	5	4	5
convention	5	3	6
session	5	3	8
seminar	8	7	8
conclave	10	-	-

25E3.0	A	B	C
gathering	3	3	1
assembly	4	3	6
audience	4	3	4
roundup	4	3	-
congregation	5	3	-

25E4.0	A	B	C
membership	5	3	7
partnership	5	4	11

SUPER CLUSTER

26. Value/Correctness

26A Right/Wrong

26A1.0	A	B	C
truth	4	3	2
justice	5	3	5
reality	6	3	7
virtue	8	5	9

26A2.0	A	B	C
fault	3	3	3
mistake	3	3	2
sin	3	3	-
crime	4	3	4
error	4	3	4
failure	4	3	5
blunder	5	6	-
flaw	5	3	9
lapse	5	5	-
wrongdoing	5	5	-
shortcoming	6	8	-
aberration	8	-	-
fallacy	8	7	-
folly	8	6	7
gaff	8	4	-
foible	13	-	-
solecism	13	-	-

26A3.0	A	B	C
just	1	3	K
right	1	3	1
real	2	3	2
true	2	3	2
correct	3	3	2
actual	4	3	3
accurate	5	4	5
constitutional	5	3	5
genuine	5	3	9
lawful	5	3	-
legal	5	3	6
authentic	6	3	6
moral	6	3	7
rightful	6	4	-
valid	6	6	6
legitimate	8	4	9
literal	8	7	10
virtual	8	4	-

26A4.0	A	B	C
fair	1	3	2
proper	3	3	2
acceptable	5	4	-
appropriate	5	3	7
apt	5	4	6
precise	5	3	6
satisfactory	5	3	9
suitable	5	3	5
eligible	6	5	7
realistic	6	4	8
congruous	8	4	-
decorous	8	-	-
opportune	8	6	-
relevant	8	7	11
apposite	10	-	-
apropos	10	-	-
condign	10	-	-
germane	10	-	-

26A5.0	A	B	C
wrong	2	3	1
false	3	3	2
incorrect	4	4	4
lawless	6	5	-
pseudo	8	-	9
apocryphal	10	7	-
illicit	10	-	-
spurious	10	-	-
specious	10	-	11

26A5.1	A	B	C
faulty	6	5	7
unfit	6	3	6
fallible	10	-	-

26A6.0	A	B	C
honesty	4	3	4
fairness	5	4	9
innocence	5	5	8
integrity	8	6	-
probity	10	-	-

26A6.1	A	B	C
honest	4	3	4
innocent	4	3	4
decent	5	3	9
honorable	5	3	6
forthcoming	6	7	-
wholesome	6	6	6
candid	8	6	11

26B Success/Failure

26B1.0	A	B	C
deserve	4	3	12
qualify	4	3	6
succeed	4	4	4
merit	5	3	4

26B2.0	A	B	C
muff	4	3	-
fail	4	3	2
err	6	7	11
bungle	6	-	-
bumble	6	7	-
botch	8	-	-
backslide	8	-	-

26C Importance/Value

26C1.0	A	B	C
important	2	3	2
elementary	3	3	4
main	3	3	4
basic	4	3	4
lifesaving	4	3	9
necessary	4	3	5
primary	4	3	5
urgent	4	3	2
essential	5	3	7
vital	5	3	7
acute	6	4	6
critical	6	4	6
crucial	6	3	-
fundamental	6	3	7
organic	6	5	11
underlying	6	5	5
exigent	10	-	-
intrinsic	10	7	-
salient	10	-	-

26C1.1	A	B	C
base	4	3	3
essence	5	3	-
crux	8	5	-
gist	8	8	-

| rudiment | 10 | - | - |
| quiddity | 13 | - | - |

26C2.0	A	B	C
best	1	3	K
perfect	2	3	2
favorite	3	3	2
major	3	3	3
super	4	3	4
superior	4	3	5
absolute	5	3	6
prime	5	3	6
superb	5	3	10
supreme	5	3	5
sublime	6	4	-
foremost	8	3	9
paramount	10	5	12

26C3.0	A	B	C
dear	2	3	2
beloved	4	3	8
precious	4	3	4
delightful	5	3	4
desirable	5	5	7
memorable	5	3	7
impressive	6	3	5

26C4.0	A	B	C
good	K	3	K
better	1	3	K
fine	2	3	2
valuable	4	3	5
noteworthy	6	7	-
worthwhile	6	4	9

26C5.0	A	B	C
wonderful	3	3	3
dandy	4	3	-
excellent	4	3	5
glorious	4	3	-
magnificent	4	3	5
remarkable	4	3	3
fabulous	5	3	3
fantastic	5	3	5
incredible	5	3	6
marvelous	5	3	6
outstanding	5	3	5
regal	5	3	9
splendid	5	3	9
terrific	5	3	7
tremendous	5	3	6
exceptional	6	5	-
extraordinary	6	3	6
invaluable	6	4	-
presidential	6	3	7
spectacular	6	3	7

imperial	8	5	9
topnotch	8	-	-
impeccable	10	8	11

26C5.1	A	B	C
masterpiece	8	5	10
paragon	8	6	-
apotheosis	10	-	-
epitome	10	7	-

26C6.0	A	B	C
miraculous	5	4	7
godsend	8	-	-
auspicious	10	7	-
propitious	13	3	-

26C7.0	A	B	C
use	1	3	1
useful	3	3	1
practical	4	3	6
adequate	5	3	5
usable	6	3	10
lucrative	8	5	-
utilitarian	8	5	-

26C7.1	A	B	C
worth	3	3	2
value	4	3	4
usefulness	5	4	6

26D Lack of Value

26D1.0	A	B	C
useless	4	3	3
unimportant	5	6	5
worthless	5	3	9
insignificant	6	5	-
petty	6	7	6
futile	8	4	10
nominal	8	5	-
nonessential	8	9	-
trite	8	-	-
vapid	8	-	-
paltry	8	3	-
inane	10	-	-
insipid	10	-	-
nugatory	10	-	-

26D1.1	A	B	C
inferior	5	3	6
shabby	6	3	7
shoddy	6	8	5
sleazy	8	8	-
tawdry	10	-	-
meretricious	13	-	-

26D2.0	A	B	C
bad	1	3	1
awful	3	3	3
evil	3	3	4
terrible	3	3	2
wicked	3	3	4
worse	3	3	3
dreadful	4	3	2
horrible	5	3	6
negative	5	3	2
corrupt	6	5	11
heinous	8	6	-
infernal	8	6	-
noxious	8	6	-
vile	8	6	-
diabolic	10	-	-
flagitious	10	-	-
pernicious	10	8	-
repugnant	10	-	-
nefarious	13	-	-
scurrilous	13	-	-

26D3.0	A	B	C
dire	6	5	-
sinister	6	6	5
unfavorable	6	7	-
baleful	8	3	-
malign	8	-	-
malevolent	10	-	-

26D4.0	A	B	C
foul	5	3	7
grim	5	3	6
ghastly	6	5	7
ghostly	6	4	6
grisly	8	7	-
gruesome	8	7	11
lurid	8	8	-
atrocious	10	-	-

26D5.0	A	B	C
foolish	3	3	3
ridiculous	4	3	4
absurd	6	3	6
harebrained	8	-	-
ludicrous	8	9	-
preposterous	8	6	7
fatuous	10	-	-
puerile	13	-	-

27. Similarity/Dissimilarity

27A Likeness

27A1.0	A	B	C
likeness	4	3	-
equality	5	4	7
similarity	6	5	-
affinity	8	5	-
monotony	8	6	8
resemblance	8	3	8

27A1.1	A	B	C
comparison	5	3	5
metaphor	6	5	10
analogy	6	7	-

27A1.2	A	B	C
anthropomorphism	13	7	-

27A2.0	A	B	C
agreement	4	3	3
accord	6	4	-
harmony	6	3	7

27A3.0	A	B	C
even	1	3	K
like	1	3	K
same	2	3	3
alike	3	3	3
exact	3	3	3
twin	3	3	1
congruent	4	4	3
equal	4	3	3
related	4	3	4
similar	4	3	4
consistent	5	3	7
equivalent	5	3	7
compatible	6	-	-
ditto	6	-	-
identical	6	3	6
homogeneous	8	6	-
invariable	8	-	-
mutual	8	3	10
unanimous	8	3	-
cognate	10	-	-
commensurate	10	-	-
qua	10	-	-
selfsame	10	-	-

27A4.0	A	B	C
match	3	3	K
approximate	4	4	3
parallel	5	3	5
resemble	5	3	4

	A	B	C
conform	6	4	11
proximate	8	-	-

27A5.0	A	B	C
example	4	3	3
imitation	4	4	4
replacement	5	4	8
substitute	6	3	6
proxy	8	-	9
replica	8	6	7
surrogate	8	-	-
travesty	10	-	-

27A5.1	A	B	C
artificial	4	3	4
synthetic	6	4	6
vicarious	8	-	-

27A6.0	A	B	C
copy	3	3	3
replace	3	3	3
echo	4	3	4
imitate	4	3	9
counterfeit	5	3	9
mimic	5	4	8
duplicate	6	3	-
mimeograph	6	5	-
emulate	10	-	-

27B Addition (Relationship Markers)

27B1.0	A	B	C
and	K	3	K
of	K	3	K
with	K	3	K
as well as	4	-	-

27B2.0	A	B	C
too	K	3	K
also	1	3	1
besides	2	3	4
as well	4	-	-
equally	4	3	4
for example	4	-	-
further	4	3	8
in addition	4	-	-
moreover	5	3	5
furthermore	6	5	6
likewise	6	3	8
anent	13	-	-

27B3.0	A	B	C
actually	4	3	4
namely	5	4	9

27C Difference

27C1.0

	A	B	C
difference	3	3	5
variety	5	3	6
variation	6	4	-
inequality	8	4	7
nuance	8	9	-

27C2.0

	A	B	C
different	2	3	3
opposite	3	3	3
contrary	4	3	8
separate	4	3	5
unlike	4	3	5
various	4	3	4
lopsided	5	3	8
unequal	6	3	-
discriminate	8	5	-
diverse	8	7	9
sundry	8	7	-
eclectic	10	8	-
heterogeneous	10	-	-

27C2.1

	A	B	C
freak	5	7	-
quirk	5	3	-
anomaly	13	7	-

27C3.0

	A	B	C
change	3	3	2
temper	4	3	-
adapt	5	3	5
develop	5	3	4
differ	5	3	5
molt	5	3	-
undergo	5	4	10
vary	5	3	7
reform	6	3	-
transform	6	4	-
deviate	10	-	12
mutate	10	-	-

27C3.1

	A	B	C
development	4	3	7
metamorphosis	6	3	10
flux	8	3	-
transit	8	7	11
vicissitude	13	-	-

27D Contrast (Relationship Markers)

27D1.0

	A	B	C
but	K	3	K
not	K	3	K
without	2	3	2
yet	2	3	4
sans	10	5	-

27D2.0

	A	B	C
than	1	3	K
else	2	3	K
against	3	3	3
instead	3	3	3
compare	5	3	4
contrast	5	3	7
otherwise	5	3	6
alternately	6	5	6
alternatively	6	-	-
by comparison	6	-	-
comparative	6	5	9
in comparison	6	-	-
on the contrary	6	-	-
on the other hand	6	-	-
or rather	6	-	-
versus	6	3	-
whereas	6	3	9
contrariwise	8	-	-
conversely	8	7	-

27D3.0

	A	B	C
or	K	3	1
either	3	3	4
neither	3	3	5
whether	3	3	5
either...or	4	-	-
neither...nor	4	-	-

27D4.0

	A	B	C
still	1	3	1
only	1	3	1
besides	2	3	4
although	3	3	3
anyway	3	3	3
though	3	3	2
unless	3	3	3
except	4	3	4
except for	4	-	-
however	4	3	4
anyhow	5	3	5
at any rate	5	-	-
in any case	5	-	-
in any event	5	-	-
nevertheless	5	3	7

A: Grade level; B: Earliest Grade of Occurrence in Textbooks; C: Earliest Grade of Occurrence on Standardized Tests.

regardless of	5	-	-
despite	6	3	6
nonetheless	6	3	9
notwithstanding	6	7	-
albeit	8	7	-
howbeit	8	-	-
howsoever	8	-	-

SUPER CLUSTER
28. Money/Finance

28A Money/Goods You Receive

28A1.0	A	B	C
savings	4	3	4
pension	8	5	7
annuity	10	-	-

28A2.0	A	B	C
gift	3	3	1
treasure	3	3	3
fortune	4	3	7
windfall	6	7	-
bonanza	8	-	-

28A3.0	A	B	C
allowance	4	3	3
salary	4	3	4
income	5	3	5
wage	6	3	9
pittance	8	-	-
revenue	8	7	9
emolument	13	-	-
perquisite	13	-	-

28A4.0	A	B	C
contribution	5	3	7
grant	6	3	7
scholarship	6	4	7
alms	8	4	-
dole	10	6	-
dower	10	-	-
grubstake	10	-	-
subsidy	10	-	-

28A5.0	A	B	C
legacy	6	5	-
inheritance	8	4	10
bequest	10	8	-

28A6.0	A	B	C
credit	5	3	7
gain	5	3	5
profit	5	3	4

28A7.0	A	B	C
reward	3	3	3
bounty	4	4	4
premium	5	4	-

28A8.0	A	B	C
insurance	6	3	6
indemnity	10	-	-

28B Money/Goods Paid Out

28B1.0	A	B	C
rent	3	3	7
fee	4	3	5
tab	4	3	-
bail	5	5	6
fare	5	3	5
mortgage	5	5	4
tariff	5	5	-
tax	5	3	4
toll	5	3	2
levy	6	3	-
taxation	6	3	6
carfare	8	-	11
excise	8	5	-
impost	8	8	-
tuition	8	3	7
usury	8	-	8
alimony	10	-	-
lien	10	-	-

28B2.0	A	B	C
cost	3	3	3
dues	5	3	5
expense	5	3	6
payment	5	3	5
price	5	3	3
ante	8	7	-

28B2.1	A	B	C
loss	4	3	5
debt	5	3	4
arrears	8	-	-

28B3.0	A	B	C
handout	5	-	-

28C Types of Money/Goods

28C1.0	A	B	C
money	1	3	1
coin	3	3	3
cash	4	3	4
wealth	4	3	5
capital	5	3	2

fund	5	4	5
payroll	5	3	9
finance	6	3	7
banknote	8	-	-
sterling	8	4	-

28C2.0	A	B	C
penny	1	3	1
cent	2	3	2
dollar	2	3	2
dime	3	3	4
nickel	3	3	4
quarter	3	3	3
shilling	5	3	-
guinea	6	3	8
greenback	8	7	-
quid	10	-	-
rand	10	-	-
sawbuck	10	-	-

28C3.0	A	B	C
check	3	3	2
ticket	3	3	K
coupon	4	3	6
postage	4	3	7
receipt	4	4	2
token	6	4	-
chit	10	-	-

28C4.0	A	B	C
souvenir	4	4	-
stock	5	3	2
ware	5	4	-
merchandise	6	4	6
commodity	8	4	9
payload	8	7	-

28D Money/Goods Related to Actions

28D1.0	A	B	C
bet	3	3	3
earn	3	3	3
afford	4	3	3
budget	4	3	5
scrimp	4	-	12
invest	5	3	9
insure	6	4	7
redeem	6	7	6

28D2.0	A	B	C
pay	1	3	K
buy	2	3	K
spend	2	3	2
owe	4	3	7

purchase	5	3	4
render	5	4	-
subscribe	5	4	-
donate	5	-	7
splurge	6	-	-
disburse	8	-	-
expend	8	7	-
remit	8	-	-
squander	8	-	9
tithe	8	-	-
bequeath	10	-	-

28D2.1	A	B	C
repay	5	4	-
compensate	8	6	11
reimburse	8	-	-
remunerate	10	-	-
requite	10	-	-

28D3.0	A	B	C
sell	2	3	2
market	3	3	3
lease	4	3	10
discount	5	6	6
auction	6	3	6
peddle	6	7	-
ransom	6	6	10
retail	6	4	6
bootleg	8	-	-
transact	8	5	8
vend	8	-	-

28D4.0	A	B	C
deal	3	3	3
sale	3	3	K
bargain	4	3	4
dicker	8	-	-

28D5.0	A	B	C
audit	8	-	9
depreciate	8	7	-
amortize	13	-	-

28E Money Related to Characteristics

28E1.0	A	B	C
costly	4	3	6
expensive	4	3	4
royal	4	3	4
wasteful	4	3	4
posh	5	3	-
extravagant	8	3	-
exorbitant	10	5	-
sumptuous	10	-	-

A: Grade level; B: Earliest Grade of Occurrence in Textbooks; C: Earliest Grade of Occurrence on Standardized Tests.

28E1.1	A	B	C
luxury	5	3	9

28E2.0	A	B	C
free	3	3	2
cheap	4	3	2
inexpensive	6	3	6
gratis	10	-	-

28E3.0	A	B	C
poor	2	3	1
broke	3	3	2
humble	4	3	2
needy	4	4	-
destitute	8	5	-
downtrodden	8	-	-
indigent	8	-	-

28E3.1	A	B	C
poverty	5	3	3
penury	10	-	-

28E4.0	A	B	C
rich	2	3	2
affluent	8	7	-
solvent	8	3	11
opulent	10	4	-

28E5.0	A	B	C
fiscal	8	7	-
pecuniary	13	-	-

28F Places Where Money/Goods Are Kept

28F1.0	A	B	C
bank	2	3	2
safe	2	3	1
account	5	3	5
vault	5	5	-
mint	6	3	5
strongbox	6	-	-

28F2.0	A	B	C
handbag	3	3	-
purse	3	3	3
pocketbook	4	3	-
billfold	5	-	-
checkbook	5	-	-
wallet	5	5	4
bankbook	6	-	-
moneybag	6	-	-

28F3.0	A	B	C
marketplace	4	3	7
commerce	5	3	7
economy	5	3	7

SUPER CLUSTER
29. Soil/Metal/Rock

29A Metals

29A1.0	A	B	C
gold	2	3	1
copper	3	3	4
iron	3	3	3
lead	3	3	2
silver	3	3	3
aluminum	4	3	4
mercury	5	3	4
zinc	5	3	6
tungsten	6	5	-

29A2.0	A	B	C
metal	3	3	3
brass	4	3	5
bronze	4	3	5
steel	4	3	3
tole	4	3	-
alloy	5	3	7
chrome	5	5	5
ore	6	3	7
solder	6	4	-
ingot	8	8	-

29A3.0	A	B	C
carbon	4	3	3
calcium	5	3	5
manganese	5	3	-
radium	5	3	-
silicon	5	3	-
uranium	5	3	6
barium	6	7	-
beryllium	6	4	6
cobalt	6	4	-
phosphorus	6	4	11
potassium	6	4	6
sulphur	6	4	-
quicksilver	8	3	-
thorium	10	7	-

29A4.0	A	B	C
magnet	2	3	3
flint	5	4	7
quartz	5	5	11
bauxite	6	3	7
feldspar	6	4	-

A: Grade level; B: Earliest Grade of Occurrence in Textbooks; C: Earliest Grade of Occurrence on Standardized Tests.

	A	B	C
gneiss	6	6	-
graphite	6	5	-
lodestone	6	5	-
mica	6	5	6
talc	6	-	-
beryl	8	9	-
hornblende	8	5	-
pitchblende	8	5	-
rock salt	8	-	-

29A5.0	A	B	C
lava	4	3	4
magma	4	4	11
obsidian	5	4	-
pumice	5	4	-
soapstone	6	-	-

29B Jewels/Rocks

29B1.0	A	B	C
diamond	3	3	4
crystal	4	3	8
jewel	4	3	3
pearl	4	4	5
ruby	4	3	2
emerald	5	5	6
gem	5	5	5
opal	5	5	-
turquoise	5	3	5
amethyst	6	5	-
jade	6	5	-
topaz	6	7	-

29B2.0	A	B	C
rock	2	3	K
cobble	3	3	-
stone	3	3	1
boulder	4	3	4
limestone	4	3	4
marble	4	3	4
sandstone	4	3	4
shale	4	3	4
bedrock	5	3	-
cobblestone	5	3	8
granite	5	3	5
gravel	5	3	5
nugget	5	3	-
rubble	5	5	11
slate	5	3	4
aggregate	6	7	-
asphalt	6	3	7
bluestone	8	-	-
flagstone	8	-	-
hardpan	10	-	-
macadam	10	4	-

	A	B	C
touchstone	10	-	-
moraine	10	5	-

29B2.1	A	B	C
charcoal	4	3	3
coal	4	3	3
coke	5	3	9
anthracite	6	3	-
bituminous	8	7	-

29B3.0	A	B	C
grindstone	5	4	-
millstone	5	3	-
whetstone	8	-	-
holystone	10	-	-

29C Characteristics of Rocks/Soil

29C1.0	A	B	C
pebble	4	3	4
volcanic	4	3	7
sedimentary	5	3	5
freestone	8	-	-

29C2.0	A	B	C
sand	2	3	1
barren	6	3	6
fallow	6	3	7
alluvial	8	5	-
arable	10	-	-

29D Actions of Metals

29D1.0	A	B	C
rust	4	3	4
corrode	6	4	-
oxidize	6	6	-
tarnish	6	6	7

29E Soil

29E1.0	A	B	C
ground	2	3	1
land	2	3	K
clay	3	3	2
dirt	3	3	2
dust	3	3	K
soil	3	3	2
earth	3	3	3
humus	5	3	-
loam	5	5	-
peat	5	3	-
sod	5	3	-
topsoil	5	3	8
turf	5	3	7

clod	6	-	-
hotbed	8	-	-
sward	8	3	-

29E2.0	A	B	C
dung	4	4	-
manure	4	3	-
dunghill	5	-	-
guano	10	-	-

29F Actions Done to Soil/Crops

29F1.0	A	B	C
plant	2	3	K
harvest	3	3	3
plow	3	3	3
sow	3	3	7
till	3	3	2
harrow	4	3	-
irrigate	4	3	6
tend	4	3	7
cultivate	5	4	9
fertilize	5	5	-
grub	5	5	-
thresh	5	3	-
mulch	8	-	11

29F1.1	A	B	C
irrigation	4	3	4
cultivation	5	3	7

SUPER CLUSTER

30. Rooms/Furnishing/Parts of Dwellings/Buildings

30A Rooms

30A1.0	A	B	C
room	1	3	K
cellar	2	3	2
kitchen	2	3	1
attic	3	3	5
balcony	3	3	5
bathroom	3	3	9
bedroom	3	3	1
garage	3	3	3
porch	3	3	3
ballroom	4	3	-
cloakroom	4	3	-
closet	4	3	4
den	4	3	4
nursery	4	3	6
pantry	4	3	-
playroom	4	4	-

veranda	4	4	-
washroom	4	3	-
chamber	5	3	7
loft	5	4	11
parlor	5	3	6
showroom	5	-	-
stateroom	5	4	-
wardroom	6	7	-
bedchamber	8	-	-
checkroom	8	-	-
garret	8	3	-
latrine	8	-	-
mezzanine	8	-	-

30A2.0	A	B	C
hall	2	3	3
doorway	3	3	2
entrance	3	3	6
aisle	4	4	5
archway	4	-	-
hallway	4	3	5
lobby	4	3	9
corridor	5	3	8
portal	6	4	-
threshold	6	5	11
cloister	8	9	-
ell	8	3	6
foyer	8	8	-
vestibule	10	6	-

30A3.0	A	B	C
rostrum	8	-	-
dais	10	6	-

30B Parts of a Home

30B1.0	A	B	C
chimney	3	3	3
fireplace	4	3	2
fireside	4	3	-
smokestack	4	4	-
flue	5	3	-
hearth	5	3	7
mantel	5	4	-
mantelpiece	5	4	-
stovepipe	5	3	-
hearthstone	6	7	-

30B2.0	A	B	C
floor	2	3	K
wall	2	3	1
ceiling	3	3	2
baseboard	5	7	-
parquet	8	-	-
wainscot	8	-	-

30B3.0	A	B	C
roof	2	3	1
rooftop	3	3	5
dome	4	3	3
housetop	4	-	-
steeple	4	3	-
eaves	5	3	-
spire	5	3	7
belfry	8	4	-
gable	8	4	-
ridgepole	10	-	-

30B4.0	A	B	C
window	1	3	1
pane	3	3	6
sill	3	3	-
shopwindow	4	-	-
shutter	4	3	-
windowseat	4	-	-
windowsill	4	6	K
awning	5	4	-
lattice	5	3	5
vent	5	7	-
dormer	6	4	-
latticework	6	-	-
wicket	6	3	-

30B5.0	A	B	C
railing	3	3	7
stair	3	3	5
stairs	3	3	2
stairway	4	3	5
bannister	5	3	-
staircase	5	3	6
stile	5	4	-

30B6.0	A	B	C
door	2	3	K
doorstep	3	3	4
doorpost	4	3	-
doorplate	5	-	-
doorstone	6	-	-
jamb	6	5	-
transom	10	3	-

30C Fences/Ledges

30C1.0	A	B	C
shelf	3	3	2
ledge	4	3	3
curb	5	3	-
gutter	5	3	4
curbstone	8	6	-

30C2.0	A	B	C
fence	2	3	2
gate	2	3	2
mailbox	3	3	3
screen	3	3	6
barbed wire	4	4	-
gatepost	4	4	-
gateway	4	3	-
hedge	4	3	5
trellis	6	3	-
trelliswork	8	-	-
palisade	8	4	-
pergola	10	-	-

30D Furniture

30D1.0	A	B	C
furniture	4	3	3
decor	6	6	-
furnishing	6	6	-

30D2.0	A	B	C
table	1	3	K
desk	2	3	3
counter	4	3	4
worktable	4	-	-
altar	5	3	11
drainboard	5	4	-
pulpit	5	4	-
tabletop	5	7	-

30D3.0	A	B	C
chair	2	3	K
seat	2	3	K
bench	3	3	3
stool	3	3	3
bleacher	4	3	-
rocker	4	3	-
sofa	4	3	7
wheelchair	4	5	-
workbench	4	3	-
armchair	5	5	-
couch	5	3	5
pew	6	4	-
throne	6	3	12
davenport	8	-	-
divan	8	-	-

30D4.0	A	B	C
drawer	3	3	1
bookcase	4	4	9
cupboard	4	3	5
hutch	4	3	-
nook	4	4	9
cabinet	5	3	2

washstand	5	4	-
bureau	6	7	9
sideboard	6	7	-
commode	8	-	-
chiffonier	10	-	-
highboy	10	-	-

30D5.0	A	B	C
bed	1	3	1
bedspring	3	3	-
bunk	3	3	3
mat	3	3	8
playpen	3	3	-
cot	4	3	-
cradle	4	3	5
crib	4	3	6
fourposters	4	3	-
mattress	4	3	-
headboard	5	6	-

30E Decorations

30E1.0	A	B	C
decoration	4	3	5
ornament	4	4	5
accessory	5	-	7
knickknack	5	-	-
trifle	6	3	-
openwork	8	7	-
whatnot	8	-	-
fretwork	10	-	-

30E1.1	A	B	C
decorate	4	3	7
beautify	5	5	5
furnish	5	3	6
varnish	5	3	-
upholster	5	-	-
adorn	6	7	12
festoon	8	6	-
shellac	8	3	-
embellish	10	-	-

30E2.0	A	B	C
rug	2	3	3
carpet	3	3	3
curtain	3	3	5
wallpaper	4	8	5
canopy	5	3	10
linoleum	5	3	-
tapestry	6	5	11

30E3.0	A	B	C
banner	4	3	4
pennant	4	3	-
spangle	4	3	-

tinsel	4	3	-
wreath	4	3	-
confetti	5	4	-
plaque	5	3	5
ironwork	6	4	-
frieze	8	-	-
gargoyle	8	7	-

30E4.0	A	B	C
centerpiece	4	4	-
flowerpot	4	3	-
pottery	4	3	4
vase	4	3	5
cornucopia	5	5	-
earthenware	5	3	-
cut glass	6	-	-
urn	6	4	11

30E5.0	A	B	C
homemade	4	3	6
domestic	5	3	7

30F Linens

30F1.0	A	B	C
blanket	2	3	K
cover	2	3	2
sheet	2	3	2
pillowcase	3	3	-
bedspread	4	3	-
drape	4	5	-
quilt	4	3	5
bedroll	5	6	-

30F2.0	A	B	C
napkin	4	3	-
tablecloth	4	3	-
doily	5	-	-

30F2.1	A	B	C
towel	3	3	4
washcloth	3	3	-
dishcloth	4	-	-

30F3.0	A	B	C
pillow	3	3	2
pad	4	3	4
cushion	5	4	4
hassock	6	-	-

SUPER CLUSTER
31. Attitudinals

31A Attitudinals (Truth)

31A1.0	A	B	C
clearly	2	3	2
flatly	2	7	-
really	2	3	2
surely	2	3	2
certainly	3	3	3
indeed	3	3	3
plainly	3	3	11
simply	3	3	6
truly	3	3	3
actually	4	3	4
definitely	4	3	7
frankly	4	4	-
honestly	4	3	-
basically	5	3	-
doubtless	5	3	-
essentially	5	4	11
obviously	5	3	9
truthfully	5	3	11
undoubtedly	5	3	11
candidly	6	-	-
fundamentally	6	6	-
literally	6	3	10
undeniably	6	4	-
unquestionably	6	7	-

31A1.1	A	B	C
ideally	5	4	8
apparently	6	3	7
evidently	6	3	9
technically	6	5	-
ostensibly	8	8	-

31A2.0	A	B	C
strictly	4	5	11
seriously	5	3	7
bluntly	6	5	-

31B Attitudinals (Lack of Truth/Doubt)

31B1.0	A	B	C
maybe	1	3	K
perhaps	3	3	3
possibly	4	3	6
conceivably	6	7	-
presumably	6	5	-
reportedly	6	7	-
seemingly	6	3	6
superficially	6	7	11

	A	B	C
supposedly	6	3	7
theoretically	6	5	-
allegedly	8	7	-
arguably	8	-	-

31C Attitudinals (Expected/Unexpected)

31C1.0	A	B	C
curiously	3	3	-
strangely	3	3	4
unexpectedly	4	4	5
oddly	5	3	-
ironically	6	5	8

31C2.0	A	B	C
appropriately	5	6	-
typically	5	5	-
inevitably	6	5	-
naturally	6	3	7
predictably	6	-	-
understandably	6	6	-

31C3.0	A	B	C
remarkably	5	3	5
amazingly	6	3	-
astonishingly	6	6	-
incredibly	6	3	-
refreshingly	6	-	-

31D Attitudinals (Fortunate/Unfortunate)

31D1.0	A	B	C
happily	1	3	2
luckily	3	3	5
thankfully	3	-	-
fortunately	4	3	6
delightfully	5	6	-

31D2.0	A	B	C
sadly	2	3	3
unhappily	3	4	-
unfortunately	5	3	6
unluckily	5	-	-
tragically	6	7	-

31E Attitudinals (Satisfaction/Dissatisfaction)

31E1.0	A	B	C
disappointingly	5	-	-
annoyingly	6	-	-
disturbingly	6	-	-
regrettably	6	-	-

A: Grade level; B: Earliest Grade of Occurrence in Textbooks; C: Earliest Grade of Occurrence on Standardized Tests.

31F Attitudinals (Correctness/Incorrectness)

31F1.0	A	B	C
rightly	2	4	11
correctly	3	3	3
justly	6	6	-

31F2.0	A	B	C
wrongly	3	5	6
incorrectly	4	4	3
unjustly	6	6	-

31G Attitudinals (Wisdom/Lack of Wisdom)

31G1.0	A	B	C
wisely	2	3	4
cleverly	3	3	3
reasonably	5	3	7
shrewdly	5	4	-
artfully	6	-	-
sensibly	6	5	9
prudently	8	-	-

31G2.0	A	B	C
foolishly	3	3	3
unwisely	5	-	-

31H Other Attitudinals

31H1.0	A	B	C
please	2	3	K
hopefully	3	3	-
preferably	5	3	9

32. Shapes/Dimensions

32A Shapes (General Names)

32A1.0	A	B	C
shape	2	3	3
cutout	3	3	-
figure	3	3	3
form	3	3	2
pattern	3	3	3
outline	5	3	5
profile	5	3	-
contour	6	5	7
silhouette	6	4	-
aperture	13	6	-

32A1.1	A	B	C
amorphous	10	5	-

32A2.0	A	B	C
skyline	5	3	-

32A3.0	A	B	C
frame	3	3	9
framework	4	3	12
chassis	8	4	-

32B Circular or Curved Shapes

32B1.0	A	B	C
circle	2	3	K
cone	3	3	1
cylinder	4	3	3
halo	4	3	-
sphere	4	3	4
crescent	5	3	7
disk	5	3	-
quadrant	8	-	-
orb	10	3	-

32B2.0	A	B	C
bend	3	3	2
curl	3	3	2
curve	3	3	3
loop	3	3	3
twist	3	3	4
coil	4	3	-
spiral	4	3	5
arc	5	3	6
circuit	5	3	6
flex	5	-	-
warp	5	3	9
curvature	6	5	-
kink	6	6	-
parabola	6	9	-
convolute	10	-	-
frizz	10	-	-
hank	10	-	-
whorl	10	-	-
trajectory	10	3	-

32B3.0	A	B	C
round	2	3	2
oval	3	3	9
circular	4	3	5
concave	5	4	11
convex	5	4	11
spherical	5	4	-
annular	10	-	-
gyre	10	5	-

32C Rectangular or Square Shapes

32C1.0	A	B	C
rectangle	3	3	4
square	3	3	3
triangle	3	3	3
parallelogram	4	3	6
polygon	4	4	6
hexagon	5	5	-
octagon	5	8	-
pentagon	5	8	6
trapezoid	5	5	-
isogon	8	-	-
decagon	10	-	-

32C1.1	A	B	C
foursquare	3	5	-
equilateral	4	6	-
quadrilateral	4	4	-
rectangular	4	3	9
triangular	4	3	5
isometric	6	5	-
quadrate	8	7	-

32C2.0	A	B	C
block	2	3	4
cube	3	3	2
prism	4	3	5
pyramid	4	4	4

32C2.1	A	B	C
cubic	5	3	5

32D Straightness/Crookedness

32D1.0	A	B	C
cross	2	3	1
line	2	3	1
strip	3	3	5
stripe	3	3	4
zigzag	5	3	7
crisscross	6	3	-
fillet	6	3	-
serrate	8	-	-

32D2.0	A	B	C
straight	3	3	3
beeline	5	4	-
linear	5	4	11

32D3.0	A	B	C
bent	3	3	3
crooked	3	3	2
sinuous	6	7	-

	A	B	C
askance	8	-	-
oblique	8	7	4

32E Sharpness/Bluntness

32E1.0	A	B	C
dull	3	3	3
sharp	3	3	2
blunt	5	3	5
keen	5	3	7

32E2.0	A	B	C
flatten	4	5	-
sharpen	4	4	3
taper	8	3	-
hone	10	-	10

32F Dimension

32F1.0	A	B	C
long	1	3	K
short	2	3	1
tall	2	3	K
wide	2	3	2
broad	4	3	3
threadlike	4	3	-
vermiform	10	-	-

32F1.1	A	B	C
height	3	3	3
length	3	3	3
width	4	3	5

32F2.0	A	B	C
deep	2	3	2
thick	3	3	2
dense	4	3	4

32F2.1	A	B	C
thickness	3	3	5
depth	4	3	4
density	5	3	6

32F3.0	A	B	C
thin	2	3	1
narrow	3	3	2
shallow	4	3	4
trim	4	3	5
hairbreadth	8	6	-
superficial	8	5	8

32F3.1	A	B	C
tier	6	5	-
stratum	8	9	-
striated	10	-	-

A: Grade level; B: Earliest Grade of Occurrence in Textbooks; C: Earliest Grade of Occurrence on Standardized Tests. 159

32F4.0	A	B	C
straighten	3	3	4
extend	4	3	7
thicken	4	3	7
widen	4	4	-
deepen	5	5	-
lengthen	5	4	-

32G Fullness/Emptiness

32G1.0	A	B	C
full	2	3	K
swollen	4	3	7
fraught	6	7	-
turgid	8	7	-
replete	10	-	-

32G1.1	A	B	C
fill	2	3	1
stuff	3	3	5
distend	10	-	-

32G2.0	A	B	C
empty	2	3	2
hollow	3	3	3
vacant	3	3	3
null	5	5	-
void	5	5	11
commodious	13	-	12

32G2.1	A	B	C
exhaust	4	3	-
deflate	5	-	-
deplete	6	-	-

32H Inclination

32H1.0	A	B	C
even	1	3	K
flat	2	3	2
level	3	3	3
plumb	6	4	4

32H1.1	A	B	C
lean	3	3	3

32H2.0	A	B	C
slant	4	3	10
steep	4	3	4
tilt	4	3	-
incline	5	3	11
erect	6	3	7
declivity	10	-	-

33. Destructive and Helpful Actions

33A Actions Destructive to Nonhumans

33A1.0	A	B	C
accident	3	3	3
crash	3	3	3
wreck	3	3	3
breakdown	4	4	11
collision	6	3	12
mishap	6	6	5

33A2.0	A	B	C
mark	2	3	2
scratch	2	3	2
dent	3	3	5
chip	4	3	K
mar	5	4	9
nick	6	3	3
overuse	8	9	-

33A3.0	A	B	C
break	2	3	3
crush	4	3	4
damage	4	3	4
mash	4	3	4
puncture	4	4	4
shatter	5	4	7
squelch	5	-	-
erode	6	7	8
fracture	6	4	6
mangle	6	-	-
rupture	6	7	-
contort	8	-	-
dismantle	8	8	8
mutilate	8	-	-
perforate	8	-	-
quash	8	-	-
rend	8	-	-
sabotage	8	3	-
efface	10	-	-

33A4.0	A	B	C
erase	3	3	6
ruin	3	3	4
waste	3	3	2
destroy	4	3	4
demolish	5	4	-
extinguish	5	-	10
devastate	6	-	7
snuff	6	4	-
obliterate	8	9	-

pulverize	8	-	-
annihilate	10	-	-
eradicate	10	-	12
raze	10	-	-
expunge	13	-	-
extirpate	13	-	-

33A4.1	A	B	C
wreckage	5	4	6
destruction	6	3	6

33B Actions Destructive to Humans

33B1.0	A	B	C
hurt	2	3	1
abuse	5	5	5
injure	5	3	6
molest	6	6	-
offend	6	3	-
rape	6	7	-
manhandle	8	-	-
violate	8	7	11

33B1.1	A	B	C
incest	8	-	-
detriment	8	7	-
bane	10	-	-

33B2.0	A	B	C
kill	2	3	4
attack	3	3	K
harm	3	3	3
shoot	3	3	2
ambush	4	3	-
murder	5	3	11
slaughter	5	4	7
slay	5	3	-
execute	6	5	7
massacre	6	4	-
persecute	6	-	-
trounce	8	-	-

33B2.1	A	B	C
suicide	5	7	-
homicide	8	-	11
manslaughter	8	-	-
genocide	10	-	-
regicide	10	7	-

33B3.0	A	B	C
overwhelm	5	3	7
paralyze	5	3	-
stun	5	-	-
afflict	6	6	-
beset	6	4	-

cripple	6	6	-
assail	8	-	-
subvert	8	-	-
undermine	8	5	-
wreak	8	-	-
inflict	10	3	9

33B4.0	A	B	C
deadly	4	4	6
painful	4	3	5
fatal	5	3	6
poisonous	5	3	5
penal	6	4	-
lethal	8	7	11
toxic	8	4	12

33B5.0	A	B	C
punish	3	3	3
discipline	4	4	5
horsewhip	5	-	-
scourge	5	4	-
vengeance	5	4	-
prosecute	6	5	-
torment	6	5	-
torture	6	4	7
flog	8	-	-
gallows	8	6	11
lynch	8	-	-
pillory	8	-	-
decapitate	10	-	-
duress	10	-	-
flay	10	-	-
immolate	10	-	-
retaliate	10	7	-

33C Fighting

33C1.0	A	B	C
fight	2	3	K
duel	4	3	-
struggle	4	3	7
wrestle	4	4	-
challenge	4	3	8
clash	5	5	-
raid	5	3	7
repel	5	3	5
rumble	5	3	11
scuffle	5	3	-
skirmish	5	3	-
invade	6	4	-
brawl	8	7	-
feud	8	7	11
maraud	8	-	-
scrimmage	8	6	7
tussle	8	-	-

	A	B	C
wrangle	8	-	-
sally	10	3	4

33C2.0	A	B	C
war	3	3	2
battle	4	3	4
friction	4	3	5
revolution	4	3	4
bloodshed	5	3	-
combat	5	3	5
conflict	5	3	5
fray	5	3	11
showdown	5	4	-
strife	5	3	11
warpath	5	4	-
disturbance	6	5	-
riot	6	6	-
unrest	6	4	11
warfare	6	3	7
coup	8	7	-
sea fight	8	-	-
throes	8	-	-
affray	10	-	-
foray	10	7	-
melee	10	-	-
sortie	10	5	-

33C3.0	A	B	C
invasion	6	5	7
onslaught	6	6	-
siege	6	5	-

33C4.0	A	B	C
peace	4	3	4
truce	8	5	-

33D Actions Helpful to Humans

33D1.0	A	B	C
help	1	3	K
behave	2	3	4
assist	5	3	7
accommodate	6	3	-
avail	6	3	-
contribute	6	3	5
abet	8	5	-
behoove	8	-	-
conduce	8	-	-
subvene	10	-	-

33D2.0	A	B	C
relieve	5	3	10
allay	8	7	-
emancipate	8	-	-
redress	8	-	-
reprieve	8	8	9

	A	B	C
alleviate	10	7	12
conciliate	10	-	-
exculpate	10	-	-
exonerate	10	-	-
mediate	10	-	-
vindicate	10	-	-

33D3.0	A	B	C
foster	5	5	5
nourish	5	5	-
promote	5	3	7
enable	6	3	7

33D4.0	A	B	C
improve	4	3	5
enrich	5	5	4
amend	8	8	-
atone	10	-	-
expiate	10	-	-
ameliorate	13	-	-

33D5.0	A	B	C
guide	4	3	3
escort	6	4	-
protector	6	5	-
chaperone	8	8	9
peacemaker	8	-	-

33D6.0	A	B	C
aid	4	3	3
cure	4	3	3
heal	4	3	5
recover	4	3	6
refresh	6	5	8
convalesce	8	-	-
recuperate	8	9	-
resurrect	8	-	-
revive	8	5	-
resuscitate	10	-	-
inure	10	-	-

33D7.0	A	B	C
save	2	3	1
protect	3	3	2
defend	4	3	5
rescue	4	3	3
fend	5	3	-
safeguard	5	5	9
forfend	13	-	-

33D7.1	A	B	C
sake	4	3	11
stead	5	3	-
behalf	6	3	-
benefit	6	3	5
vantage	8	7	-

A: Grade level; B: Earliest Grade of Occurrence in Textbooks; C: Earliest Grade of Occurrence on Standardized Tests.

34. Sports/Recreation

34A Sports/Recreation

34A1.0

	A	B	C
hobby	4	3	6
sport	4	3	3
recreation	5	3	6

34A2.0

	A	B	C
game	1	3	K
race	2	3	3
contest	3	3	2
match	3	3	K
championship	4	4	4
competition	6	3	6
derby	6	3	7
marathon	6	6	9
tournament	6	4	9
bout	8	-	1
regatta	8	6	-
sweepstakes	8	9	-

34A2.1

	A	B	C
compete	5	3	5
vie	10	-	-

34B Specific Sports

34B1.0

	A	B	C
baseball	3	3	K
basketball	3	3	2
football	3	3	4
hockey	4	3	10
soccer	4	3	5
softball	4	4	6
volleyball	4	4	4
lacrosse	5	5	-
polo	5	7	6

34B2.0

	A	B	C
golf	4	3	5
tennis	4	5	3
badminton	5	5	-
croquet	6	4	-

34B2.1

	A	B	C
backhand	6	5	-

34B3.0

	A	B	C
racing	2	3	2
skating	2	3	3
bicycling	3	3	9
swimming	3	3	2
skiing	4	3	-

34B3.1

	A	B	C
skate	2	3	2
swim	2	3	1
bicycle	3	3	2
ski	3	3	11
steeplechase	6	6	-

34B4.0

	A	B	C
boxing	3	3	6
fencing	3	3	6
wrestling	5	4	11
jousting	8	9	-
logrolling	8	-	-
swordplay	8	6	-
pugilism	13	-	-

34B4.1

	A	B	C
box	1	3	K
fence	2	3	2
joust	8	-	-

34C Equipment Used in Sports/Recreation

34C1.0

	A	B	C
ball	K	3	K
net	2	3	K
mark	2	3	2
base	4	3	3
bat	4	3	1
beanbag	4	4	-
Maypole	4	3	-
putter	4	5	-
racket	4	3	5
ski	4	3	11
tee	4	4	5
backstop	5	4	-
dumbbell	5	-	-
surfboard	5	5	-
target	5	3	4
hurdle	6	4	8
puck	6	7	-
aqualung	8	4	-
javelin	8	5	9
shuttlecock	8	-	-
quoit	10	-	-

34C2.0

	A	B	C
swing	3	3	K
hammock	4	3	7
trapeze	4	3	6

34C3.0

	A	B	C
carousel	5	4	-

A: Grade level; B: Earliest Grade of Occurrence in Textbooks; C: Earliest Grade of Occurrence on Standardized Tests.   163

34C4.0	A	B	C
out	K	3	K
touchdown	3	5	9
goal	4	3	6
inning	4	3	3
knockout	4	-	-
tackle	4	3	4
volley	5	4	-
bunt	6	3	-
homer	6	5	7
sidearm	8	-	-

34C5.0	A	B	C
backfield	6	9	-
defense	6	3	7
offense	6	3	7

34D Exercising

34D1.0	A	B	C
exercise	4	3	4
workout	4	3	-
jogging	5	3	4
sprinting	6	-	-
yoga	6	-	-

34D1.1	A	B	C
practice	2	3	2
stretch	4	3	3
jog	5	5	5
sprint	5	3	6

34D2.0	A	B	C
cartwheel	4	4	-
somersault	4	4	3

34D3.0	A	B	C
play	K	3	K
horseplay	5	-	-
roughhouse	8	-	-

34E Magic

34E1.0	A	B	C
magic	2	3	1
trick	2	3	K
stunt	5	3	5
witchcraft	5	7	-
gimmick	6	-	9
sorcery	6	7	-
astrology	6	6	9
hoodoo	10	-	-
talisman	10	6	-
wile	10	-	-

	A	B	C
necromancy	13	-	-
phrenology	13	-	-

34E1.1	A	B	C
magical	6	3	6

34F Board and Other Games

34F1.0	A	B	C
toys	1	3	2
hopscotch	3	3	5
puzzle	3	3	11
riddle	3	3	3
checkers	4	3	5
crossword	4	4	4
tiddlywinks	4	-	-
chess	5	4	8
raffle	6	-	7
billiards	8	-	-
roulette	8	-	-
acrostic	10	-	-

34F1.1	A	B	C
checkmate	5	-	-

34F2.0	A	B	C
poker	5	6	-
whist	5	3	-
craps	8	-	-
cribbage	8	-	-

34F3.0	A	B	C
doll	1	3	K
toy	1	3	K
popgun	3	3	-
puppet	3	3	2
checkerboard	4	-	7
dice	4	3	5
chessboard	5	4	-
sandbox	5	6	6
ace	6	3	3
domino	8	-	-
taw	8	7	-

SUPER CLUSTER

35. Language

35A Language and Language Conventions

35A1.0	A	B	C
language	3	3	K
grammar	4	4	7
slang	4	4	-
vocabulary	4	3	K

dialect	5	3	-
idiom	6	4	-
gender	8	-	-
jargon	8	8	9
orthography	10	-	-
syntax	10	-	-
vernacular	10	5	-

35A2.0	A	B	C
accent	4	3	5
pronunciation	4	3	4
emphasis	5	3	9
lisp	5	-	-
diction	6	7	11
alliteration	8	-	-
locution	8	-	-
rhetoric	8	5	-

35A3.0	A	B	C
apostrophe	3	3	-
comma	3	3	-
period	3	3	3
punctuation	3	3	4
capitalization	4	4	3
hyphen	4	3	9
parenthesis	4	3	-
colon	5	4	-

35B Words/Sentences

35B1.0	A	B	C
word	1	3	K
sentence	3	3	2
phrase	4	3	3
clause	5	5	11
password	5	-	-
catchword	8	-	-
watchword	8	-	-
trope	10	-	-
shibboleth	13	-	-

35B2.0	A	B	C
abbreviation	4	3	-
prefix	4	3	4
suffix	4	3	4
syllable	4	3	4
affix	6	7	4

35B3.0	A	B	C
exclamatory	5	3	7
interrogative	5	3	-
superlative	5	5	11
expletive	8	-	-
imperative	8	3	12
subjunctive	8	-	-

35B4.0	A	B	C
noun	3	3	4
pronoun	3	3	-
verb	3	3	4
adjective	4	4	4
antonym	4	3	-
conjunction	4	4	-
predicate	4	3	4
preposition	4	4	-
synonym	4	4	4
modifier	5	5	-
participle	5	5	9

35B5.0	A	B	C
homonym	4	3	-
pun	5	5	9
homograph	6	5	-
homophone	6	4	-
conundrum	10	-	-
palindrome	10	6	-

35C Letters/Alphabet

35C1.0	A	B	C
letter	1	3	K
alphabet	3	3	4
consonant	3	3	-
vowel	3	3	4
beta	5	5	7
cuneiform	5	7	-
alpha	6	5	7
italics	6	3	-
hieroglyph	10	-	-

35C1.1	A	B	C
alphabetically	4	4	-

35C1.2	A	B	C
phonetic	6	5	-
sibilant	10	-	-

35C2.0	A	B	C
code	3	3	7
symbol	3	3	3
cipher	6	6	-
notation	6	3	7
icon	10	-	-
semaphore	10	3	-
rebus	13	-	-

A: Grade level; B: Earliest Grade of Occurrence in Textbooks; C: Earliest Grade of Occurrence on Standardized Tests.   165

36. Ownership/Possession

36A Losing/Giving Up

36A1.0	A	B	C
lose	3	3	1
abandon	5	3	4
misplace	5	-	-
forfeit	8	4	8
relinquish	8	-	-
waive	8	-	-

36A1.1	A	B	C
loser	3	3	-

36A2.0	A	B	C
displace	4	3	-
dismiss	5	6	8
dispose	5	3	4
discard	6	7	9
eject	6	-	11

36A3.0	A	B	C
show	2	3	1
borrow	3	3	5
share	3	3	5
trade	3	3	5
use	3	3	1
barter	4	3	-
exchange	4	3	4
lease	4	3	10
loan	4	5	3
lend	5	3	4
swap	5	4	-

36B Freedom/Lack of Freedom

36B1.0	A	B	C
escape	3	3	2
flee	3	3	5
free	3	3	2
getaway	4	4	-
parole	5	5	-
release	5	3	7
acquit	8	5	-
elope	8	-	-
evade	8	7	10
extricate	10	-	-
manumit	13	-	-

36B2.0	A	B	C
cede	5	5	11
turnover	5	3	7
sacrifice	6	3	6

surrender	6	3	-
capitulate	8	7	-
concede	8	6	11

36C Possession/Ownership

36C1.0	A	B	C
possession	4	3	4
property	4	3	5
custody	5	5	-
ownership	5	3	7
monopoly	6	5	6
dominion	8	3	-

36C2.0	A	B	C
have	1	3	K
own	2	3	1
maintain	4	3	5
occupy	5	3	4
possess	6	3	6
arrogate	10	-	-

36C3.0	A	B	C
belong	2	3	2
inhere	8	-	-
pertain	8	9	11

36D Winning/Losing

36D1.0	A	B	C
win	3	3	3
conquer	5	3	6
defeat	5	3	5
subdue	6	5	6
dominate	8	3	9
prostrate	8	4	-
vanquish	8	7	-

36D2.0	A	B	C
excel	5	5	10
overcome	5	3	5
overrun	6	3	-
overtake	6	5	7
overthrow	6	3	-
prevail	6	7	-
supercede	10	-	-

36D3.0	A	B	C
success	4	3	3
accomplishment	5	4	-
triumph	5	3	-
conquest	6	3	5

36D3.1	A	B	C
dominant	5	3	9
triumphant	5	3	7

36D4.0	A	B	C
setback	3	3	-
loss	4	3	5
downfall	5	5	9
failure	5	3	5
washout	5	5	-
fiasco	8	7	-
debacle	10	-	-

36D5.0	A	B	C
winner	3	3	3
champion	4	3	3
victor	6	4	6

36E Taking/Receiving Actions

36E1.0	A	B	C
get	K	3	K
adopt	3	4	6
reach	3	3	2
regain	4	3	-
attain	5	4	-
obtain	5	3	6
reap	5	3	4
achieve	6	3	5
acquire	6	4	9
extract	6	3	7
evoke	8	9	-
elicit	10	-	-
extort	10	-	-
procure	10	6	-
suborn	10	-	-

36E2.0	A	B	C
accept	4	3	3
attract	4	3	4
receive	4	3	4
trespass	5	3	9
inherit	6	3	6
incur	8	-	-

36E3.0	A	B	C
seize	3	3	4
arrest	4	3	5
capture	4	3	3
kidnap	5	6	10
abduct	6	-	10
apprehend	8	9	-

36E4.0	A	B	C
rob	3	3	2
steal	3	3	5
holdup	4	-	-
loot	5	4	-
plunder	5	3	9

hijack	6	-	-
ransack	6	-	-
confiscate	8	-	-
deprive	8	9	-
embezzle	8	-	-
pillage	8	-	-
filch	10	-	-
freeboot	10	-	-
pilfer	10	-	-
purloin	10	5	-
usurp	10	-	-
peculate	13	-	-

36F Finding/Keeping

36F1.0	A	B	C
find	1	3	1
spot	1	3	2
locate	4	3	1
distinguish	5	4	12
pinpoint	6	3	-

36F2.0	A	B	C
keep	2	3	1
bury	3	3	3
tuck	4	3	6
conserve	5	3	7
reserve	5	3	8
withhold	5	4	6
hoard	6	6	-
restrict	6	5	7
retain	6	5	7
stow	8	3	-

36F3.0	A	B	C
hide	2	3	K
disguise	4	3	4
conceal	5	3	6
camouflage	6	4	8
ensconce	10	-	-

SUPER CLUSTER

37. Disease/Health

37A Disease

37A1.0	A	B	C
disease	5	3	4
sickness	5	3	6
symptom	5	4	7
illness	6	3	5
infection	6	5	6
injury	6	3	8
ailment	8	-	-

malady	8	6	-
palsy	8	8	-

37A1.1	A	B	C
ill	3	3	3
sick	3	3	3
contagious	4	4	-
seasick	4	4	-
stricken	5	3	8
allergic	8	-	8
bedridden	8	-	-
infirm	8	8	-
morbid	8	-	-

37A2.0	A	B	C
epidemic	5	4	4
plague	5	3	-
famine	6	4	7

37A3.0	A	B	C
well	2	3	K
healthful	5	3	9
hale	6	6	-
robust	6	3	-
sane	6	7	-
wholesome	6	6	6
salubrious	13	7	-

37A3.1	A	B	C
condition	4	3	4
health	4	3	3
sanity	6	7	-

37B Specific Diseases/Ailments

37B1.0	A	B	C
cold	1	3	K
mumps	3	3	-
cancer	5	5	7
croup	5	-	-
polio	5	3	-
rabies	5	3	-
scurvy	5	4	-
beriberi	6	5	-
diphtheria	6	3	-
influenza	6	4	-
malaria	6	3	-
smallpox	6	3	11
tuberculosis	6	3	-
lockjaw	8	-	-
rickets	8	4	-
ringworm	8	-	-
gout	10	6	-

37B2.0	A	B	C
blindness	5	5	-
starvation	6	3	5
eyestrain	8	7	-
hangover	8	-	-
sunstroke	8	-	-
shell shock	10	-	-

37B3.0	A	B	C
blind	4	3	4
deaf	4	3	3
lame	4	3	-
mute	5	3	-

37C Symptoms of Diseases

37C1.0	A	B	C
ache	3	3	2
pain	3	3	2
itch	4	3	4
earache	5	-	-
fever	5	3	7
headache	5	4	6
toothache	5	6	5
coma	6	7	7
exhaustion	6	3	9
nausea	6	5	-
pang	6	6	-
twinge	6	7	-
vomit	6	7	-
weariness	6	4	6
agony	8	4	-
paroxysm	8	7	-
regurgitate	8	-	-
wretch	8	-	-
lassitude	10	-	-

37C1.1	A	B	C
fatigue	6	4	6
impair	6	5	7
ail	8	-	-
constipate	10	-	-
excruciate	10	-	-
languish	10	-	7

37C2.0	A	B	C
dizzy	4	3	4
numb	4	3	4
raw	4	3	5
sore	4	3	4
exhausted	5	3	5
groggy	5	4	-
delirious	6	4	7

feverish	6	5	-
bloodshot	8	7	-

37D Specific Types of Germs/Genes

37D1.0	A	B	C
germ	3	3	5
bacteria	5	3	5
virus	5	3	9
microbe	6	3	-
organism	6	4	5

37D1.1	A	B	C
septic	6	5	-

37E Actions Related to Injury/Disease

37E1.0	A	B	C
burn	2	3	2
sunburn	3	3	8
wound	3	3	9
blister	5	5	-
frostbite	5	-	-
scab	5	7	-
whiplash	5	-	-
abscess	6	-	-
concussion	6	-	-
fester	6	-	-
gash	6	5	-
venom	6	7	9
welt	6	-	-
deathblow	8	-	-
lesion	8	-	-
ulcer	8	9	-

37E2.0	A	B	C
poison	4	3	4
sprain	4	-	-
cripple	6	6	-
infect	6	7	-
paralyze	6	3	-
convulse	8	-	-
recrudesce	13	-	-

37F Medicine

37F1.0	A	B	C
check-up	3	3	-
operation	5	3	7
surgery	5	4	7
treatment	5	4	5
vaccination	5	3	-
remedy	6	5	7

therapy	6	5	9
transfusion	6	7	-
autopsy	8	-	-
suture	8	6	-

37F1.1	A	B	C
operate	4	3	4
diagnose	5	5	5
transplant	5	7	11
dissect	6	6	8
inoculate	6	-	-
abort	8	-	-
circumcise	10	-	-

37F2.0	A	B	C
medicine	2	3	4
drug	3	3	3
aspirin	4	3	3
iodine	4	3	9
pill	4	4	4
antibiotics	5	4	9
antidote	5	-	4
ointment	5	3	9
penicillin	5	3	4
potion	5	4	-
prescription	5	5	-
vaccine	5	3	-
vitamin	5	5	4
dose	6	4	-
narcotic	6	7	-
serum	6	3	-
tonic	6	5	6
balm	8	-	-
liniment	8	-	-
poultice	8	7	-
tranquilizer	8	-	-
anodyne	10	-	-
salve	10	-	-
unction	10	-	-
unguent	10	-	-
panacea	13	-	-

37F3.0	A	B	C
bandage	4	3	5
cast	4	3	K
sling	4	3	-
crutch	5	3	-
splint	6	3	-

---

38. Light

38A Light/Lightness

38A1.0

	A	B	C
lamplight	3	4	-
moonlight	3	3	2
sunlight	3	3	3
sunshine	3	3	2
daylight	4	3	4
candlelight	5	4	-
firelight	5	4	7
starlight	5	4	-

38A2.0

	A	B	C
gleam	5	4	2
gloss	5	3	-
glimmer	6	7	-
glint	6	4	-
luster	6	3	-
sheen	6	3	-

38A3.0

	A	B	C
light	1	3	K
brightness	4	3	3
lightness	5	4	-
wavelength	5	4	-
aura	8	7	8
corona	8	6	-
afterglow	10	-	-

38A4.0

	A	B	C
bright	2	3	K
clear	3	3	2
shiny	3	3	2
brilliant	5	3	4
radiant	5	4	9
vivid	5	4	10
luminous	6	3	-
lucid	8	8	-
candescent	10	-	-
lambent	10	-	-

38B Actions of Light

38B1.0

	A	B	C
flash	3	3	2
shine	3	3	2
sparkle	3	3	6
glisten	4	4	5
glitter	4	3	3
glow	4	3	5
twinkle	4	3	5
dazzle	5	4	-
radiate	5	4	6
shimmer	5	9	-

38B2.0

	A	B	C
brighten	5	3	-
lighten	5	3	4
reflect	5	3	4
illuminate	6	5	-
illumine	8	-	-

38C Darkness

38C1.0

	A	B	C
darkness	3	3	4
shade	3	3	2
shadow	3	3	5
gloom	4	3	5
haze	5	3	5
halftone	8	9	-
umbra	8	4	-

38C1.1

	A	B	C
dark	1	3	K
shady	4	3	5
somber	5	3	7

38C2.0

	A	B	C
blot	3	3	2
darken	4	3	5
fade	4	3	-
blur	5	3	-
blacken	6	3	-
splotch	6	-	-
blear	8	-	-
pall	10	7	-

38D Producers of Light

38D1.0

	A	B	C
flare	4	3	11
torch	4	3	-
beacon	5	3	6
torchlight	5	5	-

38D2.0

	A	B	C
candle	2	3	K
candlestick	4	7	-

38D3.0

	A	B	C
light	1	3	K
lamp	2	3	K
flashlight	3	3	6
lantern	4	3	7
lamppost	5	3	-
searchlight	6	6	-

| skylight | 6 | - | - |
| gaslight | 8 | - | - |

38D4.0	A	B	C
bulb	4	3	5
lightbulb	5	-	-
filament	6	3	12

38D5.0	A	B	C
beam	3	3	3
moonbeam	4	3	-
ray	4	3	K
sunbeam	4	-	-
laser	6	6	7
sunspot	6	6	9

38E Clarity

38E1.0	A	B	C
clarity	6	5	9

38E1.1	A	B	C
transparent	6	3	5
limpid	8	5	-
vitreous	8	-	-

38E2.0	A	B	C
dim	3	3	4
dull	3	3	3
faint	3	3	3
pale	3	3	3
drab	4	4	9
fuzzy	4	3	3
murky	5	5	-
indefinite	6	3	-
opaque	6	3	6
vague	6	4	6
diaphanous	10	-	-
lackluster	10	-	-
nebulous	10	-	8

SUPER CLUSTER

39. Causality

39A Causality

39A1.0	A	B	C
effect	4	3	5
result	4	3	4
conclusion	5	3	7
outcome	5	4	7
aftereffect	6	-	-
consequence	6	4	-
impact	6	3	9

| upshot | 8 | - | - |
| denouement | 13 | - | - |

39A2.0	A	B	C
cause	3	3	2
reason	3	3	2
purpose	4	3	3
intent	5	3	7
stimulus	5	4	5
agent	5	3	5
incentive	6	4	11
motive	6	4	7
impetus	10	5	10

39A3.0	A	B	C
stimulate	5	4	9
initiate	6	7	8
spearhead	6	4	-
engender	8	-	-
entail	8	K	-
innovate	8	-	-

39A4.0	A	B	C
change	3	3	2
vary	4	3	7
affect	5	3	5
impress	5	4	7
influence	5	3	4
induce	6	7	11
redound	10	-	-

39B Causality (Relationship Markers)

39B1.0	A	B	C
for	K	3	K
from	K	3	K
so	K	3	1
to	K	3	K
by	K	3	K
because	1	3	K
since	2	3	3
because of	4	-	-
in that	4	-	-
so that	4	-	-
hereby	5	3	-
hereupon	5	-	-
herewith	5	-	-
whereas	5	3	9
whereby	5	5	-
for as much	6	-	-
for the fact that	6	-	-
herein	6	-	-
on account of	6	-	-

A: Grade level; B: Earliest Grade of Occurrence in Textbooks; C: Earliest Grade of Occurrence on Standardized Tests.

therefrom	6	-	-
wherefore	6	7	-

39B2.0	A	B	C
therefore	4	3	4
thus	4	3	6
accordingly	5	3	5
as a consequence	5	-	-
as a result	5	-	-
for all that	5	-	-
lest	5	3	-
thereby	5	4	-
consequently	6	5	7
hence	6	3	7
whereupon	6	5	-

39B3.0	A	B	C
then	K	3	K
else	1	3	K
in that case	4	-	-
wherewith	6	-	-

39B4.0	A	B	C
if	1	3	K
until...then	3	-	-
when...then	3	-	-
where...there	3	-	-
if only	4	-	-
if...then	4	5	-
now that	4	-	-

SUPER CLUSTER
40. Weather

40A Weather/Nature (General)

40A1.0	A	B	C
weather	3	3	3
climate	4	3	3

40A2.0	A	B	C
nature	4	3	3
environment	5	3	4

40A3.0	A	B	C
air	2	3	K
atmosphere	4	3	5
atmospheric	5	3	11

40B Storms/Wind

40B1.0	A	B	C
snowstorm	3	3	7
storm	3	3	2
blizzard	4	3	5
hailstorm	4	7	-

40B2.0	A	B	C
downpour	4	4	6
rainstorm	4	3	-
thundershower	4	4	-
cloudburst	5	6	-
monsoon	6	5	-
torrent	6	3	-

40B3.0	A	B	C
wind	2	3	1
breeze	3	3	2
sandstorm	4	4	-
twister	4	4	-
whirlwind	4	3	-
windstorm	4	3	-
cyclone	5	4	-
gale	5	4	5
gust	5	3	4
hurricane	5	3	4
squall	5	3	-
tempest	5	4	-
tornado	5	3	4
chinook	6	-	-
typhoon	6	7	-
zephyr	8	-	-
sirocco	10	-	-

40B4.0	A	B	C
lightning	3	3	6
thunder	3	3	3
thunderstorm	4	3	5
thunderbolt	5	3	-
thunderclap	6	-	6

40C Clouds

40C1.0	A	B	C
cloud	3	3	K
cirrus	4	3	-
cumulus	4	3	-
thundercloud	4	-	-
cirrocumulus	5	-	-
cirrostratus	5	-	-
cumulonimbus	5	6	-
thunderhead	5	3	-

40D Natural Catastrophes

40D1.0	A	B	C
drought	4	3	5
earthquake	4	3	3
flood	4	3	4

	A	B	C
avalanche	5	5	5
landslide	5	4	-
blight	6	5	-

40D1.1	A	B	C
diluvial	13	-	-

40D2.0	A	B	C
disaster	4	3	5
emergency	4	3	7
catastrophe	5	4	-
tragedy	5	3	6
calamity	6	7	7
crisis	6	5	6
ordeal	6	4	11
doomsday	8	6	-
cataclysm	10	-	-

40D2.1	A	B	C
disastrous	6	5	7

40E Characteristics of Weather

40E1.0	A	B	C
dry	1	3	1
foggy	3	3	3
sunny	3	3	3
icy	4	3	K
muggy	4	4	-
overcast	5	3	7
wintry	5	3	-
arid	6	3	11
sultry	6	4	-

SUPER CLUSTER
41. Cleanliness/Uncleanliness

41A Filth/Uncleanliness

41A1.0	A	B	C
garbage	3	3	4
trash	3	3	4
wastebasket	3	3	-
junk	4	3	4
junkyard	4	3	-
litter	4	3	2
pollution	4	4	3
slop	4	3	-
wastepaper	4	4	-
clutter	5	3	8
filth	5	3	5
grime	5	3	8
rubbish	5	3	4

	A	B	C
sewage	5	3	-
debris	6	3	8
eyesore	6	6	-
impurity	6	3	-
dregs	8	-	-
sludge	8	5	-
offal	13	-	-
ordure	13	-	-

41A1.1	A	B	C
pollute	4	5	4
infect	5	7	-
contaminate	6	-	7
infest	8	7	-
taint	8	7	-
adulterate	10	-	-
vitiate	10	-	-

41A2.0	A	B	C
smear	4	-	-
smudge	4	4	-
streak	4	3	8
bloodstain	5	-	-
darken	5	3	5
blacken	6	3	-
daub	6	-	-
defile	6	5	-
dishevel	8	-	-
tousle	8	-	-
besmirch	10	-	-

41A3.0	A	B	C
dirty	2	3	1
muddy	3	3	3
foul	4	3	7
nasty	4	3	7
bleak	5	3	4
dismal	5	4	4
dreary	5	3	6
filthy	5	3	11
dingy	6	6	6
sordid	8	7	-
squalid	8	6	-
frowsy	10	-	-

41B Cleanliness

41B1.0	A	B	C
haircut	2	3	2
wash	2	3	K
clean	3	3	1
scrub	3	3	3
sweep	3	3	2
wipe	3	3	3
bathe	4	3	-
clean-up	4	3	-

	A	B	C
polish	4	3	4
rinse	4	3	5
shoeshine	4	4	-
wax	4	3	3
whitewash	4	3	-
buff	5	3	11
launder	5	5	-
manicure	5	7	-
turnout	5	3	-
preen	6	4	-
scour	6	6	-
swab	6	-	-
burnish	8	-	-
douche	8	-	-
lave	10	-	-
ablution	13	-	-

41B2.0	A	B	C
sanitary	5	3	-
sterile	5	5	11
hygiene	6	5	7
immaculate	6	7	-

41B2.1	A	B	C
cleanliness	5	3	-
sanitation	6	5	-
consecrate	8	7	-

41B3.0	A	B	C
draft	5	3	5
filter	5	3	5
pasteurize	5	-	-
purify	5	4	7
strain	5	3	5
purge	6	7	-
sterilize	6	6	11

41C Tools for Cleaning

41C1.0	A	B	C
broom	3	3	K
brush	3	3	2
cleaner	3	3	3
mop	3	3	3
broomstick	4	4	-
washboard	4	4	-
vacuum	5	3	11

41C2.0	A	B	C
soap	3	3	2
detergent	4	3	11
lotion	4	3	8
shampoo	4	8	4
lather	5	3	-
lye	5	4	-
soapsuds	5	8	-

	A	B	C
suds	5	5	-
bleach	6	3	-

41C3.0	A	B	C
toothbrush	4	3	6
toothpaste	4	3	4
toothpick	4	3	4
floss	5	-	-

SUPER CLUSTER
42. Popularity/Familiarity

42A Popularity/Familiarity

42A1.0	A	B	C
familiar	3	3	4
famous	3	3	3
popular	4	3	3
public	4	3	3
legendary	6	3	6
prominent	6	3	7
cosmopolitan	8	5	-
eminent	8	5	-
prestigious	8	7	-

42A2.0	A	B	C
common	3	3	4
usual	3	3	3
ordinary	4	3	6
regular	4	3	4
commonplace	5	3	-
normal	5	3	5
traditional	5	3	5
typical	5	3	5
widespread	5	3	11
accustomed	6	3	6
customary	6	4	9
mainstream	6	3	-
norm	6	7	-
par	6	5	-
pedestrian	6	7	9
standard	6	3	5
universal	6	4	12
catholic	8	3	11
demotic	8	-	-
generic	8	5	-
humdrum	8	7	-
mediocre	8	7	9
mundane	8	9	9
orthodox	8	6	-
banal	10	-	-

42A2.1	A	B	C
patent	4	4	9
obvious	5	3	5

A: Grade level; B: Earliest Grade of Occurrence in Textbooks; C: Earliest Grade of Occurrence on Standardized Tests.

	A	B	C
conspicuous	6	5	9
evident	6	3	7
blatant	8	7	-
manifest	8	7	-
egregious	10	-	-
flagrant	10	6	-

42A3.0	A	B	C
honor	3	3	3
fame	4	3	4
appeal	5	3	7
attraction	5	3	6
dignity	5	3	7
glory	5	3	9
recognition	5	3	9
limelight	6	7	-
repute	6	-	-
renown	8	7	-
éclat	10	-	-

42A4.0	A	B	C
scandal	8	8	-
ignominy	10	-	-
obloquy	13	7	-
opprobrium	13	-	-

42B Lack of Popularity/Familiarity

42B1.0	A	B	C
privacy	6	4	7
secrecy	6	4	9
solitude	6	5	6
stealth	8	7	-

42B2.0	A	B	C
secret	3	3	2
private	4	3	5
unfamiliar	4	3	6
unknown	4	3	4
anonymous	6	6	6
undiscovered	6	7	7
incognito	8	-	-
intimate	8	7	-
latent	8	5	-
privy	8	7	-
ulterior	8	-	-
furtive	10	-	-
parochial	10	-	-
clandestine	13	-	-
esoteric	13	7	-
recondite	13	-	-
surreptitious	13	-	-

42C Likelihood

42C1.0	A	B	C
sure	1	3	1
likely	2	3	2
certain	3	3	3
definite	4	3	3
absolute	5	3	6

42C2.0	A	B	C
possible	2	3	4
probable	5	4	5
contingent	6	4	-
liable	6	5	7
feasible	10	6	10

42C3.0	A	B	C
indefinite	3	3	-
unlikely	3	3	6
doubtful	4	3	4
mysterious	4	3	2
uncertain	5	3	4
ambiguous	6	8	-
equivocal	10	-	8

42C4.0	A	B	C
chance	2	3	1
accidental	5	5	2
doom	5	5	5
hazard	5	4	5
casual	6	4	-
jinx	6	7	-
random	6	3	9
desultory	13	-	-

42C5.0	A	B	C
bet	3	3	3
bid	4	3	4
stake	5	3	5
gamble	6	4	-
venture	6	4	9

42C6.0	A	B	C
luck	2	3	3
fate	5	3	6
fluke	5	5	-
miracle	5	4	4
boon	6	3	-

A: Grade level; B: Earliest Grade of Occurrence in Textbooks; C: Earliest Grade of Occurrence on Standardized Tests.

43. Physical Traits of People

43A Physical Traits

43A1.0	A	B	C
athletic	4	3	5
muscular	5	4	7
rugged	5	3	6
thickset	8	-	-
virile	8	5	-

43A2.0	A	B	C
strong	2	3	1
powerful	4	3	4
potent	6	5	-
powerhouse	6	4	-
stalwart	8	4	-
puissant	10	-	-

43A3.0	A	B	C
might	2	3	K
power	2	3	2
beauty	3	3	3
health	4	3	3
strength	4	3	3
vigor	5	4	-
agility	6	6	12
brawn	6	6	-
gusto	6	6	-
dexterity	8	6	11

43A4.0	A	B	C
awkward	4	3	5
clumsy	4	3	2
gawky	6	6	-
gangling	8	-	-
ungainly	8	5	-

43A5.0	A	B	C
nimble	3	3	-
agile	6	5	7
graceful	6	3	6
spry	6	3	9

43A6.0	A	B	C
weak	3	3	3
frail	5	3	4
puny	5	5	-
rawboned	5	4	-
rickety	5	3	7
scrawny	5	4	-
feeble	6	3	6
gaunt	6	5	-
decrepit	10	-	9
flaccid	10	7	-

43A6.1	A	B	C
handicap	5	4	8
weakness	6	4	9
debility	10	-	-

43B Neatness

43B1.0	A	B	C
messy	4	3	2
sloppy	5	5	4
tangle	5	3	5
windblown	6	5	-
slipshod	8	-	-
sloven	10	-	-

43B2.0	A	B	C
neat	3	3	2
tidy	5	3	-
prim	6	6	-
shipshape	6	6	-
dapper	8	-	-
meticulous	10	6	-

43C Attractiveness

43C1.0	A	B	C
beautiful	2	3	2
lovely	2	3	3
pretty	2	3	K
cute	3	3	4
handsome	3	3	4
sightly	4	-	-
attractive	5	3	5
bonny	5	3	-
comely	6	3	-
exquisite	6	3	9
buxom	8	-	-
voluptuous	10	-	-

43C2.0	A	B	C
elegant	4	3	4
adorable	5	5	5
formal	5	3	5
classic	6	3	9
gorgeous	6	4	7
majestic	6	4	9
sleek	6	3	8

43C3.0	A	B	C
ugly	2	3	2
homely	5	4	-
unattractive	5	4	-
hideous	6	3	-

A: Grade level; B: Earliest Grade of Occurrence in Textbooks; C: Earliest Grade of Occurrence on Standardized Tests.

43D Size as a Physical Trait

43D1.0	A	B	C
lean	3	3	3
scarecrow	3	3	4
skinny	4	3	7
slender	4	3	4
slight	4	3	4
slim	4	3	4
lanky	6	3	-
scrag	6	-	-

43D1.1	A	B	C
dainty	6	3	-
mignon	8	-	-

43D2.0	A	B	C
fat	1	3	K
heavy	2	3	2
husky	3	3	6
chubby	4	3	-
plump	4	3	5
flabby	5	5	-
pudgy	5	3	-
burly	6	7	-
stout	6	3	11
obese	8	8	-
portly	8	7	-
rotund	8	-	-

43D2.1	A	B	C
potbelly	6	-	-
paunch	8	-	-

SUPER CLUSTER

44. Touching/Grabbing Actions

44A Feeling/Striking Actions

44A1.0	A	B	C
feel	2	3	1
touch	3	3	2
stroke	4	3	5
grope	5	3	-
caress	6	7	-
fondle	6	-	-
knead	6	7	-
massage	6	5	-

44A2.0	A	B	C
pat	2	3	1
tap	3	3	3
tickle	3	3	K
dab	4	4	4
nudge	4	3	-
spur	4	3	7
butt	5	3	9
jab	5	3	-
rap	5	4	5
prod	6	-	-
goad	10	-	-

44A3.0	A	B	C
hit	2	3	1
beat	3	3	1
knock	3	3	2
pound	3	3	4
slap	3	3	3
spank	3	3	-
strike	3	3	3
lash	4	4	-
punch	4	3	4
smack	4	3	-
whack	4	3	-
wham	4	3	-
buffet	5	7	4
lob	5	3	-
thrash	5	5	-
whop	5	3	-
putt	6	6	-
wallop	6	-	-
clout	8	7	-
drub	8	-	-
flail	8	7	-
maul	8	8	-
smite	8	7	-
thwack	8	-	-
bastinado	10	-	-
ferule	10	-	-
pummel	10	-	-
bludgeon	13	3	-

44B Grabbing/Holding Actions

44B1.0	A	B	C
catch	2	3	K
hold	2	3	K
grab	3	3	5
squeeze	3	3	3
clasp	4	3	-
clutch	4	3	-
grip	4	3	-
nab	4	-	-
clench	5	4	-
grasp	5	3	6
secure	5	3	5
wring	5	4	-
clinch	6	-	-

vise	6	3	-
grapple	8	7	-

44B2.0	A	B	C
pick	1	3	1
pinch	4	3	9
strum	4	3	-
tweeze	5	-	-
nip	6	5	-
pluck	6	3	-
thrum	8	-	-

44B3.0	A	B	C
hug	2	3	1
wrap	3	3	3
cling	4	3	9
cuddle	4	-	-
nuzzle	4	-	-
embrace	5	3	3
snuggle	5	3	4
dandle	10	-	-

44C Specific Actions Done with the Hands

44C1.0	A	B	C
point	2	3	K
wave	2	3	1
clap	3	3	3
fumble	4	3	-
shrug	4	3	-
handshake	5	4	-
salute	5	3	6
wield	5	5	-
gesture	8	3	8

SUPER CLUSTER

45. Pronouns

45A Pronouns and Reflexive Pronouns

45A1.0	A	B	C
he	K	3	K
I	K	3	K
it	K	3	K
me	K	3	K
she	K	3	K
them	K	3	-
they	K	3	K
we	K	3	K
you	K	3	K
him	1	3	K
us	1	3	1

	A	B	C
herself	2	3	2
himself	2	3	2
yourself	2	3	2
itself	3	3	3
ourselves	3	3	3
themselves	3	3	3
thee	4	3	-
thou	4	3	-
thy	4	3	4
thyself	4	3	11
oneself	6	4	10

45B Possessive Pronouns

45B1.0	A	B	C
its	K	3	K
my	K	3	1
your	K	3	K
yours	K	3	2
her	1	3	K
his	1	3	K
our	1	3	1
their	1	3	K
hers	2	3	2
mine	2	3	2
ours	2	3	2
theirs	2	3	2

45C Relative Pronouns

45C1.0	A	B	C
that	K	3	K
who	K	3	K
which	1	3	2
whom	3	3	3

45D Interrogative Pronouns

45D1.0	A	B	C
what	K	3	K
when	1	3	K
where	1	3	K
which	1	3	2
whose	3	3	3
whatever	4	3	6
whichever	4	3	-
whomever	6	6	-
whatsoever	8	7	-

45E Indefinite Pronouns

45E1.0	A	B	C
everyone	1	3	K
no one	1	-	-
nothing	1	3	2

A: Grade level; B: Earliest Grade of Occurrence in Textbooks; C: Earliest Grade of Occurrence on Standardized Tests.

some	1	3	K
any	2	3	1
anyone	2	3	3
anything	2	3	K
each	2	3	K
enough	2	3	1
everything	2	3	2
someone	2	3	2
something	2	3	1
anybody	3	3	9
everybody	3	3	3
nobody	3	3	3
somebody	3	3	7
whoever	4	3	5
whomsoever	5	-	-

45F Interrogative/Indefinite Adverbs

45F1.0	A	B	C
how	1	3	K
why	1	3	1
somehow	2	3	7
whenever	4	3	4
wherever	4	3	9
someway	5	4	-
whensoever	6	-	-

SUPER CLUSTER

46. Contractions

46A Contractions (Not)

46A1.0	A	B	C
can't	1	3	3
don't	1	3	K
won't	1	3	2
couldn't	2	3	K
haven't	3	3	3
isn't	3	3	5
shouldn't	3	3	3
weren't	3	3	K
aren't	4	3	3
doesn't	4	3	3
hadn't	4	3	3
hasn't	4	3	3
wasn't	4	3	2
wouldn't	4	3	2
ain't	5	3	-
mustn't	5	3	-

46B Contractions (Have)

46B1.0	A	B	C
I've	2	3	3
you've	2	3	2
they've	3	3	5
we've	3	3	3

46C Contractions (Will)

46C1.0	A	B	C
I'll	1	3	1
we'll	2	3	2
you'll	2	3	2
he'll	3	3	2
she'll	3	3	11
they'll	3	3	6
what'll	3	3	-
there'll	4	3	5

46D Contractions (Is)

46D1.0	A	B	C
he's	2	3	2
how's	2	3	-
I'm	2	3	1
it's	2	3	1
she's	2	3	2
that's	2	3	K
there's	3	3	3
'tis	4	-	-
here's	4	3	4
what's	4	3	4
where's	4	3	5

46E Contractions (Would)

46E1.0	A	B	C
I'd	2	3	2
he'd	3	3	K
she'd	3	3	3
they'd	3	3	K
you'd	3	3	2

46F Contractions (Are)

46F1.0	A	B	C
we're	2	3	2
you're	2	3	2
they're	3	3	3

47. Entertainment/The Arts

47A Plays/Movies

47A1.0	A	B	C
act	2	3	2
performance	4	3	4
program	4	3	3
scene	4	3	4
matinee	6	-	7
rehearsal	6	4	5

47A1.1	A	B	C
tryout	4	3	11
perform	5	3	3
audition	6	-	-

47A2.0	A	B	C
show	1	3	1
cartoon	3	4	5
drama	4	3	7
film	4	3	5
movie	4	3	1
comedy	5	5	7
preview	5	5	5
skit	5	5	6
cinema	6	6	-
newsreel	6	-	-
radiobroadcast	6	-	-
vaudeville	6	5	-
burlesque	8	7	-

47A2.1	A	B	C
playgoer	8	-	-

47A3.0	A	B	C
plot	4	3	6
setting	4	3	4
climax	6	4	8
epilogue	8	-	9
protagonist	13	5	-

47A4.0	A	B	C
scenery	4	3	5
stage	4	3	3
background	4	3	4
backstage	5	4	-
offstage	5	5	-
coulisse	13	-	-

47B Music/Dance

47B1.0	A	B	C
music	3	3	2
rhythm	3	3	9
tune	3	3	6
chord	4	3	4
melody	4	3	-
treble	4	3	-
octave	5	3	-
jazz	6	-	6
stave	6	6	-
unison	6	3	-
cadence	8	7	-
ragtime	8	6	9
riff	10	-	-
descant	10	3	-
euphony	13	-	-

47B1.1	A	B	C
musical	5	3	5
dulcet	10	-	-
mellifluous	13	-	-

47B2.0	A	B	C
concert	4	3	5
orchestra	4	3	5
opera	5	3	8
symphony	6	3	5

47B3.0	A	B	C
ballet	2	3	7
dance	2	3	1
jig	4	3	5
polka	4	3	12
waltz	4	3	-
minuet	5	3	-
choreography	8	7	-
rhumba	8	-	-
tango	8	7	-
arabesque	10	-	-
quadrille	13	-	-

47B4.0	A	B	C
solo	4	3	8
duet	5	4	-

47B5.0	A	B	C
conduct	6	3	12
synchronize	8	-	-

47C Instruments

47C1.0	A	B	C
drum	3	3	1
piano	3	3	3
accordion	4	3	-
cymbal	4	3	-
keyboard	4	3	-
organ	4	3	12
percussion	4	3	-

tambourine	4	3	-
tom-tom	4	3	-
xylophone	4	3	3
castanets	5	4	-
glockenspiel	6	4	-
kettledrum	6	6	-
spinet	6	4	-
tabor	8	6	-

47C2.0	A	B	C
fife	3	3	-
clarinet	4	3	8
flute	4	3	3
oboe	4	3	-
piccolo	4	4	-
saxophone	4	4	-
trombone	4	3	3
tuba	4	3	8
alto	5	4	-
bagpipe	5	3	-
bugle	5	4	-
cornet	5	4	-
recorder	5	3	6
trumpet	5	3	5
hornpipe	8	-	-
panpipe	8	-	-

47C2.1	A	B	C
mouthpiece	5	3	-
woodwind	5	3	5

47C3.0	A	B	C
guitar	3	3	3
harp	3	3	3
ukulele	3	-	-
violin	3	3	3
banjo	4	3	-
cello	4	3	-
fiddle	5	3	-
viola	5	3	-
lute	6	6	-
lyre	6	5	-
mandolin	6	5	-

47C3.1	A	B	C
tuning fork	6	-	-

47D Art

47D1.0	A	B	C
painting	1	3	1
art	3	3	3

photography	5	3	5
woodcraft	6	-	-

47D2.0	A	B	C
picture	1	3	1
album	3	3	5
photo	4	3	7
mural	5	4	6
photograph	5	3	6
portrait	5	3	6
snapshot	5	3	-
mosaic	6	6	-
caricature	8	5	-
tattoo	8	4	7
woodcut	8	-	9
fresco	10	-	-
lithograph	10	7	-
tableau	10	-	-
tintype	10	-	-
vignette	10	3	-

47D3.0	A	B	C
statue	3	3	3
sculpture	5	3	6
waxwork	8	-	-

SUPER CLUSTER

48. Walking/Running Actions

48A Running/Walking Actions

48A1.0	A	B	C
run	K	3	K
dance	2	3	1
trot	2	3	5
skip	3	3	9
lope	4	4	7
scamper	4	3	-
jog	5	5	5
romp	5	5	5
footwork	6	5	-
frisk	6	-	-
prance	6	3	-
ramble	6	-	-
gambol	8	8	-
cavort	10	-	-

48A2.0	A	B	C
walk	1	3	1
march	2	3	2
step	2	3	1
tiptoe	3	3	9
hike	4	3	3
stride	4	3	-
stroll	4	3	8

	A	B	C
amble	5	4	9
pace	5	3	6
plod	5	3	-
promenade	5	3	-
strut	5	5	-
swagger	5	4	-
trudge	5	5	4
gait	6	3	9
toddle	6	6	-
tread	6	7	6
saunter	8	-	-

48A3.0	A	B	C
limp	4	3	4
shuffle	4	3	-
stumble	4	3	4
waddle	4	3	-
hobble	5	3	-
shamble	5	5	-
stagger	5	4	-

48B Lurking/Creeping

48B1.0	A	B	C
crawl	3	3	3
creep	3	3	3
slink	5	4	-
grovel	8	-	-

48B2.0	A	B	C
prowl	4	3	5
sneak	4	3	3
lurk	6	7	-
slither	6	6	-
skulk	8	-	-

48C Kicking

48C1.0	A	B	C
stamp	2	3	K
kick	3	3	2
tramp	4	3	-
stomp	5	3	-
trample	6	3	11
punt	10	-	-

48D Jumping

48D1.0	A	B	C
hop	1	3	1
jump	1	3	K
spring	2	3	K
leap	4	3	2
lurch	4	4	-
coil	5	3	-

	A	B	C
lunge	5	3	-
pounce	5	3	-
bound	6	3	6
caper	10	3	-

48E Standing/Stationary Actions

48E1.0	A	B	C
stand	2	3	1
pose	6	3	8
straddle	6	7	-
curtsy	8	7	-
recline	8	7	-
genuflect	10	-	-

48E2.0	A	B	C
bowlegged	4	-	-
prone	6	5	11
recumbent	10	6	-
supine	10	-	-
akimbo	13	-	-
couchant	13	-	-

48E2.1	A	B	C
posture	4	3	7

SUPER CLUSTER

49. Mathematics

49A Branches of Mathematics

49A1.0	A	B	C
arithmetic	3	3	3
math	4	3	4
mathematics	4	3	1
algebra	5	5	12
geometry	5	3	11
trigonometry	6	5	-

49A1.1	A	B	C
abacus	8	3	9

49B Mathematical Quantities

49B1.0	A	B	C
maximum	6	4	9
minimum	6	4	8

49B2.0	A	B	C
average	4	3	3
fraction	4	3	3
sum	4	3	4
total	4	3	5
gross	5	3	9
percent	5	3	5

median	6	5	10
multiple	6	3	5
percentage	6	3	3
proportion	6	3	6
ratio	6	6	4
sine	6	-	-

49C Mathematical Terms

49C1.0	A	B	C
equation	5	3	7
formula	5	3	4

49C2.0	A	B	C
addend	3	3	-
denominator	3	4	6
numerator	3	4	-
quotient	4	3	-
exponent	4	4	-
pi	8	3	7

49D Mathematical Operation

49D1.0	A	B	C
addition	3	3	4
subtraction	3	3	7
division	4	3	7
multiplication	4	3	7

49D1.1	A	B	C
divisible	5	4	6

49D1.2	A	B	C
add	1	3	1
count	2	3	2
minus	2	3	11
plus	2	3	6
subtract	2	3	1
divide	4	3	3
multiply	4	3	3
tally	6	5	8

49D2.0	A	B	C
times	3	3	2
per	4	3	4

49D2.1	A	B	C
quadruple	8	7	11

50. Auxiliary/Helping Verbs

50A Auxiliary Verbs

50A1.0	A	B	C
am	K	3	1
are	K	3	K
is	K	3	K
be	1	3	K
been	1	3	K
was	1	3	K
were	1	3	K
being	3	3	3

50B Primary Auxiliaries

50B1.0	A	B	C
did	K	3	K
do	K	3	K
does	1	3	1
doing	1	3	1
done	2	3	K

50B2.0	A	B	C
had	1	3	K
has	1	3	K
have	1	3	K

50C Modals

50C1.0	A	B	C
can	K	3	K
will	K	3	K
could	1	3	K
may	1	3	1
might	1	3	K
must	1	3	1
should	1	3	3
would	1	3	K
cannot	2	3	1
shall	2	3	2
ought	3	3	3
used to	4	-	-

50D Semi-auxiliaries

50D1.0	A	B	C
get to	2	-	-
had better	2	-	-
is going to	2	-	-
have to	3	-	-
is certain to	3	-	-
is sure to	3	-	-
seems to	3	-	-

had best	4	-	-
is bound to	6	-	-
is apt to	8	-	-
is liable to	8	-	-

50E Linking Verbs

50E1.0	A	B	C
seem	2	3	3
appear	3	3	3
become	3	3	3
remain	3	3	1
becoming	4	3	4

SUPER CLUSTER

51. Events

51A Dates/Events (General)

51A1.0	A	B	C
affair	4	3	7
event	4	3	4
experience	4	3	4
happening	4	3	3
development	4	3	7
incident	5	3	5
occasion	5	3	5
instance	5	3	6
occurrence	6	5	-
prodigy	10	7	9

51A2.0	A	B	C
attempt	5	3	5
deed	5	3	11
project	5	3	4
enterprise	6	3	9
feat	6	3	7

51A3.0	A	B	C
condition	4	3	4
situation	4	3	6
environment	5	3	4
circumstance	6	6	9
context	6	3	-

51B Festive/Recreational Events

51B1.0	A	B	C
vacation	3	3	3
holiday	4	3	3
honeymoon	5	4	-
pastime	5	3	9
leisure	6	3	7
sabbatical	10	-	-

51B2.0	A	B	C
birthday	1	3	1
party	1	3	1
tea party	3	-	-
anniversary	4	4	5
celebration	4	3	4
festival	4	3	5
ceremony	5	3	4
bazaar	6	4	6
debut	6	6	-
graduation	6	3	6
gala	8	3	-
inauguration	8	5	7
prom	8	9	-
rite	8	6	-
soiree	10	-	-
bacchanal	13	-	-

51B3.0	A	B	C
parade	2	3	K
pageant	3	3	6
caravan	5	4	4
procession	5	3	5
fanfare	8	5	-
motorcade	8	7	-
pomp	8	6	-
cortege	13	-	-

51B4.0	A	B	C
circus	2	3	1
fair	2	3	2
rodeo	3	3	3
carnival	4	3	3
bullfight	5	4	-

51B5.0	A	B	C
amusement	4	3	3
entertainment	5	3	4

51C Political Events

51C1.0	A	B	C
election	5	3	3
campaign	6	3	5
crusade	8	5	9

51C2.0	A	B	C
vote	4	3	3
elect	5	3	5
nominate	5	5	-
reelect	8	-	-

51C2.1	A	B	C
voter	5	5	6
ballot	6	5	7

A: Grade level; B: Earliest Grade of Occurrence in Textbooks; C: Earliest Grade of Occurrence on Standardized Tests.

| suffrage | 8 | 7 | - |
| gerrymander | 10 | - | - |

SUPER CLUSTER
52. Temperature/Fire

52A Temperature

52A1.0	A	B	C
temperature	3	3	3
centigrade	4	5	-
Fahrenheit	4	3	4
thermal	5	5	6

52A2.0	A	B	C
cold	1	3	K
cool	3	3	2
arctic	4	4	3
frigid	6	3	-

52A2.1	A	B	C
chill	4	3	-

52A3.0	A	B	C
hot	1	3	K
warm	2	3	1
temperate	5	4	6
lukewarm	6	5	-
tepid	8	6	11

52A3.1	A	B	C
heat	2	3	1
warmth	4	3	5

52A4.0	A	B	C
parch	8	-	9
swelter	8	-	-
desiccate	13	-	-

52B Insulation

52B1.0	A	B	C
insulation	6	3	11
insulator	6	4	6

52B1.1	A	B	C
insulate	6	-	5

52B1.2	A	B	C
fireproof	6	5	-

52C Fire

52C1.0	A	B	C
fire	1	3	K
campfire	3	3	5
blaze	4	3	4
backfire	6	-	-
combustion	6	5	9
inferno	6	4	-
wildfire	6	5	7
conflagration	13	-	-

52C2.0	A	B	C
flame	3	3	4
spark	3	3	-
torch	4	3	-
firebrand	8	-	-
cresset	10	-	-

52C3.0	A	B	C
burn	2	3	2
ignite	4	3	10
scorch	5	-	8
singe	5	-	-
kindle	6	7	11
sizzle	6	3	-
char	8	-	-
incinerate	8	-	3
scathe	8	-	-

52C3.1	A	B	C
arson	6	7	-

52C4.0	A	B	C
flicker	4	3	-
stoke	5	4	-
smolder	6	7	-

52D Products of Fire

52D1.0	A	B	C
ash	4	3	7
cinder	4	3	-
ember	6	5	-
smut	6	-	-
lampblack	8	5	-

52D2.0	A	B	C
smoke	2	3	K

52D2.1	A	B	C
smokey	4	6	3

52E Fire Products

52E1.0	A	B	C
firewood	3	3	2
matchbox	4	4	-
paraffin	4	4	7
wick	4	3	-
tinder	5	3	-
woodpile	5	8	-

52E1.1	A	B	C
extinguisher	6	7	-

52E2.0	A	B	C
pipe	3	3	2
cigar	4	3	-
tobacco	5	3	7
cigarette	6	3	-
cheroot	10	-	-

SUPER CLUSTER

53. Images/Perceptions

53A Visual Images/Perception

53A1.0	A	B	C
appearance	4	3	4
image	4	3	3
reflection	5	3	5
portrayal	6	4	8
representation	6	3	6
shadowgraph	8	-	-

53A2.0	A	B	C
sight	3	3	4
scene	4	3	4
view	4	3	4
demonstration	5	3	5
panorama	5	4	-
vision	5	3	5
prospect	6	5	11
perspective	8	4	-
scope	8	6	-
vista	8	-	9
parallax	10	5	-

53A2.1	A	B	C
farsighted	6	3	-
visual	6	3	9

53A4.0	A	B	C
blindfold	5	5	4
distract	6	5	10
advert	8	-	-

53A5.0	A	B	C
witness	5	3	2
observer	6	3	9
onlooker	6	7	-

53A6.0	A	B	C
show	1	3	1
represent	4	3	4
reveal	4	3	5
display	5	3	6
reflect	5	3	4
portray	6	4	7

53A6.1	A	B	C
flaunt	6	-	-
brandish	10	-	-

53A7.0	A	B	C
flag	2	3	1
badge	3	3	3
emblem	5	3	10
effigy	10	7	-
spoor	10	-	-
vestige	13	5	-

53B Looking/Perceiving Actions

53B1.0	A	B	C
look	K	3	K
see	K	3	K
watch	2	3	K
spy	3	3	3
behold	4	3	-
monitor	4	3	4
scout	4	3	4
snoop	4	-	-
verify	5	7	9

53B2.0	A	B	C
appear	3	3	3
loom	4	3	9
reappear	4	3	4

53B3.0	A	B	C
blink	3	3	4
peek	3	3	-
wink	3	3	2
glance	4	3	6
glimpse	4	3	4
squint	5	5	5

53B4.0	A	B	C
stare	2	3	2
gaze	3	3	4
glare	4	3	5
peer	4	3	5

gape	5	4	-
glower	6	-	-
leer	8	-	-

53B5.0	A	B	C
notice	3	3	4
sense	3	3	2
attend	4	3	4
observe	4	3	4
recognize	4	3	5
detect	5	5	7
distinguish	5	4	12
identify	5	3	4
perceive	6	5	11

53B6.0	A	B	C
snub	4	4	-
ignore	5	3	4
shun	5	4	-

53B7.0	A	B	C
aim	3	3	3
focus	5	4	7

53B8.0	A	B	C
lookout	3	3	4
vigil	6	4	-

SUPER CLUSTER
54. Life/Survival

54A Life, Birth, Death

54A1.0	A	B	C
life	2	3	2
birth	3	3	3
death	4	3	5
sex	4	5	5
childbirth	5	7	-
existence	5	4	5
pollination	5	-	5
reproduction	5	3	5
afterlife	6	7	5
entity	6	4	-
demise	10	-	-
anima	13	-	-

54A2.0	A	B	C
live	1	3	K
exist	4	3	4
subsist	5	4	-

54A2.1	A	B	C
alive	3	3	2
born	3	3	2

mortal	5	3	-
animate	6	7	9
earthborn	6	6	-
biotic	8	7	12
extant	8	7	-

54A2.2	A	B	C
inhabit	5	4	-
dwell	6	4	7
reside	6	7	7

54A3.0	A	B	C
die	3	3	3
perish	5	4	6
suffocate	6	-	-
expire	8	7	-
succumb	8	9	-

54A3.1	A	B	C
dead	3	3	4
mummy	4	3	5
nonliving	4	3	5
deathbed	5	3	6
extinct	5	3	5
carcass	6	5	-
corpse	6	5	9
cadaver	8	7	-
stillborn	8	-	-
testate	8	-	-
carrion	10	3	-
defunct	10	-	11
moribund	13	-	-

54A4.0	A	B	C
wake	3	3	2
burial	6	3	7
funeral	6	3	7
cremation	8	-	-
pyre	13	9	-

54A4.1	A	B	C
inter	6	5	7
embalm	8	-	-

54A5.0	A	B	C
germinate	3	3	11
hatch	3	3	3
pollinate	4	3	4
breed	5	3	10
reproduce	5	3	6
conceive	6	7	-
incubate	6	7	-
populate	6	5	-
spawn	6	7	-
propagate	8	7	-

54A5.1	A	B	C
childbearing	5	7	-
fertile	5	3	6
pregnant	5	7	11
prolific	8	5	-
fecund	13	-	-

54A5.2	A	B	C
childbed	6	-	-
gene	6	6	7
genetic	6	5	7
natal	6	7	-

54B Survival/Growth

54B1.0	A	B	C
stamina	5	3	7
endurance	6	3	6
survival	6	3	6
tolerance	6	5	6

54B2.0	A	B	C
survive	5	3	5
withstand	5	4	-
endure	6	4	7
tolerate	6	7	10
cope	8	6	-

54B3.0	A	B	C
thrive	5	3	11
flourish	6	3	6
prosper	6	3	-
abound	8	7	-
teem	8	-	-

54B4.0	A	B	C
grow	2	3	K
bloom	3	3	3
mature	5	5	9
evolve	6	4	-
effloresce	13	-	-

55. Conformity/Complexity

55A Conformity to a Norm

55A1.0	A	B	C
special	3	3	1
original	4	3	4
distinct	5	3	4
scarce	5	3	5
distinctive	6	3	10
rare	6	3	5
uncommon	6	6	9

	A	B	C
unique	6	3	6
exotic	8	3	-
maverick	8	7	-
precocious	10	-	-
recherché	13	-	-

55A2.0	A	B	C
odd	2	3	3
strange	2	3	1
queer	3	3	-
foreign	4	3	3
peculiar	5	3	7
quaint	5	3	9
weird	5	3	7
bizarre	6	6	11
eccentric	6	3	7
grotesque	6	5	-
outlandish	6	4	-
uncanny	6	4	7
rummy	8	-	-

55A3.0	A	B	C
unfinished	4	3	6
incomplete	5	3	6
deficient	8	7	8

55B Complexity/Order

55B1.0	A	B	C
fancy	2	3	3
complex	5	3	7
ornate	5	5	9
elaborate	6	3	5
intricate	6	4	12
technical	6	3	9
wrought	6	3	-

55B1.1	A	B	C
maze	6	3	11
labyrinth	8	9	8

55B2.0	A	B	C
confusion	4	3	6
disorder	4	3	9
rout	5	4	-
tangle	5	3	5
bedlam	6	5	7
disarray	6	7	10
muddle	6	7	-
turmoil	6	4	10
havoc	8	7	-
anarchy	10	7	-

55B3.0	A	B	C
order	3	3	3
balance	4	3	3

symmetry	5	3	5
cosmos	6	4	-
equilibrium	6	6	11

55B4.0	A	B	C
bare	3	3	3
blank	4	3	2
bleak	5	3	4
void	5	5	11
stark	8	6	9

55B5.0	A	B	C
balanced	4	3	4
steady	4	3	4
unbroken	4	3	5
uniform	4	3	5
neutral	5	3	7
offset	5	4	-
unchanged	5	3	12

55B6.0	A	B	C
plain	2	3	3
pure	3	3	4
simple	3	3	2

SUPER CLUSTER
56. Difficulty/Danger

56A Difficulty/Ease

56A1.0	A	B	C
easy	2	3	1
comfortable	3	3	3
convenient	4	3	9
fluent	6	-	-
glib	8	-	-
facile	10	-	-
superable	10	-	-

56A1.1	A	B	C
simplify	5	6	10
expedite	10	-	-

56A2.0	A	B	C
ease	4	3	7
cinch	5	4	-
convenience	6	3	6

56A3.0	A	B	C
difficult	3	3	4
impossible	3	3	5
backbreaking	4	3	3
tiresome	4	3	-
troublesome	4	3	3
uneasy	4	3	8

unbearable	5	3	7
grueling	6	4	-
abstruse	10	-	-
arduous	10	5	-
onerous	10	-	-

56A4.0	A	B	C
difficulty	3	3	3
problem	3	3	3
predicament	6	7	-
dilemma	8	7	10
quandary	8	7	-
imbroglio	13	-	-

56B Danger/Safety

56B1.0	A	B	C
safety	3	3	4
prevention	4	3	9

56B1.1	A	B	C
protective	4	3	5
defensive	6	5	9

56B2.0	A	B	C
trouble	2	3	2
danger	3	3	2
hazard	4	4	5
risk	5	3	4
jeopardy	6	-	-
peril	6	4	-
pitfall	6	-	-

56B2.1	A	B	C
endanger	6	7	8

56B3.0	A	B	C
dangerous	3	3	2
harmful	4	3	4
unsafe	4	3	3
hazardous	5	4	7
breakneck	6	5	-
perilous	6	3	-
treacherous	6	4	-
noxious	10	6	-
deleterious	13	-	-

56B4.0	A	B	C
safe	2	3	1
harmless	4	3	4
secure	4	3	5
immune	5	4	-

56B4.1	A	B	C
vincible	10	-	-

A: Grade level; B: Earliest Grade of Occurrence in Textbooks; C: Earliest Grade of Occurrence on Standardized Tests.

57. Texture/Durability

57A Texture

57A1.0	A	B	C
texture	4	3	-

57A1.1	A	B	C
tangible	6	5	-
palpable	10	7	-

57A2.0	A	B	C
hard	1	3	K
soft	2	3	1
firm	3	3	2
smooth	3	3	2
stiff	3	3	3
tight	3	3	4
rigid	4	3	7
solid	4	3	3
tough	4	3	3
taut	6	3	-

57A3.0	A	B	C
crisp	3	3	7
coarse	4	3	7
rough	4	3	3
porous	5	3	7
prickly	5	3	7
stony	5	-	-
callous	8	-	-
pervious	10	-	-

57A4.0	A	B	C
bumpy	2	3	3
choppy	5	3	-

57A5.0	A	B	C
furry	3	3	4
shaggy	4	3	10
spongy	4	3	-

57B Durability

57B1.0	A	B	C
durability	6	5	-

57B2.0	A	B	C
strong	2	3	1
sturdy	4	3	2
airtight	5	3	5
durable	5	3	5
potent	6	5	-
formidable	8	5	9
stoic	8	-	-

	A	B	C
irrefragable	10	-	-
tenable	10	-	-

57B3.0	A	B	C
weak	3	3	3
brittle	5	3	-
flimsy	5	4	-
ramshackle	5	5	7
makeshift	6	6	-
perishable	6	3	8
gossamer	8	4	-
dilapidated	10	-	9

57B4.0	A	B	C
deciduous	4	5	-
delicate	5	3	4
frail	5	3	4
finespun	6	-	-
fragile	6	4	7
subtle	6	5	9
filigree	8	4	-
tenuous	8	7	-
ethereal	10	8	-
friable	13	-	-

57C Consistency

57C1.0	A	B	C
elastic	3	3	6
resilient	8	7	-
supple	8	7	-
viscous	8	4	-
malleable	10	5	11

57C2.0	A	B	C
soften	4	3	5
harden	4	3	5
stiffen	5	4	-
gel	5	5	-
ossify	10	-	-

58. Color

58A Color

58A1.0	A	B	C
blue	K	3	K
brown	K	3	K
gray	K	3	K
green	K	3	1
red	K	3	K
yellow	K	3	K
black	1	3	2
gold	1	3	1

A: Grade level; B: Earliest Grade of Occurrence in Textbooks; C: Earliest Grade of Occurrence on Standardized Tests.

white	1	3	K
orange	2	3	3
pink	2	3	2
purple	2	3	2
golden	3	3	4
silver	3	3	3
tan	3	3	3
beige	4	5	-
hazel	4	3	-
lavender	4	3	-
taupe	4	-	-
violet	4	4	7
amber	5	4	-
azure	5	3	-
buff	5	3	11
magenta	5	6	-
maroon	5	7	7
roan	5	3	-
scarlet	5	3	6
tawny	5	3	-
vermilion	5	3	-
crimson	6	3	7
ecru	6	-	-
indigo	6	3	-
livid	6	3	-
mauve	6	-	-
nutbrown	6	-	-
russet	6	-	-
tangerine	6	7	-
carmine	8	-	-
verdant	8	7	-
cerulean	10	-	-
sanguine	10	9	-

58A1.1	A	B	C
colorful	3	3	2
colorless	4	3	9
chromatic	6	5	-
iridescent	6	6	-

58A2.0	A	B	C
golden haired	4	-	-
grey-headed	4	-	-
greyhaired	4	-	-
blonde	5	3	-
brunette	5	6	-
towhead	6	-	-
piebald	8	6	-
pied	10	6	-

58A3.0	A	B	C
color	1	3	2
hue	5	3	7
pigment	5	4	-

58A3.1	A	B	C
dapple	5	-	-
tinge	5	5	10
brindle	8	4	-
grizzle	8	-	-

58B Paint

58B1.0	A	B	C
paint	1	3	K
tint	4	5	7
whitewash	4	3	-
dye	5	3	5
enamel	6	4	8
lacquer	6	5	11

SUPER CLUSTER
59. Chemicals

59A Chemicals

59A1.0	A	B	C
chemical	4	3	3
compound	4	3	7
litmus	5	5	5

59A2.0	A	B	C
oxygen	2	3	3
helium	3	3	4
hydrogen	4	3	4
nitrogen	4	3	3
boron	6	4	-

59A2.1	A	B	C
chlorinate	5	-	-
ferment	5	5	5
carbonate	6	4	-

59A3.0	A	B	C
chlorine	5	3	9
neon	5	3	5
sodium	5	3	9
bromine	6	4	-
krypton	6	5	-

59A3.1	A	B	C
chlorophyll	5	3	5
enzyme	6	6	-

59A4.0	A	B	C
dioxide	4	3	3
ammonia	5	4	-
nitrate	5	4	-
oxide	5	3	7
phosphate	5	3	-

sulfate	6	8	6
limewater	8	4	9

59B Acids

59B1.0	A	B	C
acid	4	3	3
caustic	6	8	-

59B1.1	A	B	C
hydrochloric	5	5	-
sulfuric	5	5	5

SUPER CLUSTER

60. Facial Expressions/Actions

60A Facial Expressions

60A1.0	A	B	C
grin	2	3	2
smile	2	3	K
frown	3	3	2
blush	4	3	7
scowl	4	3	2
smirk	5	4	-
sneer	5	6	-
simper	6	-	-

60A2.0	A	B	C
nod	3	3	7

60B Actions Associated with the Nose

60B1.0	A	B	C
smell	2	3	1
sneeze	3	3	4
sniff	3	3	3
snort	3	3	-
snore	4	3	-
inhale	5	3	-

60B2.0	A	B	C
perfume	4	3	9
scent	4	3	-
stink	4	4	-
aroma	5	4	-
fragrance	5	3	9
fragrant	5	3	6
fume	5	3	6
incense	5	3	6
reek	5	-	7
odor	6	3	5

stench	6	7	-
pungent	8	6	-
putrid	8	7	-
acrid	10	-	-
effluvium	10	-	-
fetid	10	-	-
redolent	10	7	-

60C Actions Associated with the Mouth

60C1.0	A	B	C
kiss	3	3	-
lick	3	3	-
suck	4	3	7
slobber	5	-	-
spew	6	-	-

60C1.1	A	B	C
spit	4	3	-
expectorate	10	-	-

60D Breathing

60D1.0	A	B	C
blow	2	3	2
breath	3	3	3
breathe	3	3	3
pant	3	3	3
puff	3	3	2
exhale	4	3	-
whiff	4	3	10
respire	6	7	-

60D1.1	A	B	C
choke	4	3	-
strangle	5	5	-

SUPER CLUSTER

61. Electricity/Particles of Matter

61A Electricity

61A1.0	A	B	C
electricity	2	3	3
magnet	3	3	3

61A1.1	A	B	C
electric	3	3	3
electrical	4	3	6
electronic	4	3	4
hydroelectric	5	3	11

A: Grade level; B: Earliest Grade of Occurrence in Textbooks; C: Earliest Grade of Occurrence on Standardized Tests.

electromagnetic	6	3	-
galvanic	10	-	-

61A2.0	A	B	C
radiation	6	3	9

61A2.1	A	B	C
radioactive	6	6	9

61B Molecules/Atoms

61B1.0	A	B	C
molecule	5	3	5

61B1.1	A	B	C
molecular	5	3	7

61B2.0	A	B	C
atom	4	3	4
electron	4	3	4
neutron	4	5	4
nucleus	4	3	4
proton	4	5	4
ion	5	6	7
nuclei	5	6	11
isotope	6	6	-
photon	8	8	-

61B2.1	A	B	C
atomic	6	3	6

Appendix B: Words in Alphabetical Order

A

a, 3I
a bit, 3J
a great deal, 3K
a little, 3J
abacus, 49A
abandon, 36A
abash, 5I
abate, 2R
abbot, 1W
abbreviation, 35B
abdicate, 1d
abduct, 36E
aberration, 26A
abet, 33D
abeyance, 2B
abhor, 5E
ability, 5R
abjure, 10G
able, 12K
ablution, 41B
aboard, 14I
abode, 21B
abolish, 2F
aborigine, 9I
abort, 2F, 37F
abound, 54B
about, 2X
above, 14I
abrade, 8G
abreast, 14K
abridge, 2U
abroad, 14K
abrogate, 10G
abrupt, 7J
abscess, 37E
abscond, 2G
absence, 14L
absent, 14L

absolute, 26C, 42C
absolute(ly), 3K
absolve, 5O
absorb, 16B
abstain, 2F
abstract, 12D
abstruse, 56A
absurd, 26D
abundance, 3G
abundant, 3G
abuse, 33B
abusive, 5F
abyss, 20C
academic, 9L
academy, 21F
accede, 10G
accelerate, 7J
accent, 10C, 35A
accept, 36E
acceptable, 26A
access, 2G
accessory, 30E
accident, 33A
accidental, 42C
accolade, 10D
accommodate, 33D
accompany, 2V
accomplish, 2E
accomplishment, 36D
accord, 27A
accordion, 47C
accordingly, 39B
accost, 10B
account, 28F
accountant, 1S
accouter, 17I
accretion, 3G
accrue, 25A
accurate, 26A

accuse, 10B
accustomed, 42A
ace, 9L, 34F
ache, 37C
achieve, 36E
acid, 59B
acknowledge, 10D
acme, 14I
acorn, 6J
acoustic, 19A
acquaint, 10C
acquaintance, 9E
acquire, 36E
acquit, 36B
acre, 20A
acreage, 20A
acrid, 60B
acrimony, 5E
acrobat, 1D
acropolis, 21C
across, 14H
acrostic, 34F
act, 47A
action, 2A
active, 13B
activity, 2A
actor, 1H
actress, 1H
actual, 26A
actually, 27B, 31A
acute, 26C
ad, 15F
adage, 15B
adamant, 13H
adapt, 27C
add, 49D
addend, 49C
addict, 9G
addition, 49D

additional, 3G
addle, 12G
address, 14A
adduce, 12D
adept, 12K
adequate, 3J, 26C
adipose, 23B
adjacent, 14K
adjective, 35B
adjoin, 2V
adjourn, 2B
adjust, 22F
administer, 10G
administrator, 1B
admiration, 5O
admire, 5O
admit, 10H
admonish, 10G
adobe, 22D
adolescence, 7F
adolescent, 9D
adopt, 36E
adorable, 43C
adore, 5O
adorn, 30E
adroit, 12K
adulate, 5O
adult, 9D
adulterate, 41A
advance, 2G
advent, 2G
adventure, 2G
adventurous, 13N
adverse, 5E
advert, 10C, 53A
advertise, 10C
advertisement, 15F
advice, 10G, 12G
advise, 10E

adviser, 1I
advocate, 5O
aerial, 11G
aerie, 4M
aeronaut, 1V
aesthetic, 13J
affable, 13A
affair, 51A
affect, 39A
affection, 5O
affectionate, 13A
affiliate, 2V
affinity, 27A
affirm, 10C
affix, 2V, 35B
afflatus, 12G
afflict, 33B
affluent, 28E
afford, 28D
affray, 33C
affront, 10B
afloat, 16H
aforementioned, 7G
aforesaid, 7G
afraid, 5B
Africa, 18B
after, 7G
after that, 7H
afterdeck, 11F
aftereffect, 39A
afterglow, 38A
afterlife, 54A
afternoon, 7C
afterwards, 7H
again, 7K
against, 27D
age, 7D
agent, 1M, 39A
aggravate, 5E
aggregate, 25A, 29B
aggression, 5F
aghast, 5J

agile, 43A
agility, 43A
agitate, 5E
agnostic, 13J
ago, 7G
agog, 5J
agony, 37C
agrarian, 20B
agree, 10D
agreement, 27A
agriculture, 1K
ah, 10K
aha, 10K
ahead, 14F
ahead of, 14F
aid, 8E, 33D
ail, 37C
ailment, 37A
aim, 53B
aimless, 13C
ain't, 46A
air, 40A
air force, 25D
airborne, 11G
aircraft, 11D
airfield, 11H
airline, 11D
airliner, 11D
airmail, 2I
airman, 1J
airplane, 11D
airport, 21J
airship, 11D
airstrip, 11H
airtight, 57B
airway, 11H
aisle, 30A
ajar, 2U
akimbo, 48E
Alabama, 18C
alacrity, 13B
alarm, 5B, 19B

alas, 10K
Alaska, 18C
albatross, 4J
albeit, 27D
albino, 23B
album, 15C, 47D
alcohol, 6H
ale, 6H
alehouse, 21D
alert, 12K
alfalfa, 24E
algae, 24E
algebra, 49A
alias, 15A
alibi, 10B
alien, 9I
alike, 27A
aliment, 6B
alimony, 28B
alive, 54A
all, 3G
all over, 14D
allay, 33D
allege, 10C
allegedly, 31B
allegiance, 13N
allegory, 15B
allergic, 37A
alleviate, 33D
alley, 11H
alligator, 4C
alliteration, 35A
allocate, 12J
allot, 12J
allow, 10G
allowance, 28A
alloy, 25A, 29A
allspice, 6G
allude, 10C
alluvial, 29C
ally, 9E
almanac, 15C

almond, 6J
almost, 3J
alms, 28A
alone, 3J, 5I
alongside, 14K
aloof, 5I
alp, 20D
alpha, 35C
alphabet, 35C
alphabetically, 35C
already, 7G
also, 27B
altar, 30D
alter, 17I
alternately, 27D
alternatively, 27D
although, 27D
altitude, 14A
alto, 47C
altogether, 3K
altruism, 13A
aluminum, 29A
alumnus, 1I
always, 7K
am, 50A
amalgam, 25A
amateur, 9L
amaze, 5J
amazement, 5J
amazingly, 31C
ambassador, 1C
amber, 58A
ambient, 2X
ambiguous, 42C
ambition, 13B
ambitious, 13B
amble, 48A
ambrosia, 6L
ambulance, 11A
ambush, 33B
ameliorate, 33D
amend, 33D

amendment, 15H

amenity, 13A

America, 18B

amethyst, 29B

amiable, 13A

ammonia, 59A

ammunition, 8N

amnesia, 12A

amnesty, 13D

among, 14F

amorphous, 32A

amortize, 28D

amount, 3G

amour, 5O, 9E

amphibian, 4A

ample, 3G

amputate, 8G

amuck, 13O

amulet, 17G

amuse, 5K

amusement, 51B

an, 3I

anachronism, 7F

anaconda, 4C

analogy, 27A

analyze, 12C

anarchy, 55B

anathema, 9G

anatomy, 1L

ancestor, 9N

ancestry, 7F

anchor, 11F

ancient, 7F

and, 27B

anemone, 24D

anent, 27B

angel, 9F

anger, 5E

angle, 3D

angry, 5E

anguish, 5H

anima, 54A

animal, 4A

animate, 54A

animated, 13B

ankle, 23G

annals, 15C

annex, 2V

annihilate, 33A

anniversary, 51B

announce, 10C

announcement, 15F

announcer, 1E

annoy, 10B

annoyingly, 31E

annual, 7K

annuity, 28A

annul, 10G

annular, 32B

anodyne, 37F

anoint, 12J

anomaly, 27C

anonymous, 42B

another, 3G

answer, 10F

ant, 4K

Antarctica, 18B

ante, 28B

anteater, 4E

antecedent, 7G

antelope, 4E

antenna, 4L

anterior, 7G

anthem, 15D

anthology, 15C

anthracite, 29B

anthropoid, 4G

anthropology, 1L

anthropomorphism, 27A

antibiotics, 37F

antic, 5K

anticipate, 5Q

antidote, 37F

antipathy, 5E

antipodes, 14A

antique, 7F

antler, 4L

antonym, 35B

anvil, 8J

anxiety, 5D

anxious, 5D

any, 45E

anybody, 45E

anyhow, 27D

anymore, 7K

anyone, 45E

anything, 45E

anyway, 27D

anywhere, 14D

apartment, 21B

apathy, 13C

ape, 4G

aperture, 32A

apex, 14I

aphorism, 10A

apocalypse, 15C

apocryphal, 26A

apologize, 10H

apology, 10D

apostasy, 13M

apostle, 1W

apostrophe, 35A

apothecary, 1U

apothegm, 15B

apotheosis, 26C

appall, 5J

apparatus, 8A

apparel, 17A

apparently, 31A

appeal, 10E, 42A

appear, 2G, 50E, 53B

appearance, 53A

appellation, 15A

appetite, 6N

applaud, 19C

applause, 19C

apple, 6I

applesauce, 6I

appliance, 8A

apply, 2D

appoint, 12J

apposite, 26A

appraise, 12D

appreciate, 5O

appreciation, 5O

apprehend, 12G, 36E

apprentice, 1B

apprise, 10C

approach, 2G

appropriate, 26A

appropriately, 31C

approve, 5O

approximate, 27A

approximate(ly), 3J

apricot, 6I

April, 7E

apron, 17C

apropos, 26A

apt, 26A

aqua, 16A

aqualung, 34C

aquarium, 4M, 16I

aquatic, 4A

aqueduct, 16I

arabesque, 47B

arable, 29C

arbitrate, 12J

arbor, 24A

arc, 32B

arch, 23G

archeologist, 1L

archeology, 1L

archer, 1D

archipelago, 16G

architect, 1G

architecture, 1L

archive, 21F

archway, 11H, 30A

arctic, 52A
arduous, 56A
are, 50A
area, 20A
arena, 21G
aren't, 46A
arguably, 31B
argue, 10B
argument, 10B
aria, 15D
arid, 40E
arise, 2O
aristocracy, 25C
arithmetic, 49A
Arizona, 18C
ark, 11E
Arkansas, 18C
arm, 23F
armchair, 30D
armor, 17H
armpit, 23F
arms, 8N
army, 25D
aroma, 60B
around, 2X
arouse, 5J
arraign, 10G
arrange, 25A
arrangement, 25A
array, 17A, 25A
arrears, 28B
arrest, 36E
arrival, 2G
arrive, 2G
arrogant, 13E
arrogate, 36C
arrow, 8N
arrowhead, 8N
arsenal, 21K
arson, 52C
art, 47D
artery, 23I

artfully, 31G
article, 15C
articulate, 10C
artifice, 12G
artificial, 27A
artillery, 8N
artist, 1G
artistic, 13J
as, 7I
as a consequence, 39B
as a result, 39B
as good as, 3J
as well, 27B
as well as, 27B
as yet, 7G
asbestos, 22D
ascend, 2O
ascent, 2O
ascetic, 13H
ascot, 17G
ash, 52D
ashore, 16H
Asia, 18B
aside, 14K
ask, 10F
askance, 32D
asleep, 12E
aspect, 5R
aspen, 24B
asperity, 5E
asperse, 10B
asphalt, 29B
aspic, 6G
aspire, 5Q
aspirin, 37F
ass, 4E
assail, 33B
assassin, 9G
assay, 12C
assemble, 25A
assembly, 25E
assent, 10G

assert, 10C
assess, 12D
assiduous, 13B
assign, 12J
assignment, 12C
assist, 33D
assistant, 1B
assizes, 15H
associate, 2V
association, 25E
assortment, 25A
assuage, 5L
assume, 12D
assure, 10D
aster, 24D
astern, 14F
astonish, 5J
astonishingly, 31C
astonishment, 5J
astound, 5J
astral, 20H
astrology, 34E
astronaut, 1L
astronomer, 1L
astronomy, 1L
astute, 12K
at, 7I, 14G
at any rate, 27D
at first, 7G
at least, 3J
at the same time, 7I
at this point, 7I
athlete, 1D
athletic, 43A
atlas, 15C
atmosphere, 40A
atmospheric, 40A
atoll, 16G
atom, 61B
atomic, 61B
atone, 33D
atop, 14I

atrocious, 26D
attach, 2V
attack, 33B
attacker, 9G
attain, 36E
attempt, 51A
attend, 53B
attendance, 14L
attendant, 1B
attention, 12F
attentive, 13A
attenuate, 3G
attest, 10C
attic, 30A
attire, 17A
attitude, 5R
attorney, 1Y
attract, 36E
attraction, 42A
attractive, 43C
attribute, 5R
attrition, 3G
auction, 28D
audacity, 13N
audible, 19A
audience, 25E
audio, 19A
audit, 28D
audition, 47A
auditorium, 21G
auger, 8E
augment, 3G
August, 7E
aunt, 9N
aura, 38A
auricle, 23E
auspices, 10G
auspicious, 26C
austere, 13H
Australia, 18B
authentic, 26A
author, 1E

authority, 10G
auto, 11A
autobiography, 15C
autocracy, 25C
autograph, 15A
automate, 8A
automatic, 7J
automatically, 7J
automobile, 11A
autonomy, 13D
autopsy, 37F
autumn, 7D
auxiliary, 25E
avail, 33D
available, 14L
avalanche, 40D
avarice, 5Q
avenue, 11H
aver, 10C
average, 49B
averse, 13P
aviary, 4M
aviation, 11G
avid, 13B
avoid, 2F
aw, 10K
await, 2B
awake, 12E
aware, 12K
away, 14K
awe, 5J, 10D
awful, 26D
awhile, 7K
awkward, 43A
awl, 8E
awning, 30B
ax, 8F
axe, 8F
axiom, 12D
axis, 14A
axle, 11F
ay, 10K

aye, 10K
azure, 58A

B

baa, 19D
babble, 19C
babe, 9D
baboon, 4G
baby, 9D
babysitter, 1c
bacchanal, 51B
bachelor, 9C
back, 14F
backbone, 23J
backbreaking, 56A
backfield, 34C
backfire, 52C
background, 14F, 47A
backhand, 34B
backlash, 2D
backslide, 26B
backstage, 47A
backstop, 34C
backward, 14F
backwards, 14F
backwater, 16F
backwoods, 20E
backwoodsman, 9I
bacon, 6E
bacteria, 37D
bad, 26D
bad tempered, 5G
badge, 53A
badger, 4E
badly, 3K
badminton, 34B
baffle, 12G
bag, 22A
baggage, 22A
bagpipe, 47C
bail, 28B

bailiwick, 18A
bait, 10E
bake, 6K
baker, 1N
bakery, 21D
balance, 55B
balanced, 55B
balcony, 30A
bald, 23B
bale, 25A
baleful, 26D
balk, 5I
ball, 34C
ballad, 15D
ballet, 47B
ballistics, 8N
balloon, 11D
ballot, 51C
ballplayer, 1D
ballroom, 30A
balm, 37F
balsa, 24B
bamboo, 24E
ban, 10G
banal, 42A
banana, 6I
band, 25B
bandage, 37F
bandanna, 17G
bandbox, 22A
bandit, 9G
bane, 33B
bangle, 17G
banjo, 47C
bank, 28F
bankbook, 28F
banker, 1S
banknote, 28C
banner, 30E
bannister, 30B
banquet, 6A
banter, 10B

baptism, 2C
bar, 22D
barb, 8F
barbaric, 13O
barbecue, 6K
barbed wire, 30C
barber, 1N
barbershop, 21D
bare, 17J, 55B
bareback, 4O
barefoot, 17J
bareheaded, 17J
barely, 3J
bargain, 28D
barge, 11E
barium, 29A
bark, 19D, 24C
barker, 1H
barley, 6J
barn, 21K
barnacle, 4I
barnyard, 20G
baron, 1C
barracks, 21B
barrel, 22A
barren, 29C
barrio, 18A
barroom, 21D
barrow, 11B
bartender, 1a
barter, 36A
base, 26C, 34C
baseball, 34B
baseboard, 30B
baseman, 1D
bashful, 13L
basic, 26C
basically, 31A
basin, 22A
bask, 2B
basket, 22A
basketball, 34B

bass, 4H
basswood, 22C
baste, 17I
bastinado, 44A
bat, 34C
batch, 25A
bath, 22A
bathe, 41B
bathrobe, 17C
bathroom, 30A
bathtub, 22A
baton, 8J
batten, 22C
batter, 1D, 6G
battery, 8B
battle, 33C
battlefield, 20F
battlefront, 14B
battleground, 20F
battleship, 11E
bauble, 17G
bauxite, 29A
bawdy, 13K
bawl, 19C
bay, 16F
bazaar, 51B
be, 50A
beach, 16G
beacon, 38D
bead, 17G
beagle, 4B
beak, 4L
beam, 38D
bean, 6J
beanbag, 34C
beanstalk, 24E
bear, 2I, 4E
beard, 23B
bearded, 23B
bearing, 5R
bearskin, 4L
beast, 4A

beat, 44A
beater, 8M
beautiful, 43C
beautify, 30E
beauty, 43A
beaver, 4F
becalm, 5L
because, 39B
because of, 39B
beckon, 10F
become, 50E
becoming, 50E
bed, 30D
bedchamber, 30A
bedclothes, 17C
bedfellow, 9E
bedgown, 17C
bedlam, 55B
bedridden, 37A
bedrock, 29B
bedroll, 30F
bedroom, 30A
bedspread, 30F
bedspring, 30D
bedtime, 7A
bee, 4K
beech, 24B
beechnut, 6J
beef, 6E
beefsteak, 6E
beehive, 4M
beeline, 32D
been, 50A
beer, 6H
beeswax, 4M
beet, 6J
beetle, 4K
before, 7H
before now, 7G
before that, 7G
beforehand, 7G
beg, 10E

beggar, 9M
begin, 2C
beginner, 9L
beginning, 2C
begone, 10K
behalf, 33D
behave, 33D
behavior, 5R
behind, 14F
behold, 53B
behoove, 33D
beige, 58A
being, 9A, 50A
belch, 19C
beleaguer, 5I
belfry, 30B
belief, 5N, 12L
believe, 5O
bell, 19B
belle, 9B
bellhop, 1Z
bellicose, 5E
belligerent, 5E
bellow, 19C
belly, 23A
belong, 36C
beloved, 26C
below, 14J
belt, 17C
bench, 30D
bend, 32B
beneath, 14J
benediction, 10D
benefit, 33D
benevolent, 13A
benign, 13A
bent, 32D
bequeath, 28D
bequest, 28A
beret, 17D
berg, 16A
beriberi, 37B

berry, 6I, 24D
berth, 16I
beryl, 29A
beryllium, 29A
beseech, 10E
beset, 33B
besides, 27B, 27D
besmirch, 41A
best, 26C
bestow, 2I
bet, 28D, 42C
beta, 35C
betray, 10B
betroth, 2V
better, 26C
between, 14K
beverage, 6H
bevy, 25B
beware, 10K
bewilder, 12G
beyond, 14K
bias, 10E
bib, 17B
bible, 15C
bibliography, 15C
bibliophile, 1e
biceps, 23F
bicker, 10B
bicycle, 11A, 34B
bicycling, 34B
bid, 10F, 42C
bide, 2B
big, 3A
bigamy, 2V
bighorn, 4E
bight, 16F
bigot, 9G
bike, 11A
bile, 23I
bill, 4L
billboard, 15F
billet, 15F

billfold, 28F

billiards, 34F

billion, 3H

billow, 2S

bin, 22A

binary, 3G

bind, 22G

binoculars, 8K

biography, 15C

biologist, 1L

biology, 1L

biotic, 54A

biped, 4A

birch, 24B

bird, 4J

birdcall, 19C

birdhouse, 4M

birdlime, 4O

birth, 54A

birthday, 51B

birthmark, 23B

birthplace, 18A

birthrate, 3D

biscuit, 6D

bisect, 2W

bishop, 1W

bison, 4E

bit, 3F

bitch, 4B

bite, 6M

bitter, 6L

bitterness, 5E, 6L

bittersweet, 6L

bituminous, 29B

bizarre, 55A

blab, 10A

black, 58A

blackball, 5P

blackberry, 6I

blackbird, 4J

blackboard, 15G

blacken, 38C, 41A

blackguard, 9G

blackhead, 23B

blackjack, 8N

blackmail, 10E

blacksmith, 1N

blacksnake, 4C

blackthorn, 24B

blade, 8F

blame, 10B

blanch, 6K

bland, 6L

blank, 55B

blanket, 30F

blare, 19A

blas, 13C

blaspheme, 10B

blast, 2S

blast-off, 2O

blatant, 42A

blaze, 52C

bleach, 41C

bleacher, 30D

bleak, 41A, 55B

blear, 38C

bleat, 19D

bleed, 23I

blemish, 23B

blend, 25A

bless, 10D

blessing, 10D

blight, 40D

blimp, 11D

blind, 37B

blindfold, 53A

blindness, 37B

blink, 53B

bliss, 5K

blister, 37E

blithe, 5K

blizzard, 40B

bloat, 2S

block, 32C

blockhead, 9G

blockhouse, 21C

blonde, 58A

blood, 23I

bloodcurdling, 5B

bloodhound, 4B

bloodshed, 33C

bloodshot, 37C

bloodstain, 41A

bloodstream, 23I

bloodthirsty, 5F

bloom, 54B

blossom, 24D

blot, 38C

blouse, 17C

blow, 60D

blubber, 23B

bludgeon, 44A

blue, 58A

blue bottle, 4K

blue jay, 4J

bluebell, 24D

blueberry, 6I

bluebird, 4J

bluefish, 4H

blueprint, 15E

bluestocking, 9B

bluestone, 29B

bluff, 20D

blunder, 26A

blunt, 32E

bluntly, 31A

blur, 38C

blurt, 19C

blush, 60A

bluster, 10C, 19A

board, 22C

boardinghouse, 21B

boast, 10C

boat, 11E

boathouse, 21K

boatswain, 1V

bob, 2N

bobcat, 4B

bobsled, 11C

bobtail, 4L

bode, 10B

body, 23A

bodyguard, 1N

bog, 16F

boggle, 5J

bogus, 10B

boil, 6K, 16B

boiler, 8D

boisterous, 19A

bold, 13N

boldface, 15I

bologna, 6E

bolster, 5O

bolt, 8H

bomb, 8N

bombast, 10B

bombshell, 8N

bonanza, 28A

bonbon, 6C

bond, 2V

bondholder, 9M

bondman, 1T

bondservant, 1T

bondsman, 1T

bone, 23J

bonnet, 17D

bonny, 43C

book, 15C

bookcase, 30D

bookkeeper, 1S

bookkeeping, 10J

booklet, 15C

bookshop, 21D

bookstore, 21D

boom, 19E

boomerang, 8N

boon, 42C

boor, 9G

boost, 2O
boot, 17E
bootblack, 1N
booth, 21D
bootleg, 28D
border, 14B
borderland, 14B
boreal, 14E
born, 54A
boron, 59A
borough, 18A
borrow, 36A
bosom, 23A
boss, 1B
botanist, 1L
botany, 1L
botch, 26B
both, 3G
bother, 5I
bottle, 22A
bottom, 14J
bough, 24C
bouillon, 6H
boulder, 29B
boulevard, 11H
bounce, 2N
bound, 14G, 48D
boundary, 14B
bounty, 28A
bouquet, 24D
bout, 34A
bovine, 4E
bow, 8N
bowel, 23H
bower, 24A
bowl, 8M
bowlegged, 48E
bowstring, 8N
box, 22A, 34B
boxer, 1D
boxing, 34B
boxwood, 24B

boy, 9C
boycott, 2F
boyfriend, 9E
boyhood, 7F
brace, 22D
bracelet, 17G
bracket, 22D
brackish, 6L
brad, 8H
brag, 10C
braid, 17I
brain, 23C
brainstorm, 10A
braise, 6K
brake, 8B
brakeman, 1V
bran, 6J
branch, 24C
brand, 15A
brandish, 53A
brandnew, 7G
brandy, 6H
brass, 29A
brassiere, 17C
brave, 13N
bravery, 13N
bravo, 10K
brawl, 33C
brawn, 43A
bray, 19D
brazier, 1N
breach, 10I
bread, 6D
breadbasket, 22A
breadfruit, 24B
breadwinner, 1A
break, 33A
breakdown, 33A
breakfast, 6A
breakneck, 56B
breakthrough, 12G
breakwater, 16I

breast, 23A
breastbone, 23J
breastplate, 17H
breastwork, 21C
breath, 60D
breathe, 60D
breathless, 19A
breech, 14F
breed, 54A
breeze, 40B
brew, 6K
bribe, 10E
brick, 22D
brickbat, 8N
bricklayer, 1X
brickwork, 22D
brickyard, 20G
bride, 9N
bridegroom, 9N
bridesmaid, 9N
bridge, 11H
bridgehead, 21C
bridle, 4N
brief, 7J
brier, 24D
brigade, 25D
bright, 38A
brighten, 38B
brightness, 38A
brilliant, 12K, 38A
brim, 14B
brindle, 58A
brine, 6G
bring, 2I
brink, 14B
brisk, 7J
brisket, 6E
bristle, 4L
brittle, 57B
broad, 32F
broadbrim, 17D
broadcast, 10C

broadcloth, 17K
broadleaf, 24C
broadloom, 17I
broadly, 3J
broadside, 14C
broadsword, 8N
brogue, 17E
broil, 6K
broke, 28E
broker, 1M
bromine, 59A
bronco, 4E
bronze, 29A
brood, 25B
brook, 16F
broom, 41C
broomstick, 41C
broth, 6H
brother, 9N
brotherhood, 25B
brow, 23E
browbeat, 10B
brown, 58A
brownie, 6C
brownstone, 22D
browse, 15I
bruise, 23B
brunch, 6A
brunette, 58A
brunt, 3G
brush, 15G, 17G, 41C
brushwood, 24B
brusque, 5G
brute, 9G
bubble, 16B
buck, 4O
bucket, 22A
buckle, 17G
buckshot, 8N
buckskin, 17K
buckwheat, 6J
bucolic, 20B

bud, 24D
buddy, 9E
budge, 2N
budget, 28D
buff, 41B, 58A
buffalo, 4E
buffet, 6A, 44A
buffoon, 9G
bug, 4K
bugaboo, 9F
buggy, 11A
bugle, 47C
build, 22F
builder, 1P
building, 21A
bulb, 24D, 38D
bulge, 2S
bulk, 3A
bulkhead, 11F
bull, 4E
bulldog, 4B
bulldoze, 8G
bulldozer, 11B
bullet, 8N
bulletin, 15F
bulletproof, 17H
bullfight, 51B
bullfinch, 4J
bullfrog, 4C
bully, 9G
bum, 9M
bumble, 26B
bumblebee, 4K
bump, 23B
bumpkin, 9G
bumpy, 57A
bun, 6D
bunch, 25A
bundle, 25A
bung, 22B
bungalow, 21B
bungle, 26B

bunk, 30D
bunker, 21C
bunkhouse, 21B
bunny, 4D
bunt, 34C
bunting, 17K
buoy, 11F
bureau, 30D
burg, 18A
burgh, 18A
burglar, 9G
burial, 54A
burlesque, 47A
burly, 43D
burn, 37E, 52C
burner, 8D
burnish, 41B
burp, 19C
burr, 19C
burro, 4E
burrow, 8G
burst, 2S
bury, 36F
bus, 11A
busboy, 1a
bush, 24A
bushel, 3E
bushman, 9I
business, 1K
businessman, 1O
businesswoman, 1O
bustle, 7J
busy, 13B
busybody, 9G
but, 27D
butcher, 1N
butler, 1Z
butt, 44A
butte, 20D
butter, 6F
buttercup, 24D
butterfly, 4K

buttermilk, 6H
butternut, 6J
butterscotch, 6C
button, 17B
buttonhole, 17B
buttonhook, 17B
buttress, 22D
buxom, 43C
buy, 28D
buyer, 1M
buzz, 19D
by, 14K, 39B
by comparison, 27D
by far, 3K
bye, 10K
bygone, 7F
bypass, 11H
byway, 11H
byword, 15B

C
cab, 11A
cabaret, 21G
cabbage, 6J
cabdriver, 11G
cabin, 21B
cabinet, 30D
cabinetmaker, 1N
cable, 8H
caboose, 11A
cachet, 15A
cackle, 19D
cad, 9G
cadaver, 54A
caddie, 1Z
cadence, 47B
cafe, 21D
cafeteria, 21D
cage, 21C
cairn, 21M
cajole, 10E

cake, 6C
calamity, 40D
calcium, 29A
calculate, 12D
calculation, 12D
calendar, 7B
calf, 4D
calfskin, 17K
caliber, 3D
calico, 17K
California, 18C
calk, 22F
call, 10F
calligraphy, 15I
callous, 13C, 57A
callow, 12K
calm, 5L
calorie, 6B
calumny, 10B
calves, 23G
camel, 4E
cameo, 17G
camera, 8K
cameraman, 1X
camouflage, 36F
camp, 18A
campaign, 51C
camper, 1F
campfire, 52C
campsite, 18A
campus, 21F
can, 50C
Canada, 18B
canaille, 25B
canal, 16I
canape, 6A
canary, 4J
cancel, 2F
cancer, 37B
candescent, 38A
candid, 26A
candidate, 1C

cent, 28C

centennial, 7D

center, 14F

centerpiece, 30E

centigrade, 52A

centimeter, 3E

centipede, 4K

central, 14F

century, 7D

ceramic, 22D

cereal, 6D

cerebellum, 23C

cerebrum, 23C

ceremony, 51B

certain, 13E, 42C

certainly, 31A

certify, 10G

cerulean, 58A

chafe, 8G

chaff, 24E

chagrin, 5D

chain, 8H

chair, 30D

chairman, 1B

chairperson, 1B

chairwoman, 1B

chalet, 21B

chalk, 15G

chalkboard, 15G

challenge, 10B, 33C

chamber, 30A

chambermaid, 1Z

champagne, 6H

champion, 36D

championship, 34A

chance, 42C

chancellor, 1C

change, 27C, 39A

channel, 16I

chant, 19C

chap, 9A

chapel, 21I

chaperone, 33D

chaplet, 17G

chaps, 4N

chapter, 15C

char, 52C

character, 9A

characteristic, 5R

charade, 10B

charcoal, 29B

charge, 7J

chariot, 11A

charity, 13A

charm, 10D

chart, 15E

charter, 15H

chary, 13P

chase, 2H

chasm, 20C

chassis, 32A

chaste, 13K

chastise, 10B

chat, 10A

chattel, 1T

chatter, 19C

chatterbox, 9G

chauffeur, 1Z

cheap, 28E

cheat, 10B

check, 28C

check-up, 37F

checkbook, 28F

checkerboard, 34F

checkers, 34F

checkmate, 34F

checkroom, 30A

cheek, 23C

cheekbone, 23J

cheep, 19D

cheer, 19C

cheerful, 5K

cheese, 6F

cheesecloth, 17K

chef, 1a

chemical, 59A

chemise, 17C

chemist, 1L

chemistry, 1L

cherish, 5O

cheroot, 52E

cherry, 6I

cherub, 9F

chess, 34F

chessboard, 34F

chest, 23A

chesterfield, 17F

chestnut, 6J

chew, 6M

Cheyenne, 18D

Chicago, 18D

chicanery, 12G

chick, 4D

chicken, 4J

chickweed, 24E

chide, 10B

chief, 1C

chiffon, 17K

chiffonier, 30D

child, 9D

childbearing, 54A

childbed, 54A

childbirth, 54A

childhood, 7F

chili, 6H

chill, 52A

chime, 19B

chimera, 4C

chimney, 30B

chimpanzee, 4G

chin, 23C

China, 18B

china, 8M

chinaware, 8M

chinook, 40B

chip, 33A

chipmunk, 4F

chips, 6D

chirp, 19D

chisel, 8E

chit, 28C

chivalrous, 13A

chivalry, 13N

chlorinate, 59A

chlorine, 59A

chlorophyll, 59A

chock, 8E

chocolate, 6C

choice, 12J

choke, 60D

choler, 5E

choose, 12J

chop, 8G

choppy, 57A

chopsticks, 8M

chord, 47B

chore, 1A

choreography, 47B

chortle, 19C

chorus, 25B

chow, 6A

chowder, 6H

chromatic, 58A

chrome, 29A

chronic, 7K

chronicle, 15C

chronology, 25A

chrysanthemum, 24D

chubby, 43D

chuck, 2J

chuckle, 19C

chug, 19E

chum, 9E

chunk, 3F

church, 21I

churchwarden, 1W

churchyard, 20G

churl, 9G

churn, 6K

chute, 11H

cicada, 4K

cider, 6H

cigar, 52E

cigarette, 52E

cinch, 56A

Cincinnati, 18D

cinder, 52D

cinema, 47A

cinnamon, 6G

cipher, 35C

circa, 3J

circadian, 7K

circle, 32B

circuit, 32B

circular, 32B

circulate, 23I

circulation, 2X, 23K

circulatory, 23K

circumcise, 37F

circumference, 3D

circumspect, 13K

circumstance, 51A

circus, 51B

cirrocumulus, 40C

cirrostratus, 40C

cirrus, 40C

cistern, 22A

cite, 10C

citizen, 9I

citrus, 24B

city, 18A

civic, 25C

civil, 13A

civilization, 25C

civilize, 5L

clack, 19E

clad, 17I

claim, 10C

clairvoyant, 9F

clam, 4I

clamber, 2O

clamor, 19A

clamp, 8H

clan, 25C

clandestine, 42B

clang, 19E

clank, 19E

clap, 44C

clapboard, 22D

claptrap, 10B

clarinet, 47C

clarity, 38E

clash, 33C

clasp, 44B

class, 25B

classic, 43C

classification, 25A

classify, 25A

classmate, 9E

classroom, 21F

clatter, 19A

clause, 35B

claw, 4L

clay, 29E

clean, 41B

clean-up, 41B

cleaner, 41C

cleanliness, 41B

clear, 38A

clearing, 20A

clearly, 31A

cleave, 2V

cleft, 20C

clement, 13A

clench, 44B

clergyman, 1W

clerical, 1W

clerk, 1O

Cleveland, 18D

clever, 12K

cleverly, 31G

clew, 17K

click, 19E

client, 1M

cliff, 20D

climate, 40A

climax, 47A

climb, 2O

clinch, 44B

cling, 44B

clinic, 21H

clink, 19E

clip, 8G

clipper, 8F

clique, 25B

cloak, 17F

cloakroom, 30A

clock, 7B

clockmaker, 1N

clockwise, 2X

clockwork, 8A

clod, 29E

clodhopper, 17E

clog, 2F

cloister, 21I, 30A

clop, 19E

close, 14K

closeness, 14K

closet, 30A

closure, 2R

clot, 23I

cloth, 17K

clothe, 17I

clothes, 17A

clothesline, 8H

clothespin, 8H

clothing, 17A

cloud, 16D, 40C

cloudburst, 40B

clout, 44A

clover, 24E

cloves, 6G

clown, 1H

cloy, 6M

club, 25B

clubhouse, 21G

cluck, 19D

clue, 12D

clump, 25A

clumsy, 43A

cluster, 25A

clutch, 44B

clutter, 41A

coach, 1D, 12G

coachman, 1Z

coagulate, 23I

coal, 29B

coalesce, 2V

coarse, 57A

coast, 16G

coastal, 20B

coastland, 16G

coat, 17F

coax, 10E

cob, 24E

cobalt, 29A

cobble, 29B

cobbler, 1N

cobblestone, 29B

cock, 4J

cock-eyed, 13O

cockcrow, 19D

cockle, 4I

cockleshell, 4I

cockpit, 11F

cockroach, 4K

cocksure, 13E

cocktail, 6H

cocoa, 6C

coconut, 6I

cocoon, 4M

cod, 4H

coddle, 5K

code, 35C

codfish, 4H

coerce, 10G

coeval, 7I
coffee, 6H
coffeehouse, 21D
coffeepot, 22A
coffer, 22A
coffin, 22A
cog, 8B
cogent, 12K
cogitate, 12A
cognate, 27A
cognition, 12A
cohere, 2V
cohort, 9E
coif, 17D
coil, 32B, 48D
coin, 28C
coke, 29B
colander, 8M
cold, 37B, 52A
coliseum, 21G
collapse, 2P
collar, 4N, 17B
collarbone, 23J
collect, 25A
collection, 25A
collective, 25A
collector, 1e
college, 21F
collide, 2V
collie, 4B
collision, 33A
colloquy, 10A
collude, 10B
cologne, 17G
colon, 35A
colonel, 1J
colonial, 7F
colonist, 9I
colony, 18A
colophon, 15A
color, 15I, 58A
Colorado, 18C

colorful, 58A
colorless, 58A
colossus, 3A
colt, 4D
Columbus, 18D
column, 15C
coma, 37C
comb, 17G
combat, 33C
combination, 25A
combine, 2V
combustion, 52C
come, 2G
comeback, 10F
comedy, 15B, 47A
comely, 43C
comestible, 6B
comet, 20H
comfort, 5L
comfortable, 5L, 56A
comic, 1H
comity, 13A
comma, 35A
command, 10G
commandment, 15H
commend, 10D
commensurate, 27A
comment, 10A
commerce, 28F
commercial, 15F
commissary, 21D
commission, 10G, 25E
commit, 2D
committee, 25E
commode, 30D
commodious, 32G
commodity, 28C
common, 7K, 42A
commonplace, 42A
commonwealth, 25C
commotion, 19A
commune, 10A

communicate, 10A
communist, 9O
community, 25C
commute, 2G
compact, 3A
company, 25E
comparative, 27D
compare, 27D
comparison, 27A
compartment, 22A
compass, 3C
compatible, 27A
compel, 10G
compendium, 15C
compensate, 28D
compete, 34A
competent, 12K
competition, 34A
compile, 25A
complacent, 13C
complain, 10B
complaint, 10B
complete, 2E
complete(ly), 3K
completion, 2E
complex, 55B
complexion, 23B
complicate, 12G
compliment, 10D
comply, 10G
component, 3F
comport, 10G
compose, 12D
composer, 1G
composite, 25A
composition, 15B
compote, 8M
compound, 25A, 59A
comprehend, 12G
compress, 2R
compression, 2R
compressor, 8B

comprise, 2V
compromise, 10G
compulsive, 13B
compunction, 5D
compute, 12D
computer, 8L
comrade, 9E
con, 10B
concatenate, 2V
concave, 32B
conceal, 36F
concede, 36B
conceit, 13E
conceivably, 31B
conceive, 12D, 54A
concentrate, 12A
concentration, 12F
concern, 5D
concert, 47B
conciliate, 5L, 33D
concise, 10A
conclave, 25E
conclude, 12D
conclusion, 39A
concoct, 6K
concomitant, 7I
concord, 10D
concrete, 22D
concur, 10D
concurrently, 7I
concussion, 37E
condemn, 10B
condensation, 16D
condense, 2R
condign, 26A
condiment, 6G
condition, 37A, 51A
condole, 5L
condone, 5O
conduce, 33D
conduct, 47B
conductor, 1G

crewel, 17I

crib, 30D

cribbage, 34F

cricket, 4K

crime, 26A

criminal, 9G

crimp, 2R

crimson, 58A

cringe, 5C

crinkle, 2R

cripple, 33B, 37E

crisis, 40D

crisp, 57A

crisscross, 32D

criterion, 12D

critic, 1E

critical, 26C

criticism, 10B

criticize, 10B

croak, 19D

crochet, 17I

crock, 8M

crocodile, 4C

crony, 9E

crook, 9G

crooked, 32D

crop, 6B

cropland, 20F

croquet, 34B

croquette, 6D

cross, 32D

crossbar, 22D

crossbones, 9F

crossbow, 8N

crossbred, 25A

crosscut, 8G

crosspiece, 22D

crossroad, 11H

crosstrees, 11F

crossway, 11H

crossword, 34F

crotch, 23G

crouch, 2Q

croup, 37B

croupier, 1S

crouton, 6D

crow, 4J

crowbar, 8E

crowd, 25B

crown, 17D

crucial, 26C

crucible, 8D

crude, 12K

cruel, 5F

cruelty, 5F

cruet, 22A

cruise, 11G

cruller, 6C

crumb, 3F

crumble, 2R

crumple, 2R

crunch, 19E

crusade, 51C

cruse, 22A

crush, 33A

crust, 6D

crutch, 37F

crux, 26C

cry, 19C

crypt, 21M

crystal, 29B

cub, 4D

cubbyhole, 22A

cube, 32C

cubic, 32C

cuckoo, 4J

cucumber, 6J

cud, 4L

cuddle, 44B

cudgel, 8N

cue, 10E

cuff, 17B

cuirass, 17H

cuisine, 6B

culinary, 6B

cull, 12J

culminate, 2E

culprit, 9G

cult, 25C

cultivate, 29F

cultivation, 29F

culture, 25C

culvert, 22D

cumber, 2P

cumulate, 25A

cumulonimbus, 40C

cumulus, 40C

cuneiform, 35C

cunning, 13M

cup, 8M

cupbearer, 1Z

cupboard, 30D

cupcake, 6C

cupful, 3E

cupid, 9F

curator, 1L

curb, 30C

curbstone, 30C

curd, 6F

cure, 33D

curfew, 15H

curiosity, 12F

curious, 12K

curiously, 31C

curl, 32B

current, 7G, 16F

curriculum, 25A

curry, 6G

curse, 10B

cursory, 7J

curt, 5G

curtail, 2U

curtain, 30E

curtsy, 48E

curvature, 32B

curve, 32B

cushion, 30F

cusp, 14I

cuspid, 23D

custard, 6C

custodian, 1R

custody, 36C

custom, 12L

customary, 7K, 42A

customer, 1M

cut, 8G

cut glass, 30E

cutaneous, 23B

cutaway, 17F

cute, 43C

cuticle, 23F

cutlass, 8N

cutlet, 6E

cutoff, 8G

cutout, 32A

cutter, 11E

cutthroat, 9G

cycle, 7D

cyclone, 40B

cylinder, 32B

cymbal, 47C

cynic, 9G

cynosure, 9K

czar, 1C

D

dab, 44A

dad, 9N

daddy, 9N

daffodil, 24D

daft, 13O

dagger, 8N

daily, 7K

dainty, 43D

dairy, 21L

dais, 30A

daisy, 24D

dale, 20C
Dallas, 18D
dally, 2B
dam, 16I
damage, 33A
dame, 9B
damn, 10B
damp, 16B
damselfly, 4K
dance, 47B, 48A
dancer, 1H
dandelion, 24D
dander, 5E
dandle, 44B
dandruff, 23B
dandy, 26C
danger, 56B
dangerous, 56B
dangle, 2B
dank, 16B
dapper, 43B
dapple, 58A
dare, 10B
daredevil, 1D
dark, 38C
darken, 38C, 41A
darkness, 38C
darling, 9E
darn, 17I
dart, 8N
dash, 7J
dashboard, 11F
dastard, 9G
data, 3H
date, 7B
daub, 41A
daughter, 9N
daunt, 5C
davenport, 30D
dawdle, 2B
dawn, 7C
day, 7C

daybreak, 7C
daydream, 12E
daylight, 38A
daytime, 7A
daze, 12E
dazzle, 38B
deacon, 1W
dead, 54A
deadline, 2E
deadlock, 2B
deadly, 33B
deaf, 37B
deafening, 19A
deal, 28D
dean, 1I
dear, 26C
dearth, 3G
death, 54A
deathbed, 54A
deathblow, 37E
debacle, 36D
debate, 10B
debauch, 10E
debility, 43A
debonair, 13A
debris, 41A
debt, 28B
debut, 51B
decade, 7D
decagon, 32C
decant, 16B
decapitate, 33B
decay, 6K
deceit, 10B
deceive, 10B
decelerate, 7J
December, 7E
decent, 26A
decide, 12J
deciduous, 57B
decimal, 3H
decimeter, 3E

decision, 12J
deck, 11F
declaration, 10A
declare, 10C
decline, 10B
declivity, 32H
decoct, 6K
decor, 30D
decorate, 30E
decoration, 30E
decorous, 26A
decoy, 12G
decrease, 3G
decree, 10G
decrepit, 43A
dedicate, 12J
deduce, 12D
deduct, 3G
deed, 2E, 15H, 51A
deem, 12D
deep, 32F
deepen, 32F
deeply, 3K
deer, 4E
deerskin, 4L
defeat, 36D
defend, 33D
defendant, 1Y
defense, 34C
defensive, 56B
defer, 2B
deficient, 55A
defile, 41A
define, 12I
definite, 42C
definitely, 31A
definition, 12I
deflate, 32G
deflect, 2N
deft, 12K
defunct, 54A
defy, 10B

degenerate, 9G
degrade, 10B
degree, 3E
deign, 10G
deity, 9F
deject, 5I
Delaware, 18C
delay, 2B
delectable, 6L
delegate, 1C
deleterious, 56B
deliberate, 12A
delicacy, 6B
delicate, 57B
delicious, 6L
delight, 5K
delightful, 26C
delightfully, 31D
delinquent, 9G
delirious, 37C
deliver, 2I
dell, 20C
delta, 16F
delude, 10B
delve, 12C
demagogue, 1C
demand, 10G
demented, 13O
demise, 54A
democracy, 25C
democratic, 9O
demography, 1L
demolish, 33A
demon, 9F
demonstrate, 10C
demonstration, 53A
demote, 10G
demotic, 42A
demure, 13K
den, 30A
denizen, 9I
denomination, 15A, 25B

denominator, 49C

denouement, 39A

denounce, 10B

dense, 32F

density, 32F

dent, 33A

dental, 23D

dentist, 1U

Denver, 18D

deny, 10G

depart, 2G

department, 3F

departure, 2G

depend, 5O, 13B

dependability, 13B

dependable, 13B

dependent, 13D

deplete, 32G

deplore, 5H

deport, 2I

depose, 1d

deposit, 2I

deposition, 10A

depot, 21J

deprave, 10E

deprecate, 10B

depreciate, 28D

depress, 5I

deprive, 36E

depth, 32F

depute, 12J

derange, 12G

derby, 34A

derelict, 5P

deride, 10B

derive, 12D

derma, 23B

derogate, 10B

derrick, 11B

dervish, 1W

Des Moines, 18D

descant, 47B

descend, 2P

descendant, 9N

descent, 2P

describe, 10C

desert, 20B

deserve, 26B

desiccate, 52A

design, 12D, 17A

designer, 1G

desirable, 26C

desire, 5Q

desist, 2F

desk, 30D

desolate, 5H

despair, 5N

desperate, 5N

desperation, 5N

despise, 5E

despite, 27D

despond, 5H

despot, 1C

dessert, 6A

destination, 14A

destine, 12J

destitute, 28E

destroy, 33A

destroyer, 11E

destruction, 33A

destructive, 5F

desultory, 42C

detach, 2W

detail, 25D

detain, 2B

detect, 53B

detective, 1J

deter, 2F

detergent, 41C

deteriorate, 6K

determination, 13B

determine, 12D

detest, 5E

detonate, 2S

detour, 11H

detract, 10B

detriment, 33B

Detroit, 18D

deuce, 3G

devastate, 33A

develop, 22F, 27C

developed, 20B

development, 27C, 51A

deviate, 27C

device, 8E

devil, 9F

devise, 12D

devoir, 13B

devolve, 2I

devote, 5O

devotion, 13N

devour, 6M

dew, 16D

dewberry, 6I

dewdrop, 16D

dexter, 14E

dexterity, 43A

diabolic, 26D

diadem, 17D

diagnose, 37F

diagonal, 14C

diagram, 15E

dial, 8J

dialect, 35A

dialogue, 10A

diameter, 3D

diamond, 29B

diaper, 17C

diaphanous, 38E

diaphragm, 23H

diary, 15C

dibble, 8E

dice, 34F

dichotomy, 2W

dickens, 10K

dicker, 28D

dickey, 17C

dictate, 10G

dictator, 1C

diction, 35A

dictionary, 15C

did, 50B

didactic, 12G

die, 54A

diesel, 8C

diet, 6B

differ, 27C

difference, 27C

different, 27C

difficult, 56A

difficulty, 56A

diffident, 13L

diffuse, 2S

diffusion, 2S

dig, 8G

digest, 23K

digestion, 23K

digestive, 23K

digger, 1F

digit, 3H

dignitary, 1C

dignity, 42A

digress, 10A

dike, 16I

dilapidated, 57B

dilate, 2S

dilatory, 13C

dilemma, 56A

dilettante, 9L

diligent, 13B

dilute, 16B

diluvial, 40D

dim, 38E

dime, 28C

dimension, 3A

diminish, 2R

din, 19A

dine, 6M

dinghy, 11E
dingle, 20C
dingo, 4B
dingy, 41A
dinner, 6A
dinnertime, 7A
dinosaur, 4C
dioxide, 59A
dip, 2P
diphtheria, 37B
diploma, 15H
diplomat, 1C
dipper, 8M
dire, 26D
direct, 10G
direction, 10G, 12G,
  14A
director, 1B
directory, 25A
dirge, 15D
dirigible, 11D
dirt, 29E
dirty, 41A
disagree, 10B
disagreeable, 5G
disappear, 2G
disappoint, 5I
disappointingly, 31E
disappointment, 5N
disarray, 55B
disaster, 40D
disastrous, 40D
disbelief, 5J
disburse, 28D
discard, 36A
discern, 12G
discharge, 2S
disciple, 1I
discipline, 5R, 33B
discomfort, 5H
disconcert, 5I
disconnect, 2W

discontent, 5I
discord, 10B
discount, 28D
discourage, 5I
discourse, 10A
discover, 12G
discoverer, 1L
discovery, 12D
discreet, 13K
discriminate, 12J, 27C
discuss, 10A
discussion, 10A
disdain, 5E
disease, 37A
disgrace, 10B
disguise, 36F
disgust, 5E
dish, 8M
dishcloth, 30F
dishevel, 41A
dishonest, 13M
dishpan, 8M
dishwasher, 1a
disk, 32B
dislike, 5E
disloyalty, 13M
dismal, 41A
dismantle, 33A
dismay, 5H
dismiss, 36A
disobey, 10B
disorder, 55B
disparage, 10B
dispatch, 2I
dispel, 2S
dispense, 2I
disperse, 2S
displace, 36A
display, 53A
displease, 5E
dispose, 36A
dispute, 10B

disquisition, 10A
disrupt, 5I
dissatisfied, 5I
dissect, 37F
dissemble, 10B
disseminate, 2S
dissent, 10B
dissertation, 15C
dissipate, 2S
dissolve, 2G, 16B
dissuade, 10E
distance, 14A
distant, 14K
distend, 32G
distill, 6K
distinct, 55A
distinctive, 55A
distinguish, 36F, 53B
distort, 10B
distract, 53A
distraught, 5D
distress, 5I
distribute, 2I
district, 18A
disturb, 5I
disturbance, 33C
disturbingly, 31E
ditch, 20C
ditto, 27A
ditty, 15D
diurnal, 7K
divan, 30D
dive, 16B
diver, 1D
diverge, 2W
diverse, 27C
divert, 2W
divest, 17I
divide, 49D
divine, 13J
divisible, 49D
division, 49D

divorce, 2W
divulge, 10H
dizzy, 37C
do, 2D, 50B
docile, 13L
dock, 16I
docket, 25A
dockyard, 16I
doctor, 1U
doctrine, 12L
document, 15C
dodder, 2L
dodge, 2F
doe, 4E
does, 50B
doeskin, 4L
doesn't, 46A
doff, 17I
dog, 4B
doggerel, 15D
doghouse, 4M
dogie, 4D
dogma, 12L
dogsled, 11C
dogwood, 24B
doily, 30F
doing, 50B
doldrums, 5H
dole, 28A
doll, 34F
dollar, 28C
dolor, 5H
dolphin, 4H
dolt, 9G
domain, 20A
dome, 30B
domestic, 30E
domicile, 21B
dominant, 36D
dominate, 36D
dominion, 36C
domino, 34F

don, 17I
donate, 28D
done, 50B
donkey, 4E
don't, 46A
doodle, 15I
doom, 42C
doomsday, 40D
door, 30B
doorbell, 19B
doorkeeper, 1Z
doorknob, 8I
doorman, 1Z
doorplate, 30B
doorpost, 30B
doorstep, 30B
doorstone, 30B
doorway, 30A
dooryard, 20G
dope, 9G
dormant, 13C
dormer, 30B
dormitory, 21B
dory, 11E
dose, 37F
dot, 3F
dote, 5O
double, 3G
doubt, 5N
doubtful, 42C
doubtless, 31A
douche, 41B
dough, 6G
doughboy, 1J
doughnut, 6C
doughty, 13N
dour, 5I
douse, 16B
dove, 4J
dovecote, 4M
dovetail, 2V
dowdy, 17J

dowel, 8H
dower, 28A
down, 14J
downcast, 5H
downfall, 36D
downgrade, 10B
downhearted, 5H
downhill, 14J
downpour, 40B
downright, 3K
downstairs, 14J
downstream, 16H
downtown, 18A
downtrodden, 28E
downward, 14J
downwind, 14J
doze, 12E
dozen, 3H
drab, 38E
draft, 15I, 41B
draftsman, 1X
draftsperson, 1X
drag, 2K
dragon, 4C
dragonfly, 4K
drain, 16B
drainboard, 30D
drainpipe, 22D
drake, 4J
dram, 3E
drama, 47A
drape, 30F
drastic, 5F
draw, 15I
drawbridge, 11H
drawer, 30D
drawing, 15E
drawl, 10A
drawstring, 8H
dread, 5B
dreadful, 26D
dream, 12E

dreamland, 12E
dreary, 41A
dredge, 8G
dregs, 41A
drench, 16B
dress, 17C
dressmaker, 1N
dressmaking, 17I
dribble, 16B
drift, 16B
driftwood, 22C
drill, 8E
drink, 6M
drip, 16B
drive, 11G
drivel, 10B
driver, 1V
driveway, 11H
drizzle, 16A
droll, 13I
drone, 4K
droop, 2P
drop, 2P
droplet, 16D
dropper, 22A
drought, 40D
drown, 16B
drowsy, 12E
drub, 44A
drudge, 1d
drug, 37F
drugstore, 21D
drum, 47C
drummer, 1G
drumstick, 47C
dry, 40E
dry goods, 17K
dub, 15A
duchess, 1C
duck, 4J
duckbill, 4L
duckling, 4D

duckweed, 24E
duct, 22D
dude, 9C
due, 7G
duel, 33C
dues, 28B
duet, 47B
duff, 24E
dugout, 21C
duke, 1C
dulcet, 47B
dull, 32E, 38E
Duluth, 18D
dumb, 12K
dumbbell, 34C
dump, 2P
dunce, 9G
dune, 20D
dung, 29E
dungarees, 17C
dungeon, 21C
dunghill, 29E
dunk, 2P
duplex, 3G
duplicate, 27A
durability, 57B
durable, 57B
duration, 7D
duress, 33B
during, 7I
dusk, 7C
dust, 29E
duty, 13B
dwarf, 9J
dwell, 54A
dweller, 9I
dwelling, 21B
dwindle, 2R
dye, 58B
dynamite, 8N
dynamo, 8B
dynasty, 25C

enamel, 58B
enchant, 5J
encircle, 2X
enclose, 2X
encompass, 2X
encore, 7K
encounter, 2V
encourage, 10D
encroach, 2G
encyclopedia, 15C
end, 2E, 14F
endanger, 56B
endeavor, 1d
endemic, 9I
endless, 7K
endorse, 5O
endpoint, 14F
endurance, 54B
endure, 54B
enemy, 9G
energetic, 13B
enforce, 10G
engage, 1d, 2V
engender, 39A
engine, 8B
engineer, 1L
engrave, 15I
engross, 12F
engulf, 16B
enhance, 3G
enigma, 12D
enjoy, 5O
enjoyable, 5K
enjoyment, 5K
enlarge, 2S
enlighten, 12G
enlist, 10E
enliven, 5J
enmesh, 2J
ennui, 12E
enormous, 3A
enough, 3J, 45E

enrage, 5E
enrich, 33D
enroll, 10J
ensconce, 36F
ensemble, 25B
ensue, 2D
entail, 39A
enter, 14H
enterprise, 51A
entertain, 5K
entertainer, 1H
entertainment, 51B
enthrall, 5J
enthuse, 5J
enthusiasm, 13B
enthusiastic, 13B
entice, 10E
entire, 3G
entire(ly), 3K
entitle, 15A
entity, 22E, 54A
entomology, 1L
entourage, 25B
entrails, 23H
entrance, 30A
entreat, 10E
entrust, 5O
enunciate, 10C
envelope, 22A
environ, 2X
environment, 40A, 51A
envoy, 1C
envy, 5M
enzyme, 59A
epaulet, 17B
ephemeris, 15C
epic, 15B
epicure, 9L
epidemic, 37A
epigram, 15D
epilogue, 47A
episode, 15C

epistle, 15F
epitaph, 15F
epithet, 15A
epitome, 26C
epoch, 7D
equal, 27A
equality, 27A
equally, 27B
equanimity, 5L
equation, 49C
equestrian, 1D
equilateral, 32C
equilibrium, 55B
equinox, 7D
equip, 8A
equipment, 8A
equivalent, 27A
equivocal, 42C
era, 7D
eradicate, 33A
erase, 33A
eraser, 15G
erect, 32H
eremite, 1W
erode, 33A
err, 26B
errand, 1A
errant, 2G
error, 26A
erudite, 12K
erupt, 2S
escalate, 2O
escalator, 11B
escape, 36B
escarp, 20D
eschew, 2F
escort, 33D
escutcheon, 17H
esoteric, 42B
especially, 3K
essay, 15C
essence, 12B, 26C

essential, 26C
essentially, 31A
establish, 22F
establishment, 21A
estate, 21B
esteem, 5O
estimate, 12D
estuary, 16F
etch, 15I
eternal, 7K
eternity, 7F
ethereal, 57B
ethics, 12L
ethnic, 9I
etiquette, 5R
etymology, 1L
eucalyptus, 24B
eulogy, 10A
eunuch, 9C
euphemism, 15A
euphony, 47B
Europe, 18B
evade, 36B
evaporate, 16B
evaporation, 16D
eve, 7C
even, 27A, 32H
evening, 7C
event, 51A
eventual, 7H
eventually, 7H
ever, 7K
evergreen, 24B
everlasting, 7K
every, 3I
everybody, 45E
everyday, 7F
everyone, 45E
everything, 45E
everywhere, 14D
evict, 2I
evidence, 12D

evident, 42A
evidently, 31A
evil, 26D
evildoer, 9G
evince, 12D
evoke, 36E
evolve, 54B
ewer, 22A
exact, 27A
exactly, 3J
exaggerate, 10B
exaggeration, 10B
exam, 12C
examination, 10F, 12C
examine, 12C
example, 27A
exasperate, 5I
excavate, 8G
exceed, 3G
exceedingly, 3K
excel, 36D
excellent, 26C
excelsior, 22C
except, 27D
except for, 27D
exceptional, 26C
exceptionally, 3K
excerpt, 15C
excess, 3G
exchange, 36A
excise, 28B
excite, 5J
excitement, 5J
exclaim, 10C
exclamation, 10A
exclamatory, 35B
exclude, 5P
exclusively, 3J
excrescence, 23B
excrete, 2K
excruciate, 37C
exculpate, 33D

excursion, 2G
excursive, 10A
excuse, 10G
execrate, 5E
execute, 33B
exempt, 10G
exercise, 34D
exert, 2D
exhale, 60D
exhaust, 32G
exhausted, 37C
exhaustion, 37C
exhibit, 10C
exhilarate, 5J
exhort, 10E
exhume, 8G
exigent, 26C
exist, 54A
existence, 54A
exit, 2G
exodus, 2G
exonerate, 33D
exorable, 13A
exorbitant, 28E
exorcise, 2I
exordium, 2C
exotic, 55A
expand, 2S
expanse, 20A
expansion, 2S
expatiate, 10A
expect, 5Q
expectant, 13F
expectorate, 60C
expedite, 56A
expedition, 2G
expel, 2S
expend, 28D
expense, 28B
expensive, 28E
experience, 51A
experiment, 12C

experimentation, 12C
expert, 9L
expiate, 33D
expire, 54A
explain, 10C
expletive, 35B
explicate, 10C
explicit, 10A
explode, 2S
exploit, 10G
exploration, 2G
explore, 12C
explorer, 1L
explosion, 2S
explosive, 8N
exponent, 49C
export, 2I
expose, 10H
expound, 10C
express, 10C
expression, 10A
expressway, 11H
expunge, 33A
exquisite, 43C
extant, 54A
extempore, 7J
extend, 2S, 32F
extension, 2S
extensive, 3G
extent, 3A
extenuate, 2R
exterior, 14H
external, 14H
extinct, 54A
extinguish, 2F, 33A
extinguisher, 52E
extirpate, 33A
extol, 10D
extort, 36E
extra, 3G
extract, 36E
extraordinary, 26C

extrapolate, 12D
extravagant, 28E
extreme(ly), 3K
extricate, 36B
extrude, 2K
exuberant, 13B
exult, 5J
eye, 23E
eyeball, 23E
eyebrow, 23E
eyeglasses, 17D
eyelash, 23E
eyelid, 23E
eyepiece, 8K
eyeshade, 17D
eyesight, 23E
eyesore, 41A
eyestrain, 37B

F

fable, 15B
fabric, 17K
fabricate, 22F
fabulous, 26C
face, 23C
facetious, 13I
facile, 56A
fact, 12D
faction, 25B
factor, 3F
factory, 21E
factotum, 1A
faculty, 5R
fad, 17A
fade, 38C
Fahrenheit, 52A
fail, 26B
failure, 26A, 36D
faint, 38E
fainthearted, 13L
fair, 26A, 51B

fair-minded, 13N
fairness, 26A
fairway, 11H
fairy, 9F
fairyland, 12E
faith, 5N
faithful, 13N
fake, 12G
falcon, 4J
fall, 2P, 7D
fallacy, 26A
fallible, 26A
fallout, 3F
fallow, 29C
false, 26A
falsehood, 10B
falter, 2B
fame, 42A
familiar, 42A
family, 9N, 25C
famine, 37A
famish, 6N
famous, 42A
fan, 17G
fanatic, 13O
fanatical, 13O
fancy, 55B
fanfare, 51B
fang, 23D
fantail, 4J
fantasize, 12E
fantastic, 26C
fantasy, 12E
far, 14K
faraway, 14K
farce, 5K
fare, 28B
farewell, 10K
farina, 6D
farm, 21L
farmer, 1F
farmhouse, 21B

farmland, 20F
farmyard, 4M
farseeing, 12K
farsighted, 53A
fascinate, 5J
fascism, 9O
fashion, 17A
fashionable, 17J
fast, 7J
fasten, 2V
fastidious, 13H
fat, 43D
fatal, 33B
fate, 42C
father, 9N
fatherland, 18A
fathom, 3B
fatigue, 37C
fatuous, 26D
faubourg, 18A
faucet, 16C
fault, 26A
faulty, 26A
fauna, 4A
favor, 5O
favorite, 26C
fawn, 4D
fear, 5B
fearful, 5B
fearless, 13N
feasible, 42C
feast, 6A
feat, 51A
feather, 4L
featherbedding, 1d
February, 7E
fecund, 54A
federal, 25C
federate, 2V, 25A
federation, 25C
fee, 28B
feeble, 43A

feed, 6M
feel, 44A
feeling, 5A
feet, 23G
feign, 12G
feldspar, 29A
felicity, 5K
feline, 4B
fellow, 9C
felon, 9G
felt, 17K
female, 9B
feminine, 9B
fence, 30C, 34B
fencing, 34B
fend, 33D
ferment, 59A
fern, 24E
ferocious, 5F
ferrule, 8H
ferry, 11E
ferryboat, 11E
fertile, 54A
fertilize, 29F
ferule, 44A
fervent, 13B
fester, 37E
festival, 51B
festoon, 30E
fetch, 2I
fetid, 60B
fetish, 5O
fetter, 2V
fetus, 9D
feud, 33C
feudal, 9O
feudalism, 9O
fever, 37C
feverish, 37C
few, 3G
fez, 17D
fiance, 9E

fiasco, 36D
fiat, 15H
fib, 10B
fiber, 17K
fickle, 13O
fiction, 15B
fiddle, 47C
fidelity, 13N
fidget, 2N
fief, 20A
field, 20F
fielder, 1D
fiend, 9G
fierce, 5F
fife, 47C
fifteen, 3H
fifteenth, 3H
fifth, 3H
fiftieth, 3H
fifty, 3H
fig, 6I
fight, 33C
fighter, 1D
figment, 12E
figure, 32A
figurehead, 1C
filament, 38D
filbert, 6J
filch, 36E
file, 25A
filial, 9N
filibuster, 2B
filigree, 57B
fill, 32G
fillet, 32D
fillip, 2N
film, 47A
filter, 41B
filth, 41A
filthy, 41A
fin, 4L
final, 2E

finance, 28C

finch, 4J

find, 36F

fine, 26C

finespun, 57B

finger, 23F

fingernail, 23F

fingerprint, 23F

fingertip, 23F

finicky, 13H

finish, 2E

finite, 3G

fir, 24B

fire, 52C

firearms, 8N

fireball, 8N

firebox, 19B

firebrand, 52C

firecracker, 8N

firefly, 4K

firelight, 38A

firelock, 8N

fireman, 1J

fireplace, 30B

fireproof, 52B

fireside, 30B

firewood, 52E

fireworks, 8N

firm, 57A

first, 3H

fiscal, 28E

fish, 4H, 4O

fisher, 1F

fisherman, 1F

fishery, 21L

fishhook, 8H

fishline, 8H

fishmonger, 1N

fishtail, 2M

fishwife, 9G

fission, 2W

fissure, 20C

fist, 23F

fit, 17I

five, 3H

fix, 22F

fizz, 19E

fjord, 16F

flabby, 43D

flaccid, 43A

flag, 53A

flagitious, 26D

flagon, 22A

flagpole, 22D

flagrant, 42A

flagship, 11E

Flagstaff, 18D

flagstone, 29B

flail, 44A

flair, 5R

flake, 3F

flame, 52C

flange, 22D

flank, 14B

flannel, 17K

flapjack, 6D

flare, 38D

flash, 38B

flashlight, 38D

flask, 22A

flat, 32H

flatboat, 11E

flatfoot, 23G

flatiron, 8D

flatly, 31A

flatten, 32E

flatter, 10D

flatworm, 4K

flaunt, 53A

flavor, 6L

flaw, 26A

flax, 24D

flay, 33B

flea, 4K

fleck, 3F

flee, 36B

fleece, 4L

fleet, 7J

flesh, 23B

flex, 32B

flick, 2J

flicker, 52C

flier, 1V

flight, 2G

flimsy, 57B

flinch, 5C

fling, 2J

flint, 29A

flintlock, 8N

flip, 2J

flipper, 4L

flirt, 5Q

flit, 2L

flitch, 6E

float, 16B

flock, 25B

floe, 16A

flog, 33B

flood, 40D

floor, 30B

floorwalker, 1B

flop, 2Q

flora, 24A

Florida, 18C

florist, 1N

floss, 41C

flotilla, 11E

flounce, 2N

flounder, 4H

flour, 6G

flourish, 54B

flow, 16B

flower, 24A

flowerpot, 30E

fluctuate, 2L

flue, 30B

fluent, 10A, 56A

fluff, 3F

fluid, 16A

fluke, 42C

flume, 16I

flurry, 7J

flush, 16B

fluster, 12G

flute, 47C

flutter, 2L

flux, 16B, 27C

fly, 4K, 4O, 11G

flying fish, 4H

flyleaf, 15G

flytrap, 24D

flywheel, 8B

foam, 16E

focus, 53B

foe, 9G

fog, 16D

foggy, 40E

foghorn, 19B

foible, 26A

foil, 22B

fold, 17I

folder, 22A

foliage, 24C

folio, 15C

folk, 9A

follow, 2H

folly, 26A

fond, 5O

fondle, 44A

food, 6B

foodstuff, 6B

fool, 9G

foolhardy, 13P

foolish, 26D

foolishly, 31G

foolishness, 10B

foot, 3E, 23G

football, 34B

foothill, 20D
footwear, 17E
footwork, 48A
fop, 9G
for, 39B
for all that, 39B
for as much, 39B
for example, 27B
for the fact that, 39B
forage, 4O
foray, 33C
forbid, 10G
force, 2T, 10G
forceps, 8H
ford, 16B
fore, 14F
forecast, 12D
forehead, 23C
foreign, 55A
foreigner, 9I
foreman, 1B
foremost, 26C
forensic, 1Y
foresee, 12D
forest, 20E
forester, 1F
forever, 7K
forevermore, 7K
forfeit, 36A
forfend, 33D
forge, 22F
forget, 12A
forgive, 5O
forgiveness, 13A
fork, 8M
forklift, 11B
forlorn, 5H
form, 22F, 32A
formal, 43C
formation, 22F
former, 7G
formidable, 57B

formula, 49C
fort, 21C
forth, 14F
forthcoming, 26A
forthright, 13N
forthwith, 7H
fortification, 21C
fortress, 21C
fortunate, 13G
fortunately, 31D
fortune, 28A
fortuneteller, 1H
fortunetelling, 10B
forty, 3H
forum, 21I
forward, 14F
fosse, 20C
fossil, 4A
foster, 33D
foul, 26D, 41A
found, 22F
foundation, 25E
founder, 1B
fountain, 16C
fountainhead, 16F
four, 3H
fourposters, 30D
fourscore, 3H
foursquare, 32C
fourteen, 3H
fourteenth, 3H
fourth, 3H
fowl, 4J
fox, 4B
foxglove, 24D
foxhound, 4B
foyer, 30A
fracas, 19C
fraction, 49B
fractional, 3G
fracture, 33A
fragile, 57B

fragment, 3F
fragrance, 60B
fragrant, 60B
frail, 43A, 57B
frame, 32A
framework, 32A
France, 18B
franchise, 10G, 21D
frank, 13E
frankfurter, 6D
frankly, 31A
frantic, 5B, 13O
fraternal, 9N
fraternity, 25B
fraud, 10B
fraught, 32G
fray, 33C
freak, 27C
freckle, 23B
free, 13D, 28E, 36B
freeboot, 36E
freeborn, 13D
freedom, 13D
freeman, 9I
freestone, 29C
freethinker, 13J
freeway, 11H
freeze, 16B
freezer, 8D
freight, 22A
freighter, 11E
frenzy, 7J
frequent, 7K
fresco, 47D
fresh, 7G
freshman, 1I
fret, 5D
fretwork, 30E
friable, 57B
friar, 1W
fricassee, 6K
friction, 33C

Friday, 7E
friend, 9E
friendship, 13N
frieze, 30E
fright, 5B
frighten, 5C
frightful, 5B
frigid, 52A
frill, 17B
fringe, 17B
frippery, 17A
frisk, 48A
fritter, 6D
frivolous, 13P
frizz, 32B
frock, 17C
frog, 4C
frogman, 1L
frolic, 5K
from, 14G, 39B
front, 14F
front-page, 15C
frontier, 20A
frontiersman, 1L
frontierswoman, 1L
frost, 16A
frostbite, 37E
froth, 16E
frown, 60A
frowsy, 41A
frugal, 13P
fruit, 6B
frump, 9G
frustrate, 5I
fry, 6K
fuddle, 12G
fudge, 6C
fuel, 8C
fugitive, 9H
fulcrum, 8J
fulfill, 2E
full, 32G

fully, 3K
fulminate, 2S
fumble, 44C
fume, 60B
fun, 5K
function, 2D
fund, 28C
fundamental, 26C
fundamentally, 31A
funeral, 54A
fungus, 24E
funnel, 16C
funny, 13I
fur, 4L
furbish, 22F
furious, 5E
furl, 17I, 22G
furlong, 3E
furnace, 8D
furnish, 2I, 30E
furnishing, 30D
furniture, 30D
furrow, 20C
furry, 57A
further, 27B
furthermore, 27B
furtive, 42B
fury, 5E
fuse, 2V
fuselage, 11F
fusion, 2V
fuss, 7J
futile, 26D
future, 7F
fuzzy, 38E

G

gable, 30B
gad, 10K
gadabout, 9G
gadfly, 4K

gadget, 8A
gaff, 26A
gag, 5K
gage, 10I
gaggle, 25B
gain, 28A
gait, 48A
gala, 51B
galaxy, 20H
gale, 40B
gall, 5E
gallant, 13N
galleon, 11E
gallery, 21F
galley, 11F
gallon, 3E
gallop, 4O
gallows, 33B
galore, 3K
galosh, 17E
galvanic, 61A
galvanometer, 3C
gamble, 42C
gambol, 48A
game, 34A
gamekeeper, 1Z
gamesman, 9L
gamin, 9C
gamut, 25A
gander, 4J
gang, 25B
gangling, 43A
gangplank, 11F
gangway, 11H
gannet, 4J
gantry, 8J
gap, 20C
gape, 2U, 53B
garage, 30A
garb, 17A
garbage, 41A
garbageman, 1R

garble, 12G
garden, 20G
gardener, 1F
gardenia, 24D
gargle, 6M
gargoyle, 30E
garish, 17J
garland, 17G
garlic, 6G
garment, 17A
garnish, 6B
garret, 30A
garrison, 21C
garrulous, 10A
garter, 17E
gas, 8C
gash, 37E
gasket, 8B
gaslight, 38D
gasoline, 8C
gasp, 19C
gate, 30C
gatekeeper, 1Z
gatepost, 30C
gateway, 30C
gather, 25A
gathering, 25E
gauche, 12K
gauge, 3C
gaunt, 43A
gauntlet, 17E
gauze, 17K
gavel, 8E
gawky, 43A
gay, 5K
gaze, 53B
gazelle, 4E
gazette, 15C
gazetteer, 1E
gear, 8B
gearbox, 8B
gee, 10K

gel, 57C
gelatin, 6G
gem, 29B
gender, 35A
gene, 54A
general, 7K
general(ly), 3J
generate, 22F
generation, 7D
generator, 8B
generic, 42A
generous, 13A
genesis, 2C
genetic, 54A
genial, 5K, 13A
genie, 9F
genital, 23K
genius, 9L
genocide, 33B
gentle, 13A
gentlefolk, 9A
gentleman, 9C
gentlemen, 9C
gentlewoman, 9B
genuflect, 48E
genuine, 26A
genus, 25B
geographer, 1L
geographic, 20B
geographical, 20B
geography, 1L
geological, 20B
geologist, 1L
geology, 1L
geometry, 49A
Georgia, 18C
geranium, 24D
germ, 37D
germane, 26A
Germany, 18B
germinate, 54A
gerrymander, 51C

gesture, 44C
get, 2I, 36E
get to, 50D
getaway, 36B
gewgaw, 17G
geyser, 16F
ghastly, 26D
ghetto, 18A
ghost, 9F
ghostly, 26D
ghoul, 9F
giant, 3A, 9J
gibberish, 10B
gibe, 10B
giblet, 6E
giddy, 13O
gift, 28A
gig, 11E
giggle, 19C
gill, 4L
gimlet, 8E
gimmick, 34E
gin, 6H
ginger, 6G
gingerbread, 6C
gingersnap, 6C
giraffe, 4E
gird, 2X
girl, 9B
girlfriend, 9E
gist, 26C
give, 2I
gizzard, 6E
glac, 16A
glacier, 16A
glad, 5K
glade, 20E
gladiator, 1T
glair, 6F
glamour, 17A
glance, 53B
gland, 23H

glare, 53B
glass, 8M
glasses, 17D
glassware, 8M
glaze, 22F
gleam, 38A
glean, 12G
glee, 5K
gleeful, 5K
glen, 20C
glib, 56A
glide, 11G
glider, 11D
glimmer, 38A
glimpse, 53B
glint, 38A
glisten, 38B
glitter, 38B
gloat, 5M
global, 20H
globe, 20H
glockenspiel, 47C
glomerate, 25A
gloom, 5H, 38C
glorious, 26C
glory, 42A
gloss, 38A
gloves, 17E
glow, 38B
glower, 53B
glowworm, 4K
glucose, 6B
glue, 8H
glut, 6M
gnarl, 24C
gnash, 8G
gnat, 4K
gnaw, 6M
gneiss, 29A
gnome, 9F
gnostic, 12K
go, 2G

goad, 44A
goal, 34C
goalkeeper, 1D
goat, 4E
goatskin, 4L
gob, 3F
gobble, 19D
goblet, 8M
goblin, 9F
god, 9F
godchild, 9N
goddaughter, 9N
godfather, 9N
godhead, 9F
godmother, 9N
godsend, 26C
godson, 9N
goggles, 17D
gold 29A, 58A
golden, 58A
golden haired, 58A
goldenrod, 24D
goldfish, 4H
goldsmith, 1N
golf, 34B
gondola, 11E
gong, 19B
goo, 16E
good, 26C
good-bye, 10K
goodby, 10K
goodness, 13A
goose, 4J
gooseberry, 6I
gore, 23I
gorge, 6M
gorgeous, 43C
gorilla, 4G
gossamer, 57B
gossip, 9G
gouge, 8E
gourmand, 9G

gout, 37B
govern, 10G
government, 25C
governor, 1C
gown, 17C
grab, 44B
grace, 13A
graceful, 43A
gracious, 13A
grade, 3E
graduate, 1I, 2E
graduation, 51B
graft, 2V
graham, 6G
grain, 6J
gram, 3E
grammar, 35A
grand, 3A
grandchildren, 9N
granddaughter, 9N
grandfather, 9N
grandma, 9N
grandmother, 9N
grandnephew, 9N
grandpa, 9N
grandparent, 9N
grandson, 9N
grandstand, 21G
grange, 21L
granite, 29B
granny, 9N
grant, 28A
grape, 6I
grapefruit, 6I
grapevine, 24E
graph, 15E
graphite, 29A
grapple, 44B
grasp, 44B
grass, 24E
grasshopper, 4K
grassland, 20F

grate, 8G

grateful, 13A

gratis, 28E

gratitude, 5O

grave, 13H

gravedigger, 1F

gravel, 29B

gravestone, 21M

graveyard, 20G

gravity, 2K

gravy, 6G

gray, 58A

graze, 4O

grease, 8C

greasy, 6L

great, 3A

greatcoat, 17F

greatly, 3K

greatness, 3A

greed, 5Q

greedy, 5Q

green, 58A

greenback, 28C

greenery, 24A

greenhorn, 9L

greenhouse, 21K

Greenland, 18B

greenwood, 20E

greet, 10D

greeting, 10D

gregarious, 13A

grenade, 8N

grey-headed, 58A

greyhaired, 58A

greyhound, 4B

griddle, 8D

grief-stricken, 5H

grieve, 5H

grill, 6K

grim, 26D

grime, 41A

grin, 60A

grind, 8G

grindstone, 29B

grip, 8I, 44B

gripe, 10B

grisly, 26D

grist, 6J

gristle, 23J

gristmill, 21E

grit, 13N

grizzle, 58A

groan, 19C

grocer, 1N

grocery, 21D

grog, 6H

groggy, 37C

groom, 9N

groove, 20C

grope, 44A

gross, 49B

grotesque, 55A

grotto, 20C

ground, 29E

groundwork, 22F

group, 25A

grout, 22D

grove, 20E

grovel, 48B

grow, 54B

grower, 1F

growl, 19D

grown-up, 9D

growth, 24A

grub, 29F

grubstake, 28A

grudge, 5M

gruel, 6D

grueling, 56A

gruesome, 26D

gruff, 5G

grumpy, 5G

grunt, 19D

guano, 29E

guaranty, 10I

guard, 1T

guardhouse, 21C

guardian, 9N

guardroom, 21C

guerilla, 1J

guess, 12D

guest, 9H

guffaw, 19C

guide, 33D

guidebook, 15C

guideline, 10G

guild, 25E

guildhall, 21I

guile, 13M

guillotine, 8N

guilt, 5D

guilty, 5D

guinea, 28C

guise, 5R, 10B

guitar, 47C

gulch, 20C

gulf, 16F

gull, 4J

gullet, 23D

gulley, 20C

gulp, 19C

gum, 6C, 23D

gumdrop, 6C

gun, 8N

gunboat, 11E

gunfighter, 9G

gunny, 17K

gunnysack, 22A

gunpowder, 8N

gunshot, 8N

gunsmith, 1N

gunstock, 8N

gunwale, 11F

guppy, 4H

gurgle, 19E

gush, 16B

gusher, 16F

gusset, 17B

gust, 40B

gustatory, 6L

gusto, 43A

gut, 23H

gutter, 30C

guttural, 23D

guy, 9C

guzzle, 6M

gym, 21G

gymnast, 1D

gypsy, 9H

gyrate, 2X

gyre, 32B

H

ha, 10K

haberdasher, 1N

habiliments, 17A

habit, 12L

habitat, 21B

habitual, 7K

hack, 8G

hackle, 4L

hackney, 4E

hacksaw, 8E

had, 50B

had best, 50D

had better, 50D

hadn't, 46A

haft, 8I

hag, 9F

haggle, 10B

hail, 16A

hailstone, 16A

hailstorm, 40B

hair, 23B

hairbreadth, 32F

haircloth, 17K

haircut, 41B

hairline, 23B

hairpin, 17G

hale, 37A

half, 3G

halfback, 1D

halftone, 38C

halfway, 14F

halibut, 4H

hall, 30A

hallucinate, 12E

hallucination, 12E

hallway, 30A

halo, 32B

halt, 2F

halter, 4N

halyard, 11F

ham, 6E

hamburger, 6D

hamlet, 18A

hammer, 8E

hammerhead, 4H

hammock, 34C

hamper, 22A

hamster, 4F

hand, 23F

handbag, 28F

handbill, 15F

handbook, 15C

handcuff, 8H

handful, 3E

handicap, 43A

handkerchief, 17G

handle, 8I

handmade, 17J

handmaid, 1Z

handout, 28B

handshake, 44C

handsome, 43C

handspike, 8E

handwork, 17I

handwriting, 15I

handwritten, 15I

hang, 2B

hangar, 21J

hangdog, 5H

hangman, 1T

hangover, 37B

hank, 32B

hanker, 5Q

happen, 2D

happening, 51A

happily, 31D

happiness, 5K

happy, 5K

harangue, 10A

harass, 5I

harbinger, 10B

harbor, 16I

hard, 57A

harden, 57C

hardly, 3J

hardpan, 29B

hardtack, 6D

hardware, 8A

hardwood, 22C

hare, 4E

harebrained, 26D

harem, 9N

hark, 19A

harlequin, 1H

harm, 33B

harmful, 56B

harmless, 56B

harmony, 27A

harness, 4N

harp, 47C

harpoon, 8N

Harrisburg, 18D

harrow, 11B, 29F

harry, 5I

harsh, 19A

Hartford, 18D

harvest, 29F

has, 50B

hash, 6B

hasn't, 46A

hasp, 8H

hassock, 30F

haste, 7J

hasten, 7J

hastily, 7J

hasty, 7J

hat, 17D

hatch, 54A

hatchet, 8F

hatchway, 11F

hate, 5E

hatred, 5E

haughty, 13E

haul, 2K

haunch, 23G

haunt, 5C

have, 36C, 50B

have to, 50D

havelock, 17D

haven, 21C

haven't, 46A

havoc, 55B

haw, 10K

Hawaii, 18C

hawk, 4J

hay, 24E

hayfield, 20F

hayloft, 21K

hayrack, 11A

haystack, 24E

haywire, 13O

hazard, 42C, 56B

hazardous, 56B

haze, 38C

hazel, 58A

hazelnut, 6J

he, 45A

head, 23C

headache, 37C

headband, 17D

headboard, 30D

headdress, 17D

headfirst, 7J

headgear, 17D

heading, 15A

headland, 16G

headlight, 11F

headline, 15C

headlong, 7J

headmaster, 1B

headmistress, 1B

headpiece, 17D

headquarters, 21E

headstone, 21M

headstrong, 13H

headwaters, 16F

headway, 2G

heal, 33D

health, 37A, 43A

healthful, 37A

heap, 25A

hear, 19A

hearsay, 10B

hearse, 11A

heart, 23H

heartache, 5H

heartbreak, 5H

heartfelt, 13B

hearth, 30B

hearthstone, 30B

heartrending, 5H

heartsick, 5H

heartstrings, 5A

heartwood, 22C

heat, 52A

heater, 8D

heath, 20B

heathen, 13J

heave, 2J

heaven, 18A

heavy, 43D

heavyweight, 1D

heckle, 10B	herd, 25B	highbrow, 9L	hobgoblin, 9F
hectic, 13O	herdsman, 1F	highland, 20D	hobnail, 8H
he'd, 46E	here, 14D	highly, 3K	hobnob, 10A
hedge, 30C	hereafter, 7H	highness, 9A	hobo, 9H
hedgehog, 4E	hereby, 39B	highroad, 11H	hockey, 34B
hedgerow, 24A	herein, 39B	highway, 11H	hod, 22A
heed, 10G	hereinafter, 7H	hijack, 36E	hoe, 8E
heel, 23G	hereon, 14I	hike, 48A	hog, 4E
hegemony, 10G	here's, 46D	hilarious, 13I	hogan, 21B
height, 32F	heretofore, 7G	hill, 20D	hogshead, 22A
heinous, 26D	hereupon, 39B	hillside, 20D	hoist, 2O
heir, 9N	herewith, 39B	hilltop, 20D	hold, 44B
Helena, 18D	hermit, 1W	hilt, 8I	holder, 22A
helicopter, 11D	heroic, 13N	him, 45A	holdup, 36E
helium, 59A	heroine, 9K	himself, 45A	hole, 20C
hell, 18A	herring, 4H	hind, 14F	holiday, 51B
he'll, 46C	herringbone, 17K	hinder, 2B	Holland, 18B
hello, 10K	hers, 45B	hinge, 8H	holler, 19C
helm, 11F	herself, 45A	hint, 10E	hollow, 32G
helmet, 17D	he's, 46D	hippodrome, 21G	holly, 24D
help, 33D	hesitate, 2B	hips, 23G	holster, 8N
helpless, 13L	heterogeneous, 27C	hire, 1d	holy, 13J
helpmate, 9N	hew, 8G	hirsute, 23B	holystone, 29B
helter-skelter, 7J	hexagon, 32C	his, 45B	homage, 5O
helve, 8I	hey, 10K	hiss, 19D	home, 21B
hem, 17B	hi, 10K	historian, 1E	homecoming, 2I
hemlock, 24B	hiatus, 2B	historic, 7F	homeland, 18A
hemoglobin, 23I	hibernate, 12E	historical, 7F	homely, 43C
hemorrhage, 23I	hiccup, 19C	history, 7F	homemade, 30E
hemp, 24D	hickory, 24B	hit, 44A	homemaker, 1A
hemstitch, 17I	hidalgo, 1C	hitch, 2V	homer, 34C
hen, 4J	hide, 4L, 36F	hitchhike, 2G	homesick, 5I
hence, 39B	hidebound, 13H	hither, 14G	homespun, 17K
henceforth, 7H	hideous, 43C	hitherto, 7G	homestead, 21B
henceforward, 7H	hie, 7J	hive, 4M	hometown, 18A
henchman, 9G	hierarch, 1W	ho, 10K	homeward, 14K
hencoop, 4M	hieratic, 13J	hoar, 7F	homework, 12C
henhouse, 4M	hieroglyph, 35C	hoard, 36F	homicide, 33B
henpeck, 5I	high, 14I	hoarfrost, 16A	homily, 10A
her, 45B	highball, 6H	hoarse, 19A	hominy, 6J
herald, 10C	highborn, 13N	hobble, 48A	homogeneous, 27A
herb, 6G	highboy, 30D	hobby, 34A	homograph, 35B

homonym, 35B

homophone, 35B

hone, 32E

honest, 13N, 26A

honestly, 31A

honesty, 26A

honey, 6C

honeybee, 4K

honeycomb, 4M

honeydew, 6I

honeymoon, 51B

honeysuckle, 24D

honk, 19D

honor, 42A

honorable, 26A

hood, 17D

hoodoo, 34E

hoodwink, 12G

hoof, 4L

hoofbeat, 19D

hook, 8H

hookup, 2V

hookworm, 4K

hoop, 22D

hoot, 19D

hop, 48D

hope, 5N

hopeful, 13E

hopefully, 31H

hopeless, 5N

hopper, 22A

hopscotch, 34F

horde, 25B

horizon, 14B

horizontal, 14C

horn, 19B

hornblende, 29A

hornbook, 15C

hornet, 4K

hornpipe, 47C

horrible, 26D

horrify, 5C

horror, 5B

horse, 4E

horseback, 4O

horsecar, 11A

horseflesh, 4E

horsehair, 4L

horsehide, 4L

horseless, 4O

horseman, 1D

horseplay, 34D

horseradish, 6G

horseshoe, 4N

horsetail, 24E

horsewhip, 33B

horsewoman, 1D

hose, 16C

hospital, 21H

hospitality, 13A

host, 9C

hostage, 9G

hostess, 9B

hostile, 5E

hot, 52A

hotbed, 29E

hotel, 21B

hotfoot, 7J

hothead, 9G

hothouse, 21K

hound, 4B

hour, 7C

hourglass, 7B

hourly, 7K

house, 21B

houseboat, 11E

housefly, 4K

household, 9N

housekeeper, 1Z

housekeeping, 1A

housetop, 30B

housewife, 9B

housework, 1A

Houston, 18D

hovel, 21B

hover, 2B

how, 45F

howbeit, 27D

howdy, 10K

however, 27D

howl, 19D

how's, 46D

howsoever, 27D

hub, 11F

hubbub, 5J

huckleberry, 24D

huckster, 9G

huddle, 25B

hue, 58A

huff, 5E

hug, 44B

huge, 3A

hulk, 11E

hull, 11F

hullabaloo, 19C

hum, 19C

human, 9A

humble, 28E

humdrum, 42A

humid, 16B

humiliation, 5D

hummingbird, 4J

humor, 5K

humorous, 13I

hump, 23B

humpback, 4H

humus, 29E

hunch, 12D

hunchback, 9G

hundred, 3H

hunger, 6N

hungry, 6N

hunt, 4O

hunter, 1F

hurdle, 34C

hurl, 2J

hurrah, 10K

hurricane, 40B

hurry, 7J

hurt, 33B

hurtle, 7J

husband, 9N

hush, 19A

husk, 24E

husky, 43D

hustle, 7J

hut, 21K

hutch, 30D

hybrid, 25A

hydrant, 16C

hydraulic, 16C

hydrochloric, 59B

hydroelectric, 61A

hydrogen, 59A

hydrostatic, 16C

hyena, 4B

hygiene, 41B

hymn, 15D

hymnal, 15C

hyperbole, 10B

hyphen, 35A

hypnosis, 12E

hypocrisy, 10B

hysteria, 5B

I

I, 45A

ice, 16A

iceberg, 16A

icebox, 8D

icebreaker, 11E

icecap, 16A

icehouse, 21A

icicle, 16A

icon, 35C

icy, 40E

I'd, 46E

Idaho, 18C
idea, 12A
ideal, 12L
ideally, 31A
identical, 27A
identify, 15A, 53B
ides, 7D
idiom, 35A
idiosyncrasy, 5R
idle, 13C
idol, 9K
idyll, 15D
if, 39B
if only, 39B
if...then, 39B
igloo, 21B
ignite, 52C
ignominy, 42A
ignorance, 12K
ignorant, 12K
ignore, 53B
ill, 37A
I'll, 46C
illicit, 26A
Illinois, 18C
illness, 37A
illuminate, 38B
illumine, 38B
illusion, 12E
illustrate, 15I
illustration, 15E
I'm, 46D
image, 53A
imagination, 12A
imaginative, 12K
imbecile, 9G
imbibe, 6M
imbroglio, 56A
imbue, 16B
imitate, 27A
imitation, 27A
immaculate, 41B

immediate, 7J
immediately, 7I
immense, 3A
immerse, 16B
immigrant, 9I
imminent, 7H
immolate, 33B
immune, 56B
immure, 13D
imp, 9F
impact, 39A
impair, 37C
impale, 8G
impartial, 13N
impatient, 13F
impeach, 10G
impeccable, 26C
impede, 2B
impel, 10E
imperative, 35B
imperial, 26C
impertinent, 5G
impetuous, 13P
impetus, 39A
impinge, 2G
implement, 8E
implore, 10E
imply, 10C
import, 2I
important, 26C
importune, 10E
impose, 5I
impossible, 56A
impost, 28B
impound, 13D
imprecate, 10B
impresario, 1B
impress, 39A
impression, 5A
impressive, 26C
imprison, 13D
improve, 33D

improvise, 12D
impudent, 5G
impugn, 10B
impulse, 5A
impunity, 13D
impurity, 41A
in, 14H
in addition, 27B
in all respects, 3K
in any case, 27D
in any event, 27D
in comparison, 27D
in part, 3J
in particular, 3J
in some respect, 3J
in that, 39B
in that case, 39B
in the beginning, 7G
in the end, 7H
in the interim, 7I
in the least bit, 3J
in the meantime, 7I
in the slightest, 3J
inactive, 13C
inane, 26D
inasmuch, 3J
inaugurate, 2C
inauguration, 51B
incarcerate, 13D
incendiary, 8N
incense, 5E, 60B
incentive, 39A
incessant, 7K
incest, 33B
inch, 3E
inchoate, 2C
incident, 51A
incinerate, 52C
incipient, 2C
incise, 8G
incite, 10E
incline, 32H

include, 2V
incognito, 42B
income, 28A
incoming, 14H
incommode, 5I
incomplete, 55A
incorrect, 26A
incorrectly, 31F
increase, 3G
incredible, 26C
incredibly, 31C
incubate, 54A
inculcate, 12G
incumbent, 1C
incur, 36E
indeed, 31A
indefinite, 38E, 42C
indemnity, 28A
indent, 15I
indenture, 15H
independence, 13D
independent, 13D
index, 15C
Indiana, 18C
Indianapolis, 18D
indicate, 10C
indication, 12D
indicator, 12D
indict, 10B
indigenous, 9I
indigent, 28E
indignant, 5E
indignation, 5E
indigo, 58A
individual, 9A
indolent, 13C
indoor, 14H
indoors, 14H
induce, 10E, 39A
induct, 2C
indulge, 5K
industrious, 13B

invertebrate, 4A
invest, 28D
investigate, 12C
investigation, 12C
inveterate, 7K
invite, 10F
invoice, 25A
invoke, 10G
involve, 2V
inward, 14H
iodine, 37F
ion, 61B
iota, 3F
Iowa, 18C
Iran, 18B
ire, 5E
iridescent, 58A
irk, 5I
iron, 29A
ironclad, 17H
ironically, 31C
ironwork, 30E
irony, 5K
irrefragable, 57B
irregular, 7K
irrigate, 29F
irrigation, 29F
irritable, 5G
irritate, 5E
is, 50A
is apt to, 50D
is bound to, 50D
is certain to, 50D
is going to, 50D
is liable to, 50D
is sure to, 50D
island, 16G
isle, 16G
ism, 12L
isn't, 46A
isogon, 32C
isolate, 5P

isometric, 32C
isotope, 61B
Israel, 18B
issue, 15C
isthmus, 16G
it, 45A
italicize, 15I
italics, 35C
Italy, 18B
itch, 37C
item, 3F
iterate, 7K
itinerary, 25A
its, 45B
it's, 46D
itself, 45A
I've, 46B
ivory, 4L

J

jab, 44A
jabber, 10A
jack, 8E
jackal, 4B
jackass, 4E
jackboot, 17E
jacket, 17F
jackknife, 8F
Jackson, 18D
Jacksonville, 18D
jade, 29B
jag, 2G
jail, 21C
jailbird, 9G
jalopy, 11A
jam, 6C
jamb, 30B
jangle, 19E
janitor, 1R
January, 7E
Japan, 18B

jar, 22A
jargon, 35A
jaunt, 2G
jaunty, 5K
javelin, 8N, 34C
jaw, 23D
jawbone, 23J
jay, 4J
jazz, 47B
jealous, 5M
jealousy, 5M
jeans, 17C
jeep, 11A
jeer, 10B
jellyfish, 4I
jeopardy, 56B
jerk, 2N
jersey, 17C
jest, 5K
jet, 8B
jettison, 2J
jewel, 29B
jewelry, 17G
jibe, 2V
jiffy, 7J
jig, 47B
jigsaw, 8E
jilt, 10B
jimmy, 8E
jingle, 19E
jinx, 42C
jitter, 2L
job, 1A
jog, 34D, 48A
jogging, 34D
johnnycake, 6D
join, 2V
joist, 22D
joke, 5K
jolly, 5K
jolt, 2N
joss, 9F

jostle, 2M
jot, 3F, 15I
jounce, 2N
journal, 15C
journey, 2G
journeyman, 1B
joust, 34B
jousting, 34B
jovial, 5K
jowl, 23D
joy, 5K
joyful, 5K
joyous, 5K
jubilant, 5K
jubilation, 5J
judge, 1Y, 12J
judgement, 12J
jug, 22A
juggle, 2L
juggler, 1H
juice, 6H
juicy, 6L
jukebox, 8D
July, 7E
jumble, 2L
jumbo, 3A
jump, 48D
June, 7E
jungle, 20E
junior, 9C
junk, 41A
junket, 2G
junkyard, 41A
junta, 25C
Jupiter, 20H
juror, 1Y
just, 3J, 26A
justice, 26A
justly, 31F
jut, 2S
jute, 24D
juvenile, 9D

lath, 22C

lathe, 8F

lather, 41C

latitude, 3D

latrine, 30A

latter, 7H

lattice, 30B

latticework, 30B

laud, 10D

laugh, 19C

laughter, 19C

launch, 11G

launder, 41B

laurel, 24B

lava, 29A

lave, 41B

lavender, 58A

lavish, 3G

law, 1K, 15H

lawbreaker, 9G

lawful, 26A

lawgiver, 1C

lawless, 26A

lawmaker, 1J

lawmaking, 25C

lawn, 24E

lawnmower, 8F

lawsuit, 10B

lawyer, 1Y

lax, 13C, 13P

lay, 2P

layette, 17A

layoff, 1d

layout, 12B

layperson, 1W

lazar, 9G

lazy, 13C

lea, 20F

leach, 16B

lead, 29A

leader, 1B

leadership, 10G

leaf, 24C

league, 25E

leak, 16B

lean, 32H, 43D

leap, 48D

learn, 12G

lease, 28D, 36A

leasehold, 20A

leash, 4N

least, 3G

leather, 17K

leave, 2G

leaven, 6G

lecture, 10A

ledge, 30C

ledger, 15C

lee, 21C

leer, 53B

leeway, 14C

left, 14E

leftover, 3G

leg, 23G

legacy, 28A

legal, 26A

legate, 1C

legend, 15B

legendary, 42A

legible, 15I

legion, 25D

legislative, 25C

legislature, 25C

legitimate, 26A

legume, 6B

leisure, 51B

lemon, 6I

lemonade, 6H

lend, 36A

length, 32F

lengthen, 32F

lenient, 13A

lens, 8K

leopard, 4B

leper, 9G

lesion, 37E

less, 3G

lesson, 12C

lest, 39B

let, 10G

letdown, 5H

lethal, 33B

lethargy, 12E

letter, 15F, 35C

letterhead, 15G

lettuce, 6J

letup, 2R

levee, 16I

level, 32H

lever, 8E

levity, 5K

levy, 28B

lex, 15H

lexicon, 15C

liable, 42C

liaison, 2V

liar, 9G

libation, 6H

libel, 10B

liberal, 13A

liberator, 1C

liberty, 13D

librarian, 1I

library, 21F

libretto, 15D

license, 10G

licentious, 13K

lichen, 24E

lick, 60C

licorice, 6C

lid, 22B

lie, 2Q, 10B

liege, 1C

lien, 28B

life, 54A

lifeblood, 23I

lifeboat, 11E

lifeguard, 1D

lifeline, 11F

lifelong, 7D

lifesaver, 1D

lifesaving, 26C

lifetime, 7A

lifework, 1A

lift, 2O

ligament, 23J

light, 38A, 38D

lightbulb, 38D

lighten, 38B

lighthouse, 16I

lightness, 38A

lightning, 40B

lightship, 11E

lightweight, 3A

like, 5O, 27A

likely, 42C

likeness, 27A

likewise, 27B

lilac, 24D

lily, 24D

limb, 24C

limbo, 18A

limbs, 23A

lime, 6I

limelight, 42A

limerick, 15D

limestone, 29B

limewater, 59A

limit, 14B

limousine, 11A

limp, 48A

limpid, 38E

line, 32D

linear, 32D

lineman, 1D

linen, 17K

liner, 11E

linger, 2B

M

ma, 9N
ma'am, 9B
macadam, 29B
macaroni, 6D
macaroon, 6C
mace, 6G
machine, 8A
machinery, 8A
mackinaw, 17F
mackintosh, 17F
madam, 9B
madame, 9B
madhouse, 21H
madrigal, 15D
magazine, 15C
magenta, 58A
magic, 34E
magical, 34E
magician, 1H
magistrate, 1C
magma, 29A
magnanimous, 13A
magnet, 29A, 61A
magnificent, 26C
magnify, 2S
magnum, 22A
mahogany, 24B
maid, 1Z
maiden, 9B
mail, 2I
mailbox, 30C
mailman, 1b
main, 26C
Maine, 18C
mainland, 16G
mainly, 3J
mainstay, 11F, 22D
mainstream, 42A
maintain, 36C
maintenance, 22F
maize, 6J

majestic, 43C
majesty, 9A
major, 26C
majority, 3G
make, 22F
makeshift, 57B
malady, 37A
malaria, 37B
male, 9C
malefactor, 9G
malevolent, 26D
malice, 5F
malign, 26D
mall, 11H
mallard, 4J
malleable, 57C
malmsey, 6H
malt, 6J
mama, 9N
mamma, 9N
mammal, 4A
mammoth, 3A
man, 9C
manacle, 8H
manage, 10G
manager, 1B
mandate, 10G
mandolin, 47C
mane, 4L
maneuver, 12H
manganese, 29A
mangle, 33A
mangonel, 8N
manhandle, 33B
manhole, 20C
mania, 5O
manicure, 41B
manifest, 42A
manipulate, 10G
mankind, 9A
manner, 5R
manor, 21B

mansion, 21B
manslaughter, 33B
mantel, 30B
mantelpiece, 30B
mantilla, 17D
mantis, 4K
mantle, 17F
manual, 15C
manufacture, 22F
manufacturer, 1P
manumit, 36B
manure, 29E
manuscript, 15C
many, 3G
map, 15E
maple, 24B
mar, 33A
maraschino, 6H
marathon, 34A
maraud, 33C
marble, 29B
March, 7E
march, 48A
mare, 4E
margarine, 6F
margin, 14B
marigold, 24D
marinate, 16B
marine, 11G
marines, 25D
mark, 15A, 33A, 34C
market, 21D, 28D
marketplace, 28F
marksman, 1D
markswoman, 1D
marmalade, 6C
maroon, 5P, 58A
marquis, 1C
marriage, 2V
marrow, 23J
marry, 2V
Mars, 20H

marsh, 16F
marshal, 1J
marshland, 16F
marshmallow, 6C
mart, 21D
martial, 1J
martyr, 9G
marvel, 5J
marvelous, 26C
Maryland, 18C
mascot, 4A
masculine, 9C
mash, 33A
mask, 17D, 22B
mason, 1X
mass, 25B
Massachusetts, 18C
massacre, 33B
massage, 44A
massive, 3A
mast, 11F
master, 9C
masterpiece, 26C
masthead, 11F
masticate, 6M
mat, 30D
match, 27A, 34A
matchbox, 52E
matchlock, 8N
mate, 3G, 9E
material, 17K, 22E
maternal, 9N
math, 49A
mathematician, 1L
mathematics, 49A
matinee, 47A
matriculate, 10J
matrimony, 2V
matrix, 25A
matron, 9N
matter, 22E
mattress, 30D

mature, 54B

maul, 44A

maunder, 10A

mausoleum, 21M

mauve, 58A

maverick, 55A

maw, 23D

mawkish, 5H

maxim, 10A

maximum, 49B

May, 7E

may, 50C

maybe, 10K, 31B

mayfly, 4K

mayonnaise, 6G

mayor, 1C

Maypole, 34C

maze, 55B

me, 45A

mead, 6H

meadow, 20F

meadowlark, 4J

meager, 3G

meal, 6A

mealtime, 7A

mealworm, 4K

mean, 5F

meander, 2G

meaning, 12I

meanness, 5F

meantime, 7D

meanwhile, 7I

measure, 3B

measurement, 3A

meat, 6B

mechanic, 1X

mechanical, 8A

mechanism, 8A

meddle, 5I

median, 49B

mediate, 33D

medicine, 1K, 37F

medieval, 7F

mediocre, 42A

meditate, 12A

medium, 14F

medley, 25A

medulla, 23C

meek, 13L

meet, 2V

melancholy, 5H

melee, 33C

mellifluous, 47B

mellow, 5L

melody, 47B

melon, 6I

melt, 16B

member, 3F

membership, 25E

membrane, 23B

memo, 15F

memorable, 26C

memorial, 21M

memorize, 12A

memory, 12A

Memphis, 18D

menace, 10B

menagerie, 25A

mend, 17I

mendacity, 10B

mendicant, 9M

menfolk, 9C

menial, 1Z

mental, 23A

mention, 10C

mentor, 1I

menu, 25A

meow, 19D

mercenary, 1J

mercer, 1N

mercerize, 17I

merchandise, 28C

merchant, 1M

merciless, 5F

Mercury, 20H

mercury, 29A

mercy, 13A

mere(ly), 3J

meretricious, 26D

merge, 2V

meridian, 3D

merit, 26B

mermaid, 4C

merry, 5K

merrymaker, 9E

mesa, 20D

mesmerize, 12G

message, 15F

messenger, 1b

messmate, 9E

messy, 43B

metal, 29A

metamorphosis, 27C

metaphor, 27A

meteor, 20H

meteorologist, 1L

meter, 3E

method, 12H

meticulous, 43B

metric, 3E

metropolis, 18A

metropolitan, 20B

Mexico, 18B

mezzanine, 30A

Miami, 18D

mica, 29A

Michigan, 18C

microbe, 37D

microscope, 8K

microscopic, 3A

mid, 14F

midday, 7C

middle, 14F

middleman, 1M

midget, 9J

midmost, 14F

midnight, 7C

midst, 14F

midstream, 16H

midway, 14F

midwest, 14E

might, 43A, 50C

mignon, 43D

migrate, 2G

migration, 2G

mil, 3E

mild, 13L

mild(ly), 3J

mildew, 24E

mile, 3E

military, 1K

milk, 6H

milkmaid, 1F

milkman, 1N

milkweed, 24E

mill, 21E

millennium, 7D

miller, 1N

milliner, 1N

million, 3H

millionaire, 9M

millionth, 3H

millipede, 4K

millpond, 16F

millrace, 16F

millstone, 29B

Milwaukee, 18D

mime, 1H

mimeograph, 27A

mimic, 27A

mince, 8G

mind, 23C

mine, 45B

miner, 1F

mingle, 2V

miniature, 3A

minimum, 49B

minister, 1W

mink, 4E
Minnesota, 18C
minnow, 4H
minor, 9D
minstrel, 1G
mint, 28F
minuet, 47B
minus, 49D
minute, 7C
miracle, 42C
miraculous, 26C
mirage, 12E
mire, 16F
mirror, 11F
mirth, 5K
misanthropy, 5E
miscellany, 25A
mischief, 13M
mischievous, 13M
miscreant, 9G
miser, 9M
miserable, 5H
misery, 5H
mishap, 33A
misjudge, 12J
misplace, 36A
miss, 5Q
missile, 8N
mission, 21I
missionary, 1W
Mississippi, 18C
missive, 15F
Missouri, 18C
misspell, 15I
mist, 16A
mistake, 26A
mister, 9C
mistress, 9B
mite, 4K
mitigate, 2R
mitt, 17E
mittens, 17E

mix, 6G
mixture, 25A
moan, 19C
moat, 16I
mob, 25B
mobile, 2A
moccasin, 17E
mock, 10B
mockingbird, 4J
model, 1H
moderate(ly), 3J
modern, 7G
modernize, 22F
modest, 13K
modesty, 13K
modifier, 35B
modify, 22F
module, 3F
moiety, 3G
moist, 16B
moisten, 16B
moisture, 16A
molar, 23D
molasses, 6C
mold, 22F
mole, 4E
molecular, 61B
molecule, 61B
molest, 5I, 33B
mollify, 5L
mollusk, 4I
molt, 27C
mom, 9N
moment, 7C
momentarily, 7H
momentary, 7K
monarch, 1C
monastery, 21I
Monday, 7E
money, 28C
moneybag, 28F
moneymaker, 9M

monger, 9G
monition, 10B
monitor, 53B
monk, 1W
monkey, 4G
monocle, 17D
monogram, 15A
monograph, 15C
monolith, 21M
monologue, 10A
monopoly, 36C
monotony, 27A
monsoon, 40B
monster, 4C, 9F
monstrous, 3A
Montana, 18C
Montgomery, 18D
month, 7D
monument, 21M
moo, 19D
mood, 5A
moon, 20H
moonbeam, 38D
moonlight, 38A
moonshine, 6H
moonstruck, 13O
moor, 20B
mooring, 11F
moorland, 16F
mop, 41C
mope, 5H
moraine, 29B
moral, 26A
morbid, 37A
mordant, 5F
more, 3G, 3K
more or less, 3J
moreover, 27B
mores, 12L
morgue, 21H
moribund, 54A
morning, 7C

moron, 9G
morose, 5H
morphology, 1L
morrow, 7F
morsel, 3F
mortal, 54A
mortar, 22D
mortgage, 28B
mortify, 10B
mortise, 22D
mortuary, 21H
mosaic, 47D
mosquito, 4K
moss, 24E
most, 3G, 3K
mostly, 3J
mote, 3F
motel, 21B
moth, 4K
mother, 9N
motion, 2A
motionless, 2B
motive, 39A
motor, 8B
motorboat, 11E
motorbus, 11A
motorcade, 51B
motorcar, 11A
motorcycle, 11A
mottle, 15I
motto, 15F
mount, 2O
mountain, 20D
mountainous, 20B
mountainside, 20D
mountaintop, 20D
mourn, 5H
mouse, 4F
mousetrap, 4O
mousse, 6C
mouth, 23D
mouthful, 3E

mouthpiece, 47C
movable, 2A
move, 2I
movement, 2A
movie, 47A
mow, 8G
mower, 8F
much, 3K
mucilage, 8H
muck, 16E
mucus, 23I
muddle, 55B
muddy, 41A
muff, 26B
muffin, 6D
muffle, 2F
muffler, 17G
mug, 8M
muggy, 40E
mulberry, 24B
mulch, 29F
mulct, 10B
mule, 4E
mull, 12A
multiple, 49B
multiplication, 49D
multiply, 49D
mum, 19A
mumble, 19C
mummy, 54A
mumps, 37B
munch, 6M
mundane, 42A
municipal, 20B
munificent, 13A
mural, 47D
murder, 33B
murky, 38E
murmur, 19C
muscle, 23J
muscular, 43A
muse, 12A

museum, 21F
mush, 6D
mushroom, 24E
music, 15D, 47B
musical, 47B
musician, 1G
musket, 8N
muskrat, 4F
must, 50C
mustache, 23B
mustang, 4E
mustard, 6G
muster, 25A
mustn't, 46A
mutate, 27C
mute, 37B
mutilate, 33A
mutt, 4B
mutter, 19C
mutton, 6E
mutual, 27A
muzzle, 4N
my, 45B
myriad, 3G
mysterious, 42C
mystery, 12D
mystify, 12G
myth, 15B
mythology, 12L

N
nab, 44B
nag, 10B
nail, 8H
nails, 23F
naive, 12K
naked, 17J
name, 15A
namely, 27B
namesake, 15A
nap, 12E

nape, 23A
napkin, 30F
narcotic, 37F
narrator, 1E
narrow, 32F
Nashville, 18D
nasty, 41A
natal, 54A
nation, 18B, 25C
national, 25C
nationalist, 9O
nationwide, 18A
native, 9I
naturalist, 1L
naturally, 31C
nature, 40A
naughty, 13M
nausea, 37C
nautical, 11G
naval, 11G
navigable, 16F
navigate, 11G
navy, 25D
near, 14K
nearby, 14K
nearly, 3J
neat, 43B
Nebraska, 18C
nebulous, 38E
necessary, 26C
neck, 23A
neckband, 17G
neckcloth, 17G
necklace, 17G
necktie, 17G
necromancy, 34E
necropolis, 20G
nectar, 6H
need, 5Q
needle, 8H
needlepoint, 17I
needy, 28E

nefarious, 26D
negate, 10G
negative, 26D
neglect, 5P
negligee, 17C
negotiate, 10A
neigh, 19D
neighbor, 9E
neighborhood, 18A
neither, 27D
neither...nor, 27D
neon, 59A
neophyte, 9L
nephew, 9N
nepotism, 1d
Neptune, 20H
nerve, 23J
nest, 4M
net, 34C
nether, 14J
network, 25A
neuron, 23J
neutral, 55B
neutron, 61B
Nevada, 18C
never, 7K
nevermore, 7K
nevertheless, 27D
new, 7G
New Hampshire, 18C
New Jersey, 18C
New Mexico, 18C
New Orleans, 18D
New York, 18C
New York City, 18D
newborn, 9D
newcomer, 9I
news carrier, 1b
newscaster, 1E
newspaper, 15C
newspaperman, 1E
newsreel, 47A

next, 7H
nibble, 6M
nice, 13A
niche, 14A
nick, 33A
nickel, 28C
nickname, 15A
niece, 9N
niggard, 9M
nigh, 14K
night, 7C
nightcap, 17D
nightdress, 17C
nightfall, 7C
nightgown, 17C
nightingale, 4J
nightly, 7K
nightmare, 12E
nightshade, 24D
nightshirt, 17C
nimble, 43A
nine, 3H
nineteen, 3H
nineteenth, 3H
ninety, 3H
ninny, 9G
ninth, 3H
nip, 44B
nitrate, 59A
nitrogen, 59A
no, 3I, 10K
no one, 45E
noble, 13A
nobleman, 1C
nobody, 45E
nod, 60A
node, 23B
noise, 19A
noisy, 19A
nomad, 9H
nomadic, 2G
nominal, 26D

nominate, 51C
nonchalant, 13C
nonessential, 26D
nonetheless, 27D
nonfiction, 15B
nonliving, 54A
nonplus, 12G
nonsense, 10B
noodles, 6D
nook, 30D
noon, 7C
noonday, 7C
noontime, 7C
noose, 8N
norm, 42A
normal, 42A
north, 14E
North America, 18B
North Carolina, 18C
North Dakota, 18C
northeast, 14E
northeastern, 14E
northerly, 14E
northern, 14E
northernmost, 14E
northland, 14E
northward, 14E
northwest, 14E
northwestern, 14E
nose, 23E
nostalgia, 12A
nostril, 23E
not, 27D
notably, 3K
notary, 1J
notation, 35C
notch, 20C
note, 15F
notebook, 15G
noteworthy, 26C
nothing, 45E
notice, 53B

notify, 10C
notwithstanding, 27D
noun, 35B
nourish, 33D
nourishment, 6B
nova, 20H
novel, 15C
November, 7E
novice, 9L
now, 7I
now that, 7G, 39B
nowadays, 7I
nowhere, 14D
noxious, 26D, 56B
nozzle, 16C
nuance, 27C
nuclei, 61B
nucleus, 61B
nude, 17J
nudge, 44A
nugatory, 26D
nugget, 29B
nuisance, 9G
null, 32G
numb, 37C
number, 3H
numeral, 3H
numeration, 3H
numerator, 49C
numerous, 3G
nun, 1W
nuptial, 2V
nurse, 1U
nursemaid, 1c
nursery, 30A
nut, 6J
nutbrown, 58A
nutcracker, 8M
nutmeg, 6G
nutrition, 6B
nutshell, 6J
nuzzle, 44B

nylon, 17K
nymph, 4C

O

oak, 24B
oar, 11F
oarlock, 11F
oasis, 24A
oatmeal, 6D
oats, 6J
obdurate, 13H
obedience, 13N
obedient, 13D
obelisk, 21M
obese, 43D
obey, 10G
obituary, 15C
object, 10B, 22E
objection, 10B
objective, 12B
oblige, 13B
oblique, 32D
obliterate, 33A
oblivion, 12E
obloquy, 42A
oboe, 47C
obscene, 13K
obsequious, 13B
observatory, 21F
observe, 53B
observer, 53A
obsess, 5C
obsidian, 29A
obsolete, 7F
obstacle, 2F
obstetrics, 1L
obstinate, 13H
obstruct, 2F
obtain, 36E
obtrude, 5I
obverse, 14F

obviate, 2F
obvious, 42A
obviously, 31A
occasion, 51A
occasional, 7K
occlude, 2U
occupation, 1A
occupy, 36C
occur, 2D
occurrence, 51A
ocean, 16F
o'clock, 7B
octagon, 32C
octave, 47B
October, 7E
octogenarian, 9D
octopus, 4I
ocular, 23E
odd, 55A
oddly, 31C
ode, 15D
odious, 5F
odor, 60B
of, 7I, 27B
off, 14I
offal, 41A
offend, 5E, 33B
offense, 34C
offer, 10F
offhand, 7J
office, 21E
officeholder, 1C
officer, 1J
official, 1C
offset, 55B
offshoot, 24C
offshore, 16H
offspring, 9N
offstage, 47A
often, 7K
ogle, 5Q
oh, 10K

Ohio, 18C
ohm, 3E
oil, 8C
oilskin, 17K
ointment, 37F
ok, 10K
okay, 10K
Oklahoma, 18C
Oklahoma City, 18D
old, 7F
ol, 10K
oligarchy, 25C
olive, 6J
Omaha, 18D
omen, 10B
omit, 5P
omnibus, 11A
omniscient, 12K
on, 7I, 14I
on account of, 39B
on the contrary, 27D
on the other hand, 27D
on top of, 14I
once, 7K
oncoming, 2G
one, 3H
onerous, 56A
oneself, 45A
onion, 6J
onlooker, 53A
only, 3G, 3J, 27D
onrush, 2T
onset, 2C
onslaught, 33C
ontology, 1L
ooh, 10K
ooze, 16B
opal, 29B
opaque, 38E
open, 2U
opener, 8M
openwork, 30E

opera, 21G, 47B
operate, 37F
operation, 37F
operator, 1b
opinion, 12L
opossum, 4E
opponent, 9G
opportune, 26A
oppose, 10B
opposite, 14K, 27C
oppress, 10G
opprobrium, 42A
optic, 23E
optimism, 5N
opulent, 28E
or, 27D
or rather, 27D
oracle, 10B
oral, 23D
orange, 6I, 58A
orate, 10C
orb, 32B
orbit, 2X
orbital, 2X
orchard, 20F
orchestra, 47B
ordain, 12J
ordeal, 40D
order, 2O, 55B
ordinary, 42A
ordure, 41A
ore, 29A
Oregon, 18C
organ, 47C
organic, 26C
organism, 37D
organization, 25E
organize, 25A
Orient, 18B
orifice, 23D
origin, 2C
original, 7G, 55A

originate, 2C
oriole, 4J
ornament, 30E
ornate, 55B
ornery, 13H
ornithology, 1L
orphan, 9D
orthodox, 13J, 42A
orthography, 35A
oscillate, 2L
osmosis, 2A
ossify, 57C
ostensibly, 31A
ostentation, 13E
ostracize, 10B
ostrich, 4J
other, 3G
otherwise, 27D
ought, 50C
ounce, 3E
our, 45B
ours, 45B
ourselves, 45A
oust, 2I
out, 14H, 34C
outback, 20A
outboard, 11F
outcome, 39A
outdoors, 14H
outer, 14K
outfit, 17A
outlandish, 55A
outlaw, 9G
outlet, 16F
outline, 32A
outlying, 14K
outnumber, 3G
outpost, 21C
outrage, 5E
outright, 3K
outside, 14H
outskirts, 18A

outsmart, 12G
outstanding, 26C
outward, 14H
outwit, 12G
oval, 32B
ovary, 23H
ovation, 19C
oven, 8D
over, 14I
overall, 3J
overalls, 17C
overboard, 14H
overcast, 40E
overcoat, 17F
overcome, 36D
overflow, 16B
overhead, 14I
overland, 14I
overlook, 5P
overnight, 7C
overrun, 36D
overseas, 14K
overseer, 1B
overtake, 36D
overthrow, 36D
overuse, 33A
overwhelm, 33B
overwork, 1d
ow, 10K
owe, 28D
owl, 4J
own, 36C
owner, 1B
ownership, 36C
ox, 4E
oxide, 59A
oxidize, 29D
oxygen, 59A
oyster, 4I

P

pa, 9N
pabulum, 6D
pace, 7J, 48A
pacify, 5L
pack, 22G
package, 22A
packet, 22A
packsack, 22A
packthread, 17K
pact, 10I
pad, 30F
paddle, 11F
paddock, 4M
paddy, 20F
padrone, 1B
pagan, 13J
page, 15G
pageant, 51B
pail, 22A
pain, 37C
painful, 33B
painstaking, 13P
paint, 15I, 58B
paintbrush, 15G
painter, 1G
painting, 47D
pair, 3G
pajamas, 17C
pal, 9E
palace, 21B
palate, 23D
pale, 38E
paleolithic, 7F
paleontology, 1L
palette, 22C
palindrome, 35B
palisade, 30C
pall, 38C
pallet, 8J
palm, 23F
palpable, 57A

palpitate, 2L
palsy, 37A
palter, 10B
paltry, 26D
pamper, 5K
pamphlet, 15C
pan, 8M
panacea, 37F
pancake, 6D
pander, 5K
pane, 30B
panegyric, 10D
panel, 22C
pang, 37C
panhandle, 20A
panic, 5B
pannier, 22A
panoply, 17H
panorama, 53A
panpipe, 47C
pant, 60D
pantheon, 25B
panther, 4B
pantry, 30A
pants, 17C
pap, 6D
papa, 9N
paper, 15G
paperback, 15C
paperboy, 1c
papoose, 9D
par, 42A
parable, 15B
parabola, 32B
parachute, 11F
parade, 51B
paradise, 18A
paradox, 12D
paraffin, 52E
paragon, 26C
paragraph, 15C
parakeet, 4J

parallax, 53A
parallel, 27A
parallelogram, 32C
paralyze, 33B, 37E
paramount, 26C
parasite, 4K
parasol, 17G
parcel, 22A
parch, 52A
parchment, 15G
pardon, 5O
pare, 8G
parent, 9N
parenthesis, 35A
parfait, 6C
pariah, 9G
park, 20G
parka, 17F
parkway, 11H
parley, 10A
parliament, 25C
parlor, 30A
parochial, 42B
parody, 15B
parole, 36B
paroxysm, 37C
parquet, 30B
parrot, 4J
parry, 2F
parsley, 6G
parson, 1W
part, 3F
parterre, 20G
partial, 3G
participate, 10D
participle, 35B
particle, 3F
particular, 3G
particularly, 3J
partly, 3J
partner, 9E
partnership, 25E

partridge, 4J
party, 51B
parvenu, 9G
pass, 2J, 11H
passage, 11H
passageway, 11H
passenger, 9H, 11G
passion, 5J
passive, 13C
passport, 15H
password, 35B
past, 7F, 14K
paste, 22D
pasteboard, 15G
pastel, 15G
pasteurize, 41B
pastime, 51B
pastor, 1W
pastoral, 20B
pastry, 6C
pastry cook, 1N
pasture, 20F
pat, 44A
patch, 17I
patent, 42A
paternal, 9N
path, 11H
pathology, 1L
pathway, 11H
patience, 13F
patient, 13F
patio, 20G
patriarch, 9N
patrician, 1C
patriot, 9I
patriotic, 13N
patrol, 25D
patrolman, 1J
patron, 1M
patten, 17E
pattern, 32A
patty, 6C

paunch, 43D
pauper, 9M
pause, 2B
pave, 22F
pavement, 22D
pavilion, 21G
paw, 4L
pawnbroker, 1S
pawnshop, 21D
pay, 28D
payload, 28C
payment, 28B
payroll, 28C
peace, 33C
peaceful, 5L
peacemaker, 33D
peacetime, 7A
peach, 6I
peak, 14I
peal, 19A
peanut, 6J
pear, 6I
pearl, 29B
peas, 6J
peasant, 9M
peat, 29E
pebble, 29C
pecan, 6J
peck, 8G
pectoral, 23A
peculate, 36E
peculiar, 55A
pecuniary, 28E
pedagogue, 1I
pedal, 8J
peddle, 28D
peddler, 1M
pedestal, 22D
pedestrian, 42A
pediatrics, 1L
pedigree, 9N
peek, 53B

peel, 8G
peep, 19D
peer, 9E, 53B
peeve, 5E
peg, 8H
pelisse, 17F
pellet, 8N
pelt, 4L
pemmican, 6E
pen, 15G
penal, 33B
pencil, 15G
pendant, 17G
penetrate, 16B
penicillin, 37F
peninsula, 16G
penitent, 5H
penmanship, 15I
pennant, 30E
Pennsylvania, 18C
penny, 28C
pension, 28A
pensive, 5H
pentagon, 32C
penthouse, 21B
penury, 28E
peon, 1B
people, 9A
Peoria, 18D
pep, 13B
pepper, 6G
peppercorn, 6G
peppermint, 6C
per, 49D
perceive, 53B
percent, 49B
percentage, 49B
percolate, 16B
percussion, 47C
perdition, 18A
peregrine, 4J
perfect, 26C

perfectly, 3K
perforate, 33A
perform, 47A
performance, 47A
performer, 1H
perfume, 17G, 60B
pergola, 30C
perhaps, 31B
perihelion, 14A
peril, 56B
perilous, 56B
perimeter, 14B
period, 7D, 35A
periodic, 7K
periphery, 14B
periscope, 8K
perish, 54A
perishable, 57B
permanent, 7K
permeate, 16B
permit, 10G
pernicious, 26D
perpendicular, 14C
perpetual, 7K
perpetuate, 7K
perplex, 12G
perquisite, 28A
persecute, 33B
persevere, 7K
persist, 7K
person, 9A
personality, 5R
perspective, 53A
perspicuous, 12K
perspiration, 23I
perspire, 23K
persuade, 10E
pert, 5G
pertain, 36C
perturb, 5I
peruse, 15I
perverse, 13H

pervious, 57A

pessimism, 5N

pest, 9G

pestle, 8E

pet, 4A

petal, 24D

petite, 3A

petition, 10E

petrify, 5C

petroleum, 8C

petticoat, 17C

petty, 26D

petulant, 5G

petunia, 24D

pew, 30D

phantom, 9F

pharmacy, 21D

phase, 7D

pheasant, 4J

Philadelphia, 18D

philander, 5Q

philanthropy, 13A

philosophy, 12L

phlegm, 23I

Phoenix, 18D

phone, 19B

phonetic, 35C

phonograph, 8D

phony, 13M

phosphate, 59A

phosphorus, 29A

photo, 47D

photograph, 47D

photographer, 1G

photography, 47D

photon, 61B

phrase, 35B

phrenology, 34E

phylum, 25B

physical, 23A

physician, 1U

physics, 1L

physiognomy, 23C

physiology, 1L

pi, 49C

piano, 47C

piccolo, 47C

pick, 12J, 44B

picker, 1F

pickle, 6J

pickpocket, 9G

pickup, 11A

picnic, 6A

picot, 17I

picture, 47D

pie, 6C

piebald, 58A

piece, 3F

piecemeal, 3J, 7K

pied, 58A

pierce, 8G

pierhead, 16I

pig, 4E

pigeon, 4J

pigeonhole, 25A

pigment, 58A

pigpen, 4M

pigskin, 17K

pigsty, 4M

pigtail, 23B

pike, 4H

pile, 25A

pilfer, 36E

pilgrim, 9I

pill, 37F

pillage, 36E

pillar, 22C

pillbox, 22A

pillory, 33B

pillow, 30F

pillowcase, 30F

pilot, 1V

pimple, 23B

pin, 8H, 17G

pinafore, 17C

pinch, 3E, 44B

pine, 24B

pineapple, 6I

pinfold, 4M

ping, 19E

pink, 58A

pinna, 4L

pinnacle, 14I

pinpoint, 36F

pint, 3E

pinto, 4E

pinwheel, 2X

pioneer, 9I

pious, 13J

pip, 3F

pipe, 22D, 52E

pipeline, 22D

pique, 5E

pirate, 9G

pirouette, 2X

pistil, 24D

pistol, 8N

piston, 8B

pit, 20C

pitch, 2J, 19A

pitchblende, 29A

pitcher, 22A

pitchfork, 8E

pitfall, 56B

pith, 24C

pitiful, 5H

pittance, 28A

Pittsburgh, 18D

pity, 5L

pivot, 2X

pixy, 9F

pizza, 6D

placate, 5L

place, 2I, 14A, 20A

placid, 5L

placket, 17B

plagiary, 10B

plague, 37A

plaid, 17K

plain, 55B

plainly, 31A

plaint, 10B

plait, 23B

plan, 12B

plane, 11D

planet, 20H

planetarium, 21F

plank, 22C

plant, 24A, 29F

plantation, 21L

plaque, 30E

plaster, 22D

plastic, 22D

plate, 8M

platform, 8J

platitude, 10A

platoon, 25D

platter, 8M

platypus, 4E

play, 2A, 5K, 34D

playbill, 15F

playboy, 9E

player, 1D

playfellow, 9E

playful, 5K

playgoer, 47A

playground, 20G

playhouse, 21G

playmate, 9E

playpen, 30D

playroom, 30A

playwright, 1E

plaza, 20G

plea, 10I

plead, 10E

pleasant, 13A

please, 5K, 31H

pleasure, 5K

pleat, 17I

pledge, 10I

plenty, 3G

plethora, 3G

pliers, 8E

plod, 48A

plop, 19E

plot, 20A, 47A

plover, 4J

plow, 29F

ploy, 12G

pluck, 44B

plug, 22B

plum, 6I

plumb, 32H

plumber, 1X

plume, 4L

plummet, 2P

plump, 43D

plunder, 36E

plunge, 2P

plunk, 19E

plural, 3G

plus, 49D

plush, 17K

Pluto, 20H

plutocracy, 25C

plywood, 22C

poach, 6K

pock, 23B

pocket, 17B

pocketbook, 28F

pocketknife, 8F

pod, 24D, 25B

poem, 15D

poet, 1E

poetic, 15D

poetry, 15B

poignant, 5H

point, 14A, 44C

pointer, 8J

poise, 13E

poison, 37E

poisonous, 33B

poker, 34F

polar, 20B

pole, 22D

poleax, 8N

polecat, 4E

polemic, 10B

polestar, 20H

police, 25D

policeman, 1J

policewoman, 1J

policy, 15H

polio, 37B

polish, 41B

polite, 13A

political, 25C

politician, 1C

politics, 1K

polka, 47B

poll, 10F

pollen, 24D

pollinate, 54A

pollination, 54A

pollute, 41A

pollution, 41A

polo, 34B

poltroon, 9G

polygamy, 2V

polyglot, 9L

polygon, 32C

pomp, 51B

pom-pom, 17B

poncho, 17F

pond, 16F

ponder, 12A

ponderous, 3A

pone, 6D

poniard, 8N

pontiff, 1W

pontoon, 11E

pony, 4E

poodle, 4B

pooh, 10K

pool, 16I

poolroom, 21D

poop, 11F

poor, 28E

poorhouse, 21C

pop, 6H

popcorn, 6J

pope, 1W

popgun, 34F

popinjay, 9G

poplar, 24B

popover, 6C

poppy, 24D

popular, 42A

populate, 54A

porcelain, 22D

porch, 30A

porcupine, 4F

pore, 23B

pork, 6E

porous, 57A

porpoise, 4H

porridge, 6D

port, 16I

portable, 2A

portal, 30A

portend, 10B

porter, 1V

porterhouse, 6E

porthole, 11F

portion, 3F

Portland, 18D

portly, 43D

portrait, 47D

portray, 53A

portrayal, 53A

pose, 48E

posh, 28E

position, 14A

posse, 25B

possess, 36C

possession, 36C

possessive, 5M

possible, 42C

possibly, 31B

postage, 28C

postcard, 15F

poster, 15F

posterior, 14F

posterity, 7D

posthaste, 7J

postmark, 15A

postmaster, 1b

postpone, 2B

postulate, 10C, 12D

posture, 48E

pot, 8M

potassium, 29A

potation, 6H

potato, 6J

potbelly, 43D

potent, 43A, 57B

potion, 37F

potpourri, 25A

potter, 1G

pottery, 30E

pouch, 4L

poultice, 37F

poultry, 6E

pounce, 48D

pound, 3E, 44A

pour, 16B

poverty, 28E

powder, 3F

power, 43A

powerful, 43A

powerhouse, 43A

powwow, 10A

practical, 12K, 26C

practically, 3J

practice, 7K, 12L, 34D

praetor, 1C

prairie, 20F

praise, 10D

prance, 48A

prattle, 10A

pray, 10D

prayer, 10D

preach, 10C

preamble, 2C

precede, 7G

precept, 15H

precincts, 18A

precious, 26C

precipice, 20D

precise, 26A

precisely, 3J

preclude, 2F

precocious, 55A

precursor, 7G

predicament, 56A

predicate, 35B

predict, 12D

predictably, 31C

prediction, 12D

predilection, 12J

preempt, 2F

preen, 41B

preface, 2C

prefect, 1C

prefer, 5O

preferably, 31H

prefix, 35B

pregnant, 54A

prehistoric, 7F

prelate, 1W

preliminary, 7G

prelude, 2C

premises, 20A

premium, 28A

premonition, 10B

prepare, 22F

preposition, 35B

preposterous, 26D

presage, 10B

prescience, 12K

prescribe, 10G

prescription, 37F

presence, 14L

present, 2I, 7F, 10C, 14L

presently, 7I

preserve, 22F

preside, 10G

president, 1C

presidential, 26C

press, 15G

pressure, 2T

prestigious, 42A

presto, 7J

presumably, 31B

presume, 12D

pretend, 12E

pretext, 10B

pretty, 43C

pretzel, 6D

prevail, 36D

prevaricate, 10B

prevent, 2F

prevention, 56B

preview, 47A

previous, 7G

prey, 9G

price, 28B

prick, 8G

prickly, 57A

pride, 13E

priest, 1W

prig, 9G

prim, 43B

primal, 7F

primary, 26C

primate, 4A

prime, 26C

primer, 15C

primitive, 7F

primogenitor, 9N

primordial, 7F

prince, 1C

princess, 1C

principal, 1I

principle, 12D

print, 15I

printer, 1Q

prior to, 7G

prism, 32C

prison, 21C

prisoner, 1T

pristine, 7F

privacy, 42B

private, 42B

privateer, 11E

privy, 42B

pro, 9L

probable, 3J, 42C

probation, 2B

probe, 12C

probity, 26A

problem, 56A

procedure, 12H

proceed, 2G

process, 12H, 22F

procession, 51B

proclaim, 10C

proclamation, 10A

procrastinate, 2B

proctor, 1I

procure, 36E

prod, 44A

prodigy, 51A

produce, 22F

producer, 1B

production, 1A

productive, 13B

profane, 10B

profess, 10C

profession, 1A

professional, 1A

professor, 1I

proficient, 12K

profile, 32A

profit, 28A

profligate, 13K

profuse, 3G

progeny, 9N

program, 47A

progress, 2G

prohibit, 2F

project, 51A

proletarian, 9M

prolific, 54A

prolix, 10A

prologue, 2C

prom, 51B

promenade, 48A

prominent, 42A

promiscuous, 13K

promise, 10I

promontory, 16G

promote, 33D

prompt, 7J

promulgate, 10C

prone, 48E

pronoun, 35B

pronounce, 10C

pronunciation, 35A

proof, 12D

proofread, 15I

prop, 22D

propaganda, 10B

propagate, 54A

propel, 2K

propeller, 11F

proper, 26A

property, 36C

prophecy, 10B

prophet, 1W

propinquity, 14K

propitious, 26C

proportion, 49B

proposal, 10A

propose, 10F
propulsion, 2T
proscribed, 10G
prose, 15B
prosecute, 33B
prosecutor, 1Y
proselyte, 10E
prospect, 53A
prosper, 54B
prosperous, 13G
prostitute, 9G
prostrate, 36D
protagonist, 47A
protect, 33D
protective, 56B
protector, 33D
protectorate, 25C
protein, 6B
protest, 10B
protocol, 12H
proton, 61B
protract, 7K
protractor, 3C
protrude, 2S
protuberant, 2S
proud, 13E
prove, 12D
provide, 2I
Providence, 18D
province, 18A
provisions, 6B
provoke, 5E
provost, 1C
prow, 11F
prowl, 48B
proximate, 14K, 27A
proxy, 27A
prude, 9G
prudence, 13K
prudent, 13P
prudently, 31G
prune, 6I

prurient, 5Q
pry, 2O
psalm, 15D
pseudo, 26A
pseudonym, 15A
psyche, 23C
psychiatrist, 1U
psychology, 1L
ptomaine, 6K
puberty, 7F
public, 42A
publication, 15C
publish, 15I
publisher, 1Q
puck, 34C
pucker, 17I
pudding, 6C
puddle, 16F
pudgy, 43D
pueblo, 21C
puerile, 26D
puff, 60D
pug, 4B
pugilism, 34B
puissant, 43A
pule, 19C
pull, 2K
pulley, 8J
pullover, 17C
pulp, 6B
pulpit, 30D
pulverize, 33A
puma, 4B
pumice, 29A
pummel, 44A
pump, 16C
pumpkin, 6J
pun, 35B
punch, 44A
punctilio, 5D
punctuate, 15I
punctuation, 35A

puncture, 33A
pungent, 60B
punish, 33B
punt, 48C
puny, 43A
pup, 4D
pupil, 1I
puppet, 34F
puppy, 4D
purchase, 28D
pure, 55B
purely, 3J
purge, 41B
purify, 41B
puritan, 9I
purl, 17I
purlieu, 18A
purloin, 36E
purple, 58A
purport, 10C
purpose, 39A
purr, 19D
purse, 28F
pursue, 2H
pursuit, 2H
purvey, 2I
pus, 23I
push, 2K
pusillanimous, 5B
puss, 4B
put, 2I
putrid, 60B
putt, 44A
puttee, 17C
putter, 2B, 34C
putty, 22D
puzzle, 34F
pygmy, 9J
pyramid, 32C
pyre, 54A

Q
qua, 27A
quack, 19D
quadrant, 32B
quadrate, 32C
quadrilateral, 32C
quadrille, 47B
quadruped, 4A
quadruple, 49D
quaff, 6M
quail, 4J
quaint, 55A
quake, 2L
qualify, 22F, 26B
quality, 5R
qualm, 5D
quandary, 56A
quantity, 3G
quarantine, 21C
quarrel, 10B
quarry, 20C
quart, 3E
quarter, 28C
quarterback, 1D
quarterdeck, 11F
quarterly, 7K
quartet, 25B
quarto, 15C
quartz, 29A
quash, 33A
quasi, 3J
quaver, 2L
quay, 16I
queen, 1C
queer, 55A
quell, 5L
quench, 6M
quest, 2G
question, 10F
queue, 25A
quick, 7J
quicklime, 22D

quicksand, 16E
quicksilver, 29A
quid, 28C
quiddity, 26C
quiet, 19A
quill, 4L
quilt, 30F
quint, 3H
quintet, 25B
quip, 5K
quire, 15G
quirk, 27C
quit, 1d, 2F
quite, 3J, 3K
quiver, 2L
quixotic, 13O
quiz, 10F
quoit, 34C
quorum, 25A
quota, 3F
quotation, 10J
quote, 10J
quotient, 49C

R

rabbi, 1W
rabbit, 4E
rabble, 25B
rabies, 37B
raccoon, 4E
race, 7J, 34A
racecourse, 11H
racehorse, 4E
racer, 1D
racetrack, 11H
racing, 34B
racket, 34C
radiant, 38A
radiate, 38B
radiation, 61A
radiator, 8D

radio, 8D
radioactive, 61A
radiobroadcast, 47A
radiophone, 19B
radish, 6J
radium, 29A
radius, 3D
raffle, 34F
raft, 11E
rag, 17K
rage, 5E
ragtime, 47B
ragweed, 24E
raid, 33C
rail, 11H
railing, 30B
railroad, 11H
railway, 11H
rain, 16A
rainbow, 16A
raincoat, 17F
raindrop, 16A
rainfall, 16A
rainstorm, 40B
rainwater, 16A
raise, 2O
raisin, 6I
rake, 8E
ram, 4E
ramble, 48A
ramp, 11H
ramrod, 10G
ramshackle, 57B
ranch, 21L
rancher, 1F
rancid, 6L
rancor, 5E
rand, 28C
random, 42C
range, 20D
ranger, 1F
rank, 2O

ransack, 36E
ransom, 28D
rant, 19C
rap, 44A
rape, 33B
rapid, 7J
rapier, 8N
rapport, 10D
rapprochement, 10D
rapt, 12F
rare, 7K, 55A
rascal, 9G
rash, 23B
rasp, 8E
raspberry, 6I
rat, 4F
rate, 2O
rather, 3J
ratify, 10G
ratio, 49B
ration, 2I
rational, 12K
rattle, 19E
rattlesnake, 4C
rattletrap, 11A
raucous, 19A
rave, 19C
ravel, 2W, 17I
raven, 4J
ravenous, 6N
ravine, 20C
ravish, 5J
raw, 37C
rawboned, 43A
rawhide, 4L
ray, 38D
rayon, 17K
raze, 33A
razor, 8F, 17G
razorback, 4E
reach, 36E
react, 2D

reaction, 2D
reactor, 21F
read, 15I
ready, 7G
real, 26A
realistic, 26A
reality, 26A
realize, 12G
really, 31A
realm, 18A
ream, 15G
reap, 36E
reaper, 11B
reappear, 53B
rear, 14F
rearrange, 22F
reason, 39A
reasonably, 31G
rebel, 10B
rebuff, 10G
rebuild, 22F
rebuke, 10G
rebus, 35C
rebut, 10B
recalcitrant, 13H
recall, 12A
recede, 2G
receipt, 28C
receive, 36E
receiver, 19B
recent, 7G
receptionist, 1O
recherch, 55A
recipe, 12H
reciprocal, 2X
recite, 10C
reckless, 13P
reckon, 12A
recline, 48E
recluse, 9G
recognition, 42A
recognize, 53B

repute, 42A

request, 10F

require, 10G

requite, 28D

rescue, 33D

research, 12C

researcher, 1L

resemblance, 27A

resemble, 27A

resent, 5E

reserve, 36F

reservoir, 16I

reside, 54A

residue, 3G

resign, 1d

resilient, 57C

resin, 24C

resist, 2F

resolute, 13H

resolution, 15H

resolve, 12D

resort, 18A

respect, 5O

respectful, 13A

respiratory, 23K

respire, 60D

respond, 10F

responsibility, 13B

responsible, 13B

rest, 2B

restaurant, 21D

restless, 13F

restore, 22F

restrain, 2F

restrict, 2U, 36F

result, 39A

resume, 7K

resurrect, 33D

resuscitate, 33D

retail, 28D

retain, 36F

retaliate, 33B

reticent, 13L

retina, 23E

retire, 1d

retort, 10F

retract, 2G

retreat, 21C

retrench, 2R

retrieve, 2I

retrograde, 2X

retrospect, 12A

return, 2I

revamp, 22F

reveal, 10H, 53A

reveille, 15D

revel, 5K

revenge, 5E

revenue, 28A

reverberate, 19A

revere, 5O

reverie, 12E

reverse, 2X

review, 12C

revise, 12D

revive, 33D

revoke, 10G

revolt, 10B

revolution, 33C

revolve, 2X

revolver, 8N

revulsion, 5E

reward, 28A

rewrite, 15I

rhapsody, 15D

rhetoric, 35A

Rhode Island, 18C

rhumba, 47B

rhyme, 15D

rhythm, 47B

rib, 23J

ribald, 13K

ribbon, 17G

rice, 6J

rich, 28E

Richmond, 18D

rickets, 37B

rickety, 43A

ricochet, 2N

rid, 2I

riddle, 5K, 34F

ride, 11G

rider, 11G

ridge, 14B, 20D

ridgepole, 30B

ridicule, 10B

ridiculous, 26D

riff, 47B

riffraff, 25B

rifle, 8N

rifleman, 1J

rift, 20C

rig, 8A

right, 14E, 26A

rightful, 26A

rightly, 31F

rigid, 57A

rigmarole, 12H

rigor, 13H

rile, 5E

rill, 16F

rim, 14B

rind, 24E

ring, 17G, 19E

ringleader, 9G

ringmaster, 1H

ringside, 21G

ringworm, 37B

rink, 21G

rinse, 41B

riot, 33C

rip, 17I

ripe, 6L

ripen, 6K

ripple, 16B

rise, 2O

risk, 56B

rite, 51B

rival, 9G

river, 16F

riverbank, 16G

riverside, 16G

rivet, 8H

road, 11H

roadbed, 11H

roadside, 11H

roadway, 11H

roam, 2G

roan, 58A

roar, 19C

roast, 6K

rob, 36E

robber, 9G

robe, 17C

robin, 4J

robot, 8L

robust, 37A

rock, 2M, 29B

rock salt, 29A

rocker, 30D

rocket, 11D

rod, 22D

rodent, 4F

rodeo, 51B

rogue, 9G

roister, 19C

role, 1A

roll, 2X

roller, 8J

rollicking, 5K

romance, 5O

romp, 48A

roof, 30B

rooftop, 30B

rookie, 9L

room, 30A

roommate, 9E

roost, 4M

rooster, 4J
root, 24E
rope, 8H
rose, 24D
rosebud, 24D
rosebush, 24B
rosewater, 17G
rosewood, 22C
roster, 25A
rostrum, 30A
rot, 6K
rotate, 2X
rotation, 2X
rote, 12H
rotor, 11F
rotten, 6L
rotund, 43D
rouge, 17G
rough, 57A
roughhouse, 34D
roughly, 3J
roughneck, 9G
roughrider, 1F
roughshod, 4O
roulette, 34F
round, 32B
roundabout, 14K
roundhouse, 21K
roundup, 25E
roundworm, 4K
rouse, 12E
rout, 55B
route, 11H
routine, 12H
rove, 2G
rover, 9H
row, 11G
rowboat, 11E
rowdy, 19A
rowlock, 11F
royal, 28E
rub, 8G

rubber, 24C
rubbish, 41A
rubble, 29B
rubric, 15A
ruby, 29B
ruckus, 19C
rudder, 11F
ruddy, 23B
rude, 5G
rudiment, 26C
rue, 5H
ruff, 17B
ruffian, 9G
ruffle, 17B
rug, 30E
rugged, 43A
ruin, 33A
rule, 15H
ruler, 3C
rum, 6H
rumble, 33C
ruminate, 12A
rummage, 12C
rummy, 55A
rumor, 10B
rump, 23A
rumple, 17I
rumpus, 19C
run, 48A
runaway, 9H
rung, 22D
runnel, 16F
runner, 1D
runoff, 16F
runt, 9J
runway, 11H
rupture, 33A
rural, 20B
ruse, 12G
rush, 7J
rusk, 6D
russet, 58A

rust, 29D
rustic, 20B
rustle, 19E
rustler, 9G
rut, 20C
rye, 6J

S

sabbatical, 51B
saber, 8N
sabot, 17E
sabotage, 33A
sac, 4L
saccharine, 6G
sack, 22A
sackcloth, 17K
sacred, 13J
sacrifice, 36B
sad, 5H
saddle, 4N
saddlebag, 4N
sadly, 31D
sadness, 5H
safari, 2G
safe, 28F, 56B
safeguard, 33D
safety, 56B
sag, 2P
saga, 15B
sage, 9L
sagebrush, 24E
sail, 11G
sailboat, 11E
sailcloth, 17K
saint, 9F
sake, 33D
salad, 6D
salary, 28A
sale, 28D
salesclerk, 1M
salesman, 1M

salesperson, 1M
saleswoman, 1M
salient, 26C
saliva, 23I
salivary, 23K
sally, 33C
salmagundi, 25A
salmon, 4H
salon, 21D
saloon, 21D
saloonkeeper, 1N
salt, 6G
Salt Lake City, 18D
saltcellar, 8M
salubrious, 37A
salute, 44C
salve, 37F
salver, 8M
same, 27A
sample, 3F
San Antonio, 18D
San Francisco, 18D
sanction, 10G
sanctum, 21I
sand, 29C
sandal, 17E
sandalwood, 22C
sandbag, 22A
sandbank, 16G
sandbox, 34F
sandman, 9F
sandpaper, 8E
sandpiper, 4J
sandstone, 29B
sandstorm, 40B
sandwich, 6D
sane, 37A
sanguine, 13E, 58A
sanitary, 41B
sanitation, 41B
sanity, 37A
sans, 27D

Santa Fe, 18D
sap, 24C
sapient, 12K
sapsucker, 4J
sarcasm, 5K
sardine, 4H
sardonic, 5F
sartorial, 17J
sash, 17G
satchel, 22A
sate, 5L, 6M
satellite, 20H
satin, 17K
satinwood, 22C
satisfactory, 26A
satisfy, 5L
saturate, 16B
Saturday, 7E
Saturn, 20H
satyr, 4C
sauce, 6G
saucepan, 8M
saucer, 8M
saucy, 5G
sauerkraut, 6D
saunter, 48A
sausage, 6E
saut, 6K
savage, 5F
savanna, 20E
savant, 9L
save, 33D
savings, 28A
savior, 9K
savor, 6L
saw, 8E
sawbuck, 28C
sawdust, 3F
sawhorse, 8J
sawmill, 21E
saxophone, 47C
say, 10C

scab, 37E
scabbard, 17H
scaffold, 8J
scald, 6K
scale, 3C
scallop, 4I
scalp, 23B
scalpel, 8F
scamp, 9G
scamper, 48A
scan, 15I
scandal, 42A
scandalmonger, 9G
scant, 3G
scar, 23B
scarce, 55A
scarcely, 3J
scarcity, 3G
scare, 5C
scarecrow, 43D
scarf, 17G
scarlet, 58A
scarp, 20D
scathe, 52C
scatter, 2S
scatterbrain, 9G
scavenge, 25A
scene, 47A, 53A
scenery, 47A
scent, 60B
scepter, 17G
schedule, 25A
scheme, 12B
schism, 2W
scholar, 9L
scholarship, 28A
school, 21F
schoolbook, 15C
schoolboy, 9C
schoolfellow, 9C
schoolgirl, 9B
schoolhouse, 21F

schoolmaster, 1I
schoolmate, 9E
schoolmistress, 1I
schoolroom, 21F
schoolteacher, 1I
schoolwork, 12C
schoolyard, 20G
schooner, 11E
science, 1K
scientific, 12K
scientist, 1L
scintilla, 3F
scion, 9N
scissors, 8F
scoff, 10B
scold, 10B
scone, 6D
scoop, 8G, 8M
scoot, 7J
scooter, 11A
scope, 12B, 53A
scorch, 52C
score, 10J, 15D
scorn, 5E
scornful, 5G
scotch, 6H
scoundrel, 9G
scour, 41B
scourge, 33B
scout, 53B
scow, 11E
scowl, 60A
scrag, 43D
scramble, 2L
scrap, 3F
scrapbook, 15G
scrape, 8G
scraper, 8E
scratch, 8G, 33A
scrawl, 15I
scrawny, 43A
screech, 19C

screen, 30C
screw, 8H
screwdriver, 8E
scribble, 15I
scribe, 1E
scrimmage, 33C
scrimp, 28D
script, 15C
scripture, 15C
scroll, 15G
scrub, 41B
scruff, 23A
scruple, 5D
scrutiny, 12C
scud, 2M
scuff, 8G
scuffle, 33C
scullion, 1Z
sculpt, 22F
sculptor, 1G
sculpture, 47D
scum, 16E
scurrilous, 26D
scurry, 7J
scurvy, 37B
scut, 4L
scuttle, 22A
scythe, 8F
sea, 16F
sea fight, 33C
seaboard, 16G
seacoast, 16G
seafaring, 11G
seafood, 6B
seagirt, 20B
seagoing, 11G
seagull, 4J
seahorse, 4H
seal, 4H
sealskin, 4L
seam, 2V, 17B
seaman, 1V

seaplane, 11D
seaport, 16I
search, 12C
searchlight, 38D
seashore, 16G
seasick, 37A
season, 7D
seat, 30D
seatbelt, 11F
Seattle, 18D
seaway, 11H
seaweed, 24E
seaworthy, 11G
sec, 6L
seclude, 5P
second, 3H, 7C
secondary, 3H
secondhand, 7F
secrecy, 42B
secret, 42B
secretary, 1O
secrete, 16B
sect, 25C
section, 3F
secure, 44B, 56B
sedan, 11A
sedate, 13H
sedge, 24E
sediment, 16E
sedimentary, 29C
sedition, 10B
seduce, 10E
sedulous, 13B
see, 53B
seed, 6J, 24D
seek, 5Q
seem, 50E
seemingly, 31B
seems to, 50D
seep, 16B
seethe, 5E
segment, 3F

segregate, 2W
seismograph, 3C
seize, 36E
seldom, 7K
select, 12J
selection, 12J
self, 9A
selfish, 5Q
selfsame, 27A
sell, 28D
seller, 1M
semantics, 12I
semaphore, 35C
seminar, 25E
seminary, 21F
senate, 25C
senator, 1C
send, 2I
senior, 9D
señor, 9C
sensation, 5A
sense, 5A, 53B
sensible, 13K
sensibly, 31G
sensitive, 13A
sensory, 23K
sentence, 35B
sentiment, 5A
sentinel, 1J
sentry, 1J
separate, 2W, 27C
September, 7E
septic, 37D
sequence, 25A
sequester, 2W
sequin, 17G
sequoia, 24B
serenade, 15D
serene, 19A
serf, 1F
sergeant, 1J
series, 25A

serious, 5I
seriously, 31A
sermon, 10A
serpent, 4C
serrate, 32D
serum, 37F
servant, 1Z
serve, 6K
service, 13B
session, 25E
set, 2I
setback, 36D
setting, 47A
settle, 2B
settlement, 18A
settler, 9I
setup, 25A
seven, 3H
seventeen, 3H
seventeenth, 3H
seventh, 3H
seventy, 3H
sever, 8G
several, 3G
severe, 13H
sew, 17I
sewage, 41A
sewer, 22D
sex, 54A
shabby, 26D
shack, 21K
shackle, 2V
shade, 38C
shadow, 38C
shadowgraph, 53A
shady, 38C
shaft, 20C
shaggy, 57A
shake, 2L
shale, 29B
shall, 50C
shallow, 32F

sham, 10B
shamble, 48A
shame, 5D
shampoo, 41C
shank, 23G
shanty, 21B
shape, 22F, 32A
shard, 3F
share, 36A
sharecropper, 1F
shark, 4H
sharp, 32E
sharpen, 32E
sharpshooter, 1D
shatter, 33A
shave, 8G
shawl, 17F
she, 45A
sheaf, 25A
shear, 8G
sheath, 17H
shed, 21K
she'd, 46E
sheen, 38A
sheep, 4E
sheepskin, 17K
sheer, 17J
sheet, 30F
sheik, 1C
shelf, 30C
shell, 4I
shell shock, 37B
she'll, 46C
shellac, 30E
shellfish, 4I
shelter, 21C
shepherd, 1F
sherbet, 6C
sheriff, 1J
sherry, 6H
she's, 46D
shibboleth, 35B

shield, 17H
shift, 2M
shilling, 28C
shim, 8E
shimmer, 38B
shin, 23G
shinbone, 23G
shine, 38B
shingle, 22C
shiny, 38A
ship, 2I, 11E
shipbuilder, 1P
shipbuilding, 1P
shipload, 22A
shipmate, 1V
shipment, 22A
shipowner, 1V
shipshape, 43B
shipwreck, 11E
shipwright, 1X
shipyard, 16I
shirk, 2F
shirr, 6K
shirt, 17C
shirtband, 17C
shirtwaist, 17C
shiver, 2L
shoal, 16F
shock, 5B
shoddy, 26D
shoe, 17E
shoelace, 8H
shoemaker, 1N
shoeshine, 41B
shoestring, 8H
shoot, 33B
shop, 21E
shopkeeper, 1M
shopper, 1M
shopwindow, 30B
shore, 16G
shorebird, 4J

shoreline, 16G
short, 32F
shortage, 3G
shortcake, 6C
shortcoming, 26A
shortcut, 11H
shorten, 2R
shorthand, 15I
shorthorn, 4E
shortly, 7H
shorts, 17C
shortstop, 1D
shortwave, 8D
shotgun, 8N
should, 50C
shoulders, 23F
shouldn't, 46A
shout, 19C
shove, 2K
shovel, 8E
show, 36A, 47A, 53A
showboat, 11E
showdown, 33C
showman, 1H
showroom, 30A
shrapnel, 8N
shred, 8G
shrew, 4F
shrewd, 12K
shrewdly, 31G
shriek, 19C
shrill, 19A
shrimp, 4I
shrine, 21I
shrink, 2R
shrivel, 2R
shroud, 17F
shrub, 24A
shrug, 44C
shuck, 6K
shudder, 2L
shuffle, 48A

shun, 53B
shut, 2U
shutdown, 2U
shutter, 30B
shuttle, 2I
shuttlecock, 34C
shy, 13L
sibilant, 35C
sibling, 9N
sick, 37A
sickle, 8F
sickness, 37A
side, 14B
sidearm, 34C
sideboard, 30D
sideburns, 23B
sideline, 1A
sidelong, 14C
sidereal, 20H
sidetrack, 11H
sidewalk, 11H
sideways, 14C
siege, 33C
sierra, 20D
sieve, 8M
sift, 6K
sigh, 19C
sight, 53A
sightly, 43C
sightseeing, 2G
sign, 15I
signature, 15A
signboard, 15F
signify, 10C
signpost, 15F
silence, 19A
silent, 19A
silhouette, 32A
silicon, 29A
silk, 17K
silkworm, 4K
sill, 30B

silly, 5K
silo, 20C, 21A
silt, 16E
silver, 29A, 58A
silverfish, 4K
silversmith, 1N
silverware, 8M
similar, 27A
similarity, 27A
simmer, 6K
simony, 1d
simper, 60A
simple, 55B
simplify, 56A
simply, 3J, 31A
simultaneously, 7I
sin, 26A
since, 7G, 39B
sincere, 13B
sincerity, 13B
sine, 49B
sinecure, 1d
sinew, 23J
sing, 19C
singe, 52C
singer, 1G
single, 3G
singsong, 19C
singular, 3G
sinister, 26D
sink, 16B
sinuous, 32D
sip, 6M
siphon, 16B
sir, 9C
sire, 1C
siren, 19B
sirocco, 40B
sisal, 24D
sissy, 9N
sister, 9N
sit, 2Q

site, 20A
situation, 51A
six, 3H
sixteen, 3H
sixteenth, 3H
sixth, 3H
sixtieth, 3H
sixty, 3H
size, 3A
sizzle, 52C
skate, 17E, 34B
skater, 1D
skating, 34B
skein, 17K
skeletal, 23K
skeptic, 13J
sketch, 15I
skew, 2M
skewer, 6K
ski, 34B, 34C
skid, 2M
skier, 1D
skiff, 11E
skiing, 34B
skill, 5R
skillet, 8M
skillful, 12K
skim, 15I
skin, 23B
skinny, 43D
skip, 48A
skipper, 1V
skirmish, 33C
skirt, 17C
skit, 47A
skittish, 13L
skulk, 48B
skull, 23C
skullcap, 17D
skunk, 4E
sky, 20H
skylark, 4J

skylight, 38D
skyline, 32A
skyrocket, 2O
skysail, 11F
skyscraper, 21A
skyward, 14I
slab, 3F
slack, 13P
slacks, 17C
slake, 6M
slam, 19E
slander, 10B
slang, 35A
slant, 32H
slap, 44A
slash, 8G
slat, 22C
slate, 29B
slaughter, 33B
slave, 1T
slaveholder, 1T
slaw, 6D
slay, 33B
sleazy, 26D
sled, 11C
sledge, 8E
sleek, 43C
sleep, 12E
sleet, 16A
sleeve, 17B
sleigh, 11C
slender, 43D
sleuth, 1J
slice, 3F, 8G
slick, 16B
slicker, 17F
slide, 2M
slight, 43D
slightly, 3J
slim, 43D
slime, 16E
sling, 8N, 37F

slingshot, 8N
slink, 48B
slip, 2M
slipper, 17E
slippery, 16B
slipshod, 43B
slit, 8G
slither, 48B
sliver, 3F
slobber, 60C
slogan, 15F
sloop, 11E
slop, 41A
slope, 20D
sloppy, 43B
slosh, 16B
slot, 8H
sloth, 4E
slouch, 2P
sloven, 43B
slow, 7J
slowdown, 7J
slowpoke, 9G
sludge, 16E, 41A
slug, 4K
sluice, 16I
slum, 18A
slumber, 12E
slump, 2P
slur, 10B
slush, 16A
sly, 13M
smack, 44A
small, 3A
smallpox, 37B
smart, 12K
smear, 41A
smell, 60B
smelt, 4H
smile, 60A
smirk, 60A
smite, 44A

smith, 1N
smock, 17C
smog, 16D
smoke, 52D
smokehouse, 21D
smokestack, 30B
smokey, 52D
smolder, 52C
smooth, 57A
smother, 2F
smudge, 41A
smug, 13E
smut, 52D
snack, 6D
snag, 2J
snail, 4I
snake, 4C
snap, 2N
snapdragon, 24D
snapper, 4H
snapshot, 47D
snare, 4O
snarl, 19D
sneak, 48B
sneer, 60A
sneeze, 60B
snicker, 19C
sniff, 60B
snip, 8G
snipe, 4J
snob, 9G
snoop, 53B
snooze, 12E
snore, 19C, 60B
snorkel, 16B
snort, 19D, 60B
snout, 4L
snow, 16A
snowball, 16A
snowberry, 24B
snowcap, 16A
snowdrift, 16A

snowfall, 16A
snowflake, 16A
snowman, 16A
snowplow, 11C
snowshoe, 17E
snowstorm, 40B
snub, 53B
snuff, 33A
snuffbox, 22A
snug, 5L
snuggle, 44B
so, 3K, 39B
so far, 7G
so that, 39B
soak, 16B
soap, 41C
soapstone, 29A
soapsuds, 41C
soar, 4O
sob, 19C
sober, 13H
soccer, 34B
social, 13A
socialist, 9O
society, 25C
sock, 17E
socket, 22A
sod, 29E
soda, 6H
sodden, 16B
sodium, 59A
sofa, 30D
soft, 57A
softball, 34B
soften, 57C
soggy, 16B
soil, 29E
soiree, 51B
sol, 20H
solar, 20H
solder, 29A
soldier, 1J

sole, 3G
solecism, 26A
solemn, 5I
solicit, 10E
solid, 57A
solitude, 42B
solo, 47B
soloist, 1G
solution, 12D
solve, 12D
solvent, 28E
somber, 5I, 38C
some, 45E
somebody, 45E
someday, 7F
somehow, 45F
someone, 45E
someplace, 14D
somersault, 34D
something, 45E
sometimes, 7K
someway, 45F
somewhat, 3J
somewhere, 14D
somnolent, 12E
son, 9N
sonar, 19B
song, 15D
songbird, 4J
sonnet, 15D
soon, 7H
soothe, 5L, 10D
sop, 16B
sophist, 9L
sophisticate, 9L
sophomore, 1I
soporific, 12E
soprano, 1G
sorcery, 34E
sordid, 41A
sore, 37C
sorority, 25B

sorrel, 4E
sorrow, 5H
sorrowful, 5H
sorry, 5H
sort, 12J
sort of, 3J
sortie, 33C
sot, 9G
soubrette, 9B
souffle, 6A
soul, 9F
sound, 19A
soundproof, 19A
soup, 6H
sour, 6L
source, 2C, 7G
sourdough, 6G
souse, 16B
south, 14E
South America, 18B
South Carolina, 18C
South Dakota, 18C
southeast, 14E
southeastern, 14E
southern, 14E
southland, 14E
southpaw, 1D
southward, 14E
southwest, 14E
southwestern, 14E
souvenir, 28C
sow, 4E, 29F
soybean, 6J
spa, 18A
space, 20H
spacecraft, 11D
spaceman, 1L
spaceship, 11D
spade, 8E
spaghetti, 6D
Spain, 18B
span, 11H

spangle, 30E
spaniel, 4B
spank, 44A
spare, 3G
spark, 52C
sparkle, 38B
sparrow, 4J
sparrow hawk, 4J
sparse, 3G
spasm, 2N
spat, 10B
spate, 7J
spatter, 16B
spatula, 8M
spawn, 54A
speak, 10A
speaker, 1E
spear, 8N
spearhead, 39A
spearmint, 6C
special, 55A
specialist, 9L
species, 3F, 25B
specifically, 3J
specify, 10C
specimen, 3F
specious, 26A
speck, 3F
speckle, 3F
spectacles, 17D
spectacular, 26C
spectator, 9H
specter, 9F
speculate, 12D
speech, 10A
speed, 7J
speedometer, 3C
speedway, 11H
speedy, 7J
spell, 15I
spencer, 17F
spend, 28D

spendthrift, 9M

spew, 60C

sphere, 32B

spherical, 32B

sphinx, 21M

spice, 6G

spider, 4K

spigot, 16C

spike, 8H

spill, 16B

spillway, 16I

spin, 2X

spinach, 6J

spinal, 23A

spindle, 8J

spine, 23J

spinet, 47C

spinster, 9B

spiral, 32B

spire, 30B

spirit, 13B

spiritual, 13J

spit, 60C

spite, 5M

splash, 16B

splatter, 16B

splay, 2S

spleen, 23H

splendid, 26C

splice, 2V

splint, 37F

splinter, 3F

split, 2W

splotch, 38C

splurge, 28D

spoil, 6K

Spokane, 18D

spokesman, 1E

spokesperson, 1E

spokeswoman, 1E

sponge, 4I

spongy, 57A

sponsor, 1B

spontaneous, 7J

spook, 9F

spool, 8J

spoon, 8M

spoonful, 3E

spoor, 53A

sporadic, 7K

spore, 24D

sport, 34A

sportscaster, 1E

sportsman, 1F

sportswoman, 1F

spot, 14A, 36F

spouse, 9N

spout, 16C

sprain, 37E

sprawl, 2Q

spray, 16B

spread, 2S

spree, 2G

sprig, 24C

spring, 7D, 48D

springboard, 8J

Springfield, 18D

springtime, 7A

sprinkle, 16B

sprinkler, 16C

sprint, 34D

sprinting, 34D

sprocket, 8B

sprout, 24D

spruce, 24B

spry, 43A

spur, 44A

spurious, 26A

spurn, 10B

spurt, 16B

sputter, 2L

sputum, 23I

spy, 53B

spyglass, 8K

squabble, 10B

squad, 25D

squadron, 25D

squalid, 41A

squall, 40B

squander, 28D

square, 32C

squash, 6J

squat, 2Q

squaw, 9B

squawk, 19D

squeak, 19E

squeal, 19C

squeamish, 13L

squeeze, 44B

squelch, 33A

squib, 8N

squid, 4I

squint, 53B

squire, 1C

squirm, 2L

squirrel, 4F

squirt, 16B

St. Louis, 18D

stab, 8G

stable, 4M

stack, 25A

stadium, 21G

staff, 25E

stag, 4E

stage, 47A

stagecoach, 11A

stagehand, 1X

stagger, 48A

stagnant, 2B

stair, 30B

staircase, 30B

stairs, 30B

stairway, 30B

stake, 42C

stale, 6L

stalk, 24E

stall, 4M

stallion, 4E

stalwart, 43A

stamen, 24D

stamina, 54B

stammer, 19C

stamp, 48C

stampede, 4O

stanch, 2F

stanchion, 22D

stand, 48E

standard, 42A

standpoint, 14A

standstill, 2B

stanza, 15D

staple, 8H

star, 9K, 20H

starboard, 14E

starch, 6G

stare, 53B

starfish, 4I

stark, 55B

starlight, 38A

starling, 4J

start, 2C

starter, 8B

startle, 5C

starvation, 37B

starve, 6N

state, 10C, 18A

statement, 10A

stateroom, 30A

statesman, 1C

static, 2B

station, 21J

stationary, 2B

stationery, 15G

statistics, 12D

statue, 47D

staunch, 13H

stave, 47B

stay, 2B

swallow, 6M
swallowtail, 4K
swamp, 16F
swan, 4J
swap, 36A
sward, 29E
swarm, 4O
swarthy, 23B
swash, 16B
swath, 25A
swathe, 22G
sway, 2M, 10E
swear, 10B
sweat, 23I
sweater, 17C
sweatshop, 21E
sweep, 41B
sweepstakes, 34A
sweet, 6L
sweetbread, 6E
sweetbrier, 24D
sweetheart, 9E
sweetmeats, 6C
sweetness, 6L
sweets, 6B
swell, 2S
swelter, 52A
swerve, 2X
swift, 7J
swill, 6M
swim, 16B, 34B
swimmer, 1D
swimming, 34B
swindle, 10B
swine, 4E
swineherd, 1F
swing, 34C
swirl, 2X
swish, 19E
switch, 8J
switchboard, 19B
switchman, 1V

swivel, 2X
swollen, 32G
swoon, 2P
swoop, 4O
sword, 8N
swordfish, 4H
swordplay, 34B
sycophant, 9G
syllable, 35B
syllabus, 15C
syllogism, 12H
sylvan, 20B
symbol, 35C
symbolize, 12I
symmetry, 55B
sympathetic, 13A
sympathize, 5L
sympathy, 5L
symphony, 47B
symposium, 10A
symptom, 37A
synagogue, 21I
synchronize, 47B
syndicate, 25E
synod, 25E
synonym, 35B
synopsis, 15C
syntax, 35A
synthesis, 2V
synthetic, 27A
syringe, 22A
syrup, 6C
system, 12H

T

tab, 28B
tabby, 4B
tabernacle, 21I
table, 30D
tableau, 47D
tablecloth, 30F

tableland, 20D
tablespoon, 3E, 8M
tablet, 15G
tabletop, 30D
tableware, 8M
taboo, 10G
tabor, 47C
tacit, 19A
tack, 8H
tackle, 34C
tact, 13A
tactful, 13A
tactics, 12H
tadpole, 4D
taffy, 6C
tag, 15A
tail, 4L, 11F
tailor, 1N
tailrace, 16F
taint, 6K, 41A
take, 2I
takeoff, 2G
talc, 29A
tale, 15B
talebearer, 9G
talent, 5R
talisman, 34E
talk, 10A
talkative, 10A
tall, 32F
tallow, 8C
tally, 49D
talon, 4L
tambourine, 47C
tame, 5L
tamp, 2R
Tampa, 18D
tan, 58A
tandem, 11A
tang, 6L
tangerine, 6I, 58A
tangible, 57A

tangle, 43B, 55B
tango, 47B
tank, 22A
tankard, 8M
tanker, 11E
tanner, 1N
tannery, 21E
tantalize, 5J
tantrum, 5E
tap, 44A
tape, 22G
taper, 32E
tapestry, 30E
tapeworm, 4K
tapioca, 6C
taproom, 21D
tar, 22D
tardy, 7H
target, 34C
tariff, 28B
tarn, 16F
tarnish, 29D
tarpaulin, 22B
tarry, 2B
tart, 6C
tartan, 17K
tartar, 6G
task, 1A
tassel, 17B
taste, 6L
tasty, 6L
tatter, 17I
tattle, 10H
tattoo, 47D
taunt, 10B
taupe, 58A
taut, 57A
tautology, 10A
tavern, 21D
taw, 34F
tawdry, 26D
tawny, 58A

tax, 28B
taxation, 28B
taxi, 11A
taxicab, 11A
taxidermy, 1L
taxpayer, 9I
tea, 6H
tea party, 51B
teach, 12G
teacher, 1I
teacup, 8M
teahouse, 21D
teak, 24B
teakettle, 8M
teakwood, 22C
team, 25B
teammate, 9E
teamwork, 10D
teapot, 8M
tear, 17I
tearoom, 21D
tease, 10B
teaspoon, 8M
teaspoonful, 3E
teat, 23A
technical, 55B
technically, 31A
technician, 1X
technique, 12H
technology, 1K
tee, 34C
teem, 54B
teen, 9D
teepee, 21B
teeter, 2L
teeth, 23D
teetotaler, 9G
telecast, 10C
telegram, 15F
telegraph, 10C
telegrapher, 1b
telepathy, 10A

telephone, 19B
telescope, 8K
teletype, 8L
television, 8D
tell, 10C
teller, 1S
telltale, 9G
temerity, 13N
temper, 5E, 27C
temperate, 52A
temperature, 52A
tempest, 40B
temple, 21I
tempo, 7J
temporary, 7K
tempt, 10E
ten, 3H
tenable, 57B
tenacity, 13H
tenant, 9I
tend, 29F
tender, 13A
tenderfoot, 9L
tendon, 23J
tenet, 12L
Tennessee, 18C
tennis, 34B
tenon, 22D
tenor, 1G
tense, 5D
tension, 5D
tent, 21B
tentative, 7K
tenth, 3H
tenuous, 57B
tepid, 52A
tergiversate, 10B
term, 7D
termagant, 9G
terminal, 8L, 21J
terminate, 2F
termite, 4K

tern, 4J
terrace, 20G
terrain, 20A
terrible, 26D
terribly, 3K
terrier, 4B
terrific, 26C
terrify, 5C
territory, 20A
terror, 5B
terry, 17K
terse, 10A
tertiary, 3H
test, 10F
test tube, 22A
testament, 15C
testate, 54A
testify, 10C
testimony, 10A
tether, 2V, 8H
Texas, 18C
text, 15C
textbook, 15C
textile, 17K
texture, 17K, 57A
than, 27D
thank, 10D
thankful, 13A
thankfully, 31D
that, 3I, 45C
thatch, 24E
that's, 46D
thaw, 16B
the, 3I
theater, 21G
thee, 45A
their, 45B
theirs, 45B
theism, 12L
them, 45A
theme, 12B
themselves, 45A

then, 7H, 39B
theoretically, 31B
theory, 12D
therapist, 1U
therapy, 37F
there, 14D
thereabout, 14K
thereabouts, 14K
thereafter, 7H
thereby, 39B
therefore, 39B
therefrom, 39B
there'll, 46C
thereof, 7I
thereon, 14I
there's, 46D
thereto, 14G
thermal, 52A
thermometer, 3C
thermostat, 8L
thesaurus, 15C
these, 3I
thesis, 12B, 15C
thews, 23J
they, 45A
they'd, 46E
they'll, 46C
they're, 46F
they've, 46B
thick, 32F
thicken, 32F
thicket, 20E
thickness, 32F
thickset, 43A
thief, 9G
thigh, 23G
thimble, 22B
thin, 32F
thing, 22E
think, 12A
third, 3H
thirst, 6N

thirsty, 6N

thirteen, 3H

thirteenth, 3H

thirty, 3H

this, 3I

thistle, 24D

thistledown, 24E

thong, 8H

thorax, 23A

thorium, 29A

thorn, 24C

thorough, 13B

thorough(ly), 3K

thoroughbred, 4E

thoroughfare, 11H

those, 3I

thou, 45A

though, 27D

thought, 12A

thoughtful, 13A

thousand, 3H

thousandth, 3H

thrall, 1T

thrash, 44A

thread, 17K

threadbare, 17J

threadlike, 32F

threat, 10B

threaten, 10B

three, 3H

threescore, 3H

thresh, 29F

threshold, 30A

thrift, 13K

thrill, 5J

thrive, 54B

throat, 23D

throb, 2L

throes, 33C

throne, 30D

throng, 25B

throttle, 8B

through, 14H

throughout, 14H

throw, 2J

thrum, 44B

thrust, 2J

thud, 19E

thug, 9G

thumb, 23F

thumbnail, 23F

thumbscrew, 8H

thumbtack, 8H

thump, 19E

thunder, 40B

thunderbolt, 40B

thunderclap, 40B

thundercloud, 40C

thunderhead, 40C

thundershower, 40B

thunderstorm, 40B

thunderstruck, 5J

Thursday, 7E

thus, 39B

thwack, 44A

thwart, 2F

thy, 45A

thyself, 45A

tiara, 17D

tick, 19E

ticket, 28C

tickle, 44A

tidal, 16F

tidbit, 6A

tiddlywinks, 34F

tide, 16F

tidewater, 16F

tidings, 15F

tidy, 43B

tie, 17G

tier, 32F

tiger, 4B

tight, 57A

tighten, 2R

tights, 17C

tile, 22D

till, 29F

tilt, 2P, 32H

tiltyard, 20G

timbale, 6D

timber, 22C

timberland, 20E

time, 7A

timekeeper, 1D

timepiece, 7B

times, 49D

timetable, 25A

timeworn, 7F

timid, 13L

timorous, 5B

tin, 22D

tinder, 52E

tinderbox, 22A

tinfoil, 22B

ting, 19E

tinge, 58A

tingle, 5J

tinker, 22F

tinkle, 19E

tinsel, 30E

tint, 17K, 58B

tintype, 47D

tiny, 3A

tip, 14I

tipple, 6M

tipsy, 13O

tiptoe, 48A

tirade, 10B

tire, 11F

tiresome, 56A

'tis, 46D

tissue, 23B

titanic, 3A

tithe, 28D

title, 15A

titter, 19C

to, 14G, 39B

to some extent, 3J

toad, 4C

toadstool, 24E

toast, 6D

toaster, 8D

tobacco, 52E

toboggan, 11C

tocsin, 19B

today, 7F

toddle, 48A

toddler, 9D

toddy, 6H

toe, 23G

toffee, 6C

toga, 17C

together, 7I

toggle, 8J

togs, 17A

toil, 1d

token, 28C

tole, 29A

Toledo, 18D

tolerance, 54B

tolerate, 54B

toll, 28B

tollgate, 11H

tom-tom, 47C

tomahawk, 8N

tomato, 6J

tomb, 21M

tomboy, 9B

tombstone, 21M

tomcat, 4B

tome, 15C

tomfoolery, 5K

tomorrow, 7F

ton, 3E

tone, 19A

tong, 8M

tongue, 23D

tonic, 37F

tonight, 7C
tonsure, 8G
too, 3K, 27B
tool, 8E
toot, 19E
tooth, 23D
toothache, 37C
toothbrush, 41C
toothpaste, 41C
toothpick, 41C
top, 14I
topaz, 29B
topcoat, 17F
Topeka, 18D
topic, 12B
topnotch, 26C
topography, 20A
topology, 1L
topple, 2P
topsail, 11F
topside, 14I
topsoil, 29E
torch, 38D, 52C
torchbearer, 9K
torchlight, 38D
torment, 33B
tornado, 40B
torpedo, 8N
torpid, 13C
torque, 2X
torrent, 40B
torso, 23A
tortilla, 6D
tortoise, 4C
torture, 33B
toss, 2J
tot, 9D
total, 49B
totally, 3K
tote, 2I
totem, 21M
totter, 2L

touch, 44A
touchdown, 34C
touchstone, 29B
tough, 57A
toupee, 23B
tour, 2G
tourist, 9H
tournament, 34A
tousle, 41A
tout, 10C
tow, 2K
toward, 14K
towel, 30F
tower, 21A
towhead, 58A
town, 18A
townsfolk, 9I
townsman, 9I
townspeople, 9I
towpath, 11H
toxic, 33B
toy, 34F
toys, 34F
trace, 15I
track, 2H, 11H
tract, 20A
tractable, 13L
traction, 2K
tractor, 11B
trade, 36A
trademark, 15A
trader, 1M
tradesman, 1M
tradition, 12L
traditional, 42A
traduce, 10B
traffic, 2A
tragedy, 40D
tragically, 31D
trail, 11H
trailer, 11A
train, 11A

trainer, 1D
trait, 5R
traitor, 9I
trajectory, 32B
tram, 11A
trammel, 2J
tramp, 48C
trample, 48C
tramway, 11H
trance, 12E
tranquil, 19A
tranquilizer, 37F
transact, 28D
transfer, 2I
transfix, 8G
transform, 27C
transfusion, 37F
transistor, 8L
transit, 2G, 27C
translate, 10J
translation, 10J
transmission, 8B
transmit, 10C
transmitter, 8L
transom, 30B
transparent, 38E
transpire, 2D
transplant, 2I, 37F
transport, 11G
transportation, 11G
transverse, 14C
trap, 4O
trapeze, 34C
trapezoid, 32C
trapper, 1F
trash, 41A
travail, 1d
travel, 2G
traverse, 2G
travesty, 27A
travois, 11B
tray, 8M

treacherous, 56B
treachery, 13M
tread, 48A
treadmill, 21E
treason, 13M
treasure, 28A
treat, 6A
treatment, 37F
treaty, 15H
treble, 47B
tree, 24A
treetop, 24C
trek, 2G
trellis, 30C
trelliswork, 30C
tremble, 2L
tremendous, 26C
trench, 20C
trenchant, 12K
Trenton, 18D
trepidation, 5B
trespass, 36E
tress, 23B
trestle, 11H
triad, 3H
trial, 10B
triangle, 32C
triangular, 32C
tribal, 25C
tribe, 25C
tribesman, 9I
tribulation, 5H
tribune, 1C
tributary, 16F
tribute, 10D
trice, 3H
trick, 12G, 34E
trickle, 16B
tricky, 13M
tricycle, 11A
trident, 8N
trifle, 30E

trigger, 8J
trigonometry, 49A
trill, 19A
trillion, 3H
trim, 32F
trimmer, 8F
trinity, 3H
trinket, 17G
trio, 25B
trip, 2G
tripe, 6E
triphammer, 8E
triple, 3H
tripod, 8J
trite, 26D
triumph, 36D
triumphant, 36D
triumvir, 1C
troll, 9J
trolley, 11A
trombone, 47C
troop, 25D
trooper, 1J
trope, 35B
tropical, 20B
tropics, 20A
trot, 48A
troubadour, 1G
trouble, 56B
troublesome, 56A
trough, 22A
trounce, 33B
troupe, 25E
trousers, 17C
trousseau, 17A
trout, 4H
trowel, 8E
troy, 3E
truant, 14L
truce, 33C
truck, 11A
truckle, 10G

truculent, 5F
trudge, 48A
true, 26A
truehearted, 13N
truly, 31A
trumpet, 47C
truncheon, 8N
trundle, 2I
trunk, 11F, 23A
truss, 22G
trust, 5N
trustworthiness, 13B
trustworthy, 13B
truth, 26A
truthfully, 31A
try, 2C
tryout, 47A
tub, 22A
tuba, 47C
tube, 22D
tuber, 24D
tuberculosis, 37B
tuck, 36F
Tuesday, 7E
tuft, 23B
tug, 11E
tugboat, 11E
tuition, 28B
tulip, 24D
tumble, 2P
tumbrel, 11A
tumor, 23B
tumult, 19A
tun, 22A
tuna, 4H
tundra, 20B
tune, 47B
tungsten, 29A
tunic, 17C
tuning fork, 47C
tunnel, 11H
turban, 17D

turbine, 8B
turbulent, 19A
tureen, 8M
turf, 29E
turgid, 32G
turkey, 4J
turmoil, 55B
turn, 2X
turncoat, 9I
turnip, 6J
turnkey, 1T
turnout, 41B
turnover, 36B
turnpike, 11H
turnspit, 8M
turntable, 8D
turpentine, 8C
turquoise, 29B
turret, 21C
turtle, 4C
turtledove, 4J
tusk, 4L
tussle, 33C
tussock, 24E
tutor, 1I
tuxedo, 17A
TV, 8D
twaddle, 10B
twang, 19E
tweed, 17K
tweeze, 44B
twelfth, 3H
twelve, 3H
twentieth, 3H
twenty, 3H
twice, 3G, 7K
twig, 24C
twilight, 7C
twill, 17K
twin, 27A
twine, 8H
twinge, 37C

twinkle, 38B
twirl, 2X
twist, 2X, 32B
twister, 40B
twit, 10B
twitch, 2N
twitter, 2L
two, 3G, 3H
tycoon, 9M
type, 3F
typewrite, 15I
typewriter, 15G
typhoon, 40B
typical, 42A
typically, 31C
typist, 1O
tyrant, 9G
tyro, 9L

U

udder, 23A
ugh, 10K
ugly, 43C
ukulele, 47C
ulcer, 37E
ulterior, 42B
ultimate, 3K
ultra, 3K
umbra, 38C
umbrage, 5E
umbrella, 17G
umpire, 1D
unanimous, 27A
unattractive, 43C
unavailable, 14L
unbearable, 56A
unbosom, 10H
unbroken, 55B
uncanny, 55A
uncertain, 42C
unchanged, 55B

uncle, 9N
uncomfortable, 5D
uncommon, 55A
unconscious, 12E
uncontrolled, 13O
uncover, 22G
unction, 37F
undeniably, 31A
under, 14J
underbrush, 24A
underdeveloped, 20B
underdog, 1D
underfoot, 14J
undergo, 2D, 27C
underground, 14J
undergrowth, 24A
underhanded, 13M
underline, 15I
underlying, 26C
undermine, 33B
underneath, 14J
undersea, 16H
underside, 14J
understand, 12G
understandably, 31C
underwater, 16H
undiscovered, 42B
undisturbed, 5L
undoubtedly, 31A
undulate, 2L
uneasy, 5D, 56A
uneducated, 12K
unequal, 27C
unexpectedly, 31C
unfair, 13M
unfaithful, 13M
unfamiliar, 42B
unfasten, 2W
unfavorable, 26D
unfinished, 55A
unfit, 26A
unfold, 17I

unfortunate, 13G
unfortunately, 31D
unfriendly, 5G
ungainly, 43A
unguent, 37F
ungulate, 4A
unhappily, 31D
unhappy, 5H
unicorn, 4C
unicycle, 11A
uniform, 17A, 55B
unimportant, 26D
union, 2V, 25E
unique, 55A
unison, 47B
unit, 3G
unite, 2V
United States, 18B
universal, 42A
universe, 20H
university, 21F
unjustly, 31F
unkind, 5F
unknown, 42B
unless, 27D
unlike, 27C
unlikely, 42C
unlimited, 3G
unload, 22G
unlock, 22G
unluckily, 31D
unpack, 22G
unpleasant, 5G
unquestionably, 31A
unravel, 22G
unrest, 33C
unroll, 22G
unsafe, 56B
unscrew, 2W
unscrupulous, 13M
unselfish, 13A
unsettled, 13O

unskilled, 12K
unstable, 13O
unsteady, 13O
untie, 22G
until, 7H
until then, 7G
until...then, 39B
unwind, 2W
unwisely, 31G
up, 14I
up to now, 7G
upbraid, 10B
uphill, 14I
upholster, 30E
upland, 14I
upon, 14I
upper, 14I
upright, 14I
upriver, 16H
uproar, 19C
uproot, 2I
upset, 5I
upshot, 39A
upside-down, 14I
upstairs, 14I
upstart, 9K
upstream, 16H
upward, 14I
uranium, 29A
Uranus, 20H
urban, 20B
urchin, 9C
urge, 10E
urgent, 26C
urine, 23I
urn, 30E
us, 45A
usable, 26C
usage, 12L
use, 2D, 26C, 36A
used to, 50C
useful, 26C

usefulness, 26C
useless, 26D
usher, 1Z
usual, 7K, 42A
usurp, 36E
usury, 28B
Utah, 18C
utensil, 8E
utilitarian, 26C
utmost, 3K
utopia, 18A
utter, 10C
utter(ly), 3K

V

vacant, 32G
vacate, 2G
vacation, 51B
vacationer, 9H
vaccination, 37F
vaccine, 37F
vacillate, 2L
vacuum, 41C
vagabond, 9H
vagrant, 9H
vague, 38E
vain, 13E
vainglory, 13E
valedictory, 10A
valentine, 15F
valet, 1Z
valid, 26A
valise, 22A
valley, 20C
valor, 13N
valuable, 26C
value, 5O, 26C
valve, 16C
vamp, 9B
van, 11A
vandal, 9G

vanilla, 6C
vanish, 2G
vanquish, 36D
vantage, 33D
vapid, 26D
vapor, 16A
variation, 27C
variety, 27C
various, 27C
varnish, 30E
varsity, 25B
vary, 27C, 39A
vase, 30E
vassal, 1Z
vast, 3A
vat, 22A
vaudeville, 47A
vault, 28F
veal, 6E
veer, 2X
vegetables, 6B
vegetation, 24A
vehement, 5E
vehicle, 11A
veil, 17D
vein, 23I
veld, 20E
vellum, 15G
velocity, 7J
velvet, 17K
venal, 5Q
vend, 28D
vendor, 1M
veneer, 22C
venerate, 5O
vengeance, 5E, 33B
venison, 6E
venom, 37E
vent, 30B
ventral, 23A
ventricle, 23I
ventriloquist, 1H

venture, 42C
Venus, 20H
veranda, 30A
verb, 35B
verbose, 10A
verdant, 58A
verdict, 12J
verge, 14B
verify, 53B
vermicelli, 6D
vermiform, 32F
vermilion, 58A
vermin, 4A
Vermont, 18C
vermouth, 6H
vernacular, 35A
vernal, 7D
versatile, 12K
verse, 15B
version, 3F
versus, 27D
vertebrae, 23J
vertex, 3D
vertical, 14C
verve, 13B
very, 3K
vesper, 7C
vessel, 11E, 23I
vest, 17C
vestibule, 30A
vestige, 53A
vet, 1L
veteran, 9I, 9L
veterinarian, 1L
veto, 10G
vex, 5I
via, 14G
viaduct, 11H
vial, 22A
viand, 6B
vibrate, 2L
vibration, 2L

vicarious, 27A
vice, 12L
vice president, 1C
vicinity, 14K
vicious, 5F
vicissitude, 27C
victim, 9G
victor, 36D
victuals, 6B
vie, 34A
view, 53A
viewpoint, 12B
vigil, 53B
vignette, 47D
vigor, 13B, 43A
vigorous, 13B
vile, 5F, 26D
villa, 21B
village, 18A
villager, 9I
villain, 9G
vim, 13B
vincible, 56B
vindicate, 33D
vine, 24E
vinegar, 6G
vineyard, 20F
vintage, 7F
viola, 47C
violate, 33B
violent, 5F
violet, 58A
violin, 47C
violinist, 1G
virgin, 9L
Virginia, 18C
virile, 43A
virtual, 26A
virtually, 3J
virtue, 26A
virtuoso, 1G
virus, 37D

visa, 15H
visage, 23C
viscous, 57C
vise, 44B
vision, 12E, 53A
visit, 2G
visitor, 9H
visor, 17D
vista, 53A
visual, 53A
visualize, 12A
vital, 26C
vitamin, 37F
vitiate, 41A
vitreous, 38E
vituperative, 5F
vivacity, 13B
vivid, 38A
vocabulary, 35A
vocal, 10A
vocation, 1A
vodka, 6H
vogue, 17A
voice, 23D
voiceless, 19A
void, 32G, 55B
volatile, 13O
volcanic, 29C
volcano, 20D
volition, 13D
volley, 34C
volleyball, 34B
volt, 3E
voluble, 10A
volume, 3G, 15C
voluntary, 13D
voluptuous, 43C
vomit, 37C
voracious, 6N
vote, 51C
voter, 51C
vouch, 5O, 10C

vouchsafe, 10G
vow, 10I
vowel, 35C
voyage, 2G
vulgar, 12K
vulture, 4J

W

wad, 25A
waddle, 48A
wade, 16B
wafer, 6C
waffle, 6D
waft, 2I
wage, 28A
wagon, 11A
wagonload, 22A
waif, 9D
wail, 19C, 19E
wain, 11B
wainscot, 30B
waist, 23A
waistband, 17C
waistcoat, 17F
waistline, 23A
wait, 2B
waiter, 1a
waitress, 1a
waive, 36A
wake, 12E, 54A
waken, 12E
walk, 48A
wall, 30B
wallboard, 22C
wallet, 28F
wallflower, 9G
wallop, 44A
wallpaper, 30E
walnut, 6J
walrus, 4H
waltz, 47B

wand, 8J
wander, 2G
wanderer, 9H
wane, 3G
want, 5Q
war, 33C
warble, 19D
ward, 9N, 21H
warden, 1T
wardrobe, 17A
wardroom, 30A
ware, 28C
warehouse, 21K
warfare, 33C
warhead, 8N
warlike, 5E
warm, 52A
warmth, 52A
warn, 10B
warning, 10B
warp, 32B
warpath, 33C
warrant, 15H
warren, 4M
warship, 11E
wart, 23B
wartime, 7A
wary, 13P
was, 50A
wash, 41B
washbasin, 22A
washboard, 41C
washbowl, 22A
washcloth, 30F
Washington, 18C
Washington DC, 18D
washout, 36D
washroom, 30A
washstand, 30D
washtub, 22A
wasn't, 46A
wasp, 4K

waste, 33A
wastebasket, 41A
wasteful, 28E
wasteland, 20B
wastepaper, 41A
watch, 7B, 53B
watchdog, 4B
watchful, 13P
watchmaker, 1N
watchman, 1T
watchtower, 21A
watchword, 35B
water, 16A
water clock, 7B
water glass, 8M
waterbottle, 22A
watercolor, 15I
watercourse, 16F
watercress, 6D
waterfall, 16F
waterfowl, 4J
waterfront, 16G
waterline, 16F
waterlog, 16B
watermelon, 6I
waterproof, 16B
watershed, 20D
waterside, 16G
waterspout, 22D
watertight, 16B
waterway, 11H
waterwheel, 16C
waterworks, 16C
watt, 3E
wattle, 22C
wave, 44C
wavelength, 38A
waver, 2L
wax, 41B
waxwork, 47D
way, 11H
wayfarer, 9H

wayfaring, 2G
waylay, 2B
wayside, 11H
we, 45A
weak, 43A, 57B
weakness, 43A
wealth, 28C
weapon, 8N
wear, 17I
weariness, 37C
weary, 12E
weasel, 4E
weather, 40A
weatherman, 1E
weave, 17I
weaver, 1N
web, 25A
wed, 2V
wedding, 2V
wedge, 8E
Wednesday, 7E
wee, 3A
weed, 12J, 24A
week, 7D
weekday, 7D
weekend, 7D
weekly, 7K
weep, 19C
weigh, 3B
weird, 55A
welcome, 10D
welfare, 5L
well, 3K, 37A
we'll, 46C
welt, 37E
were, 50A
we're, 46F
weren't, 46A
west, 14E
West Virginia, 18C
western, 14E
westernmost, 14E

westward, 14E
wet, 16B
we've, 46B
whack, 44A
whale, 4H
whaleboat, 11E
whalebone, 4L
wham, 44A
wharf, 16I
what, 45D
whatever, 45D
what'll, 46C
whatnot, 30E
what's, 46D
whatsoever, 45D
wheat, 6J
wheedle, 10E
wheel, 11F
wheelbarrow, 11B
wheelchair, 30D
wheelwright, 1N
wheeze, 19C
whelm, 16B
when, 7I, 45D
when...then, 39B
whenever, 45F
whensoever, 45F
where, 14D, 45D
where...there, 39B
whereabouts, 14A
whereas, 27D, 39B
whereby, 39B
wherefore, 39B
where's, 46D
whereupon, 39B
wherever, 45F
wherewith, 39B
whet, 5J
whether, 27D
whetstone, 29B
whey, 6H
which, 45C, 45D

whichever, 45D
whiff, 60D
while, 7I
whilst, 7I
whim, 5A
whimper, 19C
whine, 19C
whinny, 19D
whip, 8N
whiplash, 37E
whippersnapper, 9D
whir, 19E
whirl, 2X
whirlwind, 40B
whisk, 7J
whisker, 4L
whiskey, 6H
whisper, 19C
whist, 34F
whistle, 19C
whit, 3F
white, 58A
white cap, 16F
whitefish, 4H
whitewash, 41B, 58B
whittle, 8G
who, 45C
whoever, 45E
whole, 3G
wholehearted, 13B
wholesome, 26A, 37A
whom, 45C
whomever, 45D
whomsoever, 45E
whoop, 19C
whoosh, 19E
whop, 44A
whorl, 32B
whose, 45D
why, 45F
Wichita, 18D
wick, 52E

wicked, 26D
wicker, 24C
wicket, 30B
wide, 32F
widely, 3K
wide-mouthed, 22A
widen, 32F
widespread, 42A
widow, 9B
width, 32F
wield, 44C
wife, 9N
wig, 23B
wiggle, 2L
wigwam, 21B
wild, 13O
wildcat, 4B
wilderness, 20B
wildfire, 52C
wildflower, 24D
wildfowl, 4J
wildlife, 4A
wile, 34E
will, 50C
willing, 13A
willow, 24B
wilt, 2R
wimple, 17D
win, 36D
wince, 5C
winch, 8J
wind, 40B
windblown, 43B
windbreak, 21C
windfall, 28A
windflower, 24D
windlass, 8J
windmill, 21E
window, 30B
windowseat, 30B
windowsill, 30B
windpipe, 23D

windshield, 11F
windstorm, 40B
windup, 2X
wine, 6H
wineglass, 8M
winepress, 22A
wing, 11F
wingspan, 11F
wingspread, 11F
wink, 53B
winner, 1D, 36D
winnow, 2W
winter, 7D
wintergreen, 24D
wintertime, 7A
wintry, 40E
wipe, 41B
wire, 22D
wireless, 8D
wiretap, 19B
Wisconsin, 18C
wisdom, 12K
wise, 12K
wisecrack, 5K
wisely, 31G
wish, 5Q
wisp, 3F
wistful, 5H
wit, 12K
witch, 9F
witchcraft, 34E
with, 27B
withdraw, 2G
withe, 24C
wither, 2R
withers, 4L
withhold, 36F
within, 14H
without, 27D
withstand, 54B
witness, 53A
witty, 13I

wizard, 9F

wizen, 2R

wobble, 2L

woe, 5H

wolf, 4B

wolfhound, 4B

woman, 9B

womb, 23H

womenfolk, 9B

wonder, 12A

wonderful, 26C

wonderland, 18A

won't, 46A

woo, 5Q

wood, 22C

woodchuck, 4F

woodcraft, 47D

woodcut, 47D

woodcutter, 1F

woodland, 20E

woodpecker, 4J

woodpile, 52E

woodshed, 21K

woodsman, 1F

woodwind, 47C

woof, 17K

wool, 17K

woolen, 17K

word, 35B

work, 1d

workbench, 30D

workday, 7C

worker, 1A

workhouse, 21E

workingman, 1A

workman, 1A

workout, 34D

workroom, 21E

workshop, 21E

worktable, 30D

world, 20H

worm, 4K

wormwood, 24B

worn, 17J

worry, 5D

worse, 26D

worship, 10D

worth, 26C

worthless, 26D

worthwhile, 26C

would, 50C

wouldn't, 46A

wound, 37E

wow, 10K

wraith, 9F

wrangle, 33C

wrap, 22G, 44B

wrapper, 22B

wrath, 5E

wreak, 33B

wreath, 30E

wreck, 33A

wreckage, 33A

wren, 4J

wrench, 8E

wrestle, 33C

wrestler, 1D

wrestling, 34B

wretch, 37C

wretched, 5H

wriggle, 2L

wright, 1X

wring, 44B

wrinkle, 17I

wrist, 23F

wristwatch, 7B

write, 15I

writer, 1E

writhe, 2L

writing, 15B

wrong, 26A

wrongdoer, 9G

wrongdoing, 26A

wrongly, 31F

wrought, 55B

wry, 13I

Wyoming, 18C

X

xylophone, 47C

Y

yacht, 11E

yak, 4E

yam, 6J

yank, 2K

yap, 19D

yard, 3E, 20G

yardstick, 3C

yarn, 17K

yaw, 2M

yawl, 11E

yawn, 19C

year, 7D

yearbook, 15C

yearling, 4D

yearn, 5Q

yeast, 6G

yell, 19C

yellow, 58A

yellow jacket, 4K

yelp, 19D

yes, 10K

yesterday, 7F

yet, 27D

yield, 10G

yip, 19D

yodel, 19C

yoga, 34D

yoke, 4N

yolk, 6F

yonder, 14K

you, 45A

you'd, 46E

you'll, 46C

young, 7G

youngster, 9D

your, 45B

you're, 46F

yours, 45B

yourself, 45A

you've, 46B

youth, 7F

yowl, 19D

yule, 7D

Z

zany, 13O

zeal, 13B

zebra, 4E

zenith, 14I

zephyr, 40B

zest, 13B

zigzag, 32D

zinc, 29A

zip, 17I

zipper, 17B

zone, 20A

zoo, 4M

zoology, 1L

zoom, 19E